Ca ⠀⠀⠀⠀⠀ Library
Withdrawn Stock

D1685528

Early Irish history and chronology

By the same author

The Irish Sex Aetates Mundi (Dublin 1982)

Cummian's letter 'De controuersia paschali', together with a related seventh-century Irish tract 'De ratione conputandi' (Toronto 1988)*

Evangeliarium Epternacense (Universitätsbibliothek Augsburg, Cod. I.2.4°2). Codices Illuminati Medii Aevi 9 (Munich 1988)

Bernhard Bischoff, *Latin Palaeography, Antiquity and the Middle Ages* (Cambridge 1990)**

Psalterium Salabergæ. Staatsbibliothek zu Berlin, Preußischer Kulturbesitz, MS. Hamilton 553. Codices Illuminati Medii Aevi 30 (Munich 1994)

An Cúigiú Díochlaonadh (Indreabhán, Conamara 1994)

The Songs of Elizabeth Cronin, Irish traditional singer (Dublin 2000)

* with Maura Walsh
** with David Ganz

Early Irish history and chronology

❖

Dáibhí Ó Cróinín

FOUR COURTS PRESS

Set in 10.5 on 12.5 point Ehrhardt for
FOUR COURTS PRESS LTD
7 Malpas Street, Dublin 8, Ireland
e-mail: info@four-courts-press.ie
http://www.four-courts-press.ie
and in North America
FOUR COURTS PRESS
c/o ISBS, 5824 N.E. Hassalo Street, Portland, OR 97213.

CAVAN COUNTY LIBRARY
ACC No. C/134450
CLASS NO. REF 941.501
INVOICE NO 5287 C9
PRICE €44.00

© Dáibhí Ó Cróinín 2003

A catalogue record for this title
is available from the British Library.

ISBN 1–85182–635–1

All rights reserved. No part of this publication may be
reproduced, stored in or introduced into a retrieval
system, or transmitted, in any form or by any means
(electronic, mechanical, photocopying, recording or
otherwise), without the prior written permission of both
the copyright owner and the publisher of this book.

Printed in Great Britain
by MPG Books, Bodmin, Cornwall

To the memory of
Bruno Krusch, Bartholomew Mac Carthy, Charles W. Jones
quibus ego in rebus talibus non ullos inuenio doctiores

Contents

Illustrations

Abbreviations

AM	Anno Mundi
ASE	*Anglo-Saxon England*
AU	*Annals of Ulster*
ÄID	'Über die älteste irische Dichtung', Kuno Meyer
BN	Bibliothèque Nationale (Paris)
CCSL	Corpus Christianorum Series Latina
CLA	*Codices Latini Antiquiores*
CMCS	*Cambridge [Cambrian] Medieval Celtic Studies*
CSEL	Corpus Scriptorum Ecclesiasticorum Latinorum
DIL	[Contributions to a] *Dictionary of the Irish Language* (RIA)
DNR	*De natura rerum* (Isidore, Bede)
DRC	*De ratione conputandi*
DT	*De temporibus* (Bede)
DTR	*De temporum ratione* (Bede)
EEMF	Early English Manuscripts in Facsimile
EHR	*English Historical Review*
EIHM	*Early Irish history and mythology*, T.F. O'Rahilly
HBS	Henry Bradshaw Society
HE	*Historia Ecclesiastica* (Eusebius, Bede)
JRSAI	*Journal of the Royal Society of Antiquaries of Ireland*
Jnl	Journal
Jones, *Bedae opera* (1943)	Charles W. Jones, *Bedae opera de temporibus*. Mediaeval Academy of America Publications 41 (Cambridge, Mass. 1943)
Jones, 'Sirmond MS.'	Charles. W. Jones, 'The "lost" Sirmond manuscript of Bede's "computus"', *English Historical Review* 52 (1937) 204-19 [= *Bede, the schools and the computus*, chap. X]
Kenney, *Sources*	James F. Kenney, *The sources for the early history of Ireland 1: Ecclesiastical*. Columbia Records of Civilization (New York 1929; 3rd ed. Dublin 1993)
MGH	Monumenta Germaniae Historica
MGH-AA	Monumenta Germaniae Historica, Auctores Antiquissimi
MGH-SRM	Monumenta Germaniae Historica, Scriptores Rerum Merovingicarum
MPL	Jacques-Paul Migne, *Patrologia Latina*

MS. / MSS	manuscript / manuscripts
NGR	National Grid Reference
OIG	*A grammar of Old Irish*, Rudolf Thurneysen
PIMS	Pontifical Institute of Mediaeval Studies (Toronto)
PRIA	Proceedings of the Royal Irish Academy
RIA	Royal Irish Academy
Walsh and Ó Cróinín	Maura Walsh & Dáibhí Ó Cróinín (eds & transls), *Cummian's Letter 'De controuersia paschali', together with a related seventh-century Irish tract 'De ratione conputandi'.* PIMS, Studies & Texts 86 (Toronto 1988)
ZCP	*Zeitschrift für Celtische Philologie*

Acknowledgements

I would like to thank the following for granting permission to reprint articles under their copyright:

The Royal Irish Academy for chapters 1 and 5; the National University of Ireland for chapter 11; the Institut Grand-Ducal de Luxembourg, for chapter 10; Boydell & Brewer Ltd, for chapter 3; Jan Thorbecke Verlag, Stuttgart, for permission to reprint chapter 13 from ©*Tradition und Wertung. Festschrift für Franz Brunhölzl zum 65. Geburtstag*; Prof. Donnchadh Ó Corráin and the Medieval Academy of Ireland for permission to reprint chapters 2, 4, 7, 8, 9, 12, and 14; the Medieval Academy of America for chapter 6.

I would like to thank the following for granting permission to reprint photographic material under their copyright: the President and Fellows of St John's College, Oxford, for permission to publish the plate of St John's College MS. 17; the Bibliothèque Nationale de France, for permission to reproduce plates 5-10; the Bibliothèque Municipale, Angers, for permission to reproduce pl. 4; the Universitätsbibliothek Würzburg, for permission to reproduce pl. 2; the Board and Fellows of Trinity College Dublin for permission to reproduce pl. 11; the Biblioteca Antoniana, Padua, for permission to reproduce pl. 3; the Ordnance Survey of Ireland, for permission to reproduce the map on p. 167; Cambridge University, for permission to reproduce the photograph on p. 168.

Introduction

When I was an undergraduate student in University College Dublin, one of my best teachers, Denis Bethell (†1982), remarked to me once that I might profitably read Charles W. Jones' *Bedae opera de temporibus*, his edition of Bede's works 'On Time'. That simple suggestion awakened an interest on my part in the medieval science of time-reckoning or computus that has lasted to this day, and Jones' commentary revealed to me for the first time the wealth of Irish material on the subject still in manuscript that had never been studied, let alone published. I had the great privilege, in 1979, of meeting Charles Jones and his wife Sarah in their Berkeley home, and of enjoying their splendid hospitality. Jones has been numbered by Professor Michael Lapidge among the 'greats' of Anglo-Saxon studies in the first half of the twentieth century, alongside such luminaries as Max Laistner (whose student Jones was), though Jones in fact died as recently as 25 June 1989. His gentle and generous personality, and his great courtesy to me (a lowly graduate student from another country) have remained in my memory ever since. More than anything else, Jones' example, and a gift, on the occasion of that visit, of signed copies of his two great studies of Bede's computistical works, set me on the path of research which has produced the essays in this volume.

In many of these studies I have, for reasons that require no explanation, retraced some of the steps taken by Charles Jones and the other great computistical scholars who went before him, especially Bruno Krusch (1857-1940) and 'our own' Bartholomew Mac Carthy (1843-1904). Krusch was all of twenty-three years old when his great *Studien zur christlich-mittelalterlichen Chronologie* appeared in 1880. Even if it were the only book he had ever produced, his reputation as a scholar would be secure. But of course, he published a whole string of volumes in the Scriptores Rerum Merovingicarum series of the Monumenta Germaniae Historica, together with a long list of articles on Merovingian charters, chronicles, and related texts, culminating in his monumental edition of Gregory of Tours' *Libri Historiarum*. However, the editions of important computistical texts published by Krusch in his *Studien* (a second volume of which appeared in 1938) were a pioneering effort which found few followers. For his part, Mac Carthy lamented in one of his studies that he had had no pioneer in Ireland in the field of computistics. (It may be added here in parenthesis that, until recently, he had no successor, either.)

That such a wealth of manuscript material of Irish origin could have lain wholly neglected for so long will seem strange to many, particularly readers outside Ireland. Despite the pioneering early work and exemplary lead given by the great Mario Esposito and James F. Kenney (the one Italian, the other Canadian), Hiberno-Latin studies in the modern era were left entirely to non-Irish scholars such as Ludwig Bieler, Bernhard Bischoff, and Bengt Löfstedt, and their respective pupils. The one chair of Hiberno-Latin and Medieval Latin Palaeography that existed in this country (at University College Dublin) has since been abolished, and neither subject is formally taught in any (southern) Irish university today. The inevitable result of this shameful neglect of the subject in Ireland has been that, until very recently, all the serious work in these fields to date has been conducted by scholars outside this country. While Irish people have been happy to bask in the reflected glory generated by these foreign authorities, and to read about *How the Irish saved civilization*, the tedious labour of research and analysis has been left to others, in other countries, more appreciative of the part that Irish saints and scholars played, first in the christianization of the neighbouring island of Britain, and then in the wider rôle of restoring Latin and Greek culture to a Europe emerging from its 'Dark Ages'.

Despite the fact that the manuscripts described and discussed in this collection preserve the oldest Irish names for the days of the week, the earliest known manuscript Old Irish glosses, the oldest Latin writings by Irish authors, the earliest known text of an Irish Easter table (in a unique copy), the earliest evidence for scholarly links between Ireland and Spain in the era of Isidore of Seville (†636), and between Ireland and Northumbria in the age of Bede (†735), no native Irish scholar has ever examined them, let alone studied their contents. One might echo the remark of an earlier Irish savant, bishop Cormac mac Cuilennáin (†908), who chastised his contemporaries for being *rerum suarum obliviscens* ('neglectful of their own affairs'). Thankfully, however, that situation has been changing. In the concluding section of my paper announcing the rediscovery of the previously lost Irish 84-year Easter table (below, 58 ff) I expressed the hope that the implications of that find would be worked out in the years to follow. I could not have foreseen at that time just how prophetic those words were to be. My hope, however, has been more than realised by the work of my collaborator on that paper, Dan McCarthy, who has himself single-handedly gone on, in the years since then, to publish a series of ground-breaking studies in computistics and in the related field of Irish annals and historical chronology. The years of collaboration that have resulted from Dan's first contact back in 1986 have been especially rewarding for me, not just in the personal sense, but as an indication of how two very different academic trainings, the one in computer science, the other in Early Medieval History, can be brought together to produce radical new results, drawing on unpromising materials that other scholars have deemed dry and repulsive. I hope that by bringing together the studies in this volume I will help kindle similar collaborative efforts in the future.

One other scholar deserves mention here, for the formative role he has played in helping to bring computistics back to the position it once held in the medieval world (and which it retained down to the sixteenth century): Donnchadh Ó Corráin has been a friend and valued colleague ever since he pioneered the establishment, in 1981, of the Medieval Academy of Ireland, and more particularly, its journal *Peritia*. From its inception, Donnchadh assured a place in *Peritia* for the publication of studies on computistics; in fact, the paper on 'Mo Sinu maccu Min and the computus at Bangor' (below, 35 ff) was the first ever piece of sample text set in type for that journal. Several of the articles reprinted here first saw the light of day in *Peritia*; I am immodest enough to think that they may have helped contribute to the reputation that the journal enjoys today. What is certain, however, is that, without Donnchadh's initiative, many of these studies of mine might never have appeared, or if they had, they might have done so in a scatter of journals inaccessible to the average reader. By his establishment of *Peritia*, and by assuring a place in it for the esoterica of computistics and chronological studies, Donnchadh has, in his own way, championed this field of studies, and I for one am grateful to him for it.

The studies reprinted here had their beginning in a chance discovery that I made in Charles Jones' *Bedae opera de temporibus* when I was a student. In the commentary section of that volume, Jones published a series of five sets of names for the days of the week which he found in Oxford, St John's College, MS. 17, a twelfth-century computistical collection from Thorney in Cambridgeshire (a codex with no obvious Irish connections). One of those lists was of the days of the week *secundum Scottos*, and this turned out, in fact, to preserve a unique and remarkably archaic set of terms that go back in date probably to the formative period of Irish christianity in the fifth century. The papers that followed have the appearance in hindsight of being natural successors to that initial study, representing as they do a linear and chronological progression from the foundation-period of the Irish church through the fifth and sixth centuries, with new finds of texts relating to Patrick and Columbanus, and the latter's teacher, Mo Sinu maccu Min (Sinilis) of Bangor (†610).

My discovery and publication of a computus (*De ratione conputandi*), of Irish origin and composed around the mid-seventh century, brought new light on the transition period in early Irish computistical studies, when the older practices, based on the 84-year Easter table, were beginning to give way to the newer doctrines embodied in the tables of Victorius of Aquitaine and Dionysius Exiguus. By demonstrating the very close affinities between that computus and the famous Paschal Letter of Cummian (632/3), I was able to show that Cummian was, in all likelihood, the author of the computus, and that the *De ratione conputandi* represented the assembly of technical expertise that lay behind Cummian's 'diplomatic' treatment of the Easter question in his famous epistle. The intense debate that formed the backdrop to Cummian's Letter is also to be seen in the background to the papal letter of AD 640 discussed (and preserved uniquely) by the Venerable Bede in his great *History of the English Church and people*. It was also possible to show (in my paper on Cummian's computus) that the Munich Computus, compiled on Iona *c*.718, preserves a precious excerpt from that letter which Bede had omitted from his account. This chance discovery provided conclusive proof that the papal letter had indeed been received by the (northern) Irish churches, and debated by them. By then shifting the focus of that discussion to a previously unnoticed letter by Bishop Braulio of Saragossa, literary executor to the famous Isidore of Seville (†636), I was able to cast new light on the circumstances in which the papal letter to the Irish was composed and sent. Indeed, as I suggest below, I now believe that Irish links with Visigothic Spain have their orgins in that Easter problem of AD 640, and the remarkably early familiarity with Isidore's writings in Ireland is probably likewise directly connected to that episode.

The Munich Computus was for many years, since Krusch first drew attention to it in his *Studien* of 1880, the only substantial witness to the Irish Easter observations of the earlier period. But the badly corrupted nature of the sole surviving Munich copy, and the lack of any surviving Irish 84-year Easter table, made any accurate reconstruction of early Irish Easter dates impossible. My discovery of the long-lost Irish 84-year Easter table (discarded by the community of Iona in 716 and never heard of again), which surfaced quite fortuitously in 1985 in a manuscript at Padua, put an end at last to the search that Krusch and Mac Carthy, as well as Jones and other scholars in the modern era, had pursued in vain. Thanks to Dan McCarthy's reconstruction of that table, we now for the first time are in a position to know the true dates of Easter observed by the early Irish churches in the fifth and sixth centuries.

Another chance discovery, in the famous collection of computistical texts contained in the eleventh-century Oxford, Bodleian Library, MS. 309 once owned by the French Jesuit scholar Jacques Sirmond, brought to light a dating-clause (best preserved in that manuscript) which showed that Bede's own computus was, in fact, a copy of an Irish computus compiled *c*.658. That theme of Anglo-Irish intellectual and literary connections was also the subject of my paper on 'Rath Melsigi, Willibrord, and the earliest Echternach manuscripts', in which was demonstrated that the earliest surviving original 19-year Dionysiac Easter table (for the years AD 684-702), bound up in the famous Calendar of Willibrord, apostle of the Netherlands and founder of the monastery of Echternach in Luxembourg, was actually written at Rath Melsigi, a settlement of Anglo-Saxon monks in southern Ireland that flourished in the second half of the seventh century. This added further weight to the argument that Irish and Anglo-Saxon scholars and clerics worked very closely together during those decades – a fact which has been overshadowed by the distorting image of the famous Synod of Whitby (AD 664), which supposedly had as its result the severance of such relations as had existed up to that time between the two nations. Other computistical texts from the same monastery (preserved now only in fragmentary form in Paris) preserve the oldest known manuscript Old Irish glosses, older even than the earliest stratum of vernacular glosses in the famous Würzburg codex containing the letters of St Paul (usually dated to *c*.750). The same habit of glossing Latin texts in Old Irish is found also in the Munich Computus, and I published a new gloss from that manuscript in 1981.

The fact that all these computistical texts can be, to a greater or lesser extent, precisely dated (by virtue of their habitual dating-clauses) also made it possible to demonstrate that that most enigmatic of all medieval Latin authors, Virgilius Maro Grammaticus, whose writings are frequently cited by the computists, was an Irishman writing in Ireland in the second half of the seventh century, thus finally laying to rest a debate that has raged in scholarly circles for the best part of two centuries.

One final aspect of technical chronology makes its appearance in this collection: the crucial question of the earliest Irish annals and their origins. Drawing on the material cited in the other papers collected here, and some more besides, I presented anew the case for seeing annotations in Easter tables as the source of our earliest Irish historical dates. Bolstered by a newly-discovered annal recording the death in AD 549 of Finnian of Clonard, I was able to demonstrate, I believe, that the practice of entering such historical notes into Irish Easter tables goes back at least to that mid-fifth-century period, and possibly farther. I am more than ever convinced now – especially in light of Dan McCarthy's subsequent researches – that our Irish annals are the direct outcome of the computistical studies that were such a fundamental part of the scholastic curriculum in Ireland from the very beginnings of Christianity in this country. It is that fundamental fact that inspired me to give this collection its title *Early Irish history and chronology*.

It is customary, in cases such as this, when the work of twenty-odd years is brought together and re-examined, to ponder on the rights and wrongs of whatever has been written and try to weigh up the balance with the benefit of hindsight. I prefer to leave that to the judgement of my readers. For the rest, I have followed the gospel precept: *Quod scripsi, scripsi*. However, I have added references here and there in footnotes (in square brackets) to indicate the results of more recent scholarship where I thought that might be useful.

It remains only to thank those publishers that have kindly allowed me to reprint the articles in this book, and the Publications Fund of the National University of Ireland, Galway, which made a generous grant towards the cost of publication. I am particularly grateful to the Vice-President for Development and External Affairs in my university, Prof. Ruth Curtis, for her support of that grant application.

Two friends and colleagues have been mentioned already above: Dan McCarthy, whose own researches have been inspirational (and who kindly allowed me reprint the article on the Irish 84-year Easter table which he co-authored with me) and Donnchadh Ó Corráin, whose constant interest has been a great encouragement to persevere in a field of study that has sometimes been a solitary one. Other friends and colleagues have assisted with the specifically computistical aspect of my researches: Wesley Stevens in Canada, Bruce Eastwood and Steve McCloskey in the USA, Menso Folkerts in Germany (without whose collection of microfilms I would not have rediscovered the 'lost' Irish 84-year Easter table). Others still, in the general field of Hiberno-Latin studies, have, over the years, by their own work and in personal discussion, provided me with invaluable advice and support: Ludwig Bieler, who first discussed with me the meaning of the term *calcenterus*; Bernhard Bischoff, who discussed with me the Old Irish gloss in the Munich Computus and the Paris fragments with Old Irish glosses, and many other things besides; Franz Brunhölzl, who, as my mentor in Munich as long ago as 1977-78, read through my transcript of the Munich Computus and encouraged my computistical studies when they were still in their infancy; David Dumville, who initiated a lively debate in the pages of *Peritia* on the subject of Insular computistical manuscripts; Michael Herren, who, in the wide range of his publications on Hiberno-Latin literature, touched also on the vexed subject of Virgilius Maro Grammaticus; Leofranc Holford-Strevens, who discussed the intricacies of the Irish 84-year Easter table with me (and published an excellent account of it in his *Oxford companion to the year*); David Howlett, whose path-breaking studies of Hiberno-Latin literature have taken him back to several texts which I had edited, and on which he was able to cast new light; and Marina Smyth, who also entered the debate on the Irish provenance of Bede's computus, and related matters. While I do not share many of her views, I do admire the scholarship and courtesy that she has brought to bear on the discussion. Last but certainly not least, Faith Wallis very generously gave me a copy of her new translation of Bede's works 'On Time', with its excellent commentary, which has added new impetus to the study of computus. Other scholars who assisted me with individual topics are mentioned in the footnotes to the various papers. One in particular, my former friend and colleague Tom Fanning, has since passed away; his help is gratefully recalled here. Above all, though, my deepest debt is to the three scholars mentioned in the dedication to this volume.

The oldest Irish names for the days of the week?*

The first Christian missions to Ireland must have brought with them certain radical changes of basic concepts in native Irish society. Most immediate and fundamental among these should have been the introduction of Christian concepts of number-symbolism, for to the Christian all things had been ordered by God 'in measure, number, and weight'. Of these three, number was felt to be of special importance.[1]

The very first of these adjustments to be made involved the Christian concept of the seven-day week, for the reckoning of time in pre-Christian Irish society was of one-, three-, five-, ten-, or fifteen-day periods; the seven-day week was entirely unknown.[2] The names given to the days of the week in early Irish are generally assumed to have been the same as those that still survive in the modern Irish dialects. It is the purpose of this paper to review in brief the evidence for these names and to suggest that we can, perhaps, posit the existence of a set of names older still than any which has previously been known.

By the time of our earliest written records in Old Irish, the seven-day week and the names for each of the days are already clearly in evidence. From the point of view of linguistic analysis these forms present no great difficulties.[3] They have survived almost unchanged up to the modern period and are common to all the dialects, with only a very few minor variations in pronunciation. But are these the *oldest* Irish names for the weekdays? It will be argued in what follows that we can go one step in time beyond this 'canonical' list to one which, it is hoped to show, may be as old as the fifth century.

* First published in *Ériu* 32 (1981) 95-114. This is a revised version of a paper read at the Sixth International Congress of Celtic Studies held at Galway in July, 1979. I am very grateful to [the late] Prof. D.A. Binchy, who discussed the original draft with me and made many valuable corrections and suggestions for its improvement. A revised draft was read by [the late] Prof. James Carney, who also made many useful comments, and by Prof. Liam Breatnach, Dr Vera Čapková, and Prof. Próinséas Ní Chatháin, to all of whom I here express my thanks. 1 Irish computists of the seventh century saw the foundation of their beliefs in the words of Boethius, *De arithmetica* 1 2: 'Omnia quaecumque a primaeva rerum natura constructa sunt numerorum videntur ratione formata. Hoc enim fuit principale in animo conditoris exemplar'; J.-P. Migne, *Patrologia Latina* [MPL] 73, 1083. 2 See D.A. Binchy, 'Distraint in Irish law', *Celtica* 10 (1973) 22-71, and the various periods of stay on legal restraint discussed there. 3 See Rudolf Thurneysen, 'Die Namen der Wochentage in den keltischen Dialekten', one of a series of papers on the history of the names for the weekdays published in *Zeitschrift für deutsche Wortforschung* 1 (1901) 150-93: 186-91.

In the St John's College, Oxford, MS. 17,[4] which was at Ramsey *c.* AD 1043 and at Thorney in Cambridgeshire by AD 1092, there are contained the compu-tistical works of Abbo of Fleury and Byrhtferth of Ramsey, calendars and cycles, miscellaneous tracts and letters, and the computistical works of Bede. Bede wrote two works 'On Time', *De temporibus,* in AD 703 (the year of his ordination), and the more extensive *De temporum ratione* (or *De temporibus liber maior,* as he himself called it), which he issued AD 725.[5]

On fol. 71[v] of this Oxford manuscript, in the margin beside chapter VII of DTR *(De hebdomada),* there are written, in a series of ornamented circles, the names of the weekdays *secundum Hebreos, secundum antiquos gentiles, secundum Siluestrum papam, secundum Anglos,* and *secundum Scottos.*[6] These Irish names are the ones that will concern us from here on, but before we discuss them we must make some remarks concerning the place of this Oxford manuscript in the text tradition of Bede's computus.

The St John's College manuscript has been described as 'a scientific ency-clopaedia'.[7] It derives in large part from the writings of Abbo of Fleury and the school of Fleury-sur-Loîre, and reflects too the teaching of Abbo during his period at Ramsey (AD 986-88), where Byrhtferth was one of his pupils.[8] Now, many of the computistical texts found in the works of Abbo bear a strong rela-tion to earlier works circulating in Germany and Switzerland in the first half of the ninth century, especially the St Gall, Stiftsbibliothek, MS. 248 *(saec.* IX, St Denis?), and München, Bayerische Staatsbibliothek, Clm 210 *(saec.* IX, Salzburg). The scholars of Fleury seem to have combined two streams of thought, the northern French and the southern German, that had previously

---

4 The most complete description of our MS. (though it does not mention the Irish list) is in René Derolez, *Runica manuscripta, the English tradition* (Brugge 1954) 26-29; cf. André van de Vyver, 'Les œuvres inédits d'Abbon de Fleury', *Revue Bénédictine* 47 (1935) 125-69, at 144 ff.; Charles W. Jones, *Bedae pseudepigrapha: scientific writings falsely attributed to Bede* (Ithaca, N.Y. 1939) 127-28; Charles W. Haskins, *Studies in the history of medieval science* (Cambridge, Mass. 1924) 83-84, 329 n. 23; Heinrich Henel, 'Byrhtferth's Preface: the epilogue to his Manual', *Speculum* 18 (1943) 288-302. Fol. 59[v] of the MS. is reproduced in S. Harrison Thomson, *Latin bookhands of the later Middle Ages, 1100-1500* (Cambridge 1969) Pl. 83. [See now also Faith Wallis, 'MS. Oxford St John's College 17: a medieval manuscript in its context', unpubl. Ph.D. dissertation, University of Toronto, 1984. Peter Baker (ed), *Byrhtferth's Enchiridion.* Early English Texts Society, s.s., 15 (Oxford 1995) liii-lv; idem, 'Byrhtferth's *Enchiridion* and the computus in Oxford, St John's College 17', *Anglo-Saxon England* 10 (1981) 123-42.] **5** See the great edition by Charles W. Jones, *Bedae opera de temporibus.* Medieval Academy of America Publications 41 (Cambridge, Mass. 1943); the text is reproduced, but without the invaluable commentary of the first edition, in *Bedae opera didascalica* 2, *Corpus Christianorum Series Latina* [CCSL], 123 A Turnhout 1976). **6** The lists were first published by Jones, *Bedae opera,* 340-41; they are reproduced here from the plate accompanying this paper. The Trustees of the Bodleian Library, Oxford, and the President and Fellows of St John's College, Oxford, are here thanked for their permission to publish this plate. [Actually, the lists were first published by John Leland, *Collectanea de rebus Britannicis,* ed. Thomas Hearne, 6 vols, 4 (London 1715) 99, though Jones was apparently unaware of that fact, as I was myself.] **7** Van de Vyver, art. cit., 144. **8** See Charles W. Jones, 'The Byrthferth Glosses', *Speculum* 7 (1938) 81-97.

existed more or less independently. This material they transmitted to England from the time of Abbo at Ramsey. Nearly all computistical manuscripts written after Abbo show some influence from this Fleury school.[9]

The text tradition of Bede's computus shows a division into two main groups:[10] the DTR manuscripts in or near Switzerland that did not have DT, and those in northern France that did. The scriptoria in the region of Switzerland filled the hiatus in one of two ways: either by sending to northern France for an exemplar late in the ninth century, or by copying the text of the Reichenau Karlsruhe, Badische Landesbibliothek, Augiensis CLXVII (K),[11] or its exemplar. This exemplar seems to have been entirely independent of the other continental manuscripts and may have come directly from the British Isles to Reichenau. According to the editor of Bede's *De temporum ratione*, this Karlsruhe manuscript 'is possibly the most reliable single witness' to the text. This is the 'Karlsruhe Bede' that students of Old Irish prize for its collection of glosses.

Although, as we might expect, most of the English manuscripts of Bede's computus agree with manuscripts from northern France in their text of DTR, the St John's College MS. 17 provides the exception in agreeing everywhere with K. Charles Jones could find no evidence to support either of the possible answers to this puzzle: that either the text of DT in this manuscript was taken from an ancient English exemplar, or that it was derived from southern Germany. The evidence of the list of names for the days of the week in Old Irish that we are about to discuss may give renewed impetus to the possibility that the Bedan text in the Oxford manuscript did, in fact, derive from an ancient Insular exemplar.[12]

9 Jones, *Bedae pseudepigraphica*, 160.　10 Jones, *Bedae opera*, 142, 161-64.　11 See Bernhard Bischoff, 'Irische Schreiber im Karolingerreich', in *Jean Scot Érigène et l'histoire de la philosophie*. Colloques internationaux du Centre National de la Recherche Scientifique 561 (Paris 1977) 47-58: 53 (and n. 2) [repr. in idem, *Mittelalterliche Studien. Ausgewählte Aufsätze zur Schriftkunde und zur Literaturgeschichte*, 3 vols (Stuttgart 1966-67, 1981), 3, 39-54]. Hans P.A. Oskamp, 'The Irish material in the St Paul Irish codex', *Éigse* 17 (1978) 385-91.　12 Jones overlooked fragments of two *saec.* VIII manuscripts of Irish provenance, one of which contains many of the *K* Irish glosses in an obviously earlier stage of Old Irish ; see Myles Dillon, 'The Vienna glosses on Bede', *Celtica* 3 (1956) 340-44, and Josef Hofmann and Bernhard Bischoff, *Libri Sancti Kiliani. Die Würzburger Schreibschule und die Dombibliothek im VIII. und IX. Jahrhundert*. Quellen und Forschungen zur Geschichte des Bistums und Hochstifts Würzburgs 6 (Würzburg 1952) 104, No. 31.

I give here the five lists that occur in the St John's College MS., and they will be discussed below in the order in which they occur there.

I. Nomina dierum secundum Hebreos	II. Nomina dierum secundum antiquos gentiles
Prima sabbati.	.i.　Dies solis.
Secunda sabbati.	.ii.　Dies lunae.
Tercia sabbati.	.iii.　Dies Martis.
Quarta sabbati.	.iiii.　Dies Mercurii.
Quinta sabbati.	.v.　Dies Iouis.
Sexta sabbati.	.vi.　Dies Ueneris.
Septima sabbati.	.vii.　Dies Saturni

III. Item nomina dierum secundum Siluestrum papam	IV. Nomina dierum secundum Anglos
Prima feria.	.i.　Sunnandaȝ.
Secunda feria.	.ii.　Monendeȝ.
Tercia feria.	.iii.　Tiþesdaeȝ.
Quarta feria.	.iiii.　Podnosdaeȝ.
Quinta feria.	.v.　Þunresdaeȝ.
Sexta feria.	.vi.　Friȝedaeȝ.
Sabbatum.	.vii.　Saterdaeȝ.

V. Secundum Scottos

.i.　dies scrol.	.v.　Diu ethamon
.ii.　Diu luna.	.vi.　Diu triach.
.iii.　Diu mart.	.vii.　Diu satur.
.iiii.　Diu iath,	

I.　The first list, of the so-called 'Hebrew' days of the week, is the standard medieval list for such days.[13] It is based on biblical use, and such a list could be found in almost every computistical manuscript written in the middle ages, without significant variation from ours.

II.　The second list is that of the Roman names for the days of the week. Although the Romans of Republican and Early Imperial times did not reckon in terms of a seven-day week, this seven-day period was already established in Roman use by the third century AD, obviously as a result of Judeo-Christian influence. Although the Romans at first began their week with *dies Saturni*, we have by as early as the fourth century clear evidence for the use of our current

---

13　For a popular exposition of the subject, see F.H. Colson, *The week* (Cambridge 1926); good, detailed discussions are those by J.C. Hare, 'On the names of the days of the week', *Philological Museum* 1 (1832) 1-73, and the collection of papers mentioned above in n. 3.

sequence of days, beginning with *dies solis*. The change can be attributed to the influence of Constantine, who changed the order of days to conform with Christian celebratory practices. Suffice it to say for the present that the list in our Oxford manuscript is a reliable one.

III. The third list reflects a legend known in later medieval times largely through Bede's own works, though he borrowed the story from the seventh-century Irish computus; the Irish in turn had borrowed the tradition from the apocryphal *Acta Syluestri*, a fabulous concoction of *c*. AD 500 that played an important part in the dissemination of the fraud known as the Donation of Constantine, and which served also as a source for many later writers of hagiography, including Adomnán of Iona.[14]

An anecdote in the seventh-century Irish computus relates how Pope Sylvester (AD 314-35) urged Christians to abandon the pagan names for the days of the week in favour of a list more in keeping with Christian beliefs; it is this story that provides the context for our Oxford list.

> *Sanctus Siluester apostolicus sic docuit et praedicauit Christianis, ut non dies septimanae iuxta ritum gentilium, sed Christiana obseruatione sic nominarent, quasi feria prima, id est dominicus, secunda feria, tertia feria, quarta feria, quinta feria, sexta feria, septima feria.*[15]

'The holy Pope Sylvester taught and preached to the Christians that they should not name the days of the week according to the custom of the pagans, but should name them according to Christian practice thus: *feria prima*,' etc.

All the manuscript evidence that I have seen confirms the accuracy of this Oxford list.

IV. The fourth list gives the Anglo-Saxon names for the weekdays. These too are all quite correct, save that for 'Monday' we might expect *-an-* in the second syllable (as in the name for 'Sunday'); while in the word for 'Saturday' we would expect the 'ash' (*-ae-*) in the first syllable, though this word may show influence from the Latin. These details, however, are in no way unusual in a manuscript of this date and reflect the normal variations of Late Old/Early

---

14 So Jones, correcting the view of Wilhelm Levison, who thought that Bede had borrowed directly from the *Acta*; see the latter's 'Konstantinische Schenkung und Silvester-Legende', *Miscellanea Francisco Erle*, Studi e Testi 38 (1924) 159-247, repr. in his collected papers, ed. Walther Holtzmann, *Aus rheinischer und fränkischer Frühzeit* (Düsseldorf 1948) 390-465; idem, 'Bede as historian', in A. Hamilton Thompson (ed), *Bede, his life, times and writings* (Oxford 1935; repr. 1969) 111-51: 114 n. 3 = *Aus rheinischer und fränkischer Frühzeit*, 347-82: 350 n. 2. On Adomnán's use of the *Acta Silvestri* see Gertrud Brüning, 'Adamnan's Vita Columbae und ihre Ableitungen', *Zeitschrift für Celtische Philologie* [ZCP] 11 (1917) 213-304: 253. 15 I give a text based on Karlsruhe, Badische Landesbibliothek, MS. 442 (*saec.* X/XI) fol. 67[v]; a slightly less accurate recension was printed by Jones, *Bedae opera*, Appendix, 395, from a Bern MS.

Middle English orthography. On the other hand, the preservation of the 'wynn' in *Tipesdae3* is slightly unusual for this date, reflecting an archaising orthography where Early Middle English might replace it with *w*. As it stands, though, this list is quite correct.

V. We come now to the fifth and final list, the days of the week 'according to the Irish'. Seeing that the four preceding lists are all correct historical forms, we may make the a priori assumption that this Irish list too will be correct. But it is immediately obvious that we are faced in this instance not by the 'standard' forms, but by something else entirely. There are, to be sure, basic similarities between the two lists, but in the Oxford manuscript (at least in the case of four of the names) we have what is essentially a different series of names. The questions to be asked of this series of names are, (1) is the list genuine, and (2) if so, how old are the forms contained in it?

The first day in the list, *dies scrol* 'Sunday', presents special problems that are best faced before we discuss the others. The fact of *dies* preceding in this instance suggests that we may have to do with a Latin name; but no such word as *scrol* (or *strol*, or *srol*) seems to exist in Latin.[16] But this name for 'Sunday' does occur as item 1131 of *Sanas Cormaic* 'Cormac's Glossary': *Sroll .i. soillsi, unde est aput Scottos diu srol .i. dies solis.* 'Sroll, that is brightness, whence *diu srol* among the Irish, that is Sunday'.[17] We cannot be in any doubt that Cormac († AD 908) is here referring to the *dies scrol* of our Oxford list, and besides the value of his reference as an independent witness to this form, his example is doubly significant for its preservation of the form *diu*.

It will be noted immediately that all the days in the list (except this *dies scrol)* are preceded by the word *Diu*.[18] There can be little doubt that this is the same word as Classical Old Irish *dia* ('day'), which is always prefixed to the names of days of the week in adverbial use.[19] But how are we to explain the form *Diu* in the list and in Cormac's Glossary?

It has often been remarked of *dia* itself that it is a peculiar case-form that occurs only in this one usage and in one or two syntactically identical ones like *dia bliadnae*, 'a year to the day'/ 'in a year'; otherwise it is completely lost in the later language as an independent form. It is remarkable that in Old Welsh too the form *diu (dyw)* is used in exactly this construction, and again this is a case-

16 Besides the standard dictionaries, I also consulted the unpublished materials of the Mittellateinisches Wörterbuch, Munich; I take this opportunity of thanking Frau Dr Theresia Payr [†] for her permission to use these collections.   17 Kuno Meyer (ed), *Sanas Cormaic.* Anecdota from Irish Manuscripts 5 (Oxford 1913) 100 §1134: cf. John O'Donovan (ed), *Cormac's Glossary, Sanas Chormaic.* Irish Archaeological and Celtic Society (Calcutta 1868) 148; Whitley Stokes, 'On the Bodleian fragment of Cormac's Glossary', *Transactions of the Philological Society* (1891-2) 192.   18 On Old Irish *dia* and its uses see W. Havers, 'Sprachliche Beobachtungen an den altirischen Glossen', *Celtica* 3 (1956) 256-61: 256-57. The fundamental studies of this topic are by Calvert Watkins, 'The Indo-European word for "day" in Celtic and related topics', *Trivium* 1 (1966) 102-19, and the reply by Eric Hamp, '*DIEU- "day" in Celtic', *Études Celtiques* 14 (1975) 472-77.   19 See Rudolf Thurneysen, *A grammar of Old Irish* [OIG] 217 §340.3.

form that is attested only for this one usage; Modern Welsh has replaced this older word with *dydd*.[20]

In the form *Diu* we have a clear reflex of the Indo-European nominative singular, with a lengthened grade, giving arhaic Old Irish *diu*; it is suggested that what we have in the Oxford list and in Cormac's Glossary is the oldest form of Old Irish *dia*, representing the old nominative case of the noun in adverbial usage (by analogy with the Latin *dies*), a nominitive form which later underwent paradigmatic revision due to formal identity with the dative.

We need not argue about the antiquity of the Celtic designations for the days of the week. The fact that the two branches of Celtic agree in preposing the word for 'day' in these forms suggests, as Watkins has argued, that we have here 'a common Celtic syntactic feature imposed on the borrowed lexical items themselves'. Now, Watkins maintains that the *dia* of this Old Irish syntagm represents the temporal genitive, not the nominative, of the noun,[21] because (he says) the paradigm proposed for Indo-European 'day' will not yield this form for the nominative. The subsequent discussion by Watkins, however, is based on the premiss of an Old Irish nominative singular in *dia* (from an allegedly archaic (*die*), despite the fact that the nominative is, in fact, very poorly attested and the archaism of the *die* form is nowhere convincingly proved.[22] It will not be out of place, therefore, to look again at the Indo-European paradigm for 'day' and its Old Irish reflexes, for which purpose I cite here the standard paradigmatic forms for the nominative and genitive singular. The development to Old Irish is as I see it here:

> *Indo-European　　Old Irish*
> nom. sg. **diēus* → *díu*
> gen. sg. **diwos* → *dia* (earlier *die?*)

According to this paradigm we would expect the Indo-European nom. sg. **diēus* to have yielded **di̯iu* → **dīus* → Old Irish *díu*. But because it is alleged not to be the observed result for this nom. sg., both Watkins and Hamp are driven to propose a remodelling of the form in Old Irish. Watkins, on the basis of a postulated **dio* (from the Indo-European nom. sg.) sees a further development to *die* 'just as in the case of the genitive **dio(w)* > *die*'. Hamp rightly questioned this proposed development for Old Irish, pointing out that Watkins had failed to give any satisfactory motivation for such a development; but Hamp in turn states that *diu* 'is certainly not the observed result for the nom. sg.', and he therefore proposed an alternative (and, to my mind, no better motivated)

---

20 Watkins, art. cit., 107.　**21** Following Thurneysen in this, against Pedersen.　**22** The forms cited in the Royal Irish Academy's *[Contributions to a] dictionary of the Irish language* [DIL], s. v. are from *Erchoitmed Ingine Gilide*, a text that is no older than the eleventh century; a ninth-century Fianaigecht story, and an entry in Cormac's Glossary.

development based on the extension of the full-grade in the plural (*$d\underaccent{\sim}{i}\bar{i}o\underaccent{\sim}{w}$-*) to the nom., gen., and dat. sg.

We may accept without difficulty Watkins' argument that the *dia* form in the names for the weekdays shows a temporal genitive case, not a nominative. But his further arguments for a *nominative* singular **dio → die → dia* are not convincing, and we may try an alternative approach to the problem.

Watkins' views thus expressed represent, in fact, a change of heart on the matter. In an earlier discussion of related material he came to quite a different conclusion.[23] Watkins gave it as Bergin's view that Old Irish *indíu* could go back to a construction with the preposition *i n-* *(i n-díu)*, with *díu* as the dative of an analogically created stem ** díio-*, acc. sg. **díion*. Watkins pointed out, however, that this would not account for the Brittonic forms (Welsh *heddiw*, Middle Breton *hiziu*), and by way of an alternative he ventured the suggestion that *indíu* (and the parallel *innocht*) might contain the nom. sg. with the definite article, 'parallel to *(i) ndadaig* "tonight" from an imbedded nominal sentence "it is the night"'. On the basis of examples from the earliest Greek and Roman legal texts Watkins then demonstrated convincingly that the terms 'by night'/'by day' in these languages showed an archaic use of the nom. sg. as adverb, e.g., *si nox furtum faxit* 'if (someone) commits theft by night'. The occurrence of *nox* (and the parallel *fors*) as nom. sg. in adverbial use is derived by Watkins, in the terms of transformational grammar, from kernel nominal sentences, which are imbedded into other sentences by the following transformational rule:

$$nox \text{ 'night' (nom. sg.)} \rightarrow nox \text{ 'it is night'} \rightarrow nox \text{ 'by night'}$$

The result is sentences of the type: *nox, si uoles, manebo,* and *quo nox furatum ueniat (uenias);* such usages are recognized as well by the Latin grammarians: Charisius II, p. 185 K: *fors pro aduerbio ponitur;* Priscian, *Inst. Gramm.* XV, p. 78 H: *similiter fors, cum sit nominatiuus, accipitur pro aduerbio.*

According to Watkins, 'in Indo-European, and as preserved in all the older languages and some modern ones, any noun in the nominative case ... is in principle capable of constituting such a sentence'. Allowing for the caveat implied by his statement that 'the situation in Old Irish requires a special study', we note his conclusion that 'both the adverbs *in-diu* "today" and *in-nocht* "tonight" admit of the same interpretation, as nominatives with the definite article rather than datives'.

Watkins was uneasy, however, about the phonological development of *indíu*, and in his *Trivium* article he withdrew the above suggestion of a nominative case in adverbial use as being phonologically impossible, since ... **dyēus* [the IE nom. sg.] gives *die* [not *díu*, in Old Irish].[24]

23 In an article entitled 'Lat. *nox* "by night": a problem in syntactic reconstruction', in Adam Heinz (ed), *Symbolae linguisticae in honorem Georgii Kuryłowicz* (Kraków 1965) 351-58.   24 Art. cit. (*Trivium*) 100.

We have seen above how fragile is the case for Old Irish nom. sg. *dia* ('archaic' *die*), and there is no need to reject Watkins' original theory of a nom. sg. in *díu*, especially when the interpretation of *indíu* as art. + nom. sg. is perfectly borne out by the stress in Old Irish *i'ndiu* (and, for that matter, *i'nnocht*),[25] a point which Watkins acknowledged, but which he was unable to reconcile with his own theory of *indíu* as comprising a deictic particle + 'day'. On the contrary, the evidence of the Oxford list, and of the item in Cormac's Glossary, strongly suggests that *díu* was, in fact, the earliest form of the nominative in Old Irish, showing a development from the IE nom. sg. *$d\underline{i}\bar{e}us$* that is quite regular. The fact that this old nominative should have been preserved in a list of the days of the week (where, according to Watkins, we would expect the genitive) itself supports the argument that the Oxford list reflects a stage in the history of the language when the originally Latin case system had not yet been fully adapted to Irish practice; the parallelism in Cormac's Glossary between *díu sróll: dies solis* is surely confirmation of this hypothesis.

The second name in the Oxford list may be seen to add some support to the argument that these forms are very old. I suggest that *Diu luna* represents the transitional form between Latin *dies lunae* and the later, Classical Old Irish *dia luain*. It exactly bears out Thurneysen's suggestion that the Irish form is a translation of, not a calque on, the Latin. That is to say, Latin *luna* is given an Irish equivalent in *luan*, the word then following an Irish declensional pattern. *Diu luna*, then, would seem to reflect a pre-assimilation state in respect of both words.[26]

The third form, *Diu mart*, shows a marked similarity to Welsh, which has *diu mawrth;* the unpalatalized final consonants suggest that perhaps the Irish word derives from Latin forms where cases other than the genitive were used, e.g. *Marte*.[27] Fluctuation in Latin case-endings are too common to require comment, but Thurneysen once suggested that Brittonic (following British Latin) may have dispensed altogether with the gen. sg. in such circumstances as the names for the days of the week, substituting in the case of *dies Saturni*, for example, the simple nominative *Saturnus*.[28] This could easily have come

---

25 It should be noted that the form *indnocht*, which Watkins says we would expect in a construction art. + noun, actually occurs in the eighth-century *Bethu Brigte*, ed. Donncha Ó hAodha (Dublin 1978) 3, line 82 (cf. note, pp. 41-42). This is another point against Watkins' analysis of *indiu* as deictic particle + indef. case (with zero ending); see also the objections to his theory advanced by Kim McCone, 'The dative singular of Old Irish consonant stems', *Ériu* 29 (1978) 26-38: 37-38, and n. 41. Prof. Próinséas Ní Chatháin has pointed out to me that speakers of Scots English use the phrases 'the day' = 'today', 'the night' = 'tonight', and 'the now' = 'now', reflecting, apparently, the same etymologizing of *indiu* as we propose here. 26 Prof. Binchy has suggested to me that Welsh *diu llun* may also have influenced the Irish form, which – in view of the other facts here noted – is surely very possible. 27 Thurneysen, art. cit., 188-89. 28 Compare Modern Irish *saoturn = deiseal* 'sunwise' that figures in the vocabulary of fishermen, e.g. *Irish Press*, 4 March 1952: 'Dá mbeadh an ghaoth ag gabháil timpeall le saoturn agus mura dtéigheadh sí isteach leis an oidhche do coiméadfaí greim uirthi theas nó thiar theas. An ghaoth

about by analogy with forms like *dominicus* and *sabbatum,* which frequently occur.

The form *Diu satur* in our Oxford list we can explain, doubtless, as a simple error for *Diu Saturn,* by omission of the *n*-stroke. Placed beside the Old Welsh equivalent, *diw sadwrn,* we see once again the striking similarity which we remarked also in the case of Irish *Díu mart* and Welsh *diu mawrth.* Thurneysen pointed out the peculiarity of the absence of *i*-affection in the Welsh form, and cited by way of a parallel the placename *Tref Saturn,* which occurs in the *Liber Llanndavensis.* Neither the Welsh nor the Irish forms can represent the Latin *(dies) Saturni,* for the long *-i* of this word should have caused palatalization in the ending of the Celtic forms. So far, the most plausible explanation of the phenomenon seems to be Thurneysen's tentative suggestion that in the earliest period of borrowing, the word *Saturnus* (in the nominative) may have functioned in Late Latin as the adverbial form for 'on Saturday'.[29]

But with the next three weekdays in our list, *Diu iath, Diu ethamon, Diu triach,* we cannot look to Welsh for guidance: these forms are, to my knowledge, unique to Irish. But we can nevertheless bring some additional evidence to bear on the problem of their interpretation, and perhaps go some way to establishing their authenticity.

In the Book of Leinster genealogies of the saints[30] there occurs a section concerning the seven sons of one Óengus, who are said to have come to Ireland from Scotland and to have founded churches in the Meath-Leinster area. The passage reads:

> Secht meic Óengusa meic Áeda meic Eirc meic Echach Munremair meic Óengusa Fir, ut anmnigtir i ngenelach Bercháin .i. Mo Thrianóc Ruscaig, Itharnaisc Clóenta, Éoganán Leccaig, Mo Chulli Dresnada, Mo Thairean Telcha Fortchirn, Troscán Arda Brecain, Agatán ar úr Ethni. Inde dixit Colum Cille: 'Secht meic áille Óengusa' .₇.c.

There follows elsewhere in these genealogies the full nine verses of this poem, in which are detailed the various foundations of the seven sons.[31] Of the seven sons named, four were granted by God the unique privilege of dying together on the same calendar day. I give here the relevant verses (§§6, 7):

---

ag gabháil i ndiaidh na gréine – sin saoturn'. Cf. Pádraig Ó Duinnín, *Dictionary,* s.v. [See now also Seán Ó Cróinín & Donncha Ó Cróinín, *Seanchas ó Chairbre* (Baile Átha Cliath 1985) 137.] **29** Art. cit., 187-88. **30** Trinity College Dublin MS. H. 2. 18 (1339) fol. 350, col. f; I give an edited text. The prose section occurs also in the Leabhar Breac (Royal Irish Academy, Dublin, MS. 23 P 16) p. 18, col. c, in a tract headed *Do noemi Dal Messin Corb inso;* the LB text, however, has no independent value. [See now Pádraig Ó Riain (ed), *Corpus genealogiarum sanctorum Hiberniae* (Dublin 1988) 130, No. 701.] **31** I give an edition, with translation and notes, as an Appendix to this paper. Paul Grosjean made some effort to identify the placenames in 'Notes d'hagiographie celtiques 42', *Analecta Bollandiana* 76 (1958) 387-411: 402-3. [See Ó Riain, *Corpus genealogiarum sanctorum,* 130.]

Uais itge cond-ráncatar
forind ardríg find fethal;
combad óenlaé a n-estecht-som
'n-a cure comlán cethrar.

I Prid nóin Iúin etamuin
luidset a bethaid brethglan
di deoin Meic Dé datharail,
'n-a curi comlán cethrar.

'The four complete warriors found a noble grant from the High-King of
fair halidoms: that they should all die on the same day. On the day
preceding the Nones of June [8 June] the four complete warriors passed
from the right-judging life by the will of the fair (?) Son of God'.

This translation renders everything in the two verses except for one word in the
second: *etamuin*. I suggest it means simply 'on Thursday'; that is to say, 'on the,
day preceding the Nones of June, *a Thursday*', etc. Charles Plummer[32] tried to
explain the form as 'predicative acc. [of *etham*] after *luidset*'; but he could offer
no satisfactory explanation of the semantics of the phrase. I suggest rather that
it is temporal dat. of an *n*-stem (nom. sg. *etham*, gen. sg. *ethamon* – as in our
Oxford list – and acc./dat. sg. *ethamain*, as in our poem). It may or may not be
the word *etham* 'arable land' (also an *n*-stem), as Plummer thought, but the
evidence to follow suggests that it is not. Professor Binchy has proposed to me
that *etham*, might be a noun of agency from *ith* (gen. sg. *etho*), with a meaning
like 'corn-maker' or some such thing; *Diu ethamon* might then be a day for
sowing seed in a weekly regimen of activities such as we find in *Críth Gablach*.[33]

Such an archaism may well be thought remarkable in a poem which is
distinctly late in some of its language. The chronological precision of the line
I prid nóin Iúin etamuin, however, suggests that it may originally have formed
part of a metrical calendar; but the line does not occur in any of the extant Irish
martyrologies. On the other hand, the genealogical traditions of the sons of
Óengus set them firmly in the late sixth and early seventh centuries, and they
bear witness to a connection between Scottish Dál Riata and the Leinster king-
doms for this early period which is otherwise only barely attested.

According to the *Genelach Ríg nAlban*,[34] the Óengus whose seven sons
settled in Ireland would have been coeval with Domangart, grandson of Áedán

---

32 DIL, E, col. 237. 33 See D.A. Binchy (ed), *Críth Gablach*. Medieval and Modern Irish
Series (Dublin 1941; repr. 1970) 21. 34 See Michael A. O'Brien (ed), *Corpus genealogiarum
Hiberniae* 1 (Dublin 1962; repr. 1976) 328-9. This particular sub-sept is not mentioned by name
in the genealogies, perhaps because, as an ecclesiastical family, they had lost any political
importance very early.

mac Gabráin, the king of Dál Riata who figures prominently in the narrative of Adomnán's *Vita Columbae*. Some of the islands to the north of Barra in the Outer Hebrides held a saint Taran in great honour down to modern times, and his name is preserved in an island-name of Norse construction, Tarransay.[35]

Félire Óengusa for 12 June has the following verse in his memory:

> Féil in credail Chóemáin
> diand Sanctlethan slondad;
> Torannán buan bannach
> tar ler lethan longach.[36]

'The festival of Holy Cóemán, who was called Sanctlethan; (and) Torannán of the lasting deeds, (who came) over the broad, ship-abounding ocean'.

The phrase seems more suited to the Outer Hebrides than to the less remote site in eastern Scotland which is also supposed to be his. But the martyrologies have confused this Torannán with a saint Mo Thorra, abbot of Bangor (Banchory, on the Dee in Scotland), and of Drumcliff in Co. Sligo.[37] This seems to have come about as a result of Torannán's association with Columba (the genealogies make him an older contemporary of the saint), and the fact that Drumcliff was a Columban monastery, at least in later times. Our Torannán is the one who founded a church at Tulach Fortchirn *ós toraib Tulcha Tinni*, in the territory of the Uí Felmada in Leinster.[38]

Mo Thrianóc settled, according to the poem, *irRuscachaib, la hUíb Falge* (perhaps Ruscachbeg, Co. Offaly), which is recalled also in the tract on early foundations that had seven bishops, preserved in the Book of Uí Mhaine.[39] His death is commemorated in the martyrologies at 20 August.[40]

---

35 See Marjorie O. Anderson, 'Columba and other Irish saints in Scotland', in J.L. McCracken (ed), *Historical Studies* 5 (1965) 26-36.   36 Whitley, Stokes (ed), *Félire Óengusso céli Dé, the martyrology of Oengus the Culdee*. Henry Bradshaw Society [HBS] Publications 29 (London 1905) 140.   37 The gloss in LB confuses Torannán with Palladius: Torannán *i. Palladius rocartad ó chomarba Petair i nÉrinn ria Pátraic d'forcetul dóib. Ní ragbad i nÉrinn, co ndechaid i nAlbain; hic sepultus est i Liconio. Nó Mo-Thoren Tulcha Fortchirn a n[U]íb Felmada 7 ó Druim Cliab i Cairpri;* cf. Whitley Stokes & John Strachan (eds & transls), *Thesaurus Palaeohibernicus: a collection of Old Irish glosses, scholia, prose and verse* (2 vols, Cambridge 1901, 1903) 2, 312. On the name Torannán, which seems to derive from *torann* 'thunder', see T.F. O'Rahilly, *Early Irish history and mythology* (Dublin 1946; repr. 1971) 366 n. 2.   38 Probably overlooking the river Brosna (Silver-river) in Co. Offaly; see Edmund Hogan, *Onomasticon Goedelicum locorum et tribuum Hiberniae et Scotiae* (Dublin 1910; repr. 1998) 634. [See now also Dáibhí Ó Cróinín, 'Three weddings and a funeral: rewriting Irish political history in the tenth century', in A.P. Smyth (ed), *Seanchas. Studies in Early and Medieval Irish archaeology, history and literature in honour of Francis John Byrne* (Dublin 2000) 212-24: 222 (Traig Tinni).]   39 R.A.S. Macalister (ed), *The Book of Uí Maine, otherwise called 'The book of the O'Kellys'*. Irish Manuscripts Commission (Dublin 1942) fol. 110ᵛ a 5; the tract also occurs in LB, p. 24a, but without mention of Ruscach.   40 Whitley Stokes (ed), *Félire*

The third of the seven sons, Éoganán, is said in the poem to have founded a church at *Cend Leccaig* (perhaps near the Leccach which was the seat of the Uí Berraidi kings of north Leinster),[41] but I have no further information about him. However, the fourth son, Itharnaisc, is commemorated in *Félire Óengusa* at 22 December:

> Ronnáin itge tuae,
> Itharnaisc nád-labrai,
> la hEméne ngelda
> de brú Berba balbai.

According to the poem in the Book of Leinster, he settled at Clóenad (Clane, Co. Kildare), in the territory of the Uí Faéláin. The glosses on the *Félire* in the Bodl. MS. Rawlinson B 485 read: *Itharnaisc .i. ó Chlóenad i nUíb Fáelá[i]n immolle for Bran* (where the text is to be corrected to *fri Bran*, referring to Bran Brec, whose death is commemorated in the martyrologies on 18 May; he too was of Clane).

Agatán, the fifth son, is said in the poem to have founded his church *(a dísertán)* on the banks of the river Inny, which flows from Lough Sheelan (Co. Westmeath) through Loughs Keinail, Derevaragh, and Sron into Lough Ree, a distance of twenty-five miles. It formed a traditional boundary-line between the territories of the Uí Néill and those of the Leinstermen. The martyrologies record Agatán's death on 12 June,[42] and according to the poem he was the youngest of the sons.

Mo Chullian, the sixth son, settled at Dresnatha, in the territory of the Fotharta Fea,[43] and he figures in a curious anecdote which is related in the earliest sections of the Leinster genealogies. It concerns the battle of Áth Slabae, which was fought between Cellach mac Máilottraich (of the Uí Aithechdae) and the Uí Cennselaig, in alliance with the men of Munster.[44] According to this story, Cellach's fortress was at Ráith Dermage (Durrow, Co.

Huí Gormáin, the martyrology of Gorman. HBS 9 (London 1895) 160-61; James H. Lawlor and R.I. Best (eds), *The martyrology of Tallaght.* HBS 68 (London 1931) 64; cf. Paul Walsh (ed), *Genealogiae regum et sanctorum Hiberniae* (Dublin 1918) 80-81 (Do naomhaibh Dal Riata). **41** The parish of Lackagh (barony of Offaly) Co. Kildare, according to Hogan, op. cit. 479. The Leccach cited by Hogan under a separate lemma is the same as this Lackagh. **42** James H. Todd and William Reeves (eds), *The martyrology of Donegal, a calendar of the saints of Ireland.* Irish Archaeological and Celtic Society (Dublin 1864) 166. **43** The place has not been identified but indications in the genealogies (O'Brien, *Corpus*, 82) and the scholia on Broccán's hymn to Brigit (*Thes. Pal.* 2, 341) suggest a place somewhere between the Nore and the Barrow, northeast of Kilkenny town. **44** The story occurs in the genealogies of the Síl Fiachach ba hAiccid, from whom were descended the Uí Dúnlainge and Uí Cennselaig (O'Brien, *Corpus*, 74); the battle of Áth Slabae was considered momentous enough to be mentioned in the poem *A chóicid choím Chairpri cruaid*, a march-roll of Leinster victories over their Uí Néill and Munster enemies. See the edition by Maureen O Daly, *Éigse* 10 (1961-3) 177-97: 188; in her notes to the poem, p. 197, Dr O Daly (as it seems to me) has postdated this Cellach by at least a century.

Laois?), and besides gaining victory over the combined forces of the Uí Cennselaig and the Munstermen, he is also credited with the destruction of the Uí Gabla Roírenn, a sub-sept of the Dál Cormaic which seem to have occupied the territory between Mullagh Reelan and Mullaghmast in Co. Kildare. Mo Chullian appears to have had some close connection with the Uí Cennselaig, for the story tells of his having cursed Cellach mac Maílottraich *iarna sárgud do chath Átha Slabae* ('after his violation by the battle of Á. S.'). Though not mentioned in the annals, this battle must have been quite momentous in the long sixth- and seventh-century struggle between the Uí Dúnlainge and the Uí Cennselaig for political primacy in south Leinster.

The last of the seven sons mentioned in the Book of Leinster poem is Troscán, who settled at Ard Breccain (Co. Meath): I have no more information about him than is contained in this verse and in the martyrologies, which record his death on 12 June.[45]

Having seen these seven sons of Óengus pass in review, so to speak, we are now in a position to gauge the authenticity or otherwise of the traditions preserved about them in the Book of Leinster poem. It seems reasonably assured that these men did, in fact, exist, and that their floruits can be roughly set in the late sixth and early seventh centuries. More importantly, the martyrologies record the deaths of four of them (Mo Chullian, Agatán, Torannán, and Troscán) all on the same calendar day: 12 June. We recall that the poem too stated that they died on the same day, but gave that day as *I prid nóin Iúin etamuin*, the *8th* of June; the date in the martyrologies is *pridie Idus Iunii*, and it seems clear that somewhere in the course of transmission the *pridie Nonarum* became *pridie Idus* (or vice versa). But the fact that the tradition of their deaths all on the same day has survived at all – though we may regard it with characteristically modern scepticism – must lend some credence to the suggestion that the word *etamuin* in the poem in fact designates that day, a Thursday.[46]

The proposition here advanced – that the *Diu iath*, *Diu ethamon*, and *Diu triach* forms of the Oxford list are historically genuine – can be bolstered somewhat by reference to the Leinster poems in the collections of genealogies now preserved in Oxford, Bodl. MS. Rawlinson B 502.[47] Though this manuscript was written in the early 1120s, no one, I think, disputes the relative antiquity of the poems; the questions concern only the precise date to be assigned to them, whether seventh-century or eighth.[48]

---

45 Todd and Reeves, op. cit., 168.   46 It is probable that *Prid. Id. Iun.* was the original reading, which then was misinterpreted as dittography by a scribe (*Prid. Id.*), and changed to *Prid. Non.* 47 Kuno Meyer (ed), *Rawlinson B. 502, a collection of pieces in prose and verse in the Irish language*, etc. (Oxford 1909); O'Brien, *Corpus*, 1–9.   48 See Kuno Meyer, 'Über die älteste irische Dichtung [ÄID] 1, rhythmische und alliterierende Reimstrophen', *Abhandlungen der königlichen Preußischen Akademie der Wissenschaften*, phil.-hist. Kl., Nr. 6 (Berlin 1913), who dates the poems to the seventh century; Thurneysen, in a review of Meyer's work, ZCP 10 (1915) 445–8, seems to opt for an eighth-century date; O'Rahilly, *Early Irish history and mythology* (Dublin 1946)

The poems were first edited by Kuno Meyer in his pioneering work *Über die älteste irische Dichtung*, and republished in a diplomatic edition by M.A. O'Brien in his *Corpus Genealogiarum Hiberniae*. The poems were composed in what the *Mittelirische Verslehren* call *nath cethorbrechtai:*[49] rhythmic, alliterative verse that is characteristic of our earliest Irish metrics. Mac Neill thought all six poems in this series should be ascribed to Luccreth moccu Chérrai (i. e. of the Ciarraige), to whom he also ascribed the metrical innovations first evident in these early seventh-century metres.[50]

The third of these Rawlinson poems, ascribed in the manuscript to Laidcend mac Baircheda (i.e. of the Uí Bairrchi?), lists the names of thirty-five Leinster kings who are also supposed to have been kings of Tara in pre-Christian times.[51] The poem is of peculiar interest inasmuch as it gives in third- and second-last positions in the list the names of Muiredach Mo Sníthech and Móenach mac Caírthinn, both kings of the Uí Bairrchi. The evidence of early saints' Lives and of the Patrician material in general, as well as the scattered hints throughout the Leinster genealogies, suggest that the Uí Bairrchi enjoyed this kind of political predominance in south Leinster not later than the end of the seventh century.[52] In other words, the political content of the poem tells in favour of its proposed seventh-century dating. We may now turn to the third verse of the poem:

Coin milid Ailill fri agu fri cricha Crothomun
crothois Abratchain airbe iath Ethomuin[53]

Meyer translated: 'Ailill was a fair warrior in war against the borders of Crothomun; the fair-browed one shook the battleranks of the lands of Ethomun'. Professor Wagner, in a note to his recent re-edition of the *Dind ríg* poem[54] – another of these early Leinster compositions – offers an almost identical rendering. Concerning the words *Crothomun/Ethomun* Meyer remarked[55]

[EIHM], 179 n. 2, remarks: 'In regarding the poem in ÄID 1, 16-18, as a composition of the seventh century, Meyer, as it seems to me, greatly exaggerates its antiquity', but he cites no reasons for this view. Professor Carney tended toward a dating in the late sixth century, see his 'Three Old Irish accentual poems', *Ériu* 22 (1971) 23-80, and 'Aspects of archaic Irish', *Éigse* 17 (1978-9) 417-35.   **49** See Rudolf Thurneysen (ed), 'Mittelirische Verslehren', *Irische Texte* 3/1 (1891) 1-182: 39 (II 28).   **50** Mac Neill's views on the attribution of the poems are recorded by Séamus Pender (ed), *Féilscribhinn Torna* (Cork 1947) 209-17: 210; his remark on the metres is in his paper 'The mythology of Lough Neagh', *Béaloideas* 2 (1929-30) 115-21. 116 n. 2. In a withering reply to this article, 'The mythology of Lough Neagh', ibid., 246-52, Osborn Bergin remarked (with characteristic reserve): 'The credit of originating the metrical experiments of the seventh century may or may not be due to this poet.'   **51** Meyer, ÄID 1, 16-18; O'Brien, *Corpus*, 8-9.   **52** See Alfred P. Smyth, 'Húi Failgi relations with the Húi Néill in the century after the loss of the plain of Mide', *Études Celtiques* 14 (1975) 503-23: 518-19.   **53** I give the text of O'Brien's *Corpus* in all cases.   **54** 'The archaic Dind ríg poem and related problems', *Ériu* 28 (1977) 1-16: 7.   **55** ÄID 1, 14: 'Auch die Erwähnung der sonst nicht bekannten feindlichen Gebiete Crothomun und Ethomun ... wird gewiss eine historische Grundlage haben'; cf. ibid., 20.

that 'the mention of the otherwise unknown enemy territories Crothomun and Ethomun ... must certainly have a historical basis'. It is clear that M.A. O'Brien accepted this view, for in a note to these forms[56] he identified *iath n-Ethomuin* (sic) with the *cenél n-Atheman* on the Meath border, and identified *crícha Crothomun* with the Cruithne. We may assume that Professor Wagner, too, regarded them as placenames.

So convinced, indeed, was Meyer that this was the case, that he inserted the mark of nasalization before *Ethomuin* (whence O'Brien's form above); but he made the insertion unconsciously, it seems, for he gave no manuscript reading in the apparatus to indicate that he had made the change.[57] True, *iath* (n. or m. *o*-stem) is used quite frequently in these poems with the meaning 'land', but always, it seems, with the expected nasalization. That our example (and the one to follow) should diverge from this rule ought to suggest caution. I propose, as an alternative, that in this case we are dealing, not with the word *iath* 'land', but the word *iath* 'Wednesday', exactly the form that appears in our Oxford list. Likewise, in the case of *ethomuin*, we have, I suggest, not a placename, but the word for 'Thursday'.[58]

I think we have here a formulaic use of *iath ethomuin*, similar in concept to the kind of list we find in *Críth Gablach*, but the property of the encomiastic poet, not of the lawyer. We may refer to another such eulogizing formula in the second of these Leinster poems, beginning *Nuadu Necht, ní dámair anflaith*; the twenty-third verse of this poem reads as follows:

Laithe cach Luain   lui cath cnedach fri fergus
find cach Mercúir mandrais   móin cach Satuirn selgus

Meyer translated: 'On every Monday he waged a many-wounded battle with Fergus; every Wednesday he destroyed Find (?); every Saturday he laid waste a bog'.[59] We see that the pattern is exactly the same: a great deed is ascribed to the hero on a succession of separate days. What is more, we can cite another example from this poem parallel to our first example above:

Drongaib māraib mandrais   iath Iathomuin
ella oircne   oldomun crích Crothomuin

---

56 'Hibernica', ZCP 14 (1923) 309-34: 331 n. 1.   57 He noted the MS. reading in the addenda and corrigenda to pt.1, which he issued in ÄID 2 (1914) 29, but Thurneysen's and O'Brien's citations show that the damage had already been done.   58 I suggest, then, as an alternative translation: 'Ailill was a great warrior in forays; on Wednesday and Thursday [i.e. regularly] Abratcháin shook the battleranks of (lit. "against") the land of Crothom (?).'   59 Meyer read *Find* (MS. *fid*) and *Fergus* (a personal name); Professor Carney, 'Aspects', 432, translates: 'Every Monday he embarked on a bloody battle against manly vigour.' [Quite what significance Meyer saw in laying waste a bog is not immediately apparent.]

Meyer suggested that the manuscript-reading *iathomuin* was simply a scribal error, induced by the preceding word *iath*. But here again, as in the previous occurrence of the formula, he inserted the mark of nasalization before *Ethomuin* (as he had emended it), and translated: 'He crushed the land of *Ethomun* with great military hosts; (with) masterful destructive attacks against the lands of Crothomun'.[60]

It must be admitted that the interpretation of the word *iath* as 'land' in our two examples (with the following proper noun in the genitive) is attractive. Thurneysen, in discussing the (apparent) disyllabic end-words in these poems,[61] proposed to emend to *Edmuinn* and *Cremthainn* respectively; but since he was unaware of the fact (whose discovery was due to Professor Carney) that in archaic poetry of this kind disyllabic words in end-line position and with medial consonant-clusters could be counted as trisyllables for metrical purposes, his objections to the manuscript-readings can carry no weight.

I suggest that we have here, as in the previous instance, the words *iath* and *ethomuin*, 'Wednesday' and 'Thursday' used in a poetic formula. The poet is merely emphasizing that Nuadu makes a regular practice of harrying his opponents. We may note the recurrence of the verb *mandraid* ('destroys') in the *Dind ríg* poem, and in a similar kind of verse concerning the celebrated Feidlimid mac Crimthainn, where great deeds are ascribed to that warrior-abbot on a single day.[62]

This explanation of *iath ethomuin* may be objected to on the grounds that there already exists a word for 'Wednesday' in this latter Leinster poem, in the form of *Mercúir*. There can be little doubt that this is a very old form, borrowed from the Latin *(dies) Mercurii*.[63] I can only reply that I believe the word *iath*, occurring as it does in what I understand to be a formulaic use, reflects what may have been a still older Irish word for 'Wednesday'; it is possible that by the time these verses were being written down, the exact meaning of the formula might have been forgotten.

There is one further instance of the words *iath ethomuin* occurring together which we should examine. The words are found in an obscure rhetoric which prophesies the coming of Ciarán of Clonmacnoise (here called by its older name, Druim Tipraite), and which is put into the mouth of Finn mac Cumaill.[64] I give here the first few lines of the poem, and attempt a translation:

> *Cain tuir taidleuch mac saoir eo aibda ar cach aine grene*
> *gealtaithnem gries ethomoin iath ialla en netarda*
> *niab os findnime fraicc.*

60 Note that Thurneysen in his review, ZCP 10, 446, prints *iath n-Iathomuin* without comment. **61** He obviously did not extend his reading beyond the examples edited by Meyer. **62** See Gerard Murphy, *Early Irish metrics* (Dublin 1961) 65 §114. **63** In which case the form must be *Mercuir* (with short *u*), not *Mercúir*, as Meyer, O'Brien, and Carney have it. **64** Cf. Ludwig Ch. Stern, 'Le manuscrit irlandais de Leide', *Revue Celtique* 13 (1892) 1–31.

'The carpenter's son (will be) a fine, brilliant paragon, a beautiful champion, a sun's radiance on all, the glowing of bright shining perpetually (?) [= *ethomuin iath* ?], a flock of ethereal birds (?), the brilliance of the vaults of the sky (?)'. An equal case might be made for interpreting *ethomoin iath* as I suggest, or as 'of the land of Ethomun'; the location of *iath n-Ethomuin* proposed by O'Brien would suit the present context.

If my interpretation of *ethomoin iath* in the above rhetoric is correct, then we have in this instance, and in the other two that we discussed, the words *iath* and *ethomuin* apparently used in a temporal syntactic construction. *Iath* would appear to be undeclined, while *ethomuin* seems to reflect the temporal dative form of an *n*-stem. Set against the backdrop of the Oxford list's *Diu iath* and *Diu ethamon*, and the *etamuin* form in the Book of Leinster poem, there seems to be some case for regarding these occurrences in the Leinster poems as genuine archaisms.

And what are we to make of the name *Diu triach* 'Friday'? It looks as though it might be the gen. sg. of some such theoretical word as **treó*, just as *eó* 'salmon' has a gen. sg. in *iach*. But a glance at the Academy Dictionary[65] brings that train of thought to an abrupt halt, for they dismiss the word in one sentence, as a late derivative from the word *treoir* 'direction'. We must look elsewhere.

An alternative approach might be to read *Diu triath*, and posit a lexical item *iath* (< *éth* ??) in all three of the forms *Diu iath*, *Diu ethomuin* (*éthomuin* > *iathomuin* [i.e. *éth* + *emain* 'two *iatha*'], as in the poem *Nuadu Necht, ni dámair anflaith?*), *Diu triath* (*tre* + *iath* ??). But such an approach makes the exact meaning of *iath* no clearer, unless it be, in fact, the word *iath* 'land'. Farther than this we cannot go.[*]

Are these, then, the oldest Irish names for the days of the week? I think I have shown that the Oxford list at least, far from being a learned concoction, deserves to be taken seriously. These names may represent possibly the earliest Irish contacts with the Christian Roman world, a period in the history of the Irish language when native words were still being used to render new, imported concepts in Irish society, but before the characteristics of sixth-century monastic pietism had impressed themselves on the nomenclature of the days. The Oxford list, then, marks a crossroads in early Irish history.

65 DIL, T, col. 297.   * In a review of the original article that appeared in *Études Celtiques* 21 (1984) 366–68, Prof. Pierre-Yves Lambert suggested a connection between the *diu iath, diu ethamon*, and *diu triath* of our list and the entry of Cormac's Glossary §763: ith o iath 7 ith o ith nominati sunt. (cf. also DIL s.v. 2 *ith*). He then interprets *iath* as an ancient form (perhaps inflected) of *ith/īth* 'cereal', correspondent to Breton *yod*, or Welsh *iwd*. Thus *diu iath* 'est sans doute le "jour de la bouillie"', i.e., day of abstinence, as in the case in the better-known term *cét-aín* 'first fast'. He would see the archaic names, therefore, as reflecting the same system of fasting that is found in the later Irish terms ('Si cette analyse est bonne, les dénominations archaïques découvertes par l'auteur feraient référence au système des jeûnes chrétiens tout comme les dénominations actuelles').

APPENDIX

Trinity College Dublin MS. H. 2. 18 (1339) *Book of Leinster*, p. 354c 52ff. (Cf. pp. 350 f.)

Colum Cille cecinit.

1. Secht meic áille Óengusa,
   lotar co iath n-Érenn;
   Mo-Thrianóc is Itharnaisc,
   Éoganán áille rémend.

2. Mo-Thrianóc i rRuscachaib,
   la hUí Falge ro-fáemad;
   Cend Leccaig im Eóganán,
   Itharnaisc án i Clóenad.

3. In cethrur for-fácabsat
   luidset dar farge fostán:
   Torannán is Agatán,
   Mo Chullian is Troscán.

4. Troscán trén tarrasair
   i nArd Breccain co mbinni;
   Torannán in tairbertach
   ós toraib Tulcha Tinni.

5. Mo Chullian i nDresnatha –
   Fothart Feä, feidm n-ualle;
   Agatán 'na dísiurtán
   ar brú na Ethni uaire.

6. Uais itge cond-ráncatar
   forind ardríg find fethal;
   combad óenláe a n-estecht-som
   'n-a cure comlán cethrar.

7. I prid nóin Iúin etamuin
   luidset a bethaid brethglan
   di deoin Meic Dé datharail,
   'n-a curi comlán cethrar.

8. Ind lecc fora-táncatar
    dar triathmuir trethnaig,
    Agatán a sósar-som
    ros-fuc a crandchor cethruir.

9. Na manistri fuaratar,
    i nde[r]natar a ferta,
    is la hUí Néill Nóigiallaig
    co rrath in spirta sechta. S.

1. The seven beautiful sons of Óengus, they went to the land of Ireland; Mo Thrianóc and Itharnaisc, Éoganán of the beautiful coursing.

2. Mo Thrianóc was received at Ruscach, among the Uí Failge; Éoganán was at Cend Leccaig, and the famous Itharnaisc at Clane.

3. The four whom they left (behind) went across the steady sea; Torannán and Agatán, Mo Chullian and Troscán.

4. Troscán the strong settled at Ardbreccan with melodiousness; Torannán the generous (settled) above the hosts of Tulach Tinni.

5. Mo Chullian was in Dresnatha (in the territory) of the Fotharta Fea, great pride; Agatán was in his little hermitage on the banks of the cold Inny.

6. The four complete warriors found a noble grant from the High-King of fair halidoms; that they should all die on the same day.

7. On the day preceding the Nones of June (8 June) the four complete warriors passed from the right-judging life by the will of the fair (?) Son of God.

8. The flagstone on which they came over the storm-swelled sea, it was Agatán, the youngest of them, who won it in a lot-casting among the four.

9. The monasteries that they received and in which they did their great deeds, they are (now) among the Uí Néill, with the grace of the seven-fold Spirit.

NOTES

The metre is *Ae freslige* ($7^3 + 7^2$), but some lines are wanting one or more syllables. Construe-marks connect the first occurrences of each name with the abbreviated forms in the following verses; the signs used are: .. : .·.·.

Title: The words *Colum Cille cecinit* are actually enclosed within the red border that surrounds the previous item on the page; but the prose introduction cited above, p. 16, clearly indicates that the ascription is intended to accompany this poem.

1b: To make up the requisite syllable-count we must read *iäth.*

2a: *i rRuscachaib.* Cf. Hogan, *Onomasticon,* 589.

2c: *Cend Leccaig.* My suggestion that this site may have been the ecclesiastical equivalent of *Leccach* (townland in parish of Offaly, Co. Kildare), the royal site of the Uí Berraide kings, is based on comparison with other doublet names like *Emain Macha: Ard Macha, Dún Lethglaise: Dún dá Lethglaise.*

3cd: It should perhaps be noted that in the Life of Berchán edited by Charles Plummer, *Bethada náem n-Érenn* (2 vols, Oxford, 1922; repr. 1968) 1, 23-43, two saints Dicholla and Toranach are mentioned. In the light of Berach/Berchán's stated connection with Scotland, and the fact that the story of the sons of Óengus is said by the Book of Leinster prose introduction to have occurred *i ngenelach Bercháin,* it is possible that the two mentioned in the Life are the same as the Mo Chullian and Torannán of the poem.

4a: The line is a syllable short.

4d: *Tulach Tinni.* Perhaps identical with the *T(a)ul Tinne* cited by Hogan, *Onomasticon,* 621. The *Annals of the Four Masters* 3, 182, have reference to a *Droicheat Tine,* and O'Donovan suggested a bridge was intended over the river Brosna (Silver-river), Co. Offaly. That general area would suit the context here. [See now also Dáibhí Ó Cróinín, 'Three weddings and a funeral', in A. P. Smyth (ed), *Seanchas. Studies in honour of Francis John Byrne* (Dublin 2000) 212-24: 222 (*Traig Tinni*).]

7a: *etamuin.* Cf. the poem on Ard Fothaid edited by Edward Gwynn, *The metrical dindshenchas* 4 (Dublin 1924) 90, which reads: *Fothaid aingthech etamain / rotecht co cían* 'the gentle F. A. long possessed it'. Gwynn, 398, stated that *etamain* was the opposite of *tamuin,* and referred to O'Davoren's Glossary §1560: *tamuin i. borb.* However, metrical reasons preclude our equating the *etamain* of the Dindshenchas with the *etamuin* (: *datharail*) of our poem.

8b: The line is two syllables short.

2

New light on Palladius[*]

In the long and sometimes heated debate about Patrick, Palladius, and the beginnings of Christianity in Ireland much the greater part of the discussion has centred on Patrick rather than on Palladius – despite the fact that it was Palladius who was sent as 'first bishop' to the Irish at the head of an official mission from Rome. The reasons for this imbalance of treatment are obvious enough: it was Patrick's name that lived on in Irish written and oral tradition, while Palladius disappeared, apparently without trace.[1] No less important perhaps, two of Patrick's writings have come down to us, the Confession and the letter to the soldiers of Coroticus. From the Palladian mission, on the other hand, not a single document has survived – this, at any rate, has been the common perception.[2] It is, however, a mistaken one. I hope to demonstrate, from published and unpublished evidence, that one at least of the texts associated with the official mission did, in fact, survive, if only in fragmentary form. The text is Palladius' Easter table.

Traces of Palladius' Easter table are to be found in two seventh-century Irish computistical texts. The earliest and best-known of the two is Cummian's Paschal Letter.[3] Composed in AD 632-33, Cummian's letter is a collection of biblical, patristic, canonical, and computistical information remarkable in its extent and erudition. Not the least remarkable part of it is that section specifically devoted to Easter tables. Cummian states that he had to hand no fewer than ten such cycles, which he identifies by name. The first is that which he ascribes to Patrick: *Primum illum quem sanctum Patricius, papa noster, tulit et fecit; in quo luna a .xiiii. usque in .xxi. regulariter, et equinoctium a .xii. Kalendis*

---

[*] First published in *Peritia* 5 (1986) 276-83.   1 According to R.P.C. Hanson, *Saint Patrick: his origins and career* (Oxford 1968), 'Palladius must have died quite early, so that by the time Patrick wrote to Coroticus he could call himself *Hiberione constitutum episcopum* (Ep. 1) with an easy mind'. This interpretation of Patrick's Latin, and the inference drawn from it, are, I think, mistaken.   2 The accounts of Palladius in the standard discussions of the Irish church are invariably coloured by the 'Patrick problem'. This treatment continues in the most recent work, Richard Sharpe, 'Some problems concerning the organisation of the early Irish church', *Peritia* 3 (1985) 230-70, where Palladius merits only one passing reference. [In Colmán Etchingham, *The organisation of the Irish Church, AD 650-1000* (Maynooth 2000) he is not mentioned at all.]   3 A new edition of the letter, with commentary, will appear shortly in the Studies and Texts series of the Pontifical Institute of Mediaeval Studies [PIMS], Toronto. [See now Maura Walsh & Dáibhí Ó Cróinín (eds & transls), *Cummian's Letter 'De controversia Paschali' together with a related seventh-century Irish tract 'De ratione conputandi'*. PIMS, Studies & Texts 86 (Toronto 1988).]

Aprilis observatur. This cycle was based on three principles, two of them explicitly given in Cummian's wording; the third follows by natural inference from the others: (1) 'Patrick's' Easter table observed lunar limits XIIII-XXI for the Easter full moon;[4] (2) It observed the vernal/spring equinox on 21 March; (3) It observed an early Easter limit of 22 March.

Before examining these principles we must turn to the additional evidence, hitherto unpublished, because this new material provides crucial details which will help confirm the nature and origin of the 'Patrick' table.

In the collection of computistical tracts used by Bede, the archetype of which was compiled in southern Ireland *c.* AD 658,[5] there is found a brief miscellany of texts culled from the writings of Q. I. Hilarianus, Dionysius Exiguus, and Isidore of Seville, as well as from a number of pseudonymous works, including the *Epistolae* of Virgilius Maro Grammaticus.[6] Here in this seemingly random selection is a precious excerpt from the 'Prologue' to a 'Patrician' table:

> Patricius in prologo suo, secundum rationem Anatolii, hoc ius ostendit: 'Notandum est quod in .xviiii. ciclo quattuor anni contrariae regulae inueniuntur, quorum ratio diligenter arguteque animaduertenda est. Hoc est annus .viii. lunae, secundum rationem Grecorum, et annus .xxvii. Item, secundum rationem Latinorum, .iiii. lunae annus, et .xxx. Item tribus annis in .xviiii. ciclo eadem aetas super Kalendas Aprilis et Maii inuenitur. Hoc est in anno .xxvi. lunae super Kalendas Ianuarii, et in anno .xxviiii. et in anno .xxvii.

It is not necessary at this point to enter into the technical aspects of this text. Leaving aside for the moment the whole question of authorship, two statements only need be noted: (i) The text is a prologue to a 19-year table; (2) Comparison is made in it between 'Greek' and 'Latin' practice. The obvious question arises: Is this the same as Cummian's Patrician cycle? Cummian refers to a cycle that passed under Patrick's name, and the data in the unpublished collection is said to derive from Patrick's prologue. This coincidence of names and the combination of data in both sources can leave one in no doubt that they refer to one and the same work, for both embody the principles of a 19-year cycle.

But this could not be Patrick's Easter table. The author of the Confession and of the letter to Coroticus came from Britain, and he was formed by his

---

4 The lunar limits were arbitrarily 'emended' by Bartholomew Mac Carthy, *Annals of Ulster* 4 (Dublin 1901) cxxxvii (altering *xiiii* to *xv*, strangely overlooking the fact that early medieval manuscripts invariably write *iiii* not *iv*). **5** Dáibhí Ó Cróinín, 'The Irish provenance of Bede's computus', *Peritia* 2 (1983) 229-47. [See now below, 173-89.] **6** This is the earliest datable use of Virgilius in Irish (or any other) sources.

experience of the British church.[7] However, the British church in the fourth and fifth centuries reckoned the date of Easter in accordance with the rules of an 84-year cycle, not a 19-year one. This old table, the *Romana supputatio*,[8] was introduced to Rome early in the fourth century. De Rossi was the first to suggest that this cycle (or a slightly modified version of it) was brought back to Britain by the three British bishops who attended the council of Arles in AD 314, and all available evidence supports this suggestion.[9] Everything that we know about British and Irish Easter observances in the sixth and seventh centuries points to the use by churches in both countries of an 84-year cycle based on the principles of the (older) *supputatio:* equinox on 25 March; lunar limits XIIII-XX; Easter limits 25 March – 21 April.[10] Indeed, the Britons were to prove even more obstinate than the Irish in their adherence to the 84-year tables, for while Iona – the last bastion of die-hard Irish practices – adopted the 'orthodox' reckoning in AD 716, the British churches persisted in their ways for another half-century.[11]

All the available evidence, therefore, points to a continental origin, not a British one, for this Patrician table. We know, from the letters of Pope Leo for example,[12] that the practice of comparing Greek and Latin tables was standard in Rome during the fourth and fifth centuries. The practice had arisen because the Alexandrian and Roman paschal tables frequently disagreed on the date of Easter.[13] But though Latin and Greek tables diverged constantly, Alexandria and Rome actually observed the same Easters. However, this required a certain measure of give-and-take. The data for the years when Athanasius was bishop show that on three occasions (AD 333, 346, and 349) the Alexandrians celebrated Easter on a date which disagreed with their own calculations, in order

7 It is clear from what follows that I hold no brief for the view that Patrick studied for any length of time in Gaul, whether at Auxerre or Lérins, or wherever. [See now my paper, 'Who was Palladius, "first bishop of the Irish"?', *Peritia* 14 (2000) [2001] 205-37.] 8 The question of whether or not an 'older' *supputatio* was subsequently replaced by a 'newer' one at Rome during the early fourth century is too complicated to allow for full discussion here. I hope to return to the problem in a more comprehensive treatment of the Easter controversy among the British and Irish churches which I have in preparation. For the present it will suffice to remark that only an 84-year table (of whatever construction) is involved. 9 There is a useful summary of the Easter problem in the British churches in Hugh Williams, *Christianity in early Britain* (Oxford 1912) 463-73; though not necessarily acceptable in some details, the general treatment is a model of clarity. [See now also the excellent discussion in Thomas Charles-Edwards, *Early Christian Ireland* (Cambridge 2000) 391-415, and Faith Wallis, *Bede 'The Reckoning of Time'* (Liverpool 2000) xxxiv-lxiii.] 10 See Jones, *Bedae opera* 78-104 ('Easter in the British Isles'). Jones' rejection of the 21 April limit is not convincing. For general discussion see August Strobel, *Ursprung und Geschichte des christlichen Osterkalenders* (Berlin 1977) 224-80. 11 'Pasca commutatur apud Brittones emendante Elbodugo homine Dei', in Egerton Phillimore (ed), 'The *Annales Cambriae* and Old-Welsh genealogies from Harleian MS 3859', *Y Cymmrodor* 9 (1888) 141-83: 162, s.a. 768. 12 Edited by Bruno Krusch, *Studien zur christlich-mittelalterlichen Chronologie* [1] (Leipzig 1880) 251-65. 13 For what follows see Krusch, *Studien*, passim, and Eduard Schwarz, 'Christliche und jüdische Ostertafeln', *Abh. Kgl. Gesellsch. Wiss. Göttingen*, phil.-hist. Kl., N.F., 8/6 (Berlin 1905) 49-88.

to accommodate Rome. Thereafter, however, the Alexandrians decided to follow their own tables, without regard to any objections which their dates might cause at Rome. With the publication by bishop Theophilus (385-412) of a table extending over one hundred years from AD 380, the patriarchate of Alexandria signalled a final and definitive decision to observe Easter only on those dates calculated by their own 19-year tables, and they issued paschal letters every year which indicated the date in advance.

The choice now lay with the popes, whether or not to celebrate the Alexandrian Easter when that date differed from the one offered by their own tables. The evidence shows that in fact the popes were loath to make the decisive break. During the years AD 328-386 the two churches only once observed Easter on divergent dates. Where before Alexandria had yielded to Roman wishes in AD 333, 346, and 349, Rome in turn opted for Alexandrian dates against her own tables three times between AD 350 and 387: 357, 360, and 384. But the correct Easter date could only be ascertained by comparing Greek and Latin tables, precisely the practice we saw reflected in the 'Patrician' table.

The divergence of Alexandrian and Roman tables clearly caused considerable difficulties, not just for the popes. We have a letter from Ambrose of Milan to the bishops of the province of Aemilia on the subject of the thorny Easter date for AD 387,[14] which shows clearly that several bishops, including some from the Roman province, had written to him looking for an explanation of the Alexandrian methods and for a verdict on the proposed Easter date for that year (25 April, the latest possible date according to Alexandrian principles, and four days beyond the limit set by Roman tables). Ambrose's letter is clear testimony to the fact that Alexandrian rules and the 19-year tables that embodied them were known and used in the West before the end of the fourth century, and that other tables were also in use at the same time. This situation clearly persisted into the fifth century, for the years AD 444 and 455 saw further serious clashes which forced Pope Leo to write both to the emperor and to the patriarch Proterius of Alexandria in defence of Roman tables.[15]

Around the time of Palladius' mission, therefore, the practice at Rome and elsewhere on the continent was to compare the 84- and 19-year tables. It is precisely this practice that we find in the prologue to 'Patrick's' table, and the data in Cummian's letter makes it abundantly clear that – whatever its origins – the 'Patrician' table was a 19-year cycle constructed according to Alexandrian principles.

Bury, in his *Life of Saint Patrick*, was faced by the conflicting evidence in Cummian's letter that Patrick had apparently introduced an Easter table into

14 MPL 16, 1026-35. I accept the case for the letter's authenticity made by Michaela Zelzer, 'Zum Osterfestbrief des heiligen Ambrosius und zur römischen Osterfestberechnung des 4. Jahrhunderts', *Wiener Studien*, N.F., 12 (1978) 187-204. Her arguments more than outweigh the flimsy objections of Krusch and Schwarz. 15 Jones, *Bedae opera*, 55-61.

Ireland, and yet, on Cummian's own evidence, the known Irish usage was not what Patrick could have introduced. 'If we suppose', he wrote, 'that a table of Paschal computation was brought by Patrick to Ireland in the first half of the fifth century, it is not probable that he would have introduced any other than the *supputatio Romana*. This inference does not depend on the view which we adopt as to Patrick's relations to the church of Rome. It depends upon his connexion with the Gallic church. There is no evidence, so far as I can discover, that the Gallic church did not agree with the Roman in the fourth and fifth centuries as to the Paschal limits. We should have to suppose that Patrick rejected both the system prevailing in western Europe and the Alexandrine system in favour of the older usage prevailing in his native country, Britain; and this, in view of the circumstances of his career, seems extremely unlikely. The evidence, in my opinion, suggests a rather different conclusion. It suggests that the Paschal system which prevailed in Britain in the fourth century and survived to the seventh had been introduced from Britain into Ireland and taken root among the christian communities there, before the arrival of Patrick. There is no a priori objection to the possibility that, while the old method continued in the old-established communities, he may have sanctioned a different table in the new communities which he founded'.[16]

Bury's conjectures are characteristically brilliant, but his conclusions cannot stand because he worked on the supposition (advanced by Krusch and others after him) that Roman Paschal tables were universally and exclusively used in all Latin-speaking provinces in Patrick's time.[17] But this was not the case. Ambrose's letter is clear proof that Alexandrian tables were being followed at Milan in his time († AD 397), and Gaudentius of Brescia's Paschal tracts confirm that they were still in use there a decade after Ambrose's death. Gaudentius († *c*. AD 406) states unequivocally, following Exodus 12: 17-19, that Easter must be sought in the week of Unleavened Bread, between moons XIIII and XXI: *Et ideo nec intra quartam decimam lunam nec ultra uicesimam primam celebrare possumus, quia septem tantum dies sunt azymorum paschalium, in quibus dominicum quaerimus diem.*[18] These are an extension of Theophilus' words; lunar limits XIIII-XXI are Alexandrian. The same limits are repeated exactly in Augustine's letter to Ianuarius (Ep. L): *a xiiii luna uoluit obseruari, ... usque ad uicensimam uero et primam propter ipsum numerum septenarium.*[19] Augustine may have acquired this doctrine during his stay in Milan. At any rate, he observed it in Africa while bishop of Hippo. Proof that these limits were observed elsewhere in the West in the latter half of the fourth century is to be found in

---

16 *The life of Saint Patrick and his place in history* (London 1905) 373-74.   17 It was precisely in order to maintain this view that Krusch and Schwartz were forced to dismiss the Ambrosian letter of AD 386 as spurious. Zelzer (op. cit., 190 n.10) has a pointed comment on the matter: 'Das ist keine brauchbare Methode, um mit Angaben, die nicht ins Konzept passen, fertig zu werden'.   18 Ibid., n. 3.   19 Cited Jones, *Bedae opera*, 36 n. 2.

Ambrosiaster's *Quaestiones ueteris et noui testamenti: Omnia enim plena deus insti-tuit; ideoque a decima quarta usque in uigensimam primam, his septem diebus pascha nobis celebrare concessum est.*[20]

There are no grounds, therefore, for Bury's assumption that the *Romana supputatio* was the 'official' table in the Latin-speaking provinces. Different tables were being followed at Milan, and Milan in this period was almost as certain to spread its usages as the church at Rome (as Ambrose's letter eloquently proves). Milanese rites were known and followed throughout north-ern Italy and southern Gaul. After all, the seat of empire was in Milan, not in Rome.

But Bury was almost right – if we substitute Palladius for Patrick then all the pieces of the puzzle fall neatly into place. The table described by Cummian was one based on Alexandrian principles; that much cannot be in dispute. Palladius, trained at Auxerre, would have been ideally positioned to acquire such a table. He may also have spent some time at Rome between AD 429 and AD 431, if we accept literally Prosper's statements that he was instrumental in the selection of bishop Germanus of Auxerre for the anti-Pelagian mission to Britain in AD 429, and that he was subsequently ordained bishop by Celestine prior to his own departure on the Irish mission in AD 431. Either way, Palladius' background provides the perfect milieu for Cummian's 'Patrician' table.[21] Cummian's *papa noster* was Palladius, not Patrick.

Charles W. Jones wrote that 'Patrick therefore introduced into Ireland in the first part of the fifth century the paschal usage of Milan, which he may have learned at Lérins or Auxerre. It existed in Patrician establishments long enough to be known to Cummian two centuries later. Bury may be right that Patrick was not able to overcome the already firmly implanted tradition of British Easter'.[22] Much more likely, it seems to me, it was Palladius who introduced the paschal usage of Milan. The Palladian mission, based quite possibly in the south midlands (Kildare-Offaly?) seems not to have put down deep roots, and its organisation did not survive in strength. It was overwhelmed by the burgeoning monastic *paruchiae* of the sixth century, which had strong links with Britain. That British church used an 84-year Easter cycle, and the '84' was to be a characteristic feature of Irish practice down to Columbanus' time and beyond. The newer monastic churches may well have continued a usage already established in the fledgling Irish christian communities of pre-Palladian times, for those first Irish converts were certainly under British influence. In which case Bury would be right (as Jones remarked) in suggesting that Patrick (for

---

20 Jones, ibid., 37. **21** Hanson's statement (*St Patrick,* 104 n. 4) that 'Cummian in his letter to Segene would, of course, ascribe to Patrick as traditional author any Paschal Cycle of which he approved and whose immediate origin he could not trace' indicates a misunderstanding of the let-ter and its background. **22** *Bedae opera,* 86.

whom read Palladius) 'was not able to overcome the already firmly implanted British Easter'.

We know of no connection between Cummian and the Patrician community of churches. Those clerics mentioned by him as having attended the synod of Mag Léne were all from foundations in the north Munster region, not far distant from the likely location of the fifth-century Palladian mission. Patrick, on the other hand, seems to have laboured in Ulster. By an ironic twist of fate, Patrick's writings survived long enough to be incorporated into the Armagh archive in the seventh century, while Palladius' table (and perhaps other books from his mission?) passed into the southern sphere of influence, only to see its true origins obscured by the inexorable advance of the Patrician legend. But Cummian set that table at the top of his list, before any Alexandrian table and even before Augustine's, and he venerated its owner as *papa noster*, a term found nowhere else in Hiberno-Latin literature. Given the manifest confusion of Patrician and Palladian traditions that already existed in the seventh century, the obvious conclusion is that Cummian had Palladius in mind, not Patrick the Briton. If the table is Palladius' then Cummian's letter and the collection used by Bede both preserve parts of the oldest Irish christian text.*

[In printing the above text from Oxford, Bodl. 309, I unaccountably took the opening words *Patricius in prologo suo ... hoc ius ostendit* to refer to what follows in the manuscript, when, of course, it actually refers to what *precedes* it. That being the case, my arguments for asserting that Patrick's 'Prologue' must (because of its technical content) have related to a 19-year Easter table of continental origin (and specifically of Milanese derivation) cannot now stand, on this evidence at any rate. The text that precedes the reference to the Prologue (*Sed cum tres menses uernum tempus habeat ... hiemale tempus est*) is, in fact, an excerpt from Pseudo-Athanasius / Pseudo-Martin of Braga, *De Pascha*, and the details in that text – together with the reference to Patrick's Prologue as reckoning *secundum rationem Anatolii* – should have alerted me to the probability that Patrick's Prologue followed the same computistical rules, and therefore contained material more at home in discussions of an 84-year Easter table than in a 19-year one. The proposed connection with Palladius, therefore, cannot stand either. See further my recent paper, 'Who was Palladius, "first bishop of the Irish"?', *Peritia* 14 (2000) [2001] 205-37.]

* The research for this paper was undertaken with the aid of a Fellowship from the Alexander von Humboldt-Stiftung, Bonn, for which I here record my sincere thanks. In the course of my work in Munich I discovered a manuscript of the Irish 84-year Easter table, previously believed to be lost; I hope to publish the table in the near future. [See now below, 58-75.]

3

Mo Sinu maccu Min and the computus at Bangor[*]

Despite the abundant literature on the subject of the Paschal controversies in the early Irish churches, we are in some respects still as far as ever from a reconciliation of the conflicting evidence. The long story of the 84-year cycle and its use in Ireland has been brilliantly expounded by Krusch[1] and Mac Carthy,[2] even if we still do not know for certain when or whence that cycle was first introduced, and even though we are still without any solid evidence for the historical Easters celebrated in Ireland.[3]

The story of the controversies begins with St Columbanus, who, about the year AD 590, left his monastery at Bangor (Co. Down) with twelve companions and travelled to Burgundy to found there the three monasteries of Annagray, Luxeuil, and Fontaines which were to become the hub of Irish monastic influence in Europe in the succeeding centuries. Columbanus, however, found in Burgundy a number of Gallican rites which differed from his own, and the next few years comprise a well-known catalogue of contentions between the Irish and the Merovingians, for which a group of five letters written by Columbanus himself are our main evidence.[4]

Chief among these differences, it appears, was the question of the Paschal cycle. In the first of his letters,[5] directed to Pope St Gregory the Great around the year AD 600, Columbanus protested against the Paschal observance which he found in Gaul, based on the Easter cycle of Victorius of Aquitaine. He told the pope that the Victorian table had been studied by the foremost Irish scholars and computists and had been not only rejected but considered more worthy

[*] First published in *Peritia* 1 (1982) 281-95. 1 Bruno Krusch, *Studien zur christlich-mittelalterlichen Chronologie* [1]: *Der 84-jährige Ostercyclus und seine Quellen* (Leipzig 1880). 2 Bartholomew Mac Carthy (ed & transl), *Annála Uladh. Annals of Ulster, otherwise, Annála Senait, Annals of Senat* 4 (Dublin-London 1901) xiv-clx. 3 'Thatsächlich ist kein einziger Ostersonntag der irischen Observanz bekannt', the verdict of Eduard Schwarz, 'Christliche und jüdische Osterfeln', *Abh. d. Kgl. Gesellsch. d. Wiss Göttingen*, phil.-hist. Kl., N. F., 8, No. 6 (Berlin 1905) 1-196: 102. 4 Wilhelm Gundlach (ed), *Columbae sive Columbani abbatis Luxoviensis et Bobbiensis epistolae*, Mommenta Germaniae Historica Epist. Merov. Karol. aevi 1 (Berlin 1892) 154-90; G.S.M. Walker (ed & transl), *Sancti Columbani opera*. Scriptores Latini Hiberniae 2 (Dublin 1957) 2-59. There is no need here to discuss the canon of Columbanus' writings [for which see below, 48-55]; the epistles cited below are universally accepted as genuine. My citations are from Walker's edition. 5 Walker, 21-22; Gundlach, 156-60.

of ridicule than of authority.[6] In his second letter,[7] addressed to the Gallican bishops gathered in synod at Chalon-sur-Saône in AD 603, Columbanus returned to the fray and cited as his authority in this question 'the traditions of my fatherland according to the calculus of 84 years' and the work which modern computists know as the Anatolian Canon Paschalis.[8]

Our concern is not with Columbanus nor with the Irish foundations in Europe, but with the computus at Bangor. Yet the two are obviously inseparable, for Columbanus was driven from Burgundy, and his followers who remained at Luxeuil almost immediately adopted the Victorian Easter, as we know from a calendar (itself a copy) which was carried there from Corbie sometime before AD 657.[9] Scholars have maintained that Columbanus' struggle was lost 'not only in the foreign waste places but in his native Bangor, the home of the sapient computists'.[10] The evidence for this conclusion is a brief note bound in with an eighth-century Irish text (with ninth-century glosses) of the Gospel of Matthew, in the Würzburg, Universitätsbibliothek, MS. M. p. th. f. 61.[11] The fragment is one of thirty intercalated slips which have been bound in with the Matthew text, but it bears no relation either to the Gospel or to the

---

6 'Scias namque nostris magistris et Hibernicis antiquis philosophis et sapientissimis componendi calculi computariis Victorium non fuisse receptum, sed magis risu vel venia dignum quam auctoritate', Walker, 6; Gundlach, 157. 3.   7 Walker, 12-23; Gundlach, 164-65.   8 'plus credo traditionis patriae meae iuxta doctrinam et calculum octoginta quattuor annorum et Anatolium, ab Eusebio ecclesiasticae historiae auctore episcopo et sancto catalogi scriptore Hieronymo laudatum, Pascha celebrare', Walker, 18; Gundlach 162. On Anatolius see Krusch, *Studien* 1, 311-17, and Jones, *Bedae opera*, 82-85.   9 Mac Carthy, *Annals of Ulster* 4 (1901) cxxxii-iii. Prof. Wesley Stevens rightly cautioned me against a too-ready acceptance of the calendar evidence, since Mac Carthy was drawing on Krusch at this point, who in turn was depending on Ferdinand Piper, *Karls des Grossen Kalendarium und Ostertafel* (Berlin 1858) 62; Piper is not always reliable. But Columbanus himself (Ep. IV, Walker, 26-28) warned his monks at Luxeuil: 'sed interim cauete, ne sit inter uos qui unum uotum non habeat inter uos, quicumque ille fuerit; *plus enim nobis nocuerunt qui apud nos unanimes non fuerunt*' (italics mine). Moreover, we know also that Victorius was cited by Columbanus' biographer Jonas, *c.* AD 642, and also in the Milan, Biblioteca Ambrosiana, MS. H 150 Inf., which is a computistical collection (containing much seventh-century material) deriving both from Bobbio and from Columbanus' Frankish foundations. Besides, after their founder's departure, the monks of Luxeuil must have comprised almost exclusively Franks, whose commitment to the Irish 84-year cycle would have been dubious. 10 Jones, *Bedae opera*, 81, and others there cited.   11 George Schepss, *Die ältesten Evangelienhandschriften der Universitätsbibliothek Würzburg* (Würzburg 1877) 26; Karl Köberlin, 'Eine Würzburger Evangelienhandschrift (M. p. th. f. 61, S. 8)', *Programm zu dem Jahresbericht d. Kgl. Studienanstalt St Anna in Augsburg Schuljahr 1890-1* (Augsburg 1891) 3-95: 48; Whitley Stokes, 'Hibernica', *Zeitschrift für vergleichende Sprachforschung* 31 (1892) 232-55: 245-46; Whitley Stokes and John Strachan (eds & transls), *Thesaurus Palaeohibernicus, a collection of Old-Irish glosses, scholia, prose and verse* (2 vols, Cambridge 1901, 1903; repr. Dublin 1975) 2, 285; Bernhard Bischoff and Josef Hofmann, *Libri Sancti Kyliani. Die Würzburger Schreibschule und die Dombibliothek im VIII. und IX. Jahrhundert.* Quellen und Forschungen zur Geschichte des Bistums und Hochstifts Würzburg 6 (Würzburg 1952) 99 No. 16. Elias A. Lowe, *Codices Latini Antiquiores* 9 (Oxford 1959) No. 1415: 'Written in Ireland and partly glossed there in the centre where the Würzburg St Paul [M. p. th. f. 12] originated. Other Irish glosses were probably added

commentary. The note has never been satisfactorily edited in its entirety,[12] so I give here the full text with accompanying apparatus and a translation:

> Mo Sinu maccu Min, scriba et abbas Bennchuir, primus Hibernensium compotem a Graeco quodam sapiente memoraliter didicit. Deinde Mo Cuoróc maccu Neth Sémon, quem Romani doctorem totius mundi nominabant, alumnusque praefati scribae, in insola quae dicitur Crannach Dúin Lethglaisse, hanc scientiam literis fixit, ne memoria laberetur. ſ. episinon i. ui.., γ..cophe uel cosse., XC.,, ꝑ enacosse.., dcccc. Haec sunt notae tres, non literae. Sed tamen inseruntur apud Graecos inter literas, ne turbetur ordo numerorum ..,,, ,,

1) benncuir... hebernensium	2) compotem ... dedicit	
2-3) mocuoroc maccumin semon	5) -glaisṣe	8) numerſ

Mo Sinu maccu Min, scholar and abbot of Bangor, was the first of the Irish 'who learned the computus by heart from a certain learned Greek. Afterwards, Mo Chuoróc maccu Neth Sémon (*sic leg.*), whom the Romans[13] styled doctor of the whole world, and a pupil of the aforesaid scholar, in the island called Crannach of Downpatrick,[14] committed this knowledge to writing, lest it should fade from memory.'

ꝑ 'episinon', that is six; γ 4 'cophe' or 'cosse', [that is] ninety; ꝑ 'enacosse', [that is] nine hundred. These are three symbols, not letters. However, they are inserted by the Greeks among [their] letters, lest the sequence of numbers be disturbed.

on the Continent'. There is a good facsimile in Georg Baesecke, *Der Vocabularius Sti Galli in der angelsächsischen Mission* (Halle 1933) Tafel 36; cf. 57 n. 1. My edition is based on a transcript that I made at Würzburg on March 16, 1978, which I have checked against an excellent photograph generously provided by Dr G. Lehmann, University Librarian at Würzburg, and which is reproduced here with his permission. **12** Baesecke's comment is worth noting here: 'Beim Photographieren von Bl. 33 a (Tafel 36) habe ich die eingehefteten Zettel so gelegt, dass Nr. 29 mit dem Berichte über das griechische Studium von Mosinu mac Cumin scriba et abbas Benncuir (Bangor) und Mocuoroc mac Cumin Semon sichtbar wird'. Unfortunately, the crucial lines of the text were not visible in his plate! It should be noted, however, that the arrangement of the slips has been altered since Baesecke's day (as Dr Lehmann kindly informs me). **13** Pádraig Ó Néill, University of North Carolina at Chapel Hill, has made the interesting suggestion that the Romani represented a distinctive group among the seventh-century Irish writers in biblical exegesis, hagiography, canonical legislation and liturgy, as well as in the matters of the Easter controversy and the tonsure. E.g., in the Vatican, MS. Palatinus Latinus 68, a Hiberno-Saxon psalm commentary compiled probably in Northumbria *c.* AD 700, the Romani are cited by name on three occasions as having a distinctive interpretation of certain psalms. [See now Martin McNamara (ed), *Glossa in psalmos. The Hiberno-Latin gloss on the psalms of the Codex Palatinus-Vaticanus 68* (Psalms 39:11-151:7). Studi e Testi 310 (Vatican 1986)]. Prof. Ó Néill's suggestion seems to my mind preferable to that made by Richard Sharpe (Oxford), that the use of the term implied support for the claims of Armagh to primacy in the Irish Church. [On the text, see now David Howlett, 'Five experiments in textual reconstruction and analysis', *Peritia* 9 (1985) 1-50: 1-3.]

First the names: both of these men are known from other sources. Mo Sinu
maccu Min is the Sillán (Silnán), abbot of Bangor, whose death is recorded in
the Annals of Ulster s. a. AD 609 [= AD 610]. He is listed fourth in the poem *in
memoriam abbatum nostrorum* in the late-seventh-century Antiphonary of
Bangor:

> Amauit Christus Comgillum,
> Bene et ipse Dominum,
> Carum habuit Beognoum,
> Domnum ornauit Aedeum,
> Elegit sanctum Sinlanum,
> Famosum mundi magistrum,
> Quos conuocauit Dominus
> Coelorum regni sedibus.[15]

The name of the 'holy Sinlán, famous teacher of the world' suggests that he
belonged to the Menraige, a north-east Munster people who are otherwise only
rarely mentioned in historical sources.[16] Mo Chuoróc maccu Neth Sémon, for
his part, is mentioned in the Irish genealogical collections as Mo Chuaróc *ind
ecnai* ('M. the Wise'), of the Semuine, a tribe generally located in the copper-
mining district of the Déisi (Co. Waterford).[17] He is possibly the same man
who is listed, under his proper name (Mo Chuoróc being a pet form), as
Crónán *sapiens* in the early Leinster genealogies.[18] He is commemorated in the
Félire Óenguso (*c.* AD 800) on 9 Feb:

> Mo-Chuaróc ind ecnai,
> noéb ná dámair dignae.

---

14 Mac Carthy *(Annals of Ulster* 4, cxxxiv) identified the site as 'Cranny Island, in the south-
western arm of Strangford Lough, a few miles from Downpatrick'. But according to Deirdre
Flanagan, 'The names of Downpatrick', *Dinnseanchas* 4/4 (1971) 89-112: 111 n. 39, no such site
is recorded either in documents or in local tradition, and she refers to a paper by Fr Mc Keown,
Down & Connor Hist Soc Jnl 5, 33, who suggests Wood island, Hollymount townland, west of
Downpatrick.   **15** See F.E. Warren (ed), *The Antiphonary of Bangor, an early Irish manuscript in
the Ambrosian Library at Milan*, HBS 4 and 10 (London 1893, 1895) 4, 33.   **16** Thomas Charles-
Edwards, 'The social background to Irish *peregrinatio*', *Celtica* 11 (1976) 43-59: 44 n. 3, suggested
(correctly in my view) that the Sinilis whom Jonas refers to as Columbanus' teacher 'may well be
identical with Sillán (Sinlán, dimin. to Sinell, hypocoristic Mo-Sinu)'; such an identification
would resolve what has hitherto been a textual crux in the *Vita Columbani*.   **17** See John Mac
Neill, 'Early Irish population groups: their nomenclature, classification, and chronology', PRIA
29 C 7 (1911-12) 59-114: 79.   **18** See O'Brien (ed), *Corpus genealogiarum Hiberniae* 1, 137:
'Seimni na nDéisse dia mbui Mo-Chuaróc ind ecnai'; cf. 230: 'Clann Sem dia tá Semne na
nDéisse de quibus Mo-Chuaróc ind ecnae'.   The location stems from a mistaken belief that the
tribal name Semuine derives from Old Irish *sem(m)* 'rivet'; cf. Mac Neill, 'Early Irish population
groups', 81. It is worth noting, however, that Island Magee, near Larne (Co Antrim), is
referred to in Old Irish sources as *rinn Semne*.

'M. of the wisdom, a saint that endured not reproach'.[19] One manuscript of the commentary of the *Félire* says that he was also known as Mo Chuaróc *nóna* ('of the None') because of a change in the observance of the canonical hours which he is said to have introduced.[20] He was patron saint of Cell Chuaráin (Kilcoran) about a mile outside Youghal (Co. Cork), where he was remembered in local tradition as 'Cuaran of the None' as late as the turn of the century.[21] This is not the place to discuss Mo Chuoróc's alleged liturgical innovation;[22] it happens, however, that his epithet has been otherwise explained and it is to this alternative explanation that we now turn.

Charles Jones, in his great studies of the Alexandrian paschal cycle and its introduction into the West,[23] made the ingenious suggestion that the computus which Mo Sinu maccu Min learned 'from a certain learned Greek', and which was subsequently committed to writing by his pupil, Mo Chuaróc maccu Neth Sémon, was the mnemonic poem beginning *Nonae Aprilis norunt quinos*.[24] The poem consists of nineteen lines of doggerel verse, each line comprising two phrases of four or more syllables each, and each pair of phrases being inter-connected either by alliteration or by assonance; there is no rhyme in the poem. For ease of reference, I give the text here with the mnemonic features indicated:

*N*onae Aprilis *n*orunt quinos	V
*O*ctonae Kalendae *a*ssim depromunt	I
*I*dus Aprilis *e*tiam sexis	VI
*N*onae quaternae *n*amque dipondio	II

---

19 See Whitley Stokes (ed), *Félire Óengusso. The martyrology of Oengus the culdee.* HBS 29 (London 1905) 59. **20** Stokes, *Félire*, 70: 'Is aire at-berar Mo-Chuaróc nóna fris, ar is é toisech ro-delig celibrad nóna, quia cum media & ora (sic) apud antiquos celebra[ba]tur'; the Latin passage is corrupt; see Mac Carthy, *Annals of Ulster* 2 (1893) 104-5. **21** According to Mac Carthy, *Annals of Ulster* 2, 105. The connection of two possibly southern clerics with a monastery as far north as Bangor need not surprise us too much, for we know that Bangor had property in Leinster and Columbanus himself was a Leinsterman by birth. **22** See Paul Grosjean, 'Recherches sur les débuts de la controverse pascale chez les Celtes', *Analecta Bollandiana* 64 (1946) 200-44: 220-25. This paper is to be read with caution. **23** 'The Victorian and Dionysiac Paschal tables in the West', *Speculum* 9 (1934) 408-21 [repr. *Bede, the computus and the schools*, chapt. 8]; *Bedae opera*, 34-104. **24** Karl Strecker (ed), Poetae Latini aevi Carolini, MGH Poet. Lat. med. aevi 4/2 (Berlin 1923; repr. 1964) 670-1. See also Charles W. Jones, 'Carolingian aesthetics: why modular verse?', *Viator* 6 (1975) 309-40, esp. 337-38. Grosjean, 'Recherches', 244, proposed to see the acrostics NOIN (i.e. Irish for Nonae) in the intials of the first four verses, and PASQQ at the end of the poem, and offered three criteria for classifying it as a Hiberno-Latin composition: 1) 'Dans l'évangéliaire de Wurzbourg, la note en question [sc. concerning Mo Sinu] introduit-elle peut-être précisément ce petit poème? 2) Le systeme d'assonnances du poème ... ne sont-ils pas un rappel de la métrique irlandaise ...? 3) Enfin l'épithète "de None" ajoutée au nom de Mo-Chuaróc, ne viendrait-elle pas, en dernière analyse, du *Nonae aprilis*?' I am not competent to answer the second question, but the present study provides a firm *No* in answer to the other two. Jones described the poem as a 'Teutonic verse form' and claimed Visigothic origin, *c.* AD 600.

    5 *I*tem undenae *a*mbiunt quinos   V
      *Q*uatuor Idus *c*apiunt ternos   III
      *T*ernae Kalendae *t*itulant senos   VI
      *Q*uatuordenae *c*ubant in quadris   IV
      *S*eptenae Idus *s*eptem eligunt   VII
   10 *S*enae Kalendae *s*ortiunt ternos   III
      *D*enae septenae *d*onant assim   I
      *P*ridie Nonarum *p*orro quaternis   IV
      *N*ovenae Kalendae *s*ortiunt ternos   VII
      *P*ridie Idus *p*anditur quinis   V
   15 *A*prilis Kalendas *u*nus exprimit   I
      *D*uodenae namque *d*octe quaternis   IV
      *S*peciem quintam *s*peramus duobus   II
      *Q*uaternae Kalendae *q*uinque coniciunt   V
      *Q*uindenae tribus *c*onstant adeptis.   III

The first phrase in each line gives the date, in the Julian calendar, of the Easter full-moon in a particular year of the 19-year (decennovenal) cycle. The second phrase gives the so-called 'lunar regular', a number which, when combined with the 'concurrent' of the particular year, gives the day of the week on which the Easter full-moon falls. For example, the year AD 659 is the fourteenth year in the 19-year cycle (659 + 1 ÷ 19 = 34, remainder 14). In the poem, the first phrase in the fourteenth line gives as the Julian date for the Easter full-moon in that year *Pridie Idus* [Aprilis] = 12 April. To find the day of the week on which that falls we combine the 'lunar regular' for the year (which the poem gives as *quinis* = 5) with the 'concurrent' (= 1), giving 6 = *feria sexta* = Friday. Thus the Easter full-moon in AD 659 occurred on Friday, 12 April; counting forward, it follows that Easter Sunday occurred on 14 April, *luna XVI*.

In simpler terms, what the poem contains is the data from two of the eight columns in an Alexandrian cycle for a period of nineteen years; and since in fact the Easter data recur in the same sequence every nineteen years the practical value of the verses is immediately obvious, for what might otherwise be calculable only with the aid of complex Easter tables could now, by means of these easily memorized verses, be computed by anyone with a minimum of technical expertise. So popular was the poem, in fact, that almost at once a legend arose claiming that an angel had handed it in writing to St Pachomius, the Egyptian author of the first monastic rule.[25] Because of the mnemonic nature of the composition, and because the data contained in it are those of the

---

25 See Charles W. Jones, 'A legend of St Pachomius', *Speculum* 18 (1943) 198-210.

Dionysiac cycle, Jones (not unreasonably) concluded that this was the computus that Mo Sinu maccu Min had learned by heart,[26] and he further surmised that it was from a member of the Augustinian mission to England that he had received it.[27]

Père Paul Grosjean, following a similar line of reasoning, sought to add some weight to Jones' surmise by suggesting that Mo Chuoróc maccu Neth Sémon had himself composed the verses and that it was from this alleged composition of the *Nonae Aprilis* that he had acquired his epithet 'Mo Chuoróc of the None'.[28] It was then, so the scenario goes, some time before the year AD 610 (the year of Mo Sinu's death) that the Dionysiac cycle was introduced into Ireland. Computists could well appreciate the importance of such a milestone in an otherwise poorly signposted terrain.

Unfortunately, none of these scholars was familiar with the entire text of the Würzburg note, but followed the earlier, incomplete transcripts by Schepss and the editors of the *Thesaurus Palaeohibernicus*. Of the four independent transcripts known to me only one, Köberlin's, gives lines 6–8 of the edition printed above; and Köberlin's text at this point is so hopelessly garbled as to be totally unintelligible.[29] But these four lines are the key to the question of what it was that Mo Sinu maccu Min introduced into the school of Bangor. The writing at this point in the Würzburg note, though clearly by the same hand that wrote the rest of the text, is crabbed and awkward and the scribe clearly had difficulty

---

26 'The Victorian and Dionysiac Paschal tables', 419, and again in subsequent studies. Cf. Mac Carthy, *Annals of Ulster* 4, cxxxiv: 'The computus in question was, of course, the Alexandrine decemnovennal cycle'; Grosjean, 'Recherches', 228: 'Le sage grec dont Sillán de Bangor apprit par coeur la table pascale, couchée ensuite sur le parchemin par son disciple Mo-Chúaróc, serait en réalité Denys le Petit'. **27** Jones, *Bedae opera*, 82 n. 3, alone provides a motivation for the alleged change in the Bangor practice, in the letter of bishop Laurentius of Canterbury to the Irish in AD 604, reported in Bede's *Historia Ecclesiastica* II 4. **28** In a 'note complémentaire' written in response to Jones' paper of 1943. Grosjean's note, 244, reads very much as an afterthought, for having expended some six pages on Mo Chuoróc's alleged liturgical innovation, he now proposed to see in Mo Chuoróc's epithet the upshot of his alleged connection with the *Nonae Aprilis;* he can hardly have it both ways! **29** I give here Köberlin's version of these few lines: 'Epuus (vielleicht ἐχῖος) nonne (non) id est sextus (VI)? us cophe vel χοσιη (cosse), nonaginta unus duo de mille (IXCHM), ἐναχοσιοσωσιή (enacosse) nongenti (DCCCC), hae sunt natae, tres (Ill), non litterae sunt, sed tamen inseruntur apud (ap) Graecos + litteras ne turbetur ordo numerus'. Note that on slip 28, below the text here under discussion, there are two Old Irish glosses clearly visible. The gloss *tommemaid* (with 4 horizontal dashes indicating that it is Irish) stands over the Latin *medius crepuit* (Acts 1, 18). Köberlin read this as *id est actorum memories ait*! On the fourth line from the bottom of the same slip the Latin *Figuli* is glossed.i. *inne cerde uel uiri, qui imagines faciebant*, with *imagines* glossed .i. *delba*. Köberlin read all this as: *id est inanes facies dealbant vel viri, qui imagines faciebant* (darüber geschr. *id est dealbare*)! These, and the other Old Irish glosses in the MS., were correctly identified by Bernhard Bischoff, 'Wendepunkte in der Geschichte der lateinischen Exegese im Frühmittelalter', *Sacris Erudiri* 6 (1954) 189–279 = *Mittelalterliche Studien. Ausgewählte Aufsätze zur Schriftkunde und Literaturgeschichte* 1 (Stuttgart 1966) 205–73: 254. Linguistic and palaeographical considerations would suggest a seventh- or early eighth-century origin for the glosses.

understanding his exemplar, which, to judge from the linguistic and palaeographical indications, must have been a very old one, possibly even
seventh-century.[30] The text omitted by previous editors reads, again, as
follows:

> ∫ episinon.i. ui.., γ..cophe uel cosse., XC.,, ꝑ enacosse.., dcccc. Haec sunt
> notae tres, non literae. Sed tamen inseruntur apud Graecos inter literas,
> ne turbetur ordo numerorum..,,, ,

The first symbol was originally the Greek ƒ (or similar) and therefore also
called 'digamma' (i.e. double-gamma). Later, it assumed forms which were
similar to the ligature of *o* and *c* in Byzantine manuscripts and it came then to
be called 'stigma'. The symbol is here referred to as επίσημον (the episinon
of the MS.) literally 'symbol'. The second symbol is the Greek κόππα (Q in
the Phoenician alphabet), here rendered as *cophe uel cosse*,[31] another obsolete
Greek letter denoting the number nine-hundred, otherwise ἐναχόσιοι
(rendered as *enacosse* in the MS.). The commentary states that 'these are three
signs, not letters. However, they are inserted among [their] letters by the
Greeks, lest the order of numbers be disturbed.' What is this 'order of
numbers'?

The reference is to a tract on finger-reckoning which occurs in some
computistical manuscripts, including Bede's *De temporum ratione*, cap. I, *De
computo digitorum*.[32] To illustrate its use I give here the text as it stands in Bede,
with a translation of his commentary:[33]

'But it is possible likewise to learn and to do these things [sc. finger calcula-
tions] more easily with the computus and letters of the Greeks, who are not
wont – like the Latins – to express their numbers by doubling [only] a few of
these letters but rather, by using all the characters of the alphabet as figures for
the numbers (representing the three extra numbers by peculiar symbols) and
following almost the same sequence of numerical figuration as in the writing of
the alphabet, thus:

---

30 The occurrence of the *maccu* formula in the note would alone be proof enough of antiquity;
see Eoin Mac Neill, 'Mocu, Maccu', *Ériu* 3 (1907) 42–49: 42: 'The latest contemporary use of the
term in AU [Annals of Ulster] is at 690: "Cronan mocu Chualnae abbas Bennchuir obiit". It is
therefore probable that *mocu* began to go out of use about 700'.   31 The confusion probably
arose from the misreading of *coppe*, where the p's were of the Irish minuscule type (shaft with s-
shaped head), such as are clearly visible, e.g., in the Antiphonary of Bangor, fol. 15ᵛ.   32 Jones,
Bedae opera, 181.   33 'Sed haec graecorum computo literisque facilius disci simul atque agi
possunt, qui non, ut latini, paucis hisdemque geminatis suos numeros solent exprimere literis;
verum toto alphabeti sui characteres in numerorum figuras expenso, tres qui plus sunt numeros
notis singulis depingunt, eundem pene numeri figurandi, quem scribendi alphabeti ordinem
sequentes, hoc modo: ... Qui et ideo mox numeros digitis significare didicerint, nulla interstante
mora, literas quoque pariter hisdem praefigere sedunt.' Jones, *Bedae opera*, 181.

A	I	H	VIII	Ξ	LX	Υ	CCCC
C	II	Θ	IX	O	LXX	Φ	D
Γ	III	I	X	Π	LXXX	X	DC
Δ	IV	K	XX	μ	XC	Ψ	DCC
E	V	Λ	XXX	P	C	ω	DCCCC
2	VI	M	XL	C	CC	↑	DCCCC
Z	VII	N	L	T	CCC		

'Therefore, those who have learnt how to represent numbers with their fingers know, without any intervening delay, how equally to represent letters also with these numbers'.[34]

The system is relatively simple: Each letter in the Greek alphabet had also a numerical significance. The first nine letters denoted the numbers from one to nine – *alpha* 'one', *beta* 'two', *gamma* 'three', etc., with the obsolete *digamma* denoting six, and nine therefore represented by *theta*. After *iota* 'ten', the reckoning advanced by decades: *kappa* 'twenty', *lamda* 'thirty', and so on up to *pi* 'eighty' and the obsolete *koppa* 'ninety'. After *rho* '100', the reckoning advanced by hundreds, from *sigma* '200' up to *omega* '800', and the obsolete *sampi* for 900.

The numbers in the list are all that are required by the computist for calculations of almost limitless complexity. Most significant from our point of view, however, are the figures for the numbers 6, 90, and 900. These are the *tres [numeri] qui plus sunt* in Bede's words, which are here represented by the three obsolete letters of the Greek alphabet that we encountered already in the Würzburg note. The final link is provided by Bede's description of this chart as a *computus Graecorum*, for there can be no doubt that the computus which Mo Sinu maccu Min learned by heart a *quodam Graeco sapiente* was precisely this list of Greek numbers and their equivalents in Roman numerals.

A study of insular computistical manuscripts indicates that finger-calculation was a standard feature of Irish teaching, and there were at least four different versions of the Latin material in circulation before Bede's definitive treatment.[35] The text on which Bede most obviously drew was the version known as *Romana computatio*[36] – not so-called because it derived directly from Rome but doubtless to distinguish it from the *computus Graecorum* that Mo

---

34 Paul Lejay, 'Note sur un passage de Bède et sur un système de numération', *Compte rendu quatrième congrès scientifique internat. catholiques*, 6me sect., sciences philol. (Fribourg 1898) 129-36, discusses the development of the system in computistical texts; however, his contention that the tabular form here discussed was invented by Hrabanus Maurus is clearly mistaken. **35** See Jones, *Bedae pseudepigrapha: scientific writings falsely attributed to Bede* (Ithaca, N.Y. 1939) [repr. in *Bede, the schools and the computus* (Aldershot 1994) 53-54, 106-8], and the discussion in *Bedae opera*, 329-93. **36** Jones, *Bedae pseudepigrapha*, Appendix, 106-8; see his discussion of the tract ibid., 53-54, and *Bedae opera*, 329-32. Re-edited by him in *Bedae opera didascalica* 3, Corpus Christianorum Series Latina [CCSL] 123 C, 669-72.

Sinu maccu Min had learned by heart. Though the tradition of finger-calculation was well-established in the classical authors, these Insular tracts are the
first definite treatment of the subject in medieval Latin literature.[37] The
Romana computatio, like the *computatio Graecorum* of Bangor, was undoubtedly
an oral tract in origin, composed for use in the schools. Its existence and circulation before Bede's time were inferred on textual and codicological grounds by
Jones; but he overlooked the fact that in one computus, British Library, MS.
Cotton Caligula A XV (saec. VIII[1], northern France)[38] – made up almost exclusively of pre-Bedan, insular tracts – a dating formula on fol. 70[r] gives the *annus
praesens* of the original compilation as AD 688.[39] We may conclude, therefore,
that the *Romana computatio* was at least a generation older than Bede's text, and
maybe much older.

   It is clear also from the capitula of the seventh-century Irish computus *De
ratione temporum uel de compoto annali*[40] that such a tract as occurs in Bede's
DTR, cap. I, was a commonplace of the Irish schools, for one of the capitula
reads: *Deinde etiam interrogare debemus quomodo numeri nominantur apud
Graecos, ab uno usque ad mille, et myriades, et quae notae significant illos numeros
apud Graecos.* The subsequent capitulum reads: *Nec non etiam scire nos oportet
quae notae significant istos numeros, ab uno usque ad mille, et myriades, apud
Latinos.* In fact, comparison with a transcript of Bede's own computus, Oxford,
Bodleian Library, MS. Bodley 309 (sacc. XI, Vendôme) fol. 61[v], leads us to just
such a list of Greek numbers, from 1 to 10,000 (*myrias*), with their numerical
and verbal equivalents.[41] It is particularly significant that in this list, for the
number 6, the Bodleian manuscript reads: *S Nota numeri episinon eka* (i.e.
eἐa?); and for the number 90 the form *cophe* occurs – exactly the same as the
Würzburg manuscript's *cophe uel cosse.* But as the Oxford list extends only to
the number 800 we cannot know what orthography the scribe would have had
for the number 900. Nevertheless, we can be reasonably sure that he would
have written it as *enacosse*, just as the Würzburg scribe did.

   The rather garbled nature of the Greek in the Würzburg and Oxford manuscripts should not lead us to surmise that they are only poor copies of more
correct seventh-century exemplars. Knowledge of Greek being what it was at

---

37 There is a useful catalogue of classical commentators in Antonio Quacquarelli, 'Ai margini
dell' *actio*: la *loquela digitorum* (La rappresentazione dei numeri con la flesione delle dita in un
prontuario transmesso dal Beda)', *Vetera Christianorum* 7/2 (1970) 199-224, and in Jones, *Bedae
opera*, 329.   38 See Elias A. Lowe, *Codices Latini Antiquiores* 2 (Oxford 1935; repr. 1972) 19, No.
13; Jones 'The "lost" Sirmond manuscript of Bede's "computus"', *Engl. Hist. Rev.* 52 (1937) 204-
19: 210-11 [repr. in *Bede, the schools and the computus*, chap. X].   39 See Alfred Cordoliani, 'A
propos du premier chapitre du *De temporum ratione* de Bède', *Le Moyen Age* 54 (1948) 209-23.
40 The prologue and capitula of this computus were published by Jones, *Bedae opera*, Appendix
393-95: 393. I am presently engaged on a critical edition of the work.   41 See Jones, *Eng. Hist.
Rev.* 52 (1937) 213. Note that the list of Greek numbers immediately precedes the prologue and
capitula of the Irish Computus just referred to, which occurs in this MS. in a good recension.
Such lists are frequent in computistical MSS generally.

the time, we need expect no more than a fair approximation to the letters and their verbal equivalents. But the evidence of these two manuscripts, together with that of the capitula in the Irish Computus, can leave us in no doubt that the new tract introduced into Bangor before AD 610 was no more and no less than a treatise on finger-reckoning.

But what of the *quodam Graecus sapiens* from whom Mo Sinu is supposed to have acquired this tract? Bischoff thought the reference was to one of the many Latin translations of Greek tracts which circulated in computistical manuscripts.[42] More likely however, as it seems to me, the text concerned was a *littera formata* or authenticating document, common in the early Middle Ages as a 'passport' issued by bishops[43] to their clergy when despatching them on official business. In order to insure against forgery, official documents were provided with a code, best illustrated by the standard text knowm as the *Regula Formatarum:*[44]

> Greca elementa litterarum numeros etiam exprimere nullus, qui uel tenuiter Greci sermonis noticiam habet, ignorat. Ne igitur in faciendis epistolis canonicis, quas mos Latinus formatas uocat, aliqua fraus falsitatis temere agi presumeretur, hoc a patribus CCCXVIII Nicea constitutis saluberrime inuentum est et constitutum, ut formatae epistolae hanc calculationis seu supputationis habeant rationem, id est: adsumantur in supputationem prima Greca clementa Patris et Filii et Spiritus sancti, hoc est *IIYA,* quae elementa octogenarium, quadringentesimum et primum significat numeros, Petri quoque apostoli prima littera, id est II, qui numerus octuaginta significat, eius qui scribit epistolam prima littera, cui scribitur secunda littera, accipientis tertia littera, ciuitatis quoque de qua scribitur quarta et indictionis quaecumque est id temporis, id est qui fuerit numerus adsumatur. Atque ita his omnibus litteris Grecis, quae, ut diximus, numeros exprimunt, in unum ductis, unam quaecumque collecta fuerit summam epistola tenet. Hanc qui suscipit omni cum cautela requirat expressam, addat praeterea separatim in epistola etiam nonagenarium et nonum numeros, qui secundum elementa significant: *AMHN*

The *Regula* clearly implies the use of the same Greek alphabetical number system as occurs in the computi, and lists of Greek letters with their numerical equivalents and instructions for their use frequently accompany the *Regula* in the manuscripts. Moreover, Bischoff has pointed out that in all periods of

---

42 'Das griechische Element in der abendländischen Bildung des Mittelalters', *Byzantinische Zeitschrift* 44 (1951) 27-55 = *Mittelalterliche Studien* 2 (Stuttgart 1967) 246-75: 248 n.   43 See Clara Fabricius, 'Die Litterae Formatae im Frühmittelalter', *Archiv für Urkundenforschung* 9 (1926) 39-86, 168-94.   44 Fabricius, 39-40.

the Latin Church the Greek alphabet was used alongside the Latin in conse-
cration ceremonies.[45] Thus the consecrating bishop had to be able to inscribe
both alphabets (in the shape of a St Andrew's cross) on the floor of a new
building. Such a standard requirement would explain the relatively widespread
familiarity in the West with the Greek alphabet (the capitals at any rate), and
the duty of inscribing the *litterae formatae* may also have encouraged its
dissemination. It is perhaps conceivable that the system was introduced to
Bangor *c.* AD 600 in the guise of just such a *littera,* perhaps even the letter of
Laurentius of Canterbury (AD 604), as Jones suggested.

Where does this leave the theory that the Dionysiac cycle was introduced
into Ireland by Mo Sinu, before AD 610? The Bangor computus was clearly not
the poem *Nonae Aprilis,* for what purpose could be served anyway by Mo
Chuoróc maccu Neth Sémon committing to writing a poem which was already
mnemonic in construction, which has nothing to do with Greek, and which is
no more intelligible for having been written down? We have seen that the tract
received at Bangor was in all likelihood a table of Greek numbers, an *ordo
numerorum,* as the words of the Würzburg note have it. Moreover, the subsequent history of the Paschal controversies in Ireland also suggests that so early
a date as *c.* AD 610 for the first attestation of the Dionysiac cycle in northern
Ireland would be surprising.

Bearing in mind that in AD 640 the Pope-elect was writing to the leading
ecclesiastics of the northern Irish churches (among them, as I think, the abbot
of Bangor)[46] admonishing them to abandon the 84-year cycle and to adopt the
Alexandrian, it seems intrinsically unlikely that Bangor, alone of all the northern communities, should have already made the changeover. Columbanus'
letter to Gregory the Great shows clearly that the Bangor community were
practised in computistical matters and entirely confident of their own abilities
in the science. There is nothing to suggest that these staunch advocates of the
84-year cycle had been led already by the year AD 610 to abandon their mode
of reckoning in favour of the 19-year Alexandrian cycle. On the contrary, the
evidence of Cummian's famous Paschal letter[47] clearly implies that the change
in Irish practice came about first in the south, and probably because of the

45 'Das griechische Element', *Mittelalterliche Studien* 2, 252.   46 See Charles Plummer (ed),
Venerabilis Baedae opera historica (2 vols, Oxford 1896; repr. 1969) 1, 123 and 2, 112-13 [*Historia
Ecclesiastica* II 19][Colgrave & Mynors, 200-202]; Maurice P. Sheehy (ed), *Pontificia Hibernica,
medieval papal chancery documents concerning Ireland, 640-1261* (2 vols, Dublin 1962) 1, 3-4, No.
1. Plummer's hesitant identification of the Baétán mentioned in the letter as abbot of Bangor was
probably not correct. See the comments of M. O. Anderson, *Kings and kingship in early Scotland*
(Edinburgh 1973) 23.   47 Maura Walsh and Dáibhí Ó Cróinín (eds & transls*), Cummian's Letter
'De controversia Paschali' together with a related seventh-century computistical tract 'De ratione
conputandi'.* Pontifical Institute of Mediaeval Studies, Studies & Texts 86 (Toronto 1988). See
James F. Kenney, *The sources for the early history of Ireland* 1: Ecclesiastical. Columbia Records of
Civilization (New York 1929; repr. Dublin 1993) 220, No. 57, and Jones, *Bedae opera,* 89-99

letter of Pope Honorius which had been received *c*. AD 629.[48] Bede – who was usually right in such matters – when writing about the beginnings of the Irish mission to Northumbria, reported that 'the Irish who lived in the southern part of Ireland had long since learned to observe Easter according to the canonical custom, on the admonition of the Pope'.[49] The northern Irish churches clearly persevered in their ways, and neither the Würzburg note nor any other evidence permits us to single out Bangor as an exception.[50]

48 Described by Bede, *Historia Ecclesiastica* II 19 as 'sollerter exhortans, ne paucitatem suam in extremis terrae finibus constitutam, sapientiorem antiquis sive modernis, quae per orbem erant, Christi ecclesiis aestimarent; neve contra paschales computos et decreta synodalium totius orbis pontificum aliud pascha celebrarent'; Plummer 1, 122 [Colgrave & Mynors, 198]. **49** *Historia Ecclesiastica* II 3: 'Porro gentes Scottorum quae in australibus Hibemiae insulae partibus morabantur, iamdudum ad admonitionem apostolicae sedis antistitis, pascha canonico ritu observare didicerunt'; Plummer 1, 131 [Colgrave & Mynors, 218]. **50** I wish to thank Professor Wesley Stevens, University of Winnipeg, Canada, and Professor Gearóid Mac Niocaill, Galway, who read a draft of this paper and made helpful suggestions for its improvement.

4

The computistical works of Columbanus[*]

In his *Vita S. Columbani* (I. 3), Ionas relates that Columbanus, in the early flush of religious enthusiasm, abandoned his native Leinster and travelled north, first to Crannach at Downpatrick, where he received instruction from a certain Sinilis (*alias* Mo Sinu maccu Min, † AD 610), *qui eo tempore singulari religione et scripturarum sacrarum scientiae flore inter suos pollebat*.[1] According to Ionas, the young Columbanus showed such ability that he soon advanced to *dificilium quaestionum materia*, and before his departure he had composed a volume of commentary on the Psalms and many other works which were either suitable for singing or useful for teaching (*multaque alia, quae uel ad cantum digna uel ad docendum utilia, condidit dicta*).[2] From Downpatrick Columbanus moved on to Bangor, then still ruled by its founder Comgall († AD 602), where he spent several years (the exact number cannot be determined). The desire for *peregrinatio* that subsequently possessed him led eventually to his departure, *c.* AD 590, with twelve companions for Burgundy.

The evidence for Columbanus' interest in computistical problems is abundantly clear in the letters of his which have survived, and there can be little doubt that the science of computus formed an important part of his early instruction. In fact his earliest teacher Sinilis (*alias* Mo Sinu maccu Min) is credited by one source as being 'the first of the Irish who learned the computus by heart from a certain learned Greek'.[3] The intricacies of the Easter reckoning may quite conceivably have been among the *dificilium quaestionum materia* of Columbanus' early years at Downpatrick. There is abundant evidence in the surviving manuscripts to show that in Ireland, as indeed everywhere in western Europe, the computus formed one branch of a trivium with biblical exegesis and Latin grammar in the monastic curriculum. Columbanus' genuine *Epistulae* indicate that he had mastered all three to an exceptional degree.

The first three *Epistulae*, addressed to two popes and to the bishops of Gaul assembled in council, bear witness to a passionate concern with the question of

---

[*] First published in Michael Lapidge (ed), *Columbanus, studies on the Latin writings*. Studies in Celtic History 17 (Woodbridge 1997) 264-70.   1 Bruno Krusch (ed), *Ionae vitae sanctorum Columbani, Vedastis, Iohannis*, MGH SRM in usum scholarum (Hannover 1905) 69.   2 Ibid.   3 See 'Mo Sinu maccu Min and the computus at Bangor', *Peritia* 1 (1982) 281-95 [= 35-47 above].

Easter reckoning and an obvious confidence – not to say arrogance – about his abilities in the field. Columbanus shows himself fully conversant with the technical terminology of the subject (e.g. *rimarius, calcenterus,* etc.) and he was also familiar with the works of the most eminent computists, such as Anatolius of Laodicea and Victorius of Aquitaine.[4] Indeed, he scathingly remarks of Victorius' Easter tables (published in AD 457, and from AD 541 the official Easter tables of the Gallican churches) that they had long before been scrutinised and found wanting 'by the ancient scholars of Ireland and by learned computists most skilled in reckoning chronology', who thought the work 'more worthy of ridicule or pity than of authority'.[5] Columbanus also states that he had outlined his case for the Irish Easter practices in three letters to Pope Gregory (*de Pascha sancto papae per tres tomos innotui*) and again in an abridged pamphlet addressed to Bishop Arigius of Lyons (*et adhuc sancto fratri uestro Arigio breui libello hoc idem scribere praesumpsi*).[6]

These *tres tomos* and the *breuis libellus* are, unfortunately, lost, but there are a number of computistical texts still extant which are ascribed to Columbanus in some manuscripts, and one at least of these may represent a genuine composition of the saint. The works thus associated with Columbanus are the letter *De sollemnitatibus,* the short tract *De saltu lunae,* and a brief excerpt, apparently from a longer work, ascribed in several manuscripts to 'Palumbus'.

The letter, or *disputatio, De sollemnitatibus et sabbatis et neomeniis* is a short treatise on the Jewish festal practices and their relevance to Christian Paschal observances. The work is addressed to a *uenerabilis papa,* whose prayers are requested at the end. If the *disputatio* ever had a superscription it is now lost, and with it the names of both author and recipient. But wherever the work is rubricated in manuscripts it is attributed to Jerome: *Disputatio (Sancti) (H)Ieronimi de sollemnitatibus.* The letter was first published by Domenico Vallarsi from the Vatican manuscript listed below; Vallarsi's text was subsequently reproduced in Migne's *Patrologia Latina.*[7] A separate edition was published by Jean-Baptiste Pitra from the Paris and London manuscripts.[8] In 1885, strangely unaware of its previous publication (and despite the fact that four years previously he had catalogued the Köln manuscript and correctly

---

4 Columbanus is, in fact, the earliest witness to the knowledge and use of Anatolius in Ireland; [see now D. P. McCarthy, 'Easter principles and a fifth-century lunar cycle used in the British Isles', *Jnl Hist. Astron.* 24 (1993) 204-24; idem, 'The lunar and paschal tables of the *De ratione paschali* attributed to Anatolius of Laodicea', *Archive for the Hist. of Exact Sciences* 49/4 (1996) 285-320; idem, 'The origin of the *Latercus* paschal cycle of the Insular Celtic churches', *Cambr. Med. Celt. Stud.* [CMCS] 28 (1994) 24-49. See also Bonnie Blackburn & Leofranc Holford-Strevens, *The Oxford companion to the year. An exploration of calendar customs and time-reckoning* (Oxford 1999) 870-75.] 5 Walker, *Sancti Columbani opera,* 6: 'Scias namque nostris magistris et Hibernicis antiquis philosophis et sapientissimis componendi calculi computarii Victorium non fuisse receptum, sed magis risu uel uenia dignum quam auctoritate'. 6 Ibid., 16. 7 *Hieronymi opera omnia,* ed. Vallarsi, 1.1, 114-20 (Ep. CXLIX); Vallarsi's text is reprinted in MPL 32, 1220-24. 8 J.-B. Pitra, *Spicilegium Solesmense* (2 vols, Paris 1852) 1, xi-xiv, 9-13, 565-66.

identified the work there) Bruno Krusch republished the text from the Paris manuscript (where it has no rubric) and announced it as a 'rediscovered' letter from Columbanus to Gregory the Great.[9] A controversy ensued in German journals, principally between Wilhelm Gundlach and Otto Seebass, with Gundlach supporting Krusch's case and Seebass denying the alleged parallels (chiefly stylistic) between the concluding paragraph of the *De sollemnitatibus* and the opening of Columbanus' Ep.v.[10] So confident, in fact, was Gundlach of its authenticity that he republished Krusch's text as Ep. VI in the Monumenta edition of Columbanus' letters.[11] Fernand Cabrol and Henri Leclercq published yet another edition, as an anonymous pre-Nicene tract, in 1913,[12] and Isidor Hilberg then published it as part of his edition of Jerome's letters, again from the Vatican manuscript.[13] The most recent edition is Walker's.[14]

The letter has no salutation, but concludes with the words *ora pro me, uenerabilis papa*. In the concluding paragraph the author refers to his reader again as *uenerabilis papa* and describes himself as a *peregrinus*. He also states that the letter was solicited *(Haec autem et a te postulatae sunt)*, and the implication is that the writer was requested by higher authority to provide answers to questions on the Easter problem. The use of the word *papa* need not, of course, mean that the letter was addressed to a pope; Cummian, after all, refers to Patrick as *papa noster*,[15] and the term is frequently used of bishops. Although most modern commentators have dated it in the fifth century or even earlier, and suggested continental origin,[16] there are some indications in the letter that

9 Bruno Krusch, 'Chronologisches aus Handschriften'; see also his earlier description of Köln, Dombibliothek, 83/2 in *Studien* 1, 204.   10 Gundlach, 'Über die Columban-Briefe 1: Die prosaischen Briefe', *Neues Archiv* 15 (1890) 497-526, and 'Zu den Columban-Briefen; eine Entgegnung', *Neues Archiv* 17 (1892) 425-29; Seebass, 'Über die Handschriften der Sermonen und Briefe Columbans von Luxeuil', *Neues Archiv* 17 (1892) 245-59, and 'Über dem Verfasser eines in Cod. Par. 16361 aufgefundenen Briefs über die christliche Feste', *Zeit. f. Kirchengesch.* 14 (1894) 93-97.   11 'Columbani . . . epistolae', ed. Gundlach, 177-80. Krusch subsequently retracted his earlier attribution to Columbanus; see *Passiones vitaeque sanctorum aevi Merovingici* [2], (Hannover 1902) 20 n. 1.   12 Fernand Cabrol & Henri Leclercq (eds), *Monumenta ecclesiae liturgica. Reliquiae liturgicae vetustissimae ex ss. patrum necnon scriptorum ecclesiasticorum monumentis selectae*, 2 vols (Paris 1912-13), II 71-73, where the text is printed among 'Pseudepigraphi', although the pseudonymous author is not identified and the manuscript(s) on which the edition is based are not specified.   13 *Sancti Hieronymi Epistulae*, ed. Isidorus Hilberg, 3 vols (Vienna 1910-12), 3, 357-63.   14 *Sancti Columbani opera*, 198-206.   15 Walsh & Ó Cróinín, *Cummian's Letter*, 85.   16 Eligius Dekkers & Aemilius Gaar, *Clavis patrum Latinorum* (3rd ed, Steenbrugge 1995) No. 2278; Theodor Zahn, *Forschungen zur Geschichte des neutestamentlichen Kanons und der altchristlichen Literatur*, 10 vols (Erlangen 1881-93, Leipzig 1900-29), 4, 182-85; Bernard Blumenkranz, *Die Judenpredigt des Augustins* (Basel 1946), 47-49; and Johannes W. Smit, *Studies in the language and style of Columba the Younger (Columbanus)* (Amsterdam 1971), 33 n. 1: 'nowadays the work is usually dated in the fifth century or even earlier' (citing no authority but presumably following the *Clavis*). The work was first considered as a possible letter of Pelagius by de Plinval, 'L'œuvre littéraire', 40 n. 4, but subsequently rejected this view in *Pélage*, 43. Cf. Paul Grosjean, 'Recherches sur les débuts de la controverse pascale chez les Celtes', 240-[1], n. 3: 'La

would indicate an Irish milieu and perhaps an Irish author in the seventh century.

The *De sollemnitatibus* is preserved in the following manuscripts:[17]

1. Oxford, Bodleian Library, Bodley 309 (*saec.* xi) fols 82^v-84^r
2. Paris, Bibliothèque Nationale, lat. 16361 (*saec.* xii) pp 212-17
3. Köln, Dombibliothek, 83/2 (*c.* AD 805) fols 201^r-203^r
4. Geneva, Bibliothèque de l'Université, 50 (*saec.* ix^l) fols 121^r-123^r
5. London, British Library, Cotton Caligula A XV (*saec.* VIII^2) fols 86^v-90^r
6. Vatican City, Biblioteca Apostolica Vaticana, lat. 642 (*saec.* xi) fols 89^r-90^v
7. Tours, Bibliothèque Municipale, 334 (c. AD 819) fols 8^v-10^r

All these collections contain Irish material and five of them preserve copies of the Irish computus in the 'Sirmond group' of manuscripts first identified by Charles W. Jones, 'a computus used in the school at Jarrow when Bede was teaching there'.[18] The archetype of this group has since been shown to date from AD 658 and to have originated in southern Ireland.[19] The evidence of the manuscripts, therefore, speaks strongly for an Irish origin for the *De sollemnitatibus.*[20] The Cotton manuscript, dated *saec.* VIII,[2] offers a *terminus post quem non;*[21] the earliest known references to the work are in Irish texts of the seventh century. The *De sollemnitatibus* is cited, for instance, under Jerome's name, in the seventh-century Irish computus *De ratione conputandi,*[22] a work with clear

lettre VI ... reste dans le vague'. [See also James F. Kenney, *Sources for the early history of Ireland* 1, 193, No. 42 (vi); Jean Laporte, 'Sur la lettre "De sollemnitatibus ..." attribuée à S. Colomban', *Rev. Mabillon* 46 (1956) 9-14.] For alternative views, see further below. **17** I have not been able to confirm the existence of further copies in: Einsiedeln, Stiftsbibliothek, 263; Münster (Staatsarchiv ?) 198 (508), *saec.* XVI ('deperditus' according to *Clavis,* no. 2278, where the catalogue reference is given as: 'Hieronymus de celebratione paschae'); Oxford, Bodleian Library, '56', or Paris, 'Bibl. Univ., 183', all listed by Lambert, *Bibliotheca Hieronymiana Manuscripta. La tradition manuscrite des oeuvres de Saint Jérôme* (Steenbrugge 1969-), No. 149; Lambert gives no folio references for these supposed copies. [There is a German translation in August Strobel, Texte zur Geschichte des frühchristlichen Osterkalenders. Liturgiewissensch. Quellen u. Forschungen. Veröffentl. des Abt-Herwegen-Inst. der Abtei Maria Laach 64 (Münster 1984) 68-79.] **18** Jones, 'The "lost" Sirmond manuscript', 204-19, and *Bedae opera de temporibus,* 105-10. **19** See 'The Irish provenance of Bede's computus', below, pp 173-90. **20** An abbreviated version of the letter, inc. 'De Pascha autem tamquam maximo sacramento' [= *De sollemnitatibus* §§2 8] is contained in MSS 1, 2, 4, 5, 7 listed above, and in Milan, Biblioteca Ambrosiana, H. 150 inf. (AD 810), printed MPL 129, 1361-63, as §CXLIX of the *Liber de computo.* The Milan manuscript is also an Irish collection. **21** Note that Walker's statements concerning manuscript affiliations are completely mistaken; for example, he dated Cotton Caligula A. xv to 'saec. XII/XIII' (*Sancti Columbani opera,* lx), whereas Lowe (CLA II 183), gives the date as 'saec. VIII^2'. Similarly, the statement that the text in Paris, BN, lat. 16361 'is not related to that of the four previous manuscripts' is equally mistaken. Jones long ago demonstrated that the Paris MS. was derived from the same archetype as the other MSS in the Sirmond group, and in fact it was copied directly, I believe, from Tours 334 (a manuscript not known to Jones). **22** See 'A seventh-century Irish computus', pp 99-130 below.

southern Irish connections and closely related to Cummian's Paschal Letter (AD 632/33):[23]

> Item HIERONIMUS dicit: 'Cum dominus, uerus agnus, uerum Pascha progreditur', in mundum 'aliqua permanere uolens custodiuit, aliqua non obseruare cupiens motauit'.

The same passage is cited in another well-known Irish work, the 'Munich Computus' (München, Bayerische Staatsbibliothek, Clm. 14456, *saec.* ix, fol. 31v) compiled in AD 718 using earlier sources (dated AD 689).[24] In the opinion of Charles W. Jones, 'the tract was almost certainly in the Irish *computus* before Cummian',[25] although if the work is contemporary or even slightly later in date it is possible that the *De sollemnitatibus* found inspiration in a curious phrase in Cummian's letter, where he was defending his elders and predecessors: *Seniores uero nostri, quos in uelamine repulsionis habetis, quod optimum in diebus suis esse nouerunt simpliciter et fideliter sine culpa contradictionis ullius et animositatis obseruauerunt*; compare the *De sollemnitatibus*, where the author refers to his opponents as men who, *uelamine posito super faciem Moysi, spiritus et ueritatis luce illuminari nequeunt.*[26] It is noteworthy also that the *De sollemnitatibus* and Cummian's Paschal Letter are the only known sources for a peculiar reading in Colossians 2: 16-17: *nemo uos seducat in parte diei festi aut neomenia aut sabbato,*[27] thus further strengthening the case for Irish origin. But what of the authorship?

There is nothing definite in the letter to preclude Jerome's authorship, although we know of no circumstances in which he might have composed it. Despite efforts to place it in the fifth century or earlier, its separate circulation and the fact that it first appears in Irish manuscripts whose contents date from the seventh century would seem to argue against the attribution to Jerome, the manuscript rubrics notwithstanding. Jones thought that he noted 'a similarity in the opening paragraph, with its mass of biblical quotation that is only vaguely relevant, to the letter of Cummian to Seghine',[28] but this does scant justice to Cummian and does not advance us very much in our enquiry. It is true that the tone of the letter is forceful, even combative, reminiscent of Columbanus, whom Krusch described as 'homo uehemens feroxque natura'.[29] On the other hand, the author clearly supports the 'orthodox' Easter reckoning rather than that of the Irish 84-year tables,[30] and his thorough advocacy of

---

23 Walsh & Ó Cróinín, *Cummian's Letter*, 204. **24** See Ó Cróinín, 'A seventh-century Irish computus', esp. 408-9. **25** *Bedae opera*, 108. **26** *Cummian's Letter*, 74; *Columbani opera*, 198. **27** See, however, *Cummian's Letter*, 225. **28** *Bedae opera*, 109. **29** *Passiones vitaeque sanctorum aevi Merovingici* 3, 20. Coming from Krusch, the verdict has a certain piquancy about it! **30** See, e.g., the following: 'Et hoc etiam intueri debemus, quod non in decima quarta die ad uesperum ... sed decima quinta die, in quo manifestum est diem festum Iudeorum cum suo sacrificio a Domino esse solutum', and 'Unde electa et amica sponsa Christi, uniuersalis ecclesia, anathematizat eos

the Alexandrian Easter obviously precludes Columbanus' authorship, for there is no evidence whatever to show that the saint ever deviated, even in his last days, from the adherence to Irish practices which is such a marked feature of his letters.[31]

There are other possibilities. The name *Columba* and its diminutive form *Columbanus* (cf. Irish Colm/Colmán) were very common Irish names. Ionas, for instance, remarks that one of the saint's companions was 'nomen et ipse Columbanus',[32] and other examples abound. There were countless Irish *peregrini* in England and on the Continent, and Colmanus/ Columbanus is a name encountered frequently among them.[33] But since the work is nowhere attributed to Columbanus in the manuscripts we need not restrict the search to writers of the same name. One who comes to mind as a possible author is the Irishman referred to by Bede (*Historia Ecclesiastica* III 25) as *acerrimus ueri Paschae defensor nomine Ronan*, a vigorous supporter of the orthodox Easter reckoning who clashed bitterly with Fínán, bishop of Lindisfarne († AD 661) on the Paschal question. Rónán might well have been called upon by a bishop (*papa*) of the Irish Romanist party to refute the partisans of the 84-year reckoning. But of one thing there can be no doubt: the *De sollemnitatibus* is not a work of Columbanus.

The second computistical work attributed to Columbanus is the short tract *De saltu lunae*, a discussion of the day which the computists omitted at the end of every cycle in order to realign the movements of sun and moon. The work was first printed by Gabriel Meier, librarian of Einsiedeln, from a manuscript in St Gallen;[34] Walker republished it using an additional manuscript in Munich.[35] In fact, however, there are eight complete copies of the text known to me:[36]

qui cum Iudeis in festiuitate Paschali decimam quartam celebrari diffiniunt' (*Sancti Columbani opera*, 200, 202). **31** Ferdinand Loofs, *Antiquae Britonum Scotorumque ecciesiae* (Leipzig 1882) 93, was of the opinion that Columbanus eventually conformed, but there is no proof, and it seems highly unlikely. The attempt by Jean Laporte to circumvent this problem by claiming the letter for Attala, Columbanus' successor as abbot of Bobbio, is unconvincing; see Laporte, 'Étude d'authenticité des oeuvres attribuée à Saint Colomban' *Rev. Mabillon* 45 (1955) 1-28; 46 (1956) 1-14: 9-14 (Appendix: 'Sur la lettre *De Solemnitatibus* ... attribuée à Saint Colomban'). **32** *Vita S. Columbani* I 17 (Krusch, *Ionae vitae sanctorum*, 184). **33** See, e.g., the index to Lapidge & Sharpe, *Bibliography*, s.vv. Colmán, Columbanus. **34** Gabriel Meier, *Jahresbericht über die Lehr- und Erziehungsanstalt des Benediktinerstifts Marie Einsiedeln für 1886-7* (Einsiedeln 1887), Appendix, 30. **35** *Sancti Columbani opera*, 212-14; repr. MPL Supplement 4, 1609-10. **36** The work is cited in Paris, BN, lat. 2183, fol. 115ʳ, in a miscellany comprising material mostly of Irish origin. It doubtless is cited in other collections as well. I wish to acknowledge the assistance of Dr Cornel Dora and Prof. Wesley M. Stevens in this matter. [For further discussion, see now Dietrich Lohrmann, 'Alcuins Korrespondenz mit Karl dem Großen über Kalender und Astronomie', in Paul Butzer & Dietrich Lohrmann (eds), *Science in western and eastern civilization in Carolingian times* (Basel 1993) 79-114.]

1. St Gallen, Stiftsbibliothek, 250 (*saec.* X¹) pp 112-14
2. Zürich, Zentralbibliothek, Car. C.176 (*saec.* X/XI) fols 174ᵛ-175ᵛ
3. Karlsruhe, Landesbibliothek, Ac. 132 (*saec.* X) cover (destroyed)
4. München, Bayerische Staatsbibliothek, Clm. 10270 (*saec.* XI) fols 12ᵛ-13ʳ
5. München, Bayerische Staatsbibliothek, Clm. 14569 (*saec.* XI) fols 26ʳ-28ʳ
6. St Gallen, Stiftsbibliothek, 459 (*saec.* X) pp 125-26
7. Malibu, Getty Museum, Ludwig XIII.5 (*saec.* XII¹) fols 110ᵛ-114ᵛ
8. Zürich, Zentralbibliothek, C. 62 (*saec.* X) fol. 217ʳ⁻ᵛ

The work was cited as Columbanus' by Notker Labeo in his computus, and Krusch thought that it dated from the eighth or ninth century.[37] Jones, on the other hand, believed it possibly earlier than Bede.[38] The discussion of the *saltus* is expert and accurate, but Columbanus' authorship must be ruled out, since the tract is clearly based on the 19-year cycle of Dionysius Exiguus and cites that text verbatim.[39] Though Columbanus is named in the superscription, none of the manuscripts offers any indication of the work's age; a pre-Bedan date (as suggested by Jones) seems to me unlikely.

The third computistical tract ascribed to Columbanus occurs in the same Sirmond group of manuscripts which preserves the letter *De sollemnitatibus*, and it is cited in several others.[40] In every case the attribution is to Palumbus. The only person of such a name in Irish documents, to my knowledge, is Columbanus, who, in his Ep. V directed to Pope Boniface, signs himself by that name*: Rara auis scribere audet Bonifatio Patri Palumbus.*[41] That the text is seventh-century at the latest is proved by its citation in the *De ratione conputandi*, mentioned earlier as being closely related to Cummian's Paschal Letter.[42] The relevant chapter of *De ratione conputandi* (§70) is as follows:[43]

> Sciendum nobis, cum duae lunae in uno mense inueniuntur, quae est de illis luna ipsius mensis. Quae finitur in mense, ipsa est luna ipsius mensis. Luna uero sequens, si non pertingerit Kalendis mensis sequentis, abortiua luna uocabitur, quam alii dicunt lunam esse embolismi, quod non est uerum, ut PALUMBUS: 'Illi mensi conputa lunam, quae in eo finitur, non

37 *Passiones vitaeque sanctorum aevi Merovingici* 2, 20 n. 1.   38 *Bedae opera*, 376.   39 The words 'Omnis igitur lunaris cursus secundum Hebraeorum et Egyptiorum supputationem potest facere per singulos menses dies XXVIIII et semissem', 'quia nimis errant, qui lunam peragere cursum sui circuli XXX dierum spaciis aestimant', and 'cum diligens inquisitio ueritatis ostenderet in duobus lunae circulis non LX dies sed LVIIII debere computari', are cobbled together from Dionysius' Prologue; see Krusch, *Studien* 2, 65-6.   40 One sentence is quoted, e.g., in St Dunstan's 'Classbook': Oxford, Bodleian Library, MS. Auct. F. 4. 32, fol. 22ᵛ; see Ó Cróinín, 'A seventh-century computus', 426-27. The text occurs also in Strasbourg, Bibliothèque Universitaire, 326, fol. 150ʳ (not fol. 149ᵛ, as stated ibid., 427).   41 *Sancti Columbani opera*, 36; see Smit, *Studies*, 149-57.   42 *Cummian's Letter*, 178.   43 Ibid., 178-79. The text is based on that in Oxford, Bodleian Library, Bodley 309; the passage is obscure in places and possibly corrupt.

quae incipit. Unde, quae primum prioris aut initium sequentis non tenet, abortiua dicitur'.

Manuscripts of the Sirmond group preserve a more complete text:

Palumbus dicit: 'Nunc de luna pauca tractanda sunt. Luna maior lunaque minor in anno sunt, sed uicissim (ut quidam putant) sibi semper alterno succedunt cursu; licet unius temporis alios intellexisse breues. Sciendum est similiter absque una abortiua quae, si tunc illo euenerit tempore, nulla conputanda, ut aiunt: mensi nimirum neutri mensis Kalendis uindicata. Primum scilicet prioris non tenens ac usque ad secundi initium non pertingens e medio quodammodo proiecto deprehenditur. Caeterorum lunas similiter breues esse, id est lunii et Septembris et Nouimbris, et conputata ratione ab eis. Sed illam mensi conputa lunam quae in eo finitur, non quae incipit. Inde, quae primum prioris aut initium sequentis non tenet, abortiua luna dicitur. †Hoc licet alio lapsu saltus. Omnis enim .xiiii. luna semper facit anno† Idcirco, dum per menses sex (ut supradictum est), id est aut per tres ueris et alios tres supra iam nominatos, aut (ut plus firmant) per alternos uicis sex lunae .xxviiii. sunt et per sex alios .xxx. inueniuntur'.

The passage occurs usually in relation to discussion of the *abortiua luna* (an Irish technical term)[44] and there is nothing in it – in so far as it can be understood – that would tell against Columbanus' authorship; there is no incompatibility of the doctrine with the workings of the Irish 84-year tables, for instance. But did Columbanus write this text? Of all the works discussed here, this is the only one with a strong claim to be a genuine writing of Columbanus. The work is definitely Irish and was known and cited in Irish texts of the seventh century. Allowing for the same reservations which were voiced above about the frequency of the name Colmanus/Columbanus in an Irish context, the attribution to Palumbus would seem to add an extra weight to the case for Columbanus' authorship. More than that, however, it is not possible to say.[*]

44 See *Cummian's Letter*, edd. Walsh & Ó Cróinín, 177-78 (§69 and discussion).   [*] Research for this study was assisted by a generous grant from the Alexander von Humboldt Stiftung, Bonn, which is here gratefully acknowledged.

5

Hiberno-Latin *Calcenterus**

In his edition of the *Sancti Columbani opera*,[1] G.S.M. Walker offered the following text of Ep. I 3: *Quid ergo dicis de pascha vigesimac primae aut vigesimae secundae lunae, quod iam ... non esse pascha ... a multis comprobatur calcenteris.* Walker emended the forms *calcalenteris* and *cacalenteris* of the only two surviving transcripts of the letter, and rendered the form *calcenteris* as 'laborious scholars', basing both emendation and translation on Du Cange, *Glossarium mediae et infimae Latinitatis* (10 vols, Niort 1883-7) s.v. *Calcalenteris.*

   J.W. Smit, *Studies in the language and style of Columba the Younger (Columbanus)* (Amsterdam 1971) 70-77 has a detailed and valuable discussion of this Columbanian usage. He asks: 'Could it be possible that, for the Irish, the word *chalcenterus* evoked a writer who had formulated a particular, authoritative opinion on the dating of Easter?' In fact, the term *calcenterus* does occur in a number of seventh-century Irish tracts with the meaning 'computist'. Thus, for example, in a southern-Irish collection of AD 658, the following is found: *Sciendum cur hanc rationem* [sc. the computation of the year as having 360 + 5 days] *proprie tenuerunt. Hoc ita est, de quo iure alius calcenterus hoc modo dicens inquit*, etc. (Oxford, Bodleian Library, MS. Bodley 309, fol. 45ᵛ). So also in Munich, Bayerische Staatsbibliothek, Clm 14456, fol. 21ʳ: *Per quod inuenitur [bissextus]? Per artem numerationis in signis ciuilibus. Apud* calcentores *'aigis' uocatur*, etc. This example was overlooked by Walker and Smit, though it had been noted by Bartholomew Mac Carthy, *Annals of Ulster* 4 (Dublin 1901) cxix-cxx, who in fact had anticipated Smit's theory. Smit and Mac Carthy referred to the Anatolian *Canon paschalis*, a sixth-century Irish (?) forgery which is cited by Columbanus.[2] Anatolius mentions Origen specifically as an authority on the dating of Easter: *Sed et Origenis* (sic) *omnium eruditissimus et calculi conponendi perspicacissimus, quippe qui et Calcenterus vocatus est, libellum de pascha luculentissime edidit*.[3] Mac Carthy remarked that 'evidently the writer took *Calcenterus* to signify calculator'. So also Columbanus in his Ep. I, and

---

* First published in *Peritia* 1 (1982) 296-97. 1 Scriptores Latini Hiberniae 2 (Dublin 1957; repr. 1970) 2. 2 [On Anatolius, see now Daniel McCarthy, 'Easter principles and a fifth-century lunar cycle used in the British Isles', *Jnl Hist. Astron.* 24 (1993) 204-24; idem, 'The lunar and paschal tables of the *De ratione paschali* attributed to Anatolius of Laodicea', *Archive for the Hist. of Exact Sciences* 49/4 (1996) 285-320; idem, 'The origin of the *Latercus* paschal cycle of the Insular Celtic churches', *Cambr. Med. Celt. Stud.* [CMCS] 28 (1994) 24-49.] 3 Bruno Krusch (ed), *Studien zur christlich-mittelalterlichen Chronologie* [1] (Leipzig 1880) 317.

Cummian in his letter to Ségéne of Iona (AD 632), who refers also to a tract of Origenus Calcenterus on the subject of Easter.[4]

Smit has shown that the term most likely derives from Jerome's comparison of Origen with the Alexandrian grammarian Didymus, to whom the Greek epithet χαλκέντερος ('with bronze entrails') had become attached in recognition of his enormous literary activity. Jerome twice refers to Origen as *noster Chalcenterus* (Ep. XXXIII 4, *CSEL* 54/2, 40. 7; Ep. XLIII 1, ibid., 92. 25); Rufinus adopted the usage also in his *Apologia aduersus Hieronimum* II 24 *(CCSL* 20, 100. 7 ff.): ... *istum quem modo Chalcenterum tuum uocas et pro merito laboris laudabilis ais Adamantium nominatum.* From one or other of these sources, doubtless, the author of the Anatolian *Canon paschalis* derived his usage, and Cummian in turn refers to *Origenus Calcenterus et uere Adamantinus.* According to Mac Carthy, 'Cummian perhaps knew the meaning'. The form in Columbanus's Ep. 1 implies that the term was already common currency with the Irish in his time, and it came to denote any (but particularly a Greek) computist.

4 See Walsh & Ó Cróinín, *Cummian's letter*, 62. 52 and note.

6

The 'lost' Irish 84-year Easter table rediscovered[*]

ABSTRACT. The Paschal controversy in the British Isles centred on the use of an 84-year Easter table, which was abandoned by Iona only in AD 716. Previous discussions of the Irish table have been hampered by the fact that no manuscript copy was known. This paper announces the discovery of such a manuscript (Padua, Biblioteca Antoniana, MS. I. 27) and offers, for the first time, an authentic Irish Easter table for the years AD 438-521.

KEYWORDS. Anatolius, annals, British Easter, Columbanus, computus, chronology, Easter, Gildas, Irish 84-year Easter table, Irish Paschal forgeries, *latercus*, Munich Computus

INTRODUCTION

Writing to the Gallican bishops in AD 603 on the subject of the Easter controversy, Columbanus remarked defiantly that he had 'more confidence in the tradition of my native land in accordance with the teaching and reckoning of eighty-four years and with Anatolius ... for the celebration of Easter, than in ... Victorius'.[1] It is generally acknowledged that the Irish and British churches of the sixth century and earlier reckoned the date of Easter by means of an 84-year cycle.[2] That cycle, however, has long been given up for lost, and despite the efforts of Bruno Krusch,[3] Bartholomew Mac Carthy,[4] and Daniel O'Connell[5] to retrieve it from references in secondary sources, principally the

---

[*] First published in *Peritia* 6-7 (1987-88) 227-42 [with Daniel McCarthy].   1 G.S.M. Walker (ed & trans), *Sancti Columbani opera*, Scriptores Latini Hiberniae 2 (Dublin 1957, repr. 1970) 18. 2 Good general surveys are Joseph Schmid, *Die Osterfestberechnung in der abendändischen Kirche vom I. allgemeinen Konzil zu Nicäa bis zum Ende des VIII. Jahrhunderts*, Strassburger Theologische Studien 9/1 (Freiburg i. Breisgau 1907), and idem, *Die Osterfestberechnung auf den britischen Inseln vom Anfang des vierten bis zum Ende des achten Jahrhunderts: eine historischchronologische Studie* (Regensburg 1904). Alone amongst modern writers Alfred Anscombe denied that the Irish followed an 84-year cycle, but his views were demolished by Charles Plummer (ed), *Venerabilis Baedae opera historica* (2 vols, Oxford 1896; repr. London 1969) 348-54: 351 n 6. Plummer's 'Excursus' on the Easter question is still well worth reading.   3 Bruno Krusch, *Studien zur christlich-mittelalterlichen Chronologie* [1]. *Der 84-jährige Ostercyclus und seine Quellen* (Leipzig 1880) 10-23; idem, 'Die Einführung des griechischen Paschalritus im Abendlande', *Neues Archiv der Gesellschaft für ältere deutsche Geschichtskunde* 9 (1884) 101-69: 167. 4 Bartholomew Mac Carthy in *Annals of Ulster* 4 (Dublin 1901) lxvi-lxxviii.   5 Daniel J. O'Connell, 'Easter cycles in the early Irish church', *Jnl Royal Soc. Antiquaries of Ireland* 66 (1936) 67-106.

so-called Munich Computus, no convincing reconstruction has ever been possible. 'Thatsächlich ist kein einziger Ostersonntag der irischen Observanz bekannt', was Eduard Schwarz's verdict in his magisterial survey of 1905,[6] and nearly forty years later the doyen of modern computists, Charles W. Jones, was driven to the same conclusion.[7] Jones, moreover, did not believe that the Irish table could be reconstructed from the available evidence, and until now no new evidence has been brought to light.[8]

The Irish 84-year Easter table is not lost. A copy of it has come to light in Padua, Biblioteca Antoniana, MS. I. 27, and what follows in this article is a description and restoration of the table, together with some comments on the implications of the discovery for early Irish history and chronology. These comments must, of necessity, be of a preliminary nature; the full impact of this discovery will have to be worked out in the years to come.

DESCRIPTION OF THE MANUSCRIPT

Padua, Biblioteca Antoniana, MS. I. 27 (*saec.* x in) was written in northern Italy (possibly Verona) in the early years of the tenth century, to judge from the script and from the presence of dating clauses for AD 879 and 881. The codex has 133 folios, measuring 270 x 210 mm, written by several hands in long lines (except fols 130^v-133^r, which are in double columns). A full list of the contents will be found in the works listed in the note;[9] we give here a summary description.

The manuscript is a miscellany, mostly computistical. The principal text is Hrabanus Maurus, *Liber de computo* (fols 1^r-44^v), and this is accompanied by excerpts from Macrobius, Isidore, and Bede, as well as anonymous computistical *argumenta*, verses, tables, and *rotae*, plus church canons (including a previously unidentified set of excerpts from the *Collectio canonum Hibernensis*).[10] Buried in the mass of anonymous computistical material (fols

6 Eduard Schwarz, 'Christliche und jüdische Ostertafeln', *Abhandlungen der Wissenschaftlichen Akademie Göttingen*, phil.-hist. Kl., N.F. 8/6 (Berlin 1905) 1-95: 102.   7 Jones, *Bedae opera*, 93 n 1: 'there is no certain record of Irish Easters'.   8 The table in Knut Schäferdiek, 'Der irische Ostercyklus des sechsten und siebten Jahrhunderts', *Deutsches Archiv* 39 (1983) 357-78: 372-74, is based on O'Connell's table, not on any new manuscript evidence.   9 Patrick McGurk, *Catalogue of astrological and mythological illuminated manuscripts of the Latin middle ages 4: Astrological manuscripts in Italian libraries (other than Rome)* (London 1966) 64-72; Giuseppe Abate and Giovanni Luisetto, *Codici manoscritti della Biblioteca Antoniana col catalogo delle miniature*, Fonti e studi per la storia del santo a Padova (2 vols, Vicenza 1975) 28-33. Wesley M. Stevens, *Hrabanus Maurus On reckoning* [Latin text with English analysis]. PhD dissertation, Emory University 1968 (Ann Arbor, Michigan: University Microfilms Inc. 1980) 178-88. On the dating of the manuscript see esp. Luigi Guidaldi, *I più antichi codici della Biblioteca Antoniana di Padova (codici del sec. IX)* (Padua 1930) 21-28 (with plates), and Augusto Campana, 'Veronensia', *Miscellania Giovanni Mercati* ii, Studi e Testi 122 (Vatican City) 57-91 (reference kindly supplied by the late Prof. Bernhard Bischoff).   10 The late Prof. Maurice Sheehy, University College Dublin, who was preparing a new edition of the Hibernensis, was unable to shed any light on the

76^r-77^v) is our 84-year table. None of the modern cataloguers recognised it for what it was, and consequently none provided any details.[11] The data in the table, the heading attached to it, and the context in which it is found all combine to prove that the table is Irish. The restoration and discussion below will demonstrate that it is one of the oldest documents to survive from the early Irish churches.

The table has the rubric INCPTLTRCSIET TNCLTS, to be expanded tentatively as INCIPIT LATERCUS, ID EST LATENS CULTUS.[12] Both the term 'latercus' and its etymology are attested in seventh-century Irish sources. The 84-year table known to and described by the compiler of the Munich Computus (AD 718) was contained in a latercus, and Irish computists of the seventh-century and after who adopted the 'orthodox' Alexandrian reckoning referred to their more conservative fellow-countrymen as *laterci sectatores*.[13] The etymology of *latercus* as *latens cultus* also occurs in the seventh-century Irish *De ratione conputandi*, and nowhere else, to my knowledge.[14] The bare rubric of the text, and the absence of any indication of date or place of origin, are also in keeping with Cummian's statement (*c.* 633) that the Irish 84-year cycle championed by Iona was one 'whose author, place, and time we are uncertain of'.[15]

It is perhaps significant that the table is preceded in our manuscript (fols 71^v-75^v) by the sixth-century Irish computistical tract *De ratione paschali* attributed to Anatolius, bishop of Laodicea.[16] Every Irish writer, from Columbanus in AD 600 to Colman at Whitby in AD 664, and beyond, defended the Irish use of an 84-year cycle by reference to Anatolius, and the principles followed in the table are also to be found in the pseudepigraphical work. That the Irish 84 circulated together with Anatolius is more than likely, therefore,[17] and the fact that our manuscript combines the two is evidence for the relative archaism of its contents, since subsequent collections, while retaining the text of Anatolius, invariably jettison the 84-year table as obsolete.[18]

place of these excerpts in the transmission of the collection.   11 McGurk described it as 'Lunar tables(?)' and gave only the (unexpanded) rubric; Stevens is equally brief, while Abate and Luisetto describe it simply as 'Tavole da studiare. Forse un ciclo pasquale?', with no rubric and no further information.   12 It may have been the scribe's intention to provide the table deliberately with a cryptic heading or, alternatively, it may have been intended to add the missing letters in red (suggestion from the late Prof. Bernhard Bischoff).   13 For example, in the anonymous seventh-century *De ratione conputandi* §99: 'Laterci enim sectatores, qui a xiiii. luna usque ad xx. septem aetates paschae numerant'; ed by Dáibhí Ó Cróinín in Walsh & Ó Cróinín, *Cummian's Letter*, 202.   14 *De ratione conputandi* §4 (Walsh and Ó Cróinín, *Cummian's Letter*, 118): 'Isidorus dicit: Latercus quoque ita quibusdam intellegitur uelut latens cultus; latet enim scientia istius rei nisi luculenta quadam ratione culturam habeat'. I have been unable to trace the citation in any genuine Isidorian work.   15 'cuius auctorem locum tempus incertum habemus',Walsh and Ó Cróinín, *Cummian's Letter*, 86-87.   16 Edited by Bruno Krusch, *Studien*, 311-27; for commentary, see Jones, *Bedae opera*, 82-87; Walsh and Ó Cróinín, *Cummian's Letter*, 32-35. A new edition, by Dr D.P. McCarthy and Dr Aidan Breen, is in the press.   17 This was suggested also by Knut Schäferdiek, 'Der irische Osterzyklus', 362.   18 The exemplar of the Munich Computus may once have contained an 84-year table, but if so, it no longer survives.

Also of some significance, as indicating a possible Irish provenance for part of the contents of the manuscript, is the inclusion (fols 66ʳ-71ᵛ) of excerpts from Macrobius' *Saturnalia,* excerpts which circulated only in Irish or Irish-related manuscripts under the title *Disputatio Cori et Praetextati.*[19] The Padua manuscript contains the best and most complete text of the *Disputatio* – further evidence that the compiler had access to good, early Irish materials.[20]

LAYOUT AND CONTENTS OF THE TABLE

We proceed now to a discussion of the table itself, and an explanation of its layout and contents. It is arranged in six columns and is extended for a period of eighty-four years.

Col. 1   This marks the Kalends (Kl.), or incidence of 1 January every year; there is no AD date, and therefore no era.[21] Attached to the Kalends is the ferial for that date. The ferial number denotes the weekday on which 1 January falls: 1 = Sunday (*Dominicus*), 2 = Monday, and so on, up to 7 = Saturday (*sabbatum*). If each year consisted of 52 weeks and a day, the sequence would recur in order every eighth year; but the insertion every fourth year of the leap-year day (*bissextus*) interrupts the sequence, so that the recurrence is every 28 years (7 x 4). Hence in the subjoined 84-year table the sequence of ferials is the same at cyclic numbers 1-7, 29-35, 57-63, and again at year 1 of the next cycle.

Col. 2   This is prefixed by 'L' for *luna* and gives the moon's age or epact on 1 January. In the lunisolar reckoning of the computists the solar year = 365 days and the lunar year = 354. Assuming the solar and lunar years begin on 1 January, the second lunar cycle will begin eleven days before the solar one and will thus be eleven days in advance of the solar year on the 1 January next following. On 1 January of the third year the lunar cycle will be twenty-two days in advance, and so on; these incremental days are the epacts.

Col. 3   This is prefixed by 'P' for *Pascha* and gives the date of Easter Sunday in the Roman calendar.

Col. 4   This is prefixed by 'L' for *luna* and gives the age of the moon on Easter Sunday.

---

19 An edition is in preparation.   20 The computistical item that immediately follows the table (fols 77ᵛ-78ʳ), beginning 'Nuper inuenit', is acephalous. What survives, however, is remarkable, for it is the only example known to me of Dionysius Exiguus' Easter table Prologue arranged in lemmata form with accompanying commentary.   21 The Kalends marks each successive year, and that is what Cummian meant when he remarked that the so-called Nicene cycle marked the Kalends of January and the moon of that day. The usage, which is peculiarly Irish (and which explains the use of Kl. in the Irish annals), confused Jones, *Bedae opera,* 93 n 3.

Col. 5   This is prefixed by 'Ini[tium]' and gives the date of the beginning of
         Lent in the Roman calendar.
Col. 6   This is prefixed by 'L' and gives the moon's age on the first day of
         Lent.

Since the data here listed are interdependent, each column provides a cross-
check on the data in the other columns, and confirms their interrelationship.
Hence errors in one column can be detected and corrected by reference to the
other columns.

RESTORATION OF THE FERIAL AND LUNAR DATA

It may be remarked, as a working principle, that tables of Roman numerals are
always susceptible to errors in transcription. That said, however, we must
assume that the majority of entries are in fact sound, and that as few emenda-
tions as possible should be made to the received text. Single-digit errors are
possible and likely (e.g. xvii in place of xviii, or iii in place of ii; but xiiii in place
of xv is less likely).[22] It is also possible that the scribe transposed numbers or
lines, particularly from the line immediately above or below the line being
copied; several instances of this are found in our manuscript.

Starting with the ferials on 1 January, since the ordinary year has 365 days,
which when divided by seven leaves a remainder of one, the ferial should
increase by one each year. The incidence of a leap-year, however, increases the
number by two. Thus we expect a pattern of three single increments of one
followed by an increment of two, and examination of the eighty-four entries
shows this to be so in all but two cases (cyclic numbers 6 and 23), where in both
cases the ferial of the preceding year has been accidentally repeated. When the
necessary correction is made, a regular pattern of three single increments
followed by a double increment is obtained for the entire table.

Since the ferial of the first entry is 'S'= *sabbatum* = 7, it must have
Dominical Letter B or BA (the latter in a leap-year).[23] However, the pattern of
double increments in the ferial data shows that the bissextile or leap-year incidence occurs in the third, seventh, eleventh and corresponding years, so that
the first year in the table cannot have been a bissextile year. Thus the first year
must have Dominical Letter B, equivalent to year eighteen in the 28-year solar
cycle.[24] Although the table has no initial AD year, the epact and the ferial
number for the first year are sufficient to enable calculation of a small number
of possible starting years for the cycle, as will be discussed presently.

---

22 There is one example below, at cyclic number 48, where the moon's age is given as xiiii
(for xv).   23 For the terminology and usage see Mac Carthy, AU 4, pp xvii–xxiii.   24 Note that
the table entries marked 'B' (= *bissextus*) are misplaced up to year 31; thereafter they follow in the
correct sequence.

Turning next to the moon's age or epact on 1 January, we expect to see this increment by eleven every year, except in the years following the saltus or moon's leap, when the number advances by twelve. The sequence of epacts in the table shows eleven errors (cyclic numbers 4, 9, 24, 29, 40, 48, 49, 52, 66, 74, and 84); in every case the error is clearly due to scribal lapses, and the correction required is mechanical: [x]xii for xii; xvi[i] for xvi; ii[i] for ii; xxvii[ii] for xxvii; xx[x] for xx; xxviii[i] for xxviii; x(xi) for xxi; [x]iii for iii; xviii(i) for xviiii; xvi[i] for xvi; and vi[i] for vi.

Cyclic numbers 15, 29 (corrected), 43, 57, and 71 all show an epactal increment of twelve, compared to the normal increment of eleven. Since 15 = 1 + 14, and the other numbers follow at fourteen-year intervals, it seems safe to conclude that the saltus was inserted at fourteen year intervals. With the minor corrections just described, we find that the data of col. 2 present a smooth pattern of epacts, representing an 84-year cycle with insertion of the saltus every fourteenth year. This is the typical arrangement of the Irish cycle.

RE-CALCULATION OF THE PASCHAL AND INITIUM DATA FROM THE RESTORED FERIALS AND EPACTS

Since the Paschal and Initium dates and moons all derive from the ferials and epacts of 1 January, the next step is to compare the values recomputed from the restored ferials and epacts with the data in cols 3-6.[25] The rule is as follows: if E is the epact, then 45 *minus* E gives the date of the Paschal full moon in either the second half of March or the first half of April. When this Sunday falls on or before 25 March the calculation 74 *minus* E gives the date of the next full moon, in the second half of April, and similarly the next Sunday on or following that date is taken as Easter Sunday. The ferial of 1 January is then used to calculate the day of the week on that date, and the first Sunday on or after that date is taken as Easter Sunday, providing it occurs after 25 March, the date of the vernal equinox according to the old Roman reckoning. Once the weekday of the full moon is known the Paschal moon is readily computed. The Initium is then reckoned as occurring forty days before Easter Sunday, counting inclusively.

To eliminate the possibility of error in the calculation, all the manuscript data were carefully transcribed to a computer file with the corrections described above. A computer program was then written which read this file, recomputed the Paschal and Initium data, and printed the recomputed and original manuscript data side-by-side so as to facilitate comparison. When the recomputed (hereafter R) and manuscript (hereafter MS.) data pairs were examined it was found that they could be readily grouped into three classes:

---

25 For what follows see O'Connell, 'Easter cycles', 88.

Class 1: Pairs that matched exactly

Class 2: Pairs that varied in minor ways (e.g., for Paschal dates we found No. 30, vi. Id. Ap. (MS.) compared with v. Id. Ap. (R); or No. 18, xv. K. Ap. (MS.) compared with xv. K. Mai. (R); while for Paschal moons we found many differing by just one, e.g. No. 1, xvi. (MS.) compared with xv. (R)

Class 3: Pairs that did not match at all

Preliminary analysis of the Paschal dates produced 62 Class 1 entries, 9 Class 2, and 13 Class 3 entries; for the Paschal moons the results were 10 Class 1, 61 Class 2, and 13 Class 3 entries. When the 61 Paschal moon entries of Class 2 were examined it was noticed that in *every* case the manuscript Paschal moon was one day older than the recomputed moon. When the 13 Class 3 Paschal moon entries were examined it was found that in *every* case the Paschal moon was xiiii compared to a recomputed moon of xx. Finally, when the 13 Class 3 Paschal dates were examined it was found that in *every* case the manuscript date was one week in advance of the recomputed date, and for both moons and dates the Class 3 entries were identical. Corresponding discrepancies could be seen in the Initium data.

It is clear from this analysis that the manuscript Paschal and Initium data do not reconcile well with the manuscript ferial and epactal data, and amendments on a wholly improbable scale would be required to restore the table to some sort of coherence. However, it was also clear that the difference between the two sets of data was somehow systematic, for if the discrepancies were due to random scribal error we could never expect to find 61 cases where the Paschal moon differed by one day, nor 13 cases where the Paschal dates differed by a whole week. Consequently an alternative explanation was sought for the systematic discrepancies. It was soon realised that if the epact for 1 January was incremented by one, it would increment all the recomputed Paschal and Initium moons as well, bringing them into line with the original manuscript entries; in the case of the Class 3 entries, the recomputed moon would increase to xxi (that is, one day beyond the traditional Irish limit), allowing the Paschal date to move back one week to moon xiiii, in line with the original manuscript entries and with known Irish practice.

On the basis of this premise, the Paschal and Initium data were recomputed with the epacts all increased by one, and the results from this operation were much more encouraging, as the following table shows.

Table 1. Counts of the correspondence classes for MS. vs. incremented epacts

	MS. Epacts Class			Incremented Epacts Class		
Table entry	*1*	*2*	*3*	*1*	*2*	*3*
Paschal date	62	9	13	73	11	–
Paschal moon	10	61	13	76	8	–
Initium date	38	22	24	44	30	10
Initium moon	3	56	25	65	19	–

The results are particularly satisfactory for the Paschal dates, which all now come into line, or differ only in trivial details, and for the moons, where in both cases more than sixty entries came into line with the manuscript data. However, the Initium dates, which still show ten entries completely out of line, seem to have been less carefully copied, showing more omissions and scribal amendments.[26] The statistical evidence of these revised data is overwhelming, and we are driven to conclude that the Paschal and Initium data were in fact computed from epact values one higher (E *plus* 1) than those actually shown in the manuscript. The table below is based on this discovery.

DATING THE TABLE

It is naturally of crucial importance to know what historical years the table entries refer to, and we have here to guide us (a) the historical evidence and the manuscript context, (b) the ferial data, and (c) the epactal data. Regarding (a), we have seen that the preservation of the table together with material of demonstrable seventh-century Irish origin suggests a date no later than then. In any event, the 84 (14) cycle is known to have been relinquished finally on Iona in AD 716, and it seems reasonable to take this as a terminus post quem non.[27] Regarding (b), the ferial data in the manuscript, we have noted above that the table commences with ferial number 7 (S = *sabbatum*) = Saturday, with the bissextile intercalation occurring two years later. This tells us that the Dominical Letter for the year is B, giving solicyclic number 18 (i.e., the remainder when the AD is divided by 28 must be 18). Finally, turning to (c), the epactal data, we may first observe that there is very good discrimination at twenty-eight-year intervals, because in twenty-eight years the epact increments 28 x 11 and there are two insertions of the saltus, so the epact advances by 28 x 11 + 2 = 310 = 10 modulo 30. That is, if in a given year the epact is about correct,

---

26 This may be due to the fact that the *Initium* columns do not occur in standard 19-year tables, with which the scribe would have been more familiar.   27 See O'Connell, 'Easter cycle', 84.

then it will be 10 less twenty-eight years before and 10 greater twenty-eight years subsequently, so there is no serious possibility of confusing successive occurrences of a given solicyclic number.

With these points in mind we turn now to the epacts that the Irish were using in the period AD 400-700. O'Connell considered this question carefully and showed clearly that the Irish epacts lay between the Alexandrine and Roman epacts,[28] and on this basis he constructed a table of the possible Irish epacts for the period AD 432 to AD 720.[29] This table was searched for those years containing the data in our table, solicyclic number 18 and initial epact 20. The solicyclic restricts the search to the years 438, 466, 494, 522, 550, 578, 606, 634, 662, 690, and 718. However, only the following years have epactal ranges including 20: 438 (20-21), 522 (18-21), 606 (16-21), and 690 (15-21), where the figures in brackets show the range between the Alexandrine and Roman epacts. Which of these years is most appropriate to our table?

To decide which of these years 438, 522, 606, or 690 is the initial year of the Padua table we commence by considering the only other Irish 84-year *latercus* known, that described in the Munich Computus. This has been fully discussed by Krusch, Mac Carthy, Schwarz, and O'Connell; Schwarz and Mac Carthy dated it independently to AD 718, while the latter showed that it was based, in part at least, on materials dated AD 689; all writers are agreed on the Computus' Irish origin. Both Schwarz and O'Connell rejected Krusch's reconstruction of the Munich *latercus*, while Mac Carthy's, which is based completely on the improbable assumption that a fourth-century Roman cata-comb inscription provided epacts which matched the Irish ones exactly, was likewise rejected by O'Connell. To O'Connell's arguments for rejection we may add the fact that Mac Carthy's initial year AD 381 has epact 20 in the Victorian cycle, not epact 19 as the Munich Computus requires. However, by careful analysis of the ferial and epactal data described in the Munich Computus O'Connell established that the only possible initial years are 522, 541, and 560;[30] based on his assumption that the Latercus derived from the Victorian table O'Connell then selected AD 560 as his initial year.

We now consider the discrepancy that exists between a lunar calendar based upon a cycle of 84-years with six salti and the real moon. As O'Connell showed,[31] after 84 years the calendar moon is about 1.28 days ahead of the real moon, so the epact should be reduced by one to bring them back into line. That this was known in the fifth century and earlier is proven by the reduction in the Zeitz table's epacts relative to the *Supputatio Romana* such that its epact for AD 365 was two less than that of the *Supputatio*, 'thus correcting for a time (about 447) the error that had been building up'.[32] O'Connell also remarked on simi-lar effects in the two tables described by the Carthaginian computist of AD 455,

---

28 O'Connell, 'Easter cycles', 95.   29 Ibid. 97.   30 O'Connell, 'Easter tables', 88.   31 Ibid. 74.   32 Ibid. 75.

adding that 'the epacts of these [84-year] cycles were altered so as to bring the cyclic [i.e. calendar] moon nearer to the actual'.

Thus we see that both the theory and practice of an 84-year cycle with six salti require that the initial epact should be reduced from time to time in order to keep calendar and real moons in synchronism. This then provides the most likely explanation as to why the epacts of the Padua table have all been decremented by one subsequent to the calculation of the table. Furthermore, and finally, we see that if the Munich Computus refers to an Irish *latercus* commencing with epact 19 and dating from somewhere in the first half of the sixth century, as O'Connell demonstrated, then the Padua table, with initial epact 20, must refer to an earlier date. We are forced, therefore, to rule out the years 690, 606, and 522 as possible initial years for the table and conclude that AD 438 is the only year compatible with the ferial and epactal data and O'Connell's dating of the Munich *latercus*.

Is there any independent confirmation of this dating available? The only documentary evidence available regarding Irish epacts is the annals, the oldest being the Annals of Inisfallen and the most comprehensive the Annals of Ulster.[33] Both have been partially labelled with ferial and epactal data and the latter derive from the 19-year Alexandrian cycle adjusted to the Roman year (i.e. with epact for 1 January). Although their respective series of epacts are incomplete, these have been restored and correlated with AD dating.[34] Both annals are found to have the same sequence and both explicitly give epact 20 for AD 438, and it naturally follows from their 19-year cycle that they do *not* give epact 20 for the years 522, 606, or 690. It must be acknowledged that the epactal sequences of these annals were inserted retrospectively, most probably superseding earlier 84-year cycle epacts, but they do confirm that whoever added them accepted epact 20 for AD 438.

Hence we see that the documentary evidence does support our derivation of epact 20 for the year AD 438, and we feel confident accordingly in presenting the following *latercus* of Irish Easters for the years AD 438 to AD 521 based on this dating.

33 Seán Mac Airt (ed & trans), *The Annals of Inisfallen (MS. Rawlinson B. 503)* (Dublin 1951); Seán Mac Airt and Gearóid Mac Niocaill (eds & trans), *The Annals of Ulster (to AD 1131)* (Dublin 1983). 34 Mac Carthy, AU, p. xx ff.; Paul Walsh, 'The dating of the Irish annals', *Irish Historical Studies* 2 (1941) 355-75.

Early Irish history and chronology

Table 2. Reconstructed *latercus* of Irish Easters for the years AD 438 to AD 521

Cyclic No.	AD	Ferial	Epact	Paschal Date	Moon
1	438	7	20	27 Mar	16
2	439	1	1	16 Apr	17
3	440	2	12	7 Apr	19
4	441	4	23	20 Apr	14
5	442	5	4	12 Apr	16
6	443	6	15	4 Apr	19
7	444	7	26	23 Apr	20
8	445	2	7	8 Apr	15
9	446	3	18	31 Mar	18
10	447	4	29	20 Apr	20
11	448	5	10	4 Apr	14
12	449	7	21	27 Mar	17
13	450	1	2	16 Apr	18
14	451	2	13	1 Apr	14
15	452	3	25	20 Apr	16
16	453	5	6	12 Apr	18
17	454	6	17	28 Mar	14
15	455	7	28	17 Apr	16
19	456	1	9	8 Apr	17
20	457	3	20	31 Mar	20
21	458	4	1	13 Apr	14
22	459	5	12	5 Apr	17
23	460	6	23	27 Mar	19
24	461	1	4	16 Apr	20
25	462	2	15	1 Apr	16
26	463	3	26	21 Apr	18
27	464	4	7	12 Apr	19
28	465	6	15	28 Mar	15
29	466	7	30	17 Apr	18
30	467	1	11	9 Apr	20
31	468	2	22	21 Apr	14
32	469	4	3	13 Apr	16
33	470	5	14	5 Apr	19
34	471	6	25	18 Apr	14
35	472	7	6	9 Apr	15
36	473	2	17	1 Apr	18
37	474	3	28	21 Apr	20
38	475	4	9	6 Apr	15
39	476	5	20	28 Mar	17
40	477	7	1	17 Apr	18
41	478	1	12	2 Apr	14

42	479	2	23	22 Apr	16
43	480	3	5	13 Apr	18
44	481	5	16	29 Mar	14
45	482	6	27	18 Apr	16
46	483	7	8	10 Apr	18
47	484	1	19	1 Apr	20
48	485	3	30	14 Apr	15
49	486	4	11	6 Apr	17
50	487	5	22	29 Mar	20
51	488	6	3	17 Apr	20
52	489	1	14	2 Apr	16
53	490	2	25	22 Apr	18
54	491	3	6	14 Apr	20
55	492	4	17	29 Mar	15
56	493	6	28	18 Apr	17
57	494	7	10	10 Apr	20
58	495	1	21	26 Mar	16
59	496	2	2	4 Apr	16
60	497	4	13	6 Apr	19
61	498	5	24	19 Apr	14
62	499	6	5	11 Apr	16
63	500	7	16	2 Apr	18
64	501	2	27	22 Apr	20
65	502	3	8	7 Apr	15
66	503	4	19	30 Mar	18
67	504	5	30	18 Apr	19
68	505	7	11	3 Apr	14
69	506	1	22	26 Mar	17
70	507	2	3	15 Apr	18
71	508	3	15	30 Mar	14
72	509	5	26	19 Apr	16
73	510	6	7	11 Apr	18
74	511	7	18	27 Mar	14
75	512	1	29	15 Apr	15
76	513	3	10	7 Apr	17
77	514	4	21	30 Mar	20
78	515	5	2	12 Apr	14
79	516	6	13	3 Apr	16
80	517	1	24	26 Mar	19
81	518	2	5	15 Apr	20
82	519	3	16	31 Mar	16
83	520	4	27	19 Apr	17
84	521	6	-8	11 Apr	19

COMMENTARY

A few comments are called for regarding this table. Firstly, it has been presented so as to enable the reader to reconstruct the original manuscript entries by reference to Appendix 1, which shows every amendment made to the ferial, epactal, and Paschal data in the original Roman notation, except that the increment applied to every restored epact is not marked. Thus when amendments are shown to the epacts, it must be remembered to first subtract one from the epact given in col. 4 before applying that amendment. For example, cyclic number 24 shows epact 4, from which one must be subtracted (= iii) before applying the amendment E ii > iii, indicating that the manuscript actually has epact ii. Note also that with the single exception of cyclic number 48, where *luna xiiii* is amended to *luna xv*, all the other amendments involve only the insertion or deletion of one or two repeated digits.

Secondly, the table has been presented so as to facilitate comparison with O'Connell's reconstructed Irish table, where all the numeration is in Arabic numerals and dates are in the modern format; it is for this reason that the Roman calendar notation of the original has been dispensed with and the restored table converted to modern notation.

Thirdly, upon comparing this table with O'Connell's reconstruction over the years AD 438-521, four discrepancies emerge as follows.

Table 3. Discrepancies between Padua MS Paschal data
and O'Connell Table 1, AD 438-521

AD Year	Padua MS.	O'Connell
444	23 Apr. l. 20	26 Mar. l. 21
479	22 Apr. l. 16	25 Mar. l. 17
490	22 Apr. l. 18	25 Mar. l. 19
501	22 Apr. l. 20	25 Mar. l. 21

It should be noted that, with the exception of the date for AD 444, which has been emended from 24 April to 23 April, these are the dates actually shown in the Padua manuscript, and it is clear that whoever drew up the table rejected 25 March and *luna xxi* as possible criteria. His lunar limits are xiiii-xx and his Paschal limits are 26 March to 23 April, which incidentally fully accord with the limits in Anatolius.[35] O'Connell himself took his limits from the so-called 'Acts of the council of Caesaraea', otherwise known as Pseudo-Theophilus,[36] and the so-called Pseudo-Athanasius, both Irish forgeries of the sixth

35 See O'Connell, 'Easter cycles', 78.   36 These 'Acta synodi' are also called *Epistola Philippi de Pascha* in some manuscripts.

century;[37] he thus decided to accept 25 March and *luna xxi* as possible criteria.[38]

The manuscript entry we have dated to AD 444 provides further corroborating evidence when compared with the Annals of Inisfallen. The annals s.a. AD 454 have the entry 'l. xxvi. P. viii. K. Mai'. Mac Airt, in his footnote,[39] inferred that the entry alludes to the compromise Roman Easter of AD 455, which was celebrated on 24 April (three days beyond the Roman limit). But there are difficulties with this proposal, for as Mac Airt also pointed out, the epact xxvi is incorrect for both AD 454 and AD 455. He referred to the Alexandrine epact for these years, xvi and xxvii respectively, and remarked that the annal entry may be easily amended to either. However, this does not reconcile with O'Connell's tabulation of the Roman epacts,[40] which he gives as xviiii and xxx for AD 454 and 455 respectively, neither of which readily amends to xxvi. Furthermore, the epacts in the Annals of Inisfallen follow a 19-year cycle commencing with epact 9 in AD 437 and proceeding through 20, 1, 12, 23, 4, 15, 26, etc., which would place the entry under discussion here at AD 444; furthermore, Mac Airt's apparatus for the years AD 444 and 445 suggest that an entry has indeed been moved out from the chronicle at AD 444. Relocating it here we need only amend the date with a single digit, reading 'l. xxvi. P. viii[i] K. Mai', in order to obtain our Table 2 entry, and the amendment listed in Appendix 1 shows that the Padua manuscript in fact exactly matches the data in the Inisfallen entry. It seems, on the face of it, more likely that the Irish annals would refer to an extreme Irish Paschal date, rather than a Roman compromise with Alexandria at a time when, so far as we know, the Irish were not involved in controversy with either.

In conclusion we may point to the following results of our enquiries: (1) the Padua manuscript provides conclusive evidence for an Irish 84-year Easter cycle with a 14-year saltus, and with lunar limits 14-20 and Paschal limits 26 March-23 April; and (2) for the first time we now have a list of Irish Easter dates, commencing in AD 438 and running to AD 521.

THE 84-YEAR EASTER CYCLE IN BRITAIN AND IRELAND

In all the references to Easter practices in the British Isles that occur in early writers the Irish and British churches are invariably linked together. In his Paschal letter addressed to abbot Ségéne of Iona (AD 633), Cummian twice remarks on the fact that the Irish and British stand out alone in their unique observances, describing them once as 'an insignificant group of Britons and

---

37 For discussion of these texts see Jones, *Bedae opera*, 51-53 and 87-89; Walsh and Ó Cróinín, *Cummian's Letter*, 37-39, 158.48. 38 For other arguments against these limits see Schäferdiek, 'Der irische Osterzyklus', 360 n 12 and 371. 39 *Annals of Inisfallen*, 58. 40 O'Connell, 'Easter cycles', 97.

Irish who are almost at the end of the earth, and, if I may say so, but pimples on the face of the earth';[41] on the second occasion he asks sardonically: 'What, then, more evil can be thought about Mother Church than if we say Rome errs, Jerusalem errs, Alexandria errs, Antioch errs, the whole world errs; the Irish and British alone know what is right.'[42] That the Irish and British were at one in their observances is also stated by Aldhelm, in his letter to the British king Gerontius,[43] and by Bede.[44]

Given the direct and continuous involvement of the British church in the establishment and consolidation of early Christianity in Ireland, conformity of Easter practices seems, on the face of it, very likely, even if we are unable to confirm it with technical evidence. But the persistence of the statements, coming, as they do, from all sides, would appear to justify us in accepting the case as proven. That much having been said, it remains to see what the evidence of the rediscovered Irish 84-year Easter table can tell us about sixth- and seventh-century Irish and British chronology.

This subject is too vast to allow for detailed examination here, but a possible starting-point is the dating of Gildas' *De excidio Britanniae*, the only important literary survival from sixth-century Britain.[45] Apart from inferential deductions based on the supposed historical background of Gildas' account, the only data which might allow an accurate dating of the work are contained in a 'dating clause' which has defied interpretation up to now. The passage in the *De excidio* of concern to us reads as follows:

> Ex eo tempore nunc cives, nunc hostes, vincebant, ut in ista gente experiretur dominus solito more praesentem Israel, utrum diligat eum an non, usque ad annum obsessionis Badonici montis, novissimaeque ferme de furciferis non minime stragis, quique quadragesimus quartus (ut novi) oritur annus, mense iam uno emenso, qui et meae nativitatis est.[46]

> 'From then on victory went now to our countrymen, now to their enemies: so that in this people the Lord could make trial (as he tends to) of his latter-day Israel to see whether it loves him or not. This lasted

---

41 Walsh and Ó Cróinín, *Cummian's Letter,* 72: 'Britonum Scottorumque particula, qui sunt pene extremi et, ut dicam, mentagrae orbis terrarum', whom he describes as 'simul in obseruatione precipuarum sollenitatum uniti'.   **42** ibid. 80: 'Quid autem prauius sentiri potest de aecclesia matre quam si dicamus Roma errat, Ierosolima errat, Alexandria errat, Antiochia errat, totus mundus errat; soli tantum Scotti et Britones rectum sapiunt'.   **43** See Rudolf Ehwald (ed), *Aldhelmi opera,* MGH AA (Berlin 1919) 480-86.   **44** See Jones, *Bedae opera,* 99-101.   **45** See Michael Lapidge and David N. Dumville (eds), *Gildas, new approaches,* Studies in Celtic History 5 (Woodbridge 1984), and the reviews by Edward James in *Nottingham Medieval Studies* 30 (1986) 101-05, and Thomas Charles-Edwards in *Cambridge Medieval Celtic Studies* 12 (1986) 115-20. **46** Theodor Mommsen (ed), *Gildae sapientis De excidio et conquestu Britanniae,* MGH AA 13 (Berlin 1898) 1-85: 40. The translation cited is by Michael Winterbottom (ed & trans.), *Gildas: The ruin of Britain and other works,* History from the Sources (London and Chichester 1978) 28.

right up till the year of the siege of Badon Hill ... That was the year of my birth: as I know, one month of the forty-fourth year since then has passed already'.

The traditional interpretation of this passage has understood it to mean that the battle of Mons Badonicus took place in the year of Gildas' birth, forty-four years before the time of writing.[47] An alternative interpretation has been proposed by Ian Wood, but though this received guarded approval by one other writer,[48] his view has been subjected to vigorous criticism by both Thomas Charles-Edwards and the late J.M. Wallace-Hadrill,[49] principally on the grounds that Woods' translation is incompatible with the syntax of the clause.

As an alternative solution to the problem I should like to suggest that Gildas' 'forty-fourth year' refers, not to a unique chronology based on the date of the battle of Mons Badonicus, but to a universal chronology, such as would have been provided by an Easter table. In other words, Gildas' reference is to the forty-fourth year of an 84-year Easter cycle. Assuming that cycle to be identical to the Irish table recovered in the Padua manuscript, with initial year AD 438, we can deduce that Gildas means that the battle of Mons Badonicus took place in February of AD 482.[50] Any further inference about the absolute date of the *De excidio* would then depend on Gildas' age when he composed it. But it seems to me in the circumstances that the wording used by Gildas in this crucial passage is most naturally interpreted as referring to a *cycle* of years, and the only such cycle with any claims to validity for the period is the Irish/British 84-year Easter table.

The full implications of the rediscovery of the Irish/British 84-year Easter

---

47 Winterbottom, for example, in his introduction (2) dates the battle of Mons Badonicus 'in the 490s', in the belief that 'Gildas wrote his main work, the "Ruin of Britain", about 540 A.D. or just before, when he was forty-three years old' (1). This seems to be the view also of Patrick Sims-Williams, 'Gildas and the Anglo-Saxons', *Cambridge Medieval Celtic Studies* 6 (1983) 1-30: 25 (repeating Winterbottom's translation). **48** Ian Wood, 'The end of Roman Britain: continental evidence and parallels', in Lapidge and Dumville, *Gildas*, 1-25: esp 22-23. Wood remarks (rightly, as it seems to me) that 'the phrase *mense uno emenso* also seems curious – why should Gildas bother about the month in which Badon was fought, or was he writing in February?' But why would not Gildas be interested in the precise date of Mons Badonicus, particularly in a dating-clause? **49** Guarded approval of Wood's interpretation was expressed by James, *Nottingham Medieval Studies*, 104. According to Charles-Edwards, however, Wood's proposal 'only leads to syntactical or other absurdities' (118), arguing that 'we must either violate syntax ... or we must violate common sense and suppose that Gildas was writing at the precocious age of one month' (119). The verdict in Wallace-Hadrill, *Bede's 'Ecclesiastical history of the English people'* (Oxford 1988) 215-16, is a counsel of despair: 'If the traditional translation is unacceptable, it is necessary to emend'. I do not understand the translation in J.N.L. Myres, *The English settlements*, Oxford History of England Ib (Oxford 1986) 222-23 (Appendix III). **50** Charles-Edwards points out – quite correctly – that 'the whole structure has no chronological anchor' as hitherto interpreted. But since the purpose of the dating clause was obviously to provide such an anchor, it follows that the error is more likely to be in the interpretation than in the words of Gildas.

table will need to be worked out elsewhere. For the present it must suffice to say that its potential importance for the reconstruction of early Irish chronology, especially in terms of controlling and, where necessary, correcting the evidence of the Irish annals, can hardly be exaggerated. In the broader field of computistics we are now, for the first time, in a position to test the statements of writers such as Cummian and Bede, and relate their comments to our new understanding of the evidence. Only with this new discovery can the full story of the Easter controversy in the British and Irish churches be told. The publication of the long-lost Irish 84-year Easter table opens a new chapter in that story.[51]

APPENDIX I: A LIST OF THE AMENDMENTS
MADE TO THE PADUA MS.

The purpose of this Appendix is to list all the amendments made to the Padua manuscript in the course of making the reconstructed table given in Table 2 above, and thus enable the reader to derive the original manuscript readings from that table. The amendments are given by manuscript column, left to right, and each entry is identified by its cyclic number. The following conventions are employed: brackets [ ] denote digits that have been *excised*, while parentheses ( ) denote digits that have been *added*. For simplicity, the abbreviations 'f' [= feria], 'L' [= luna], 'P' [= Pascha], and 'In' [= Initium] have been omitted.

Column 1: Ferials
6.   vi[i]
23. vi[i]

Column 2: Epacts
Only those amendments that were made in order to obtain a smooth arrangement of epacts are given below. Subsequently all entries in this column were incremented by one, as discussed fully in section 3 above.
4.   x[x]ii
9.   xvi[i]
24. ii[i]
29. xxvii[ii]
40. xx[x]
48. xxviii[i]
49. x(xi)
52. [x]iii
66. xviii(i)
74. xvi[i]
84. vi[i]

---

51 The computer program used in this study and the resulting printouts are available from Dr Daniel McCarthy, Department of Computer Science, Trinity College, Dublin 2.

Column 3: Paschal Dates
7. viii[i] K.M.
15. x[ii] K.M.
18. xv K.(Ap.)[M.]
30. v(i) Id.AP.
38. vii[i] Id.Ap.
59. xviii [K.M.]
65. vii(i) Id.AP.
71. iii(i) K.Ap.
75. xvi[i] K.(Ap.)[M.]
76. vii(i) Id.Ap.
81. xvii [K.M.]

Column 4: Paschal Moon
22. xvi[i]
27. xviii[i]
29. xvii[i]
36. xviii(i)
48. x(iiii)[v]
49. xvi[i]
61. xiii[i]
67. xviii[i]

Early Irish annals from Easter tables: a case restated*

In the most recent published discussion of early Irish annals and their origins,[1] and in conversations with other historians of this period, an unspoken assumption seems to have emerged among many that the old theory of origin in Easter table marginal entries has now been set aside in favour of other hypotheses.[2] The established doctrine, as expressed for example by T.F. O'Rahilly, was that 'probably it was a common practice in the early religious communities to make brief marginal entries on Paschal tables',[3] in whose margins could be entered, opposite the data of the years in which they happened, the events thought worthy of recording.

According to Kenneth Harrison, however, the most recent writer on the subject, these views of O'Rahilly and others 'seem to lay rather too much emphasis on this secondary function of Easter tables, at the expense of another form of tradition, the writing of chronicles, begun by Eusebius, continued by Jerome, and still further carried on by compilers like Prosper and Marcellinus Comes'.[4] Harrison seems to differ somewhat from previous writers in his

---

* First published in *Peritia* 2 (1983) 74-86.   1 See esp. John Bannerman, 'Notes on the Scottish entries in the early Irish annals', *Scottish Gaelic Studies* 11 (1968) 149-70; repr. idem, *Studies in the history of Dalriada* (Edinburgh 1974) 9-26; Alfred P. Smyth, 'The earliest Irish annals: their first contemporary entries and the earliest centres of recording', PRIA 72 C 1 (1972) 1-48; Kathleen Hughes, *Early christian Ireland: introduction to the sources* (London 1972) 99-159; Gearóid Mac Niocaill, *The medieval Irish annals.* Dublin Historical Association Medieval Irish History Series 3 (Dublin 1975). Fundamental studies of an earlier period are those of Bartholomew Mac Carthy, *The codex Palatino-Vaticanus, No. 830.* Royal Irish Academy Todd Lecture Series 3 (Dublin 1892) 343-89; idem in William Hennessy & B. Mac Carthy (eds & transls), *Annála Uladh, the annals of Ulster,* 4 vols (Dublin 1887-1901) 4, introduction; Charles W. Jones, *Saints Lives and chronicles in early England* (Ithaca, New York 1947). For a good brief discussion of the general question, see Michael McCormick, *Les annales du haut moyen âge.* Typologie des Sources du Moyen Age Occidental 14 (Turnhout 1975). [See now D.P. McCarthy, 'The chronology of the Irish annals', PRIA 98 C 6 (1998) 203-55.]   2 Professor Mac Niocaill has said that 'later texts are of course not dependent on Easter tables: after the very earliest period, the Irish annals lead an independent life', *Medieval Irish annals,* 13; this is undoubtedly the case. [For a contrary view see, however, Rosamond McKitterick, 'Constructing the past in the early middle ages: the case of the Royal Frankish Annals', *Trans. Roy. Hist. Soc.,* 6th ser., 7 (1997) 101-29: 111: 'Although annal entries in Easter tables are attested in extant manuscripts dating from the ninth century onwards, I am no longer convinced that this is how annals originally developed'. Note, however, that Prof. McKitterick's date for the earliest Easter table annals is at least two centuries too late, something which has a significant bearing on the argument.]   3 *Early Irish history and mythology* (Dublin 1946) 235.   4 Kenneth Harrison, 'Epacts in Irish chronicles', *Studia Celtica* 12-13 (1977-8) 17-

apparent belief that the underlying text on which all our extant Irish annal collections are ultimately based (O'Rahilly's 'Ulster Chronicle', Hughes' 'World Chronicle') was a continuation of just such a Eusebio-Hieronimian text: 'possibly, then, a new recension of the Chronicle of Ireland was being prepared about 640 or 650. If so, the indications are that material from a Victorian Easter table could have been incorporated'.[5] While there is no doubt that the Eusebio-Hieronimian chronicle was known and used in Ireland from an early date,[6] it seems to me unlikely that its influence could have extended much (if at all) beyond the 'pre-Patrician' section of the extant annals – that period for which, of course, the Irish could have had no native historical documentation.[7] It is even more unlikely, I believe, that the very structure of those Irish annals derives from such a continuation of Eusebius-Jerome and owes little or nothing to early paschal annals, as Harrison implies.[8]

32:17; cf. his more general discussion, *The framework of Anglo-Saxon history to A.D. 900* (Cambridge 1976) esp. 44-51. **5** 'Epacts in Irish chronicles', 29. No manuscript evidence is offered in support of this claim for an Irish continuation of Eusebius-Jerome's chronicle up to the sixth and seventh centuries. Harrison has taken over the ideas in Mac Neill's paper, cited in the next note. **6** The evidence has not been brought together systematically, but see Eoin Mac Neill, 'The authorship and structure of the "Annals of Tigernach"', *Ériu* 7 (1913) 30-113; John Morris, 'The chronicle of Eusebius-Jerome: Irish fragments', *University of London Institute of Classical Studies Bulletin* 19 (1972) 80-93. Neither of these authors, however, has proved the extensive use of Eusebius-Jerome for annalistic purposes before the ninth or tenth centuries. Mac Neill maintained that 'there was a version made in Ireland, with additions and omissions ... about the year 607', 'Annals of Tigernach', 62. He further suggested that 'the compiler of the Irish continuation of Eusebius may well have been Sinlán, or Mo Sinu moccu Min, scribe and abbot of Bangor, whose death is recorded in the same annal with "finis chronici Eusebii"'. This 'continuation' then served, so he says, as the basis for what he called the 'Old-Irish chronicle of *c*. AD 712'. It is salutary to observe Mac Neill (rightly) dismissing the earlier view that the 'Tigernach' annals were the work of Tigernach of Clonmacnois – the sole basis for which was the entry *hucusque Tigernach scripsit* at the year AD 1088 – and yet making the claim to Sinlán moccu Min's alleged authorship of a 'continuation' of Eusebius-Jerome on the sole ground that his death notice follows the phrase *finis chronici Eusebii* in the annals. Unfortunately, however, these theories have been accepted *in toto* by Harrison. For trenchant criticisms of Mac Neill's views, see O'Rahilly, 249-54, and literature there cited. **7** It seems to me uncritical and misleading to discuss the 'pre-Patrician' and 'post-Patrician' sections of our Irish annals as one piece, as though they were compiled simultaneously. Even though the prehistoric section is manifestly modelled on the Eusebian chronicle, there is no evidence (to my knowledge) to prove that this section was synchronised with events in Irish prehistory at any time before the ninth or tenth century. See the good discussions on this point in Anton G. van Hamel, 'Über die vorpatrizianischen irischen Annalen', *Zeitschrift für Celtische Philologie* 17 (1928) 241-60, and David N. Dumville, 'Ulster heroes in the early Irish annals: a caveat', *Éigse* 17 (1977) 47-54. [See now Daniel McCarthy, 'The status of the pre-Patrician Irish annals', *Peritia* 12 (1998) 98-152.] **8** 'We should guard against thinking that the writing of chronicles or history was influenced by paschal annals to a decisive or even a considerable extent', *Framework of Anglo-Saxon history*, 45. But this is to ignore, for example, the clear evidence in Bede, for which see Wilhelm Levison, 'Bede as historian', in A. Hamilton Thompson, (ed), *Bede, his life, times and writings: essays in commemoration of the twelfth centenary of his death* (Oxford 1935) 111-51: 135-36, where Levison shows that Bede, in the *recapitulatio* to his chronicle, was drawing on a collection of annals which he had probably compiled in anticipation of his work on the *Historia Ecclesiastica*.

To prove that the characteristics of our earliest Irish annals do, in fact, derive from the nature of Easter tables would require a more technical discussion than I wish to enter on here. An essential prerequisite to such a study would be to establish, by whatever means possible, the presence of such paschal annals in the earliest stratum of the texts. Such a study should preferably await the appearance of the new edition of the Annals of Ulster now being seen through the press by Professor Gearóid Mac Niocaill. But in the interim there is scope at least for a preliminary examination of the problem and the purpose of this paper, therefore, is to demonstrate, by reference to a small number of specific examples which have not hitherto been discussed, that some of our earliest annals do, in fact, derive from marginal entries in Easter tables, and that such paschal annals can be verified, in at least one of these instances, even for the sixth century.[9] The consequences of such a demonstration – if it be accepted – would naturally be important. For even so meticulous a historian as Wilhelm Levison has stated that paschal annals were first recorded in England in the seventh century.[10] Moreover, the verification of an annal (or annals) for the sixth century would prove (what O'Rahilly had maintained) that such notices were being made already on tables of the 84-year cycle, that is, before the arrival of either the Victorian or Dionysiac tables.[11]

It should be stressed at the outset, however, that the habit of entering historical notices in the margins of Easter tables is not an Irish nor even an Insular innovation. The earliest example concerning the Burgundian Frankish kingdom occurs in the oldest surviving manuscript of Victorius of Aquitaine's paschal tables, Gotha, Herzogliche Bibliothek, MS. 75 (*saec.* VII, Burgundy), beside the data for the year AD 501: 'Gundubadus fuit in Abinione'.[12] There can be no reasonable doubt that this item was copied by the scribe of the Gotha manuscript from a contemporary entry in his exemplar. It records the flight of the Burgundian king Gundubad to Avignon after his defeat at the hands of

---

9 Thus bearing out the contention of Smyth ('The earliest Irish annals', 10) that the first contemporary notation of annals took place somewhere about the year AD 550. Hughes stated that 'there were probably no contemporary annals until late in the seventh century', *Early christian Ireland*, 145 – a view recently endorsed by Prof. D.A. Binchy, 'Irish history and Irish law I', *Studia Hibernica* 15 (1975) 7-36:19. 10 Wilhelm Levison and Wilhelm Wattenbach, *Deutschlands Geschichtsquellen im Mittelalter. Vorzeit und Karolinger* 1 (Weimar 1952) 57: 'zuerst in England ... sind Ostertafeln für geschichtliche Eintragungen benutzt worden'. 11 Harrison, *Framework of Anglo-Saxon history*, 44-50, talks only in terms of Victorian or Dionysiac annals. He seems not to have seriously considered the possibility that 84-year tables could have provided such annals – despite the fact that such tables were still in use on Iona (and possibly elsewhere in Ireland) at least until AD 716. For possible examples of misdated annals from 84-year tables, see O'Rahilly, 237-38, and Archibald A. Duncan, 'Bede, Iona, and the Picts', in R.H.C. Davis and J.-M. Wallace-Hadrill (ed), *The writing of history in the Middle Ages. Essays presented to Richard William Southern* (Oxford 1981) 1-42: 8 n. 1. 12 Bruno Krusch, 'Über eine Handschrift des Victurius', *Neues Archiv* 9 (1884) 269-81: 277. Cf. Theodor Mommsen (ed), *Victorii Aquitani cursus paschalis annorum DXXXII ad Hilarum archidiaconum ecclesiae Romanae a. CCCCL VII. MGH AA* 9 (Chron. Min. 1) (Berlin 1892; repr. 1961) 666-743: 729.

Chlovis, and was described by Krusch as 'the first beginnings of Frankish annal-writing'.[13]

The earliest paschal annal of this kind referring to an event in Ireland occurs not in an Irish manuscript as such but in Angers, Bibliothèque Municipale, MS. 477 (*saec.* IX, Brittany), containing Bede's works on times.[14] In the margin of Bede's (Dionysiac) paschal tables, beside the data for the year AD 549, is the following entry: *Pestilentia in aqua obiit Uuiniaus.* This refers to the death of Uinniaus/Finnianus, founder of the monastery at Clonard, whose obit occurs in Irish annals at this year.[15] That the entry derives from a contemporary document seems to me evident from a number of considerations. In the first place, though the date of Finnian's death might have been known in Brittany in the ninth century and entered retrospectively in the Angers table, the fact that his death was the result of 'pestilentia' would hardly have been known. Secondly, the archaic form of the name[16] supports the theory that the entry was copied from a contemporary notice. Furthermore, the Angers manuscript contains an extensive marginal commentary on Bede's works that derives in large part from an Irish computistical tract of *c.* AD 658, which I have shown elsewhere to have been compiled probably in the south-midlands area and hence not far from Clonard itself.[17] Thus the presence in Angers 477 of the Uuiniaus obit is not an isolated instance of Irish influence but combines with the evidence of the commentary to suggest that the whole collection may in fact have been copied from an Irish exemplar or have passed through Irish hands.[18] Whatever the history of its transmission, however, the independent occurrence of this obit in a continental computistical manuscript can only mean that the Irish annal of AD 549 is fully verified, and the probability that it too derives from an anno-

13 Ibid. For arguments in favour of even earlier paschal annals in Italy, see Jones, *Saints Lives*, 9-10. 14 I am most grateful to M. Gwenaël Leduc, who made available to me his complete photographic facsimile of this manuscript, from which the plate here is reproduced. 15 AU 549: 'Mortalitas magna in qua isti pausant: Finnio maccu (Tel)duib, Colaim nepos Craumthainn, Mac Tail Cille Cuilind, Sincheall mac Cenannáin abbas Cille Achaid Drumm(o) Foto₇ Columbae Insae Celtrae'. Doubtless the Angers annal should be read: 'Pestilentia, in qua obiit Uuiniaus'. 16 For discussion of the name see A.O. Anderson and M.O. Anderson (eds & transls), *Adomnan's Life of Columba* (Edinburgh 1961) 69; Rudolf Thurneysen, OIG (Dublin 1946) 175 §275. Considering the Britannic form of the name, it should perhaps be asked whether *Uuiniaus* might not in fact have been a Welshman or a Breton by origin [cf. the name Ninian, doubtless a misreading of Uiniaus]. It is noteworthy that the calendar in the MS., at 27 June, has 'Depositio sancti Samsonis in Pretannia', corrected to 'bre-' and then 'bri'. The original form, 'Pretannia', is very archaic. [On the name Uuiniaus/Finnian, see now David N. Dumville, 'St. Finnian of Movilla: Briton, Gael, ghost?', in L. Proudfoot (ed), *Down: history and society* (Dublin 1997) 71-84, and Pádraig Ó Riain, 'Finnio and Winniau: a return to the subject', in John Carey, John T. Koch & Pierre-Yves Lambert (eds), *Ildírech, ildánach. A Festschrift for Proinsias Mac Cana* (Aberystwyth 1999) 187-202.] 17 Dáibhí Ó Cróinín, 'A seventh-century Irish computus from the circle of Cummianus', PRIA 82 C 11 (1982) 405-30 [= 99-130 below]. 18 There are other annals in the margins of the Easter-tables, but none of them refers to Ireland.

tated Easter table is further strengthened.[19] Of course, the preservation of the Uuiniaus obit need not necessarily mean that continuous annals were being kept in Irish monasteries already in the sixth century. But, on the other hand, we must reckon at least with the possibility that certain other sixth-century entries may likewise derive from contemporary Easter tables and may therefore be fairly regarded as genuine records of sixth-century events.[20]

As one might expect, there is stronger evidence still to support the argument that certain seventh-century annals go back too, at least in part, to such paschal notices. Three selected examples will suffice to illustrate the point, because they comprise independent verification of the Irish annals in terms of content and of chronological precision. They are also interesting in their own right for the manner in which they illustrate the range of seventh-century Hiberno-Latin scholars.

In one of the oldest dateable Hiberno-Latin compositions, the synchronistic poem *Deus a quo facta fuit*,[21] the Ages of the World are given according to the arrangement found in the Eusebio-Hieronimian chronicle.[22] The closing verses of the poem provide three dating clauses for the time of writing; I give them here, based on Strecker's edition:

(15)	Sunt octo decem et sexcenti	a baptismo Domini	DCXVIII
	Anni usque ad Scottorum	mortem regis Domnali.	
(16)	A quo centum in futurum	est annorum spatium	C
	Finem usque quinquaginta	quino ad sex millium.	VI LXV
(17)	Ac retrorsum octingenti	ad prima principia	DCCC
	Quadraginta quinque anni	atque quinque milia.	VXLV

According to the first of these verses, the death of *Domnal rex Scottorum* occurred 618 years *a baptismo Domini*.[23] Now, this kind of calculation derives from the reckoning in the Prologue to Victorius' paschal tables, who derived it in turn from the chronicle of Euseblus-Jerome. Following that chronicle, Victorius set the date of the Passion at AM 5228 in the consulate of the Gemini

---

19 Of course, I mean an 84-year table, since that would have been the type in use in southern Ireland in AD 549. But the transfer of such an annal to a Dionysiac table would not have presented an insuperable problem. 20 Cf. Prof. Francis J. Byrne's statement: 'My own reading of the annals inclines me to the view that the entries began to be contemporary in the second half of the sixth century', 'Seventh-century documents', *Irish Ecclesiastical Record*, ser. 5, 108 (1967) 164-82. 21 Karl Strecker (ed), *Rhythmi computistici*, MGH Poet. lat. aevi carolini 4/2 (Berlin 1896; repr. 1964) 695-97: *Versus de annis a principio*. 22 It may be noted that the figures do not always coincide with those of Eusebius-Jerome. 23 AU 642: 'Mors Domnaill maic Aedho regis Hibernie in fine Ianuari'. Correction is therefore required of the statement in F.J. Byrne's *Irish kings and high-kings* (London 1973) 97, that 'Adomnán and Muirchú afford us the earliest unequivocal statements of the Uí Néill claims to high-kingship over all Ireland'. The present instance antedates Adomnán and Muirchú by at least a generation. Note the archaic spelling of Domnal (with single -*l* in final, unstressed position).

(= AD 28). Hence, to reduce a Victorian date in the Passion era to its AD equivalent, add 27: 618 + 27 = AD 645. But our Irish author set the date of Domnal's death in the 618th year from Christ's baptism, traditionally dated three years before his Passion. Thus the required date is AD 642. Sure enough, the Irish annals for this year record the death of Domnall mac Áedo, Uí Néill 'highking', who may indeed have been generally regarded as *rex Scottorum* by those in the northern half of Ireland at any rate.[24]

It is noteworthy that the author, in referring to the death of Domnall mac Áedo, employed a unique reckoning from the anno mundi dating of Christ's baptism, rather than the more traditional *annus passionis* one.[25] This was probably because he was composing three years after the event, and used the rather clever device of synchronizing the date of his *annus praesens* (AD 645) by the 'standard' reference to the millennium, and then synchronizing the year of Domnall's death with another significant date in mundane history. There can be no reasonable doubt that the composer of these verses, writing in AD 645 probably in the northern part of the country, provides contemporary but independent confirmation of the date AD 642 for the obit of Domnall mac Áedo. In this instance, admittedly, there would seem to be a superficial case for arguing a derivation from a continuation of the Eusebio-Hieronimian chronicle. However, the evidence to appear below is sufficient proof that the annal itself more likely derives from an Easter table.

The second example derives more explicitly from a marginal entry in Victorian paschal tables, though through the intermediary of another Hiberno-Latin composition, the Irish Augustine's tract *De mirabilibus sacrae scripturae*. To explain the miracle recorded in Joshua X 12-13, of the sun and moon standing still at the command of Ben Nun but without any resultant dislocation in their cyclical movements, the author illustrates his theory by giving in brief outline the cyclic recurrence from the Creation to the time of writing, in order to demonstrate that sun and moon are always in relative agreement at the end of every 532-year term:

> Ut enim hoc manifestis approbationibus pateat, cyclorum etiam ab initio conditi orbis recursus in se breuiter digeremus, quos semper post quingentos triginta duos annos sole ut in principio et luna per omnia conuenientibus nullis subuenientibus impedimentis in id unde coeperant

---

24 There are slight difficulties with the synchronisms in verses 16 and 17, due to the fact that the author appears to have used the mundane period of 5200, rather than Victorius' 5201 [§ 16: 6000-155 = 5845-5200 = AD 645; §17: 5845-5200 = AD 645]. The explanation of this discrepancy, which is too long to give here, will be found in Mac Carthy, *Codex Palatino-Vaticanus*, 366. That this pseudo-Victorian reckoning was not unique to this poet is clear from the fact that the same mundane period occurs also in the *De mirabilibus* discussed below. 25 MPL 35, 2149-2200. See William Reeves, 'On Augustin, an Irish writer of the seventh century', PRIA 7 (1861) 514-22; Mario Esposito, 'On the pseudo-Augustinian treatise "De mirabilibus sacrae scripturae"', PRIA 35 C 1 (1919) 189-207.

redire ostendemus. Quinto namque cyclo a mundi principio anno centesimo quarto decimo generate totius inundi diluuium sub Noe uenit, qui
post diluuium quadringentesimo decimo octauo defecit: et inde alius
incipiens, id est sextus, in octauo aetatis Abrahae anno finitur. Et nono
eius anno septimus incipiens, tricesimo quinto anno egressionis filiorum
Israhel de Aegypto quinquennio ante mortem Moysi concluditur. Post
quem octauus, in quo etiam istud signum in sole et luna factum, tricesimo sexto anno egressionis Israhel de Aegypto incipiens in tricesimum
primum annum Asa regis Iuda incedit: cuius tricesimo secundo anno
nonus exordium capiens in quo etiam aliud signum in sole, Ezechiae regis
tempore, de quo paulisper dicemus, factum legitur, centesimo octauuo
anno post templi restaurationem quae sub Dario facta est, sui cursus
spatium consumauit: donec decimus inde oriens nonagesimo secundo
anno post passionem Saluatoris, Alia et Sparsa [= Auiola et Pansa]
consulibus peractis cursibus consumatur. Post quem undecimus a
consulatu Paterni et Torquati ad nostra usque tempora decurrens,
extremo anno Hiberniensium moriente Manchiano inter ceteros sapientes peragitur. Et duodecimus nunc tertium annum agens ad futurorum
scientiam se praestans, a nobis qualem finem sit habiturus ignoratur.[26]

In the AM period the initial and final cyclic years are identified, from internal
evidence, by reference to the Eusebian chronicle. Hence the last year of cycle
one, the first of cycle five, and the first and last of cycles two, three, and four
are not specified by reference to any particular events. In the AD period the
tenth cycle ended, so our author says, in the ninety-second year after the
Passion, in the consulship of Aviola and Pansa (AD 119). The eleventh began in
the following year, in the consulship of Paternus and Torquatus (AD 120). This
much was derived by the author from the consular list appended to Victorius'
tables. The final year of the eleventh cycle ($532 \times 11 = 5852$ [$-5200 =$ AD 652])[27]
is identified by the death of Manchianus of Min Droichit and other Irish
scholars. In the third year of the twelfth cycle, AD 655, the tract itself was written. That the Irish Augustine was using Victorian tables is evident from the
fact that he was familiar with the principle of the 532-year cycle; for only
Victorius' tables, of all those current in the seventh century, covered that
period of time. Besides, the mention of consular years could only have derived
from Victorian tables, which were followed even in their errors. Equally clear
is the fact that in the margin of those tables, beside the data for the year AD 652,

---

26 Book II 4 = MPL 35, 2175-6. It is noteworthy that this very passage was quoted *in extenso* by
the eighth-century compiler of the Munich Computus, Munich, Bayerische Staatsbibliothek,
Clm 14456 (*saec.* IX, Regensburg), which contains much unique information concerning the Irish
computus.   27 Note the use of the pseudo-Victorian mundane period, referred to above, p. 81 n.
24.

there must have been noted the death of Manchianus and the other Irish scholars. The Irish annals duly record the death of Manchianus in that year.[28]

Our third example comes from a computistical collection, but this time without any intermediating text. In a number of manuscripts whose combined evidence preserves the bulk of the material used by Bede in the composition of his tracts On Time, and hence termed 'Bede's computus' by Professor Charles W. Jones, who discovered the connection,[29] there is found the usual mixture of technical tracts, letters, tables and formulae common to all such computistical collections. One such passage in the text comprises short synchronistic notes culled mainly from the Prologue to Victorius' tables. I give the text here from the best manuscript (Oxford, Bodleian Library, MS. Bodley 309 (*saec.* XI, Vendôme)) and in the apparatus the variants from three others:[30]

> *Omnibus annis temporibus diebus ac luna maxime, que iuxta Hebraeos menses facit, rite discussis, a mundi principio usque in diem, quo filii Israhel paschale mysterium initiauere anni sunt III DCLXXXVIIII, praecedente primo mense VIII Kl. Aprilis, luna XIIII, VI feria. Passum autem dominum nostrum Ihesum Christum peractis VCCXX & VIII annis ab exortu mundi, eadem cronicorum relatione monstratur, VIII Kl. Aprilis primo mense, luna XIIII, VI feria.*
>
> Inter primum pascha in Aegypto et passionem domini anni sunt I DXXXVIIII. R,. Ex domini uero passione usque in pascha quod secutum est Suibini filii Commanni anni sunt DCXXXI. A pascha autem supradicto usque ad tempus praefinitum consummationis mundi, id est sex milibus consummatis, anni sunt CXLI.

1. Victorius, *Prologus in cyclo paschali* (Krusch, *Studien* 2, 24) facis (underlined) S facT 2. usque *eras.* P; a principibus *corr.*> a principio P 3. annui G 4 luna XVII TG 5. annis et G 6 reuelatione TP 9. R, *in marg.* S, *in text* TGP; 8. domino G; sequu/um ÷ sui nri filii communi T sui nri R filii commamni G sui. Nri. R., *with* filii … dcxxxi. *om.* (*gap left*) P 12 XCLI GP

The mathematics of the text are straightforward enough: from the Passion to the year of writing is 631 (DCXXXI) years. To reduce a Victorian *anno passionis* date to its AD equivalent, add 27: 631 + 27 = AD 658. The second clause in the dating formula provides confirmation of this: from the time of writing to the end of the world – traditionally set at AM 6000 (as in the poem *Deus a quo facta*

---

28 See Esposito, 'The pseudo-Augustinian treatise *De mirabilibus*', 198 and 200. 29 See esp. 'The "lost" Sirmond manuscript of Bede's "computus"', *English Historical Review* 52 (1937) 204-19 [= *Bede, the schools and the computus*, chapter X]; idem (ed), *Bedae opera de temporibus*. Medieval Academy of America Publications 41 (Cambridge, Mass 1943). 30 Tours, Bibliothèque Municipale, MS. 334 (AD 819, Tours) = T; Geneva, Bibliothèque de l'Université, MS. 50 (*c.* AD 804, Massai) = G; Paris, Bibliothèque Nationale, MS. lat. 16361 (*saec.* XII) = P.

fuit) – is 141 (CXLI) years. 6000-141 = 5859 AM. To reduce this Victorian *anno mundi* reckoning to AD, subtract 5201: 5859-5201 = AD 658. Both formulae, therefore, give the date of writing as AD 658. But the date is further specified by the addition of a most important detail: the author counted from the Passion *usque ad pascha quod secutum est Suibinī filii Commāni*, 'the Easter of Suibine mac Commáin which has just ensued'. That is to say, the author was referring to a Victorian Easter table in the margin of which, beside the data for the current year, was noted the death of one Suibine mac Commáin. And the annal is preserved independently in the Annals of Inisfallen, s.a. AD 658: *Kl. Dub Tíre ua Maíl Ochtraig ⁊ Conaing mac Muricáin ⁊ Suibne mac Commáin.*[31] Most importantly of all, however, the Irish compiler of the computus calculated from the pasch of Suibine mac Commáin, that is the Easter of the year in which he died. Easter fell on 25 March in AD 658, so the computist must have been writing after that date. He was undoubtedly resident in southern Ireland.

It should be abundantly clear, therefore, from these few examples alone that the practice of entering notes in the margins of Easter tables was already fairly common in Ireland by the mid seventh century. That some at least of our sixth-century annals derive from earlier tables seems quite likely also, for the occurrence of random, inconsequential entries in the early stratum of the annals cannot reasonably be explained as the invention of retrospective 'editors'.[32] Nevertheless, we must make a distinction between the earliest contemporary entries (which may be isolated and without any sequential relationship to one another) and the period in which such annals began to be compiled and collated for the first time. It seems clear that the earliest contemporary entries were made in the sixth century, though how many of the details from that century may be relied upon it is very difficult to say. But the period of compilation undoubtedly came considerably later. Mac Neill maintained that the exemplar of the Annals of Ulster and the Annals of Tigernach was compiled *c*. AD 712.[33] O'Rahilly argued for a date *c*. AD 740, which has found favour with most subsequent writers.[34] All writers seem to agree that the

---

31 Seán Mac Airt (ed), *The Annals of Inisfallen (MS. Rawlinson B. 503)* (Dublin 1951) 94. For a full discussion of the annal, see below, 177-80.   32 My viewpoint is clearly irreconcileable with the statement of Prof. John V. Kelleher, 'Early Irish history and pseudo-history', *Studia Hibernica* 3 (1963) 113-27: 122: 'I believe it can be shown that everything [*sic*] in the annals up to about 590 and a large number of entries from thence to 735 (the entry on Bede's death) were either freshly composed or wholly revised not earlier than the latter half of the ninth century'. See also the explicit endorsement of this view by Prof. D.A. Binchy, 'Patrick and his biographers, ancient and modern', *Studia Hibernica* 2 (1962) 7-173: 73-74. Neither writer has published a proof of these assertions. Unfortunately, they have had their effect even on so careful a writer as Kathleen Hughes, *Early christian Ireland*, 124: 'the structure of the annals is undoubtedly provided by the activities of the Uí Néill'.   33 'Annals of Tigernach', 80-89.   34 See Gearóid Mac Niocaill, *The medieval Irish annals*, 19-20. The only exception that I know of is Binchy, who wrote in 'Patrick and his biographers' 73: 'Whether O'Rahilly's theory of an "Ulster Chronicle", compiled probably in Bangor about 740, really merits the almost universal agreement it has found ... has always seemed more than doubtful to me.'

process of compilation began in northern Ireland; most point to Iona as the probable place of origin for the earliest such compilation.

There is one final item of evidence which might support this theory, though it would necessitate a compilation date closer to *c.* AD 750.

In the (lost) Chartres manuscript of the *Historia Brittonum*[35] occurs an addition to the text that is of direct relevance to our enquiry. I give the text here first as it stands in Duchesne's transcript, and follow with an attempted restoration of it:

> Et in tempore Guorthigirni regis Britanie Saxones peruenerunt in Britanniam, K in anno incarnacionis Christi, sicut Libine abasiae inripum ciuitate inuenit vel reperit, ab incarnacione Domini anni D. usque a kl. ian. in XII luna ut aiunt alii .intis. CCC. annis a quo tenuerunt Saxones Britanniam usque ad annum supradictum.

Restored text:

> Et in tempore Guorthigirni regis Britanniae Saxones peruenerunt in Britanniam, id est in anno incarnationis Christi .CCCCLIII., sicut Slébíne abbas Iae in Ripum ciuitate inuenit uel reperit. Ab anno incarnatione Domini .CCCCLIII, quo Kl. Ian. in .XVI. luna fuerunt, et in quo tenuerunt Saxones Britanniam, ut aiunt alii, sunt .CCC. anni usque ad annum supradictum, quo Kl. Ian. in .XII. luna fuerunt.

Paul Grosjean, not unfairly, described the quality of the Chartres text as 'détestable'. That the scribe should have so bungled this precious record of the *aduentus Saxonum* is a matter for regret not only among historians of Anglo-Saxon England. Nevertheless, what remains of the text is sufficient for our immediate purposes.

Slébíne of Iona was abbot during the years AD 753-66; he died in AD 767.[36] According to the Chartres text he visited the Northumbrian monastery of Ripon, apparently while still abbot of Iona, and while there he obtained the date of the Anglo-Saxon arrival in England. Ripon had been founded as a daughter-house of Lindisfarne by king Alchfrith, but as a result of the tensions between the Irish and English in the years around AD 664 it had been abandoned by the Irish and given instead to Wilfrid, later bishop of York.[37] By the time of Slébíne's abbacy, however, these differences were a thing of the past. We do not know the precise reason for Slébíne's visit, but that it took place in

35 The manuscript was destroyed in the war. An edited transcript was published by Louis Duchesne as 'Nennius Retractatus', *Revue Celtique* 15 (1884) 174-97. See the discussion of this passage by Paul Grosjean, 'Pour la date de fondation d'Iona et celle de la mort de S. Colum Cille', Notes d'hagiographie celtique 49, *Analecta Bollandiana* 78 (1960) 381-90, and Harrison, *Framework*, 99-100. 36 A.O. and M.O. Anderson, *Adomnan*, 100. 37 Bede, HE III 25, summarized by Harrison, *Framework*, 99 n. 1.

his first year of office is suggested by the chronological detail of the text, for epact 12 on 1 Jan. (Kl. Ian. in .XII. luna) occurred only in that first year. But whether or not the figures in the text are reliable (and my own restoration of it is only very tentative), the fact of the two years concerned, that of the *aduentus Saxonum* and that of Slébíne's visit to Ripon, being specified by means of the epacts can only mean that the author of the original text was using the Irish method of dating, for the ferial and lunar notation is that of the Irish annals.[38] Moreover, the Chartres note suggests an active interest on Slébíne's part in matters chronological and in the salient events of history, and it was clearly the practice to denote those events by reference to the ferial and lunar incidence derived from Easter tables. For someone like him, annals would automatically have implied the use of such tables.

If previous scholars are right in believing that the first methodical compilation of Irish annals was undertaken on Iona sometime around the mid-eighth century, then it seems reasonable to suggest the active involvement of abbot Slébíne in that undertaking. He may have been continuing a process which had begun on the island even before his own succession to the abbacy, or he may have been himself the innovator behind the scheme. That the compilation involved the utilisation of southern Irish as well as northern Irish annals and Easter tables is abundantly clear from the evidence here presented. Such a process of extrapolation and compilation from different sets of Easter tables would readily explain the occurrence in the annals of misdated entries, for the transfer of entries from one table to another, or from tables to a continuous text, almost inevitably invited mistranscription. But that should not blind us to the fact that many of our earliest annals from the sixth and seventh centuries have strong claims to being accepted as genuine records of the events they profess to relate.[39]

38 As Harrison rightly noted, *Framework*, 99.   39 I am grateful to Prof. David Dumville, Cambridge, for comments and criticisms regarding *the Historia Brittonum* text cited on p. 85.

8

'New heresy for old': Pelagianism in Ireland and the papal letter of 640[*]

Scholars have often remarked on the surprising frequency with which medieval Irish writers referred to the heresiarch Pelagius and the extent to which they borrowed from his works.[1] While there has been nothing like unanimity on the question of why the Irish showed such a liking for him,[2] all are agreed that they were not true Pelagians, in the sense that the famous theological arguments for which Pelagius was eventually condemned never found favor with Irish writers.[3] There is one document, however, – and that an important one – which explicitly accuses the Irish of Pelagianism: the letter of AD 640 to the northern Irish clergy front the pope-elect John IV and three others of the Roman curia, as reported by Bede.[4] The letter has proved a mystery to modern writers, and one of the most recent has gone so far as to say that 'Bede's intriguing and puzzling reference must remain just that'.[5]

The problem for many has been on the one hand to reconcile the papal accusation of Pelagianism with the overwhelming evidence from native Irish sources that seems to exonerate them of any such charge, and on the other hand to explain why the Roman curia combined the themes of Pelagianism and

---

[*] First published in *Speculum* 60 (1985) 505-16.   1 For general discussion, see Louis Gougaud, *Christianity in Celtic Lands* (London 1932) 292-93; James F. Kenney, *Sources for the early history of Ireland*, 1: Ecclesiastical (New York 1929; repr. Dublin 1993) 661-63; Kathleen Hughes, *The Church in early Irish society* (London 1966) 20-21. Fundamental studies of the firsthand material are by Heinrich Zimmer, *Pelagius in Irland* (Berlin 1901), and Alexander Souter, *Pelagius. Expositions on the Thirteen Epistles of St. Paul* 1, Texts and Studies 9/1 (Cambridge 1922). 2 Reasons range from Pelagius' alleged Irish origins to the fact that commentaries on the Pauline epistles were few and Pelagius' was of acknowledged quality.   3 See the comment of one of the Irish scribes who penned the famous Pauline codex, Würzburg, Universitätsbibliothek, MS. M.p.th. f. 12, fol. 3ʳ: 'frecre inso [this is an answer] mentibus hereticorum', to Pelagius' comment on Romans 5.15; printed in Whitley Stokes and John Strachan (eds & transls), *Thesaurus Palaeohibernicus* (2 vols Cambridge 1901, 1903; repr. Dublin 1975) 1, 509. The standard work on Pelagius and his doctrine is still Georges de Plinval, *Pélage, ses écrits, sa vie et sa réforme, Étude d'histoire littéraire et religieuse* (Lausanne 1943). 4 *Historia ecclesiastica* III 19 (hereafter cited as HE), ed. Charles Plummer, *Baedae opera historica.* (2 vols, Oxford 1896; repr. London 1969) 1, 122-24; ed. and trans. Bertram Colgrave and R.A.B. Mynors, *Bede's Ecclesiastical History of the English People.* Oxford Medieval Texts (Oxford 1979) 198-202. There is a separate edition of the papal letter by Maurice P. Sheehy, (ed), *Pontificia Hibernica: Medieval papal chancery documents concerning Ireland, 640-1261* (2 vols, Dublin 1962-63) 1, 3-4. 5 Joseph F. Kelly, 'Pelagius, Pelagianism and the early christian Irish', *Mediaevalia* 4 (1978) 99-124.

the Easter question. But in wishing to separate these two themes, and especially in emphasizing the Pelagian one at the expense of the Easter question,
modern scholars have, I think, fallen victim to one of the occupational hazards
of their trade: applying to medieval documents the prejudices of their own age.
Because they have little taste for what they see as the bizarre complexities of
computus and the Easter controversy (and little inclination to acquire such a
taste),[6] they have tended to overlook the essentially doctrinal nature of that
controversy; and since Pelagius and his doctrines seem to offer a much more
substantial theme for discussion, it is this aspect of the papal letter that tends
to receive most attention.[7] But it is precisely because of this modern separation
of themes that the letter has hitherto resisted satisfactory explanation. I believe
that a different approach, beginning with the technical chronological aspects of
it that are usually ignored, can bring us to a full realization of what the Roman
church thought of the Irish at the time, and why. To begin with, therefore, it
is necessary to sketch a brief background to the letter and the circumstances in
which it is found.

The text of the papal letter has been transmitted in the *Ecclesiastical History*
of Bede,[8] whose interest in chronological matters needs no demonstration, and
whose interest in Pelagianism has also been remarked.[9] He cites selected
passages from the letter in the prelude to a discussion about the Easter question in the British and Irish churches prior to the synod of Whitby (AD 664).
Bede tells how the Irish missionaries at Lindisfarne, led by the bishops Aidan,
Fínán, and Colmán, had observed Easter in accordance with the rules of the
Irish 84-year cycle which they had inherited from 'their first father
Columba'.[10] The southern Irish, on the other hand, 'had long since learned
how to celebrate Easter in the orthodox manner at the exhortation of the papal
see' – a reference, apparently, to a letter of Honorius I (*c*.629?) which is referred
to at another point by Bede[11] and which is generally regarded as the document
that sparked off the chain of events described in Cummian's letter
(*c*.632/33).[12]

6 Plummer was a noted exception; his excursus on the Paschal controversy in *Baedae opera*, 2,
348-55, was an earnest attempt to come to grips with the problem and is still of value. But even
Plummer opens his discussion with the heading 'Tediousness of the Paschal Controversy'. [See
now also the excellent discussion in Thomas Charles-Edwards, *Early Christian Ireland*
(Cambridge 2000) chap. 9.]   7 As, for example, in Kelly, 'Pelagius', 104-5. Modern chronologists
have given only cursory attention to the letter and have never treated its twin themes as one.
8 Bede reproduces excerpts from the letter, not the whole text.   9 'His warnings against
Pelagianism and his denunciation of Pelagius . . . are so numerous and fierce that one must
suppose that Pelagianism was a living question to him'; M.L.W. Laistner, *Thought and letters in
Western Europe, AD 500-900* (Ithaca, N.Y. 1960) 160.   10 'Tum Colmanus: "Pascha", inquit,
"hoc, quod agere soleo, a maioribus meis accepi, qui me hinc episcopum miserunt, quod omnes
patres nostri, uiri Dei electi, eodem modo celebrasse noscuntur"'; HE III 25, ed. Plummer 1, 184;
Colgrave & Mynors, 298.   11 HE II 19, immediately preceding his introduction of the Roman
letter.   12 See Dáibhí Ó Cróinín, 'A seventh-century Irish computus from the circle of
Cummianus', *Proceedings of Royal Irish Academy* [PRIA] 82 C 11 (1982) 405-30; Wesley M.

It is at this point in the story that Bede introduces the Roman letter of AD 640. In it John and his curial colleagues state that a letter had arrived in Rome from Ireland sometime previously, addressed to Pope Severinus. Before it could be discussed, however, Severinus died, and in the interim between his death and the installation of his successor the Roman see was being administered by Iohannes *primicerius*, together with Iohannes *archipresbyter* and Iohannes *consiliarius*. These had opened the Irish letter and found the contents so disturbing that they felt they should respond immediately.[13] They declared sternly that they had learned how some among the Irish had been attempting to revive a new heresy from an old *(nouam ex ueteri heresim renouare conantes)* by proposing to observe Easter on the fourteenth day of the moon with the Jews.[14] They then urged conformity among the Irish in the matter of Easter observance, *euidenter astruens*, in Bede's paraphrase, *quia dominicum paschae diem a XVa luna usque ad XXIam, quod in Nicena synodo probatum est, oportet inquiri*. The assumption by scholars has invariably been that the Irish concerned (northern Irish, to judge by the names attached to the papal response)[15] still observed Easter in accordance with the principles of the 84-year cycle.[16] A recently discovered sentence from the letter, ascribed to *Iohannes consilarius* but not given by Bede,[17] states that *dies XIIII lunae ad umbras pertinebat*. This has been interpreted as confirming the usual inference, for Easter observance on *luna XIIII* (that is, at the full moon) was a distinctive feature of the Irish cycle.[18] But this is not necessarily the only possible interpretation of the papal letter, nor

Stevens, 'Scientific instruction in early insular schools', in Michael W. Herren (ed), *Insular Latin studies: Papers on Latin texts and manuscripts in the British Isles 550-1066*. Papers in Mediaeval Studies 1 (Toronto 1981) 83-111, esp. 83-96.   **13** 'Scripta, quae perlatores ad sanctae memoriae Seuerinum papam adduxerant, eo de hac luce migrante, reciproca responsa ad ea, quae postulatae fuerant, siluerunt. Quibus reseratis, ne diu tardae quaestionis caligo indiscussa remaneret'; Plummer 1, 123; Colgrave & Mynors, 200.   **14** Note that the accusation of quartodecimanism comes first; the Pelagian one follows from that.   Plummer remarked (2, 114), that 'the name "quartodeciman" was always a handy stick with which to beat the Celtic dog'. The phrase *noua ex ueteri heresis* was a favorite barb of Jerome's against Pelagius; see Siegfried Reiter (ed), *S. Hieronymi presbyteri in Hieremiam prophetam*, CCSL 74 (Turnhout 1960) 15 (1.17.3), 29 (1.46.2), 34 (1.56), 61 (2.5.2), 238 (5.5.3), 294 (6.4.4); references from Robert F. Evans, *Pelagius: inquiries and reappraisals* (London 1968) 127 n. 17; 133 n. 1.   **15** The list of addressees is headed by Bishop Tomianus of Armagh, who may have held a position of honorary precedence over the others named. But for arguments to the contrary (not very convincing, in my view) see Richard Sharpe, 'St Patrick and the See of Armagh', *Cambridge Medieval Celtic Studies* 4 (1982) 33-59.   **16** So Bartholomew Mac Carthy (ed & transl), *Annala Uladh, the Annals of Ulster* 4 (Dublin 1901) cxlviii; Charles W. Jones, *Bedae opera de temporibus* (Cambridge, Mass. 1943) 98-99: '[the papal letter] indicates that the northern Irish had written to Pope Severinus explaining why they had not changed their Paschal custom'. In following these authorities I said the same myself in my paper, Mo Sinu maccu Min and the computus at Bangor', *Peritia* 1 (1982) 281-95: 294 [= here, 35-47: 46].   **17** See Ó Cróinín, 'A seventh-century Irish computus', 409.   **18** Kenneth Harrison, *The framework of Anglo-Saxon history to AD 900* (Cambridge 1976) 60: 'there follow [in the letter] a few words directed against *luna xiv*, a principle on which the Celtic-84 rested'; by implication again in his paper, 'A letter from Rome to the Irish clergy, AD 640', *Peritia* 3 (1984) 222-29.

even the most satisfactory one, in my view. It leaves some questions unan-
swered and some unasked.

One question about the Roman letter that has hitherto been unasked is: why
was it written in 640? Of course the question should really be asked of the Irish
letter that prompted the reply from Rome. Scholars have seen no significance
in the fact that the northern Irish churches (after a synod, similar in kind and
purpose to that which Cummian describes for the south some years previously?)[19] addressed their queries to Rome in that year.[20] But it is precisely the
chronological sequence of events that explains the timing and purpose of the
Irish letter and the papal reply; the dates of the two letters are not purely
circumstantial but depend entirely on the nature of those Irish queries. What,
then, were the Irish saying that prompted such a response from Rome? And
why did they write when they did? The answer, I believe, has nothing to do
with the alleged use of the Irish 84-year cycle but concerns another Easter table
entirely, the table of Victorius of Aquitaine.[21]

Arising out of the problems that had beset the Western church up to the
mid-fifth century in the matter of calculating the date of Easter, Victorius had
been asked by the Roman archdeacon Hilarius, on papal commission, to
prepare a new set of tables which would secure uniformity of observance. In
457 the tables were published, and since by that time Hilarius had succeeded
Leo as pope, the new tables were almost assured of rapid approval at Rome.[22]
They were prescribed as mandatory for all Gallican churches at the synod of
Orléans in 541.[23] But Victorius' tables, far from resolving the problem, only
complicated matters still further, for his application of conflicting rules led to
miscalculations of the Easter dates.

Victorius' errors – which were ridiculed by Columbanus in his letter to Pope
Gregory I[24] – arose from three causes.

(1) The Nicene council (AD 325) had decreed that the lunar month of Easter
(the Hebrew month Nisan) must begin so that its fourteenth day fell on or after
21 March, the date of the vernal equinox by Alexandrian reckoning. Victorius,
disregarding this rule, began his lunar month on 5 March or thereafter,

---

19 Plummer's suggestion, 2, 114.   20 The Irish letter is datable from the reference in the papal
response to the fact that the questions were sent during the pontificate of Severinus, who died in
August 640.   21 Theodor Mommsen (ed), *Victorii Aquitani cursus Paschalis annorum DXXXII*,
MGH AA 9 (Berlin 1892) 666-743; rev. ed. by Bruno Krusch, 'Studien zur christlich-mittelalterlichen Chronologie [2]: Die Entstehung unserer heutigen Zeitrechnung', *Abhandlungen der
Preußischen Akademie der Wissenschaften*, phil.-hist. Kl., 8 (1937) 4-52.   22 For this and what
follows I have drawn heavily on Charles W. Jones, 'The Victorian and Dionysiac Paschal tables in
the West', *Speculum* 9 (1934) 408-21.   23 Harrison, *Framework*, 58, was the first to suggest that
the period of eighty-four years that elapsed between publication of Victorius' tables in 457 and
their official sanction in 541 was in all likelihood due to their having been compared for a full cycle
with the older eighty-four-year tables.   24 G.S.M. Walker (ed & trans), *Sancti Columbani opera*.
Scriptores Latini Hiberniae 2 (Dublin 1957; repr. 1972) 2-12. For background to Columbanus'
views, see Ó Cróinín, 'Mo Sinu maccu Min', passim [above 35ff].

whereas the Alexandrians, to prevent the full moon (*luna XIIII*) from occurring before the decreed date of the equinox, began their month of Nisan on 8 March or thereafter. Victorius took over his rule from the old Roman method of computation, from which he adopted another anachronistic criterion: that the Easter moon must have numbers 16-22 (*luna XVI-XXII*), whereas the Alexandrians, whose methods he professed to be following, computed the Easter moons by numbers 15-21. Knowing that his lunar limits were not Alexandrian, and on the basis of his own cycle, Victorius then computed alternative 'Alexandrian' dates for Easter, using moons 15-21. Where discrepancies arose, he placed the two results side by side in his tables, ascribing the one to 'Latini' and the other to 'Greci'; errors arising from this occurred in the years 499, 531, 536, 550, and 570.[25]

(2) The second reason for Victorius' confusion was his calculation of the *saltus* or 'moon's leap'. In the lunisolar reckonings of the computists, whose principal purpose was to make the new moons approximate as closely as possible the beginnings of the solar months, the lunar portion of the cycle extended over nineteen years. But the moon does not return to the same position it held in relation to the sun in nineteen years exactly but in nineteen years less one day. To overcome this difficulty the Alexandrian computists artificially increased the moon's age by one day at the end of their 19-year cycle, so that the moon's age (epact) at the beginning of the new cycle was the same as at the beginning of the previous one.[26] This 'skip' in the moon's age was known as the *saltus lunae*. Victorius, for reasons which have never been adequately explained, inserted this *saltus* in what would be the sixth year of the Alexandrian cycle, so that in his tables the age of the moon would be a day in advance of the true Alexandrian reckoning through all but the first six years of the cycle. Errors arising out of this occurred in the years 482, 522, 526, 546, 550, 577, 594, 597, 617, 621, 641, and 645.

(3) The third difference between Victorius' and the Alexandrian reckoning would occur in years 1-6 of the cycle, where his lunar limits 16-22 conflicted with the 'orthodox' limits of 15-21; errors occurred for this reason in the years 475, 476, 495, 516, 590.

Given the manifest confusion that must have arisen wherever Victorius' tables were used, it is hardly surprising that Columbanus should have dismissed them as 'more worthy of ridicule and condemnation that of authority'.[27] But the new tables had begun to spread in Gaul from an early date both because of the superficial advantages they seemed to offer in providing Easters

---

25 Jones, 'Victorian and Dionysiac tables', 411.   26 See Pseudo-Bede, MPL 90, 724: 'In fine xix. anni habebis epactas xviii. Adde xi. super xviii., fiunt xxix. Adde saltum lunae, fiunt xxx. Hi[n]c apparet, quod non addit, sed salit in retro, unum diem'.   27 'Magis risu uel uenia dignum quam auctoritate'; Ep. I, ed. Walker, 6. The error of Victorius' ways was apparently exposed by Bishop Victor of Capua in 550. Victor's work is unfortunately lost, but one of his criticisms was repeated by Bede in his *De temporum ratione* LV, ed. Jones, 272.

for 532 years and also, doubtless, because they appeared to enjoy papal
approval, for they were prefaced in the manuscripts by the letter of
Archdeacon (later Pope) Hilarius commissioning Victorius to draw up his
dates. 'Even so', as Charles W. Jones rightly remarked, 'churches would be slow
to adopt a new set of tables where any possibility of using an old set
remained'.[28] Hence the persistence in Ireland and elsewhere of 'uncanonical'
observances, and the resulting need for papal and episcopal exhortations to
conformity.[29] It is almost certain that the Victorian tables were received in
southern Ireland as a result of the events about which Cummian wrote,[30] and
there is other evidence that proves familiarity with and use of them in that part
of the country by the mid-seventh century.[31] I now believe that Victorius was
also being used at the same time by the northern Irish churches; the evidence
is provided by this letter of 640.

It so happens that the year 641 was one of the problem years in Victorius'
tables, a year with double Easter dates.[32] A glance at the data he gives for that
year will illustrate the nature of the problem:

Pascha Kal. Apr., lun. XV Latini VI Id. Apr., lun. XXII.[33]

Here Victorius gives the Greek date of Easter as 1 April (Kal. Apr.), *luna XV*.
This is not, however, the true Alexandrian date, for Victorius has committed an
error (number 2 above) in advancing the moon's age by one day: 1 April 641
was, in fact, *luna XIIII*, not *XV*. But by the peculiar combination of calculations
that he made, when Victorius computed the Latin Easters in these years he
actually computed the correct Greek dates, whereas the so-called Greek dates
that he gave according to his own rules were purely hypothetical and celebrated
nowhere in Christendom.[34] Charles W. Jones has suggested that Rome tried to

---

28 'Victorian and Dionysiac tables', 412. Witness the good example offered by the gradual
reception of Victorius' tables, for which see n. 23.   29 Bede reports, HE II 4, that the English
bishops Laurentius, Iustus, and Mellitus wrote to the Irish in AD 608 urging, among other things,
conformity on the Easter question.   30 This is the conclusion reached by Mac Carthy, *Annals of
Ulster* 4, cxlv, and by Jones, 'Victorian and Dionysiac tables', 417. Stevens, 'Scientific instruction',
84, is 'not at all certain', while Harrison, *Framework*, 58-60, is noncommital. Krusch confused the
delegation mentioned by Cummian with the one to which the papal letter was a response; see his
'Die Einführüng des griechischen Pascalritus im Abendlande', *Neues Archiv der Gesellschaft für
ältere deutsche Geschichtskunde* 9 (1884) 99-169: 149-50.   31 See Ó Cróinín, 'The Irish
provenance of Bede's computus', *Peritia* 2 (1983) 229-47: 238-40. [below, 173-90.]   32 In saying
that the Victorian and Dionysiac tables gave the identical day for Easter from 595 to 644, with
Victorius then offering double dates first in 645, Harrison (*Framework*, 60) was following D. J.
O'Connell, 'Easter cycles in the early Irish Church', *Jnl Royal Soc. Antiquaries of Ireland* 66
(1936) 67-106: 103. Both scholars, however, seem to have overlooked Jones' statement and the
more detailed study by Eduard Schwarz, 'Christliche und jüdische Ostertafeln', *Abhandlungen der
königlichen Gesellschaft der Wissenschaften zu Göttingen*, phil.-hist. Kl., N.F. 8/6 (1905) 76.
33 Mommsen, 692-93; Krusch, 31.   34 Jones, 'Victorian and Dionysiac tables', 413. This
crucial discovery of Jones has been completely overlooked by all subsequent writers.

circumvent this kind of problem by sending circular letters to the more important metropolitan churches in the West announcing in advance the correct date of Easter.[35] But though we know that a pontifical letter was issued every year, we know also that it did not always reach every province.[36] Jones surmised that 'probably it was merely published in Rome, and those provinces that had representatives in Rome learned of the correct date'.[37] But these letters, even if they were sent, would have recommended the dates marked 'Latini' in Victorius' tables, for only these were the correct Greek dates! In a church like the Irish, however, where there was no metropolitan authority to spread the word, uniformity of usage must have been that much harder to achieve; and if the papal letters never arrived at all, the possibility of error would have been doubled: with urgings to orthodoxy apparently arriving from several quarters,[38] the Irish must have inclined to use the dates marked 'Greci' in the tables.[39]

If the northern Irish were in fact using Victorius in 640 (doubtless in parallel with the older 84-year tables), then they would have realized that the next year in the new tables was going to cause problems. They may then have written to Rome (after discussion in synod?) announcing that they planned to celebrate Easter on 1 April 641 (marked 'Greci' in the tables) and sought confirmation of the date from the curia. The papal letter clearly states that the Irish questions had arrived during the pontificate of Severinus († 2 August 640); how soon after that they were replied to is difficult to say. With Easter occurring in 641 on 8 April (by Dionysiac reckoning), Lent would have begun on 21 February; Victorius' alternative date, 1 April, would have begun Lent a week earlier, 14 February. Either way, there was not much time for correction – four or five months at the most. Hence the obvious note of urgency in the papal response. When the Irish letter was received by the apostolic administrators they referred to their own (Dionysiac?) tables and would have seen that 1 April 641 was in fact *luna XIIII*, not *XV*. Hence the charge that the Irish were quartodecimans, celebrating Easter on *luna XIIII* with the Jews. Did they not know that *dies XIIII lunae ad umbras pertinebat*? The important point, therefore, is that the Irish would have given the calendar date (1 April); from their point

---

35 It is clear also from Ambrose's Ep. XXIII that he was regularly consulted by other Italian bishops in the matter of the Easter date. See MPL 16, 1026-35. It is not necessary to enter here into the question of that letter's authenticity.   36 Gregory of Tours, *Historia Francorum* V 17, records a *dubietas paschae* in Spain for 577, where an Easter was celebrated that was neither Latin nor Greek; and again, X 23, for 590, when he himself observed the Latin Easter while many about him celebrated on the Greek date; Wilhelm Arndt and Bruno Krusch (eds), *Gregorii episcopi Turonensis historia Francorum*, MGH SRM (3 vols, Berlin 1884) 1, 207 and 435 respectively.   37 'Victorian and Dionysiac tables', 412.   38 That is, from Canterbury as well as from Rome.   39 E.g., Jones, 'Victorian and Dionysiac tables', 412-13, wrote that 'we can well imagine that the ardent Romanists who had adopted the Victorian tables in preference to their native reckoning chose the Easter marked "Latini"', but the tenor of his whole argument suggests to me that they chose rather the Greek. Had they chosen the Latin date there would have been no problem, as Jones himself demonstrated.

of view the lunar limit did not present a problem, for they thought they were observing *luna* XV.

One further piece of information, hitherto overlooked by most writers[40] supports this suggested interpretation of events. Letter 22 in the collected correspondence of Bishop Braulio of Saragossa, dated 640,[41] touches precisely on the question about the problematic Easter date of 641.[42] The letter is a reply to a request from an otherwise almost unknown bishop Eutropius to set him right in the matter of the pending Easter.[43] The terminology of address used by Braulio gives the impression that perhaps he was not on familiar terms with his correspondent, who may therefore have been a Frankish ecclesiastic rather than a Spaniard.[44] Braulio's letter is direct and to the point and is worth citing in illustration of his method:[45]

> De festo autem paschali, quod inquirere ab humilitate nostra iussisti, nouerit sanctitas uestra hoc esse rectum, ut sexto Idus Apriles [8 April], luna uicesima prima, Pascha anno isto celebretur. Sic enim antiqui maiores nostri prescribserunt, id est ad Theudosium imperatorem Theuphilus; sic successor eius Cyrillus; sic Dionysius; sic ad papam Leonem Proterius; necnon et Pascasinus, et reliqui, quorum longum est facere mentionem, sed et nostri temporis uir insignis Spalensis Ysidorus. *Nec credo eos in negotio tam magno ac necessario pretermissa diligentia et labore potuisse delinquere.*

---

40 An exception is Joseph Schmid, *Die Osterfestberechnung in der abendländischen Kirche vom I. allgemeinen Konzil zu Nicäa bis zum Ende des VIII. Jahrhunderts*, Strassburger Theologische Studien 9/1 (Freiburg im Breisgau 1907) 92–93: 101; but he somehow misunderstood the internal dating criteria and placed it c. 630 ('zwar vermutlich vor dem Jahre 631', 101; 'in einem uns unbekannten Jahre', 93). 41 See the editions by José Madoz, *Epistolario de S. Braulio de Zaragoza*. Biblioteca de Antiguos Escritores Cristianos Españoles 1 (Madrid 1941), 132–36; and Luis Riesco Terrero, *Epistolario de San Braulio*. Anales de la Universidad Hispalense (Seville 1975) 114–16. There is an English translation by Claude Barlow, *Braulio of Saragossa, Fructuosus of Braga*, The Fathers of the Church, A New Translation 63, Iberian Fathers 2 (Washington, D.C. 1969). My translation is based on Barlow's. 42 There is a useful discussion in Charles H. Lynch, *Saint Braulio, Bishop of Saragossa (631–651): his life and writings*. Catholic University of America Studies in Medieval History, n.s. 2 (Washington, D.C. 1938) 65–68. 43 Eutropius is named as the addressee in the only surviving manuscript of the letter, but Lynch gives good reason for suspecting that the name was a later addition. 44 The technical evidence of the letter would tend to support this interpretation; all previous commentators have assumed that Eutropius was a Spaniard. [I was tempted in 1985 to suggest that Braulio's mysterious correspondent might have been an Irishman, but I did not have the courage then. However, given what we now know about the early reception of Isidore of Seville's writings into Ireland — Braulio was Isidore's literary executor — I should perhaps have been more courageous. If Braulio's reference to his correspondent's *laterculus* derived from the letter of inquiry which he received, then that correspondent may indeed have been an Irishman; see further above, 60.] 45 The text here is based on the two cited editions, which are not consistent. I have italicized passages borrowed from other writers.

In laterculo autem, quem dominus inspexisti, sicut uestra sanctitas scribit, forte mendosi codicis aut librarii error est, et ideo non ut debuit, sed ut contigit prescribtum habet. Nam in Kalendis Aprilibus [1 April] hoc anno non Christianorum, sed Pascha occurrit Iudeorum, ex ueteri et non ex nouo testamento. Sed quoniam oportet ut illorum precedat et sic nostra sequatur, quia prius uetus, postea nouum exstitit testamentum. Unde et Dominus quinta feria uetus *Pascha cum discipulis* manducauit et nobis post hoc sabbatum, quod in dominica lucescit, passione et resurrectione sua sacrauit; ideo cum illis simul celebrare non possumus, prohibente etiam Niceno concilio, quod in *septimo libro Ecclesiasticae refertur Historiae.*[46] Quocirca in sequenti dominica celebrandum est a nobis Pascha, quod erit, ut premisi, sexto Idus Apriles, luna uicesima prima, cum illorum in Kalendis Aprilibus in precedents dominica, luna celebretur quarta decima.

Since you have asked my unworthy self to inquire about the feast of Easter, your holiness should know that this is the truth: Easter this year will be celebrated on 8 April, the twenty-first day of the moon. That is how our elders of old prescribed, namely, Theophilus to the emperor Theodosius; likewise his successor Cyril; likewise Dionysius; likewise Proterius to Pope Leo, and also Pascasinus; and the rest, whom it would take too long to mention, save for the great man of our age, Isidore of Seville. I do not believe that in such a great and important matter they would have failed to display their customary carefulness and labor.

However, in the table which you, my lord, examined (as your holiness writes) there was possibly an error in the manuscript or by the scribe, and that is why it is that way and not as it should be. For on 1 April in this year falls the Pasch of the Jews, not of Christians, in accordance with the Old rather than the New Testament. Hence it is proper that theirs should come first and ours follow, since the Old Testament precedes and the New follows. Whence Our Lord ate the Last Supper with his disciples on the fifth day and after that, by his Passion and Resurrection, he consecrated for us the sabbath, which dawns on Sunday. Therefore we cannot celebrate with them because of the prohibition at the council of Nicaea, as found in book seven of the *Ecclesiastical History.* Therefore we must celebrate Easter on the following Sunday, which (as I have already said) will be 8 April, the twenty-first day of the moon, since their Easter is celebrated on 1 April, the preceding Sunday, on the fourteenth day of the moon.

---

46 Eusebius of Caesaraea, HE VII 32, has nothing to do with the Nicene council but concerns the Paschal writings of Anatolius, bishop of Laodicea. The mistaken reference was taken over verbatim from the prologue to Dionysius' tables, although this was not noted by either editor, nor by Lynch or Barlow. The correct identification of the citation is proof that Braulio was using Dionysiac tables.

Braulio's correspondent wrote to say that he was going to celebrate Easter on 1 April in the coming year, though some question seems to have entered his mind – doubtless because of the double dates in his Victorian tables. Braulio, on the other hand, consulted his own (Dionysiac) tables only to find that 1 April 641 was *luna XIIII* – hence his remark about celebration with the Jews. He suggested politely to Eutropius that his tables were faulty, citing verbatim from the letter of Proterius of Alexandria to Pope Leo (454) in which Proterius dismissed the Roman tables with an equal disdain. Eutropius seems not to have specified the source for his proposed Easter date, and Braulio may not have known that he was using Victorius, perhaps because Victorius never found favour in Spain.[47] But the points to be noted in Braulio's letter are (1) that Eutropius was proposing to celebrate Easter on the date marked 'Greci' in Victorius' table; (2) that Braulio – who was using different tables – understood Eutropius' date to imply celebration on *luna XIIII*, though Eutropius' own tables gave the moon's age as *luna XV*, which he naturally accepted as canonical; (3) that the implied quartodecimanism in Eutropius' date could only have made sense to Braulio; Eutropius himself was clearly unaware of the implication; and (4) that because of his uncertainty about the Easter of the coming year Eutropius wrote to one whom he regarded as of higher authority in a technical matter of this kind in order to ascertain the true date.

All these points apply equally to the papal letter of 640 to the Irish. (1) The northern Irish (as I believe) informed the curia of their intention to celebrate on 1 April 641, the date marked 'Greci' in their Victorian tables. (2) The curia – using different tables, presumably Dionysiac[48] – understood the Irish to be advocating celebration on *luna XIIII* (quartodecimanism). (3) The most important point of all, however, is that talk of observing Easter on *luna XIIII* need not necessarily imply that the Irish were still employing the old 84-year tables alone.[49] The papal letter censured the Irish for Pelagianism because they were

47 For the evidence, see Krusch, 'Einführung', esp. 115-22. Victorius was known to but strongly criticized by a monk Leo, writing to a Spanish bishop Sesuldus in 627; he was also known to Isidore of Seville; cf. his *Etymologiae* VI 17.1. [On the word *laterculus*, see now Bonnie Blackburn & Leofranc Holford-Strevens, *The Oxford companion to the year* (Oxford 1999) 870.] 48 This is Harrison's verdict, *Framework*, 61: 'At Rome, therefore, we may reasonably think of a swing away from the Victorian and in favour of the Dionysiac lunar limits as taking place in the decade 630 to 640. The fact of agreement between the rivals, the absence of alternatives, over a long period of years will have helped to make this change smoother and less painful'. While I would take issue with some of the reasons offered for the change, there seems little cause to doubt the general validity of the statement. 49 Note, however, that in Mac Carthy's reconstruction of the Irish Cycle (*Annals of Ulster* 4, table o) Easter falls on 1 April in 641. This is the case also in the tables compiled by O'Connell, 'Easter cycles in the early Irish Church', 103. If these reconstructions are accurate (and many have doubted whether they are), and if the northern Irish were using the Victorian and eighty-four-year tables parallel, then they would have had double reason for choosing Easter on 1 April. [See now the reconstructed Irish 84-year table in D. P. McCarthy, 'Easter principles and the fifth-century lunar cycle used in the British Isles', *Jnl Hist. Astron.* 24 (1993) 204-24.]

celebrating Easter (as Rome thought) on the fourteenth day of the moon *contra orthodoxam fidem, nouam ex ueteri heresim renouare conantes, pascha nostrum ... et XIIIIa luna cum Hebreis celebrare nitentes.* Readers of Bede's *Ecclesiastical History*, however, could be pardoned for thinking that the two problems were separate, for he omits entirely the passage in the letter that gave the detailed paschal arguments, substituting in its place the paraphrase *exposita autem ratione paschalis obseruantiae, ita de Pelagianis in eadem epistula subdunt,* followed by a verbatim passage on that subject.[50] But even the Romans realized that a Pelagian revival in Ireland would be a curious development, for they pointed out themselves that *non solum per istos CC annos abolita est, sed et cotidie a nobis perpetua anathemate sepulta damnatur.*[51]

The solution to the mystery is, however, surprisingly straightforward, and in case the reader of Bede missed the direct connection between unorthodoxy in the Easter question and Pelagianism, he could find it even more explicitly pointed out in his account of Ceolfrid's letter to King Naiton of the Picts.[52] That letter is a very accurate and concise presentation of the orthodox view on the matter of Easter in Bede's time. Ceolfrid clearly states that the seven days of Unleavened Bread (azyma) are to be observed on *luna XV-XXI: Porro dies XIIIIa extra hunc numerum separatim sub paschae titulo praenotatur.* Care must be taken, however, lest the Picts fall into the error of those 'who presume either to anticipate or go beyond' these limits. Ceolfrid therefore condemns observance of *luna XIIII-XX* (Irish practice) and *luna XVI-XXII* (Victorian doctrine). Anyone who presumes to anticipate Easter by observing on *luna XIIII* 'joins with those who believe that they can be saved without the intervening grace of Christ' (*concordat autem eis, qui sine praeueniente gratia Christi se saluari posse confidunt*).

Bede had himself referred to this same combination of errors – quartodecimanism and Pelagianism – in his *De temporum ratione* VI[53] – using words that he may have found in Ceolfrid's letter: *Nam si qui plenilunium paschale ante aequinoctium fieri posse contenderit, ostendat vel ecclesiam sanctam priusquam salvator in carne veniret extitisse perfectam, vel quemlibet fidelium ante praeventum gratiae illius aliquid posse supernae lucis habere.* The basic tenet of Pelagius' heresy was that man could achieve salvation through his own efforts, without the need of grace.[54] Man's sinfulness, while inherent in his being, was not the

---

50 Bede, HE ii 9, ed. Plummer 1, 123; Colgrave & Mynors, 200. Bede has been accused by R.L. Poole of having doctored the letter to suit his own argument, see 'The earliest use of the Easter cycle of Dionysius', *Engl. Hist. Rev.* 33 (1918) 57-62, 210-13; rev. ed. in Poole, *Studies in chronology and history* (Oxford 1934) 28-37. Jones, 'Victorian and Dionysiac tables', 408, 417-18, has defended Bede, and so has Harrison, Framework, 61; but I believe that there is more to be said for Poole's case than these eminent critics allow. However, the question requires more space than is available here.   51 HE II 19, ed. Plummer 1, 123, Colgrave & Mynors, 200.   52 The full text of the letter is given in HE V 21, ed. Plummer 1, 333-45; Colgrave & Mynors, 534-50.   53 Ed. Jones, *Bedae opera de temporibus*, 101. This reference I owe to the anonymous reader for *Speculum*.   54 The connection was seen by Plummer, of course; see his note on the passage, 2, 334.

burden of original sin, so that Christ's Passion and Resurrection were not the sole means of his redemption. To the Roman curia, therefore, anyone who advocated (or who seemed to advocate) celebration of Easter on the fourteenth of the moon was preempting the pasch and, by the same token, denying the efficacy of the Resurrection as the true instrument of man's redemption. Thus were the Irish seen to be resuscitating the *uirus Pelagianae hereseos*, though in fact they were doing no such thing. An unwarranted premise at Rome combined with fortuitous circumstances at home to deceive even men living at the time and led to a chain of reasoning which has misled scholars ever since.[55]

---

55 I am grateful to Mr. Kenneth Harrison [†] for stimulating and helpful discussion of this paper. However, he is not bound by any of my conclusions.

9

A seventh-century Irish computus
from the circle of Cummianus[*]

In its importance for the history of the Paschal controversy in the early Irish churches, the Letter of Cummian (*c*. AD 632/33)[1] stands without peer among the primary sources. Addressed to Ségéne, abbot of Iona (AD 623-52), and to a certain *Beccanoque solitario, caro carne et spiritu fratri*, the Letter is at once a report on the proceedings of a southern Irish synod held to discuss the Paschal question, and a reply to Ségéne's criticisms of that synod.[2] The remarkable tone of defiance in Cummian's words is itself clear enough indication that by this time the Paschal controversy in Ireland was already at its height.

The circumstances of the Letter are well known and are usually explained as follows: about the year AD 628, if we can infer from Bede (HE II 19),[3] the southern Irish churches received a letter from Pope Honorius I, solemnly exhorting them 'not to think that their small number, at the farthest ends of the earth, was wiser than all the ancient and modern churches of Christ through-out the world, and not to celebrate a different Easter contrary to the paschal computations and synodal decrees of all the bishops of the world'. As a result of this exhortation (it is commonly assumed) the leading clerics of the south-ern Irish churches gathered together in synod at Mag Léne, in the midlands, and after some deliberation they decided to accept the Easter reckoning urged on them by the Holy See.

But there then arose a certain *paries dealbatus* who, 'pretending that he was maintaining the tradition of the elders', introduced discord among the prelates

---

[*] First published in PRIA 82 C 11 (1982) 405-430.   1 First edited by James Ussher, *Veterum epistolarum Hibernicarum sylloge* (Dublin 1632) 24-35, No. XI. Re-edited in C.R. Elrington, *The whole works of the Most Rev. James Ussher* (17 vols, Dublin 1864) 4, 432-43; an emended version of Ussher's text in J. P. Migne, *Patrologia Latina* [MPL] 87, 969-78. A new critical edition, by Maura Walsh and myself is now near completion. I give citations from our new edition, with references to Ussher and Migne added for convenience. [See now M. Walsh & Dáibhí Ó Cróinín, *Cummian's Letter.*]   2 Best discussion by B. Mac Carthy in W. Hennessy & B. Mac Carthy, *Annals of Ulster*, 4, cxxxv-cxlix; J. Kenney, *Sources*, 220, No. 57; Jones, *Bedae opera*, 84-98. [See Walsh & Ó Cróinín, *Cummian's Letter*, 18-21.]   3 Charles Plummer (ed), *Venerabilis Baedae opera historica* (2 vols, Oxford 1896; repr. 1969) 1, 122: 'Misit idem papa Honorius litteras ... sollerter exhortans, ne paucitatem suam in extremis terrae finibus constitutam sapientiorem antiquis siue modernis, quae per orbem erant, Christi ecclesiis aestimarent; neue contra paschales computos, et decreta synodalium totius orbis pontificum aliud pascha celebrare'. Though Bede does not give the year as AD 628, that date can be inferred from other evidence.

and made uncertain a number that had previously been decided.[4] The upshot
of this confusion was a decision by the prelates to refer the matter to Rome,
iuxta decretum sinodicum, and a delegation was dispatched to ascertain what was
the true cycle in use there. When the delegation returned they confirmed that
the cycle agreed and adopted originally in council by the southern Irish clerics
was the one in use throughout the universal Church. This matter Cummian
had then turned over in his mind for a full year 'entering alone into the sanc-
tuary of God (that is Holy Scripture), then history, and [finally] whatever
cycles I could find',[5] before writing his response to Ségéne's criticisms.

To support his case Cummian cited a collection of ten different paschal
cycles (not all of them satisfactorily identified), and he brought to the support
of sacred scripture citations from Jerome and Augustine which are otherwise
unknown, together with a passage from the mysterious paschal work of
Origenus Chalcenterus.[6] His enumeration of authorities shows that Cummian
had to hand virtually the same computistical collection circulating in Spain a
generation previously and in his own time, but amplified by additional material from Irish sources.[7] The researches of Krusch, Mac Carthy and Jones[8]
have enabled us to identify most of the items in this computus, and we can say
with a reasonable degree of certainty that the collection of cycles to which
Cummian referred is still extant in the manuscripts.[9] But since only one manuscript of Cummian's Letter has come down to us (London, British Library,
MS. Cotton Vitellius A xii [*saec.* xi²/xii, provenance uncertain]), previous
scholars have been without any documentary evidence with which to test
Cummian's statements. However, I am now able to offer such evidence.

The Brussels, Bibliothèque Royale, MS. 5413-22 (*saec.* ix-x, partly
Rheims)[10] fols 77ᵛ-107ᵛ (hereafter referred to as Br) preserves a unique compu-

---

4 'Sed non post multum surrexit quidam paries dealbatus, traditionem seniorum seruare se
simulans, qui utraque non fecit unum, sed diuisit et irritum ex parte fecit quod promissum est'
[= Walsh & Ó Cróinín, *Cummian's Letter,* 92, 270-72.]   5 'Hinc per annum secretum sanctuarium
Dei ingressus (hoc est scripturam sanctam) ut ualui inuolui, deinde historias, postremo cyclos
quos inueni potui' [= Walsh & Ó Cróinín, *Cummian's Letter,* 58, 15-17.]   6 The only other
mention of this work is in the Anatolian *Canon Paschalis* [for which see D.P. Mc Carthy, 'Easter
principles and a fifth-century lunar cycle used in the British Isles', *Jnl of the History of Astronomy*
24 (1993) 204-10, and idem, 'The origin of the latercus paschal cycle of the Insular Celtic
churches', *Cambrian Medieval Celtic Studies* 28 (1994) 38-42.]   7 An excellent description of this
collection is given by Charles W. Jones 'The "lost" Sirmond manuscript', and *Bedae opera,* 105-13.
8 Bruno Krusch, *Studien zur christlich-mittelalterlichen Chronologie* [1]: *Der 84-jährige Ostercyclus
und seine Quellen* (Leipzig 1880); idem, 'Studien', etc. [2]: 'Die Entstehung unserer heutigen
Zeitrechnung', *Abhandl. der Preuß. Akad. der Wissensch.,* Jahrg. 1937, phil.-hist, Kl., Nr. 8
(Berlin 1938); Mac Carthy, op. cit., xv-clxxx; Jones, as above. [Walsh & Ó Cróinín, *Cummian's
Letter,* 225-26.]   9 Principally in the related MSS referred to by Jones as the 'Sirmond group',
after the owner of the most important of them, the Oxford, MS. Bodl. 309 (*saec.* xi, Vendôme)
[who was Jacques Sirmond, the seventeenth-century French Jesuit scholar]; see n. 7 above. [For
the Irish origin of the collection, see 'The Irish provenance of Bede's computus', below 173ff.]
10 A hopelessly inadequate description in J. Van den Gheyn, S.J., *Cat. des manuscrits de la Bibl.
Roy. de Belgique* 4 (Brussels 1904) 60-1; not much better is the cursory note by Henri Silvestre,

tus whose seventh-century Irish origins are clearly demonstrable. The manuscript contains 128 fols, measuring 192 x 160 mm, written in caroline minuscule (fols 125^r-28^v, containing Arator's *De actibus apostolorum*, are of Breton provenance). The bulk of the material concerns canon law, but fols 63^r -124^v comprise computistical and astronomical works. Our text has no heading, but follows immediately on a *Series annorum* (which gives the earliest possible date of compilation as *c.* AD 809) with the incipit: *Sciendum nobis quomodo sol in principalibus linguis uocatur;* it closes with the explicit: *paschalis solempnitatis celebrari summa breuitate notauit. FINIT AMEN AMEN.* The heading that follows (*DE SALTU LUNAE*) is preceded by the Roman numerals DCC. LXI, which might conceivably be a date of previous transcription, though the computistical rules that occur on fols 107^v-16^r do not, I believe, belong to our text. If the numerals were derived from a dating clause, it is not now possible to know for certain whether they belonged to our text (or its exemplar), or to the passages that follow it.

The computus itself is a school-text set in dialogue form, with questions introduced by the formulaic *Sciendum nobis est*, followed immediately by their answers. The questions serve to introduce the elementary aspects of computus: sun, moon, day, week, month, etc. (each with fanciful etymologies), and these questions become progressively more advanced, dealing ultimately with problems like lunar and solar calculations, the technicalities of cycles and the mechanics of Easter-tables. To aid the pupil in his understanding of these matters there are included also selections (some of them extensive) from various patristic and post-patristic authorities on the question of paschal reckoning: in matters of biblical interpretation those drawn on are Augustine, Jerome, Cyril and Proterius of Alexandria, and Paschasinus of Lilybaeum; while for computistical arguments the authors most often cited are Anatolius, Theophilus, Morinus, Victorius of Aquitaine, and Dionysius Exiguus. The latest authors cited are Isidore of Seville and Virgilius Maro Grammaticus.

Most immediately suggestive of an Irish exemplar is the frequent occurrence in the manuscript of the characteristically Insular signs of abbreviation: ħ, ħ, ħ (*hautem, hoc, haec*), .i., f, $_7$ (*id est, secundum, et*) and + (*enim*) occur throughout. Furthermore, on fol 92^v, the author announces his intention of passing over from a discussion of the solstices to the subject of the moon, in the following words: *CERTE INTERIM., Ó SOLESTIC deteIACEMUS ATQUE LINCIMUS* [= relinquimus?] *PLURA UT DE LUNA NARREMUS. DE LUNA hic incipit.* Here, the word *ó* is (apparently) the Old Irish preposition equivalent to Latin *de*, and the form *SOLESTIC* is simply an Irish calque on *solesticium;*[11] that is, *ó SOLESTIC* = *DE SOLESTITIO.* These features alone might not be sufficient to

'Notices et extraits des mss. 5413-22, 10098-105 et 10127-44 de la Bibl. Roy. de Bruxelles', *Sacris Erudiri* 4 (1953)174-92. See the Appendix below, 127-29, for fuller discussion of date and provenance. 11 The word is not noted in the Royal Irish Academy's *Dictionary of the Irish Language;* the word *grientairisem* is used by the glossator of the Karlsruhe Bede.

guarantee the manuscript's Irish origin, but besides such external indications
the contents of the computus are distinctively Irish; computistical tracts cited
at length are Anatolius, Cyril, Dionysius, Morinus, Theophilus, and Victorius.
The Anatolian *Canon Paschalis*, the *Epistola Cyrilli*, the Pseudo-Theophilan
Acta concilii Caesareae and the *Disputatio Morini* are all tracts which are extensively cited in Irish works, and all but the *Acta* are almost certainly Irish
compositions. Besides the references to those texts, the Brussels computus also
cites from a hitherto unknown work of Palumbus, i.e. Columbanus. In the
discussion to follow I will deal with these and the other authors cited by the
Brussels computist, and attempt to demonstrate the close affinities that exist
between the Brussels text and the Letter of Cummian.

The basic structure of the Brussels text follows the pattern of another
(unpublished) seventh-century Irish computus, the *De ratione temporum uel de
compoto annali* (DRT) which now no longer exists complete in any single manuscript, but the greater part of which can be reconstructed on the basis of extant
manuscript remains.[12] This computus, compiled in southern Ireland before AD
658,[13] comprised a detailed discussion of the ecclesiastical calendar to which
was prefaced an introduction largely concerned with the minutiae of time and
time-reckoning. This work differs from the Brussels computus only in as much
as the latter represents an adaptation of the doctrine that went into DRT,
combining its information with other (in some cases older) material. That this
was commonplace teaching among the seventh-century Irish is evident from
the fact that the same material occurs also in the well-known Munich computus, Bayerische Staatsbibliothek, Clm 14456 [*saec.* IX, Regensburg] – hereafter
referred to as M – another Irish compilation of *c.* AD 718, but containing
earlier material.[14] The Munich compilation consists mainly in a reworking of

---

12 The work is best preserved in the Sirmond group of MSS: Geneva, Bibl. de l'Univ., MS. 50
(AD 804, Massai); Tours, Bibl. munic., MS. 334 (AD 819, Tours); Vatican, Bibl. Rossiana, MS. 247
(*saec.* XI, provenance unknown); Oxford, Bodl. Libr., MS. Bodley 309 (*saec.* XI, Vendôme) Paris,
Bibl. nat., MS. lat. 16361 (*saec.* XII, provenance unknown). The prologue and *capitula* were
published by Jones, *Bedae opera*, 393-95 (Appendix). A part was published as *De computo dialogus*
in MPL 90, 647-52; cf. Jones, *Bedae pseudepigrapha: scientific writings falsely attributed to Bede*
(Ithaca, N.Y. 1939) 48-51[= *Bede, the schools and the computus*, pt 2]. I am preparing an edition of
this work at present.   13 The MSS of the Sirmond group have a dating-clause (best preserved
in Oxford, Bodl. Libr., MS. Bodley 309, fols 95ᵛ-95 bisʳ) which date the exemplar to AD 658; and
the inclusion in it of an identifiable Irish name makes it possible to locate that exemplar in
southern Ireland. I will discuss the origins of this Irish computus at greater length in a paper
entitled 'The Irish background to Bede's computus', to appear in *Peritia* 2 (1983). [See now, 'The
Irish provenance of Bede's computus', below 173ff.]   14 See Krusch, *Studien* 1, 10-21, *Studien*
2, 58; Eduard Schwarz, 'Christliche und jüdische Ostertafeln', *Abhandl. der kgl. Gesellsch. der
Wissensch. zu Göttingen*, phil.-hist. Kl., N.F. 8, Nr. 6 (Berlin 1905) 89-104; Mac Carthy, op. cit.,
lxvii-xcii. Mac Carthy and Krusch independently proved that the Munich Computus contained
dating formulae for the year AD 689; Schwarz showed that the latest date in it was AD 718. [In the
citations that follow, I give cross-references to the subsequent edition of the *De ratione conputandi*
which is pt 2 of Walsh & Ó Cróinín, *Cummian's Letter*.]

a DRT-type text, but to this material was also added a discussion of the 84-year cycle, and the 19-year and the 84-year cycles are contrasted in detail. The manuscript was written at Regensburg in Bavaria in the early ninth century but the exemplar was definitely an Irish manuscript, dating possibly from *c*. AD 718, for that is the latest date given in the formulae. That the compilation was Irish and not the work of Irishmen on the continent[15] can be demonstrated from one passage in particular, one which, as it happens, links the Brussels text with M. The context in M is provided by a discussion of the paschal lunar limits, which the author has just given on the authority of the so-called *Acta Synodi Caesareae* (Pseudo-Theophilus); having stated the limits from the *Acta* he then continued:

> Quicumque enim transgreditur hos terminos, transgreditur mandatum. Quirillus ait: 'Non faciamus pascha in .xiiii. luna cum Iudeis et hereticis, qui dicuntur thesserescedecadite'. Inde Iohannes consiliarius ait: '.Xiiii. dies lunae ad umbras pertinebat'. Ysidorus ait: 'Quicumque ante .xv. lunam pascha celebrari iubet, transgreditur mandatum'.

M fol. 43ᵛ; cf. **Br** fol. 104ʳ⁻ᵛ [DRC §58, pp 203-4]

The passages from Pseudo-Cyril and Isidore we will encounter again in the Brussels manuscript (103, 118 below), but the important citation is that of *Iohannes consiliarius*. This is none other than the man who, in the year AD 640 (together with three others of the Roman curia, including John, the pope-elect) addressed a joint letter to the leading ecclesiastics of the northern Irish churches, urging them to adopt the Roman method of calculating the date of Easter.[16]

This letter was hitherto known to us only from the account of it which Bede gives in his *Historia* II 19, in which he quoted a large part of the text; but this citation of the work in the Munich computus constitutes the sole native documentary evidence that the Irish had received the letter. The Munich citation is doubly significant in that it cites a sentence from the letter which Bede (doubtless deliberately) omitted. The statement of Iohannes that *luna XIIII* 'belonged to the shadows' clearly has reference to Quartodecimanism (the Jewish custom of celebrating the Passover on the fourteenth moon of their first month), and

---

15 Jones, *Bedae opera*, 110, thought these two tracts came from dissimilar backgrounds and were brought together first on the continent. But the evidence of the Brussels text, which combines material on the 19-year and 84-year cycles in a similar way, suggests that the two tracts in the Munich MS. were brought together already in Ireland. [My guess now would be: Iona.] 16 Plummer, ed. cit. 1, 122-24. Cf. Maurice P. Sheehy (ed), *Pontificia Hibernica. Medieval papal chancery documents concerning Ireland, 640-1261* (2 vols, Dublin 1962) 1, 3-4; and Kenney, *Sources*, 221-3, No. 58. [See now 'New heresy for old', above 87-98.]

it was obviously intended as a criticism of Irish practices which (rightly or wrongly) were believed to follow the Jews.

Since this citation from the Iohannes letter does not occur in Bede's account, and since the letter was directed to the northern-Irish prelates, the presence in M of this phrase points clearly to its Irish origin. Unfortunately, the work was so badly garbled in transcription that Krusch thought it hardly worth publishing,[17] and modern discussion of it has therefore concentrated only on the more intelligible passages. In fact, however, much of the material which was hitherto considered exclusive to the Munich computus occurs verbatim in the Brussels computus, and we shall see below that identical texts are found as well in a third Irish computistical compilation, the Milan, Biblioteca Ambrosiana, MS. H 150 Inf. (*c.* AD 825, N.E. France ?),[18] hereafter referred to as H. The various strata of texts in this collection are difficult to disentangle but dating clauses scattered throughout give the years AD 673, 691, 703, 784, 790, 810 and 825. The latest author cited is Isidore of Seville. That a part at least of this compilation was brought from Columbanus' Burgundian foundations seems very likely, for the paleographical affiliations of the manuscript are with north-eastern France and its *Bibliotheksheimat* was Bobbio.[19] From a comparison of these various collections, then, we can reconstruct a fairly accurate picture of the seventh-century Irish computus.

The Brussels text, for example, opens with a characteristic display of the Irish penchant for listing things in the so-called 'principal languages';[20] the identical material occurs both in M and in H:

---

17 'Aber ich bin mit [Eduard] Schwarz der Ansicht, daß er den Druck nicht verdient. Die Hs. ist sehr fehlerhaft geschrieben'; *Studien* 2, 58.   18 Edited by Ludovico Muratori, *Anecdota quae ex Ambrosianae Bibliothecae codicis primum eruit Ludovicus Antonius Muratorius* 3 (Padua 1713) 109-209. Muratori reproduced in full in MPL 129, 1273-1372. I have checked all readings from a microfilm copy, and give the MS. readings where they differ from the printed edition.   19 Professor Bischoff, in a letter of 24/iv/1978, described the work as being 'grösstenteils so irisch . . . wie nur denkbar' and characterised the script as being non-Italian. He thinks an origin in north-eastern France most likely, though he would not entirely rule out the possibility that it was written by French monks at Bobbio 'noch vor Dungal's italienischen Jahren'. See his remarks on the MS. in Bischoff, 'Panorama der Handschriftenüberlieferung aus der Zeit Karls des Grossen', in Wolfgang Braunfels and others (eds), *Karl der Grosse: Lebenswerk und Nachleben* (4 vols, Düsseldorf 1965) 2, 233-54: 252 n. 149. In his paper 'Carolingian aesthetics: why modular verse?' *Viator* 6 (1975) 309-40: 336, Jones suggested that the computistic verses *Annus solis continetur* (which occur in H) were 'quite probably composed in England in the mid-eighth century'. But apart from the fact that this would comprise the only English element in an otherwise predominantly Irish computus, the metrical grounds on which Jones based his claim are hardly convincing. The septenarial metre (8 - ˘, 7 - ˘), with two strong stresses and end rhyme in each hemistich, are all features, e. g., of the synchronistic poem *Deus, a quo facta fuit* (MGH, Poetae latini aevi Carolini 4/2 [Berlin 1896; repr. 1964] 695-7, No. 118) which is northern Irish and dated internally to AD 645. [Note, however, that a part of Alcuin's *Ep.* 148 also occurs in the collection; MPL 129, 1344C-1345D.]   20 I give all citations from Brussels with the minimum of editorial standardisation.

Sciendum nobis quomodo sol in principalibus linguis uocatur. Ita: 'Gamse'[21] uel 'Simsia' apud Ebreos; 'Elios' apud Grecos; 'Paniph' apud philosophos; 'Phoebus' apud Syros; 'Titan' apud Caldeos; 'Sol' apud Latinos.

Br fol. 77ᵛ; **M** fol. 18ʳ; **H** fol. 48ᵛ [= MPL 129, 1329] [DRC §1, pp 115-16]
1 Sciendum … ita *omm*. **MH**; **M** reads: sol dictus est eo quod solus luceat, uel a soliditate luminis 2 G. in Hebreo uel simpsé **M** Quam se in Ae. luna simplicia **H**; E. in Greco **MH** (Ae-); 3 Panath cum philosophis **MH** (Phanath **H**) Foebus cum Syris **M**, *om* **H**; T. (Tithan **H**) cum Chaldeis **MH**; 'Sol' … Latinos *om*. **M** (*cf. supra*) Sol cum latinis, de soliditate luminis, uel eo quod solus appareat obscuritatis sideribus radiis eius potentibus **H** (Cf. **M** fol. 25ᵛ: hercion in Hebreo, silene in Aegyptu (*sic*), gamsia grece)

Another such list common to the Brussels and Milan computi is that of the names of the months *secundum Egyptios*, *secundum Macedones*, and *secundum Ebreos*:

(I) Sciendum nobis quomodo Egyptii menses uocant. Ita: Thod, Pothi, Athir, Ciachi, Tebethi, Methi, Faminoth, Parnuthi, Poan, Poemi, Mensuri.

Br fol. 86ʳ; **H** fol 90ʳ [= MPL 129, 1363] [DRC §36, p. 147]. **H** lists Roman equivalents, which I omit here
1 Toth **H**; Paophi **H**; Chiach **H**; Mechir **H**; Famenoth **H**; Paschon **H**; 3 Paeni **H**; Epifa **H**, *om*. **B**

(II) Sciendum nobis quomodo Macidoniorum menses nominantur.
Ita: Dios, Appollonios, Admios, Feritios, Distrios, Paraticos, Artemessios, Dissius, Paruemus, Loos, Scorpios, Conperbentois.

Br fol. 86ᵛ; **H** fol. 90ʳ [= MPL 129, 1363] [DRC §40, pp 149-50]
1 Sciendum … Ita *om*. **H** 2 Dios *om*. **H**; Apolus **H**; Audinetus **H**; Peritus **H**; Disthor **H**; Psanticus **H** 3 Arthemesius **H**; Desios **H**; Panemos **H**; Sarpieos **H**; Hiberberetheus **H** [Another list in **H**, fol. 23ʳ = MPL 129,

---

21 This is doubtless the word that appears as *gansia* in the Hisperica Famina. See Michael W. Herren (ed & transl), *The Hisperica Famina: I. The A-Text*. Pontifical Institute of Mediaeval Studies, Studies and Texts 31 (Toronto 1974) 92, 176. Note that this list occurs also in the Irish Reference Bible (Bibelwerk); see Bischoff 'Wendepunkte in der Geschichte der lateinischen Exegese im Frühmittelalter' *Sacris Erudiri* 6 (1954) 189-279 = *Mittelalterliche Studien* (3 vols, Stuttgart 1966-67, 1981) 1, 205-73: 235.

1302: Nomina mensuum secundum Aegyptios (*sic*) ita dicunt: Dius, Apollonius, et Dyneus, Filisteus, Distreus, Antemesius, Pharamenius, Laus, Scurpeus, Ipuentius.]

(III) Sciendum nobis quomodo Ebreorum menses nominantur. Id est, Nisan, Iar, Siban, Tamini, Ebus, Ebul, Tetri, Mersiua, Coreclath, Tibiath, Sabath, Adar.

Br fol. 87ʳ ; H fol. 90ʳ [= MPL 129, 1363] [DRC §41, p. 150]
1 Sciendum ... id est *om.* H 2 Tahani H; Ab H; Elul H; Theseri H; Marsuan H Casleu H 3 Tereth H; Adare H

This theme of the 'principal languages' occurs also in the Brussels manuscript in relation to other divisions of time, as in the following example:

Sciendum nobis quomodo uocatur numerus in principalibus linguis. Ita: 'uidaber' uel 'minath' apud Ebreos; 'latercus' apud Aegyptios, qui luna proprium quidem est; 'calculus' apud Macedones; 'arithmos' apud Grecos; 'conpos' uel 'conpotus' uel 'numerus' et 'rima' apud Latinos. Sed numerus omni numerationi generalis est; rima uero et conpos propria sunt huic arti.

Br fol. 78ʳ; H fol. 26ᵛ [= MPL 129, 1306] [DRC §3, pp 117-18]
1 Scienim Br; Sciendum ... Ita *om.* H, which reads: Numerus apud Ebreos, Chaldeos et Syros mina dicitur. Cum Grecis arethimus nuncupabatur, apud Aegyptios laterculus, poenes Machedones calculus, cum Latinis compotus, *cet om.* 3 quidem] qiidum Br 4 rima, *with* -th- *supralin., manu rec.* Br

By way of a parallel to the names for the sun which are listed in the Brussels manuscript on fol. 77ᵛ the names for the moon are given on fol. 92ᵛ:

Sciendum nobis quomodo luna uocatur in tribus principalibus linguis. Ita: 'hericon' in Ebreo; 'silene' apud Aegyptios (unde lapis Silenitis dicitur); 'mane' apud Grecos (inde mensis dicitur); 'luna' apud Latinos.

Br fol. 92ᵛ M fol. 25ᵛ [DRC §63, p. 172]
1 Sciendum ... Ita *om.* M 2 hercion M; silene in Aegyptu M; gamsia grece M (*cf. list of names for sun, supra*); *cet. om.* M

A more common theme than the 'principal languages' in Hiberno-Latin texts, however, is the more specific 'Tres Linguae Sacrae' topos, which derives ultimately from the statement in John's Gospel that the inscription on Christ's cross was written *hebraice, graece et latine* (John 19: 19-20).[22] There is no need here to trace the development of that theme in Irish literature, it will suffice to say that it occurs in our Brussels text, in M, and in H. The Brussels text, for example, has a characteristic flourish regarding the names for the week:

> Sciendum nobis quomodo ebdoma in tribus principalibus linguis vocatur.
> Ita: 'ebron' in Ebreo; 'ebdoma' in Greco; 'septimana' in Latino.

Br fol. 82ᵛ [DRC §27, p. 135] M and H have only slightly related material

Another instance is the list of names for the day:

> Sciendum nobis quomodo dies in tribus linguis principalibus
> uocatur. Ita:'ella' in Ebreo; 'emera' in Greco; 'dies' in Latino.

Br fol. 81ʳ; M fol. loʳ; H fol. 26ʳ [= MPL 129, 1306] [DRC §22, p. 130]
1 Sciendum ... Ita *omm.* M H; Ema cum Ebreis, apud Grecos emera,
poene nes (*sic*) Latinos dies H; Ema in Hebreorum lingua, de denomina-
tione, quia emat dominatio dicitur. Emera in Greca a luce; emerat enim
lux dicitur. Dies latine, a diuidendo lucem a tenebris M

In these passages we have seen how the author introduces the basic vocabulary of the computus, though it must be said that the elaborate etymologising
of these various terms is not a common feature in computistical texts generally.[23] Nevertheless, the occurrence of identical items in all three collections,
Br, M and H, indicates that this etymologising (and in some respects we might
almost call it 'Hisperic') was common practice in the seventh-century Irish
schools at any rate. This trend is not so obvious in the *De ratione temporum*,
although much the same basic material was drawn on in the compilation of all
these collections.

Where the Brussels text shows an acquaintance with the earliest form of the
De ratione temporum type of material is in the discussion of computus and the
science of numbers; on fol. 79ʳ the text reads:

> Sciendum nobis quomodo nomina numeri apud Grecos uocantur. Ita: .i.
> mia, dia, tria, tessaera, penta, ecza, ebda, ogda, nia, deca, ecossi, trienta,
> serenta, pententa, eczenta, ebdenta, ogdenta, enienta, ecacon, cile.

---

22 See esp. Robert E. McNally, 'The Tres Linguae Sacrae in early Irish Bible exegesis',
Theological Studies 19 (1958) 395-403. 23 Krusch, *Studien* 2, 53-57, published a 'Merovingian
Computus' which he claimed (p. 58) had been used by the Irish compiler of the Munich
computus; but the occurrence in the 'Merovingian' work of terms that are otherwise known only
from Irish texts, together with the obviously corrupt and derivative nature of its content, suggests
that the dependence was rather the other way round.

This is clearly based on material which in DRT is listed under the following capitulum: *Dehinc etiam interrogare debemus, quomodo numeri nominantur apud Grecos, ab uno usque ad mille, et myriades, et quae notae significant illos numeros apud Grecos.*[24] But our Brussels manuscript is the only one in which the Greek numbers are actually given their Greek names; all other manuscripts that I have examined simply give the equivalents in Roman numerals. Nor, indeed, is that the only indication that the Brussels computist was using the same material as DRT in its earliest recension: besides the fact that he follows DRT's basic framework of fourteen divisions of time, he also shares verbatim passages with that work. For example, he has an interesting definition of *numerus* which also occurs in that computus:

> Sciendum nobis a quo fundamento crescit numerus. Ab uno. Sciendum nobis an sit unus numerus. Non est, quia ab eo crescit numerus, ad similitudinem in gradibus conparationis, UT AGUSTINUS DICIT: 'Unus non est numerus, sed ab eo crescunt numeri'.

Br fol. 78ᵛ [DRC §7, p. 120]
1 Scienim **Br** 2 Nonnisi **Br** 4 crescunt n. *corr.* < numerus (?) **Br**

In this instance, the Brussels computist identifies the author of the definition as Augustine, though the text of DRT cites only an anonymous author.[25] The context in which the axiom occurs in DRT is provided by Isidore's statement in *Etym.* III 1 that one is reckoned as the *semen numeri* but not as an integer: Δ *Numerus, quomodo diffinitur?* ⊁ *Isidorus diffiniuit, dicens: 'Numerus est multitudo ex unitatibus constituta. Nam unum semen numeri esse, non numerus, dicimus'. Item alius dicit: 'Unum non est numerus, sed ab eo crescunt numeri'.* Doubtless the definition ascribed merely to *alius* in DRT, and to Augustine in the Brussels text, was originally an adaptation of Isidore's definition.

We may cite other indications that the Brussels computist was drawing on the same material as is found in the earliest recension of DRT. For instance, he cites at length from Boethius, *De arithmetica institutione*,[26] which he had in a good recension. Thus, on the subject of the Roman numerals, the Brussels computist has this to say:

> Sed hoc auctores causa breuitatis non rationem sequentes sanxerunt, Boetio dicente: 'Hoc autem cognoscendum est, quod haec signa numero-

24 Jones, *Bedae opera*, 393 [DRC §10, p. 122].   25 Note that the same definition is cited in *Sanas Cormaic*, an Old Irish glossary of *c.* AD 900 which contains much ancient material; see Kuno Meyer, *Learning in Ireland in the fifth century* (Dublin 1913) 27 n. 36 = Cormac's Glossary § 447: 'unus non est numerus, sed ab eo crescunt numeri'.   26 I have used the edition of Gottfried Friedlein, *Anicii Manlii Torquati Severini Boetii de institutione arithmetica* (Leipzig 1867).

rum, quae posita sunt, quae nunc quoque homines in summarum designatione describunt, non naturali institutione formata sunt'.

Br fol. 79ᵛ = *De inst. arithmetica* II 4, Friedlein, 86-87 [DRC §11, p. 122]
3 quae (1°) *om.* **Br** 4 fornata **Br**

Besides further material from Book II, the Br computist also had access to Book I of Boethius, as is clear from the following excerpt:

Sciendum nobis quod per hanc numeri rationem omnia primitus formata sunt, ut Boetius dicit: 'Omnia quacumque a primeua rerum natura constructa sunt numerorum uidentur ratione formata'. Sciendum nobis quoque quod per hanc cursus siderum, haec est inuestigatio temporum, cognoscitur, ut Boetius: 'Propriae tamen ipsa numerorum natura omnis astrorum cursus omnisque astronomica ratio constituta est. Sic enim ortus occasusque collegimus, sicut tarditates uelocitatesque errantium siderum custodimus, sic defectus et multiplices lunae uariationes agnoscimus'.

Br fol 79ᵛ = *De Inst. Arithmetica* I 2 = Friedlein, 12 [DRC §12, p. 123]
4 quod] qui **Br** 7 ortus] artus **Br** 9 uariationes] narationes **Br**

The fact that the material from Book II of Boethius is not cited, to my knowledge, in any manuscript of DRT would tend to reinforce the impression of dependence on a common source, rather than of direct borrowing by the Brussels computist from DRT. The lengthy citations in the Brussels collection from another characteristically Irish work, the *opera grammatica* of Virgilius Maro,[27] are also slightly different in DRT. The Irish enthusiasm for Virgilius Maro's writings (borne out by the exclusively Irish textual tradition for the early period) has long been known to scholars.[28] But previous studies have referred only to his frequent occurrence in the exegetical and grammatical works of Hiberno-Latin writers; Virgil was, however, equally popular with Irish computists and is cited both in DRT and in our Brussels computus. Indeed, one of the most fantastic of Virgil's etymological extravaganzas is cited at length in Brussels, fol. 82ʳ:

27 I have used the editions of Giovanni Polara,*Virgilio Marone grammatico Epitomi ed Epistole.* Nuova Medioeve 9 (Naples 1979), and Johannes Huemer, *Virgilii Maronis Grammatici opera* (Leipzig 1886). [For Virgilius in Irish texts generally, see 'On the earliest Irish knowledge', below 191-200.] **28** A good review of the work to date by Michael Herren, 'Some new light on the life of Virgilius Maro Grammaticus', *Proceedings of the Royal Irish Academy* [PRIA] 79 C 2 (1979) 27-71. [See also Vivien Law, *Wisdom, authority and grammar in the seventh century: Decoding Virgilius Maro Grammaticus* (Cambridge 1997).]

Sciendum nobis quomodo haec nomina defferunt, id est *uespere, uespera, uesperum*. VIRGILIUS demonstrat dicens: 'Est etiam *uesper, uespere, uesperum, uespera*. Hic cassus nominatiuus quadruplex est, cuius differentia est quod uesper quidem dicitur quociescumque sol nubibus aut luna ferruginibus quacumque diei ac noctis hora obcecatur; et hoc neutrum *uesper, uesperis* facti. Aut nominatiuus uespere uocatur, ab hora nona sole discensum inchoante. Hoc nomen declinationem non habet. *Uesperum* est dum sole occidente dies defecit et sic declinatur: *uesperum, uesperi, uespero*. *Uespera* est, cum lucis oriente aurora nox finitur, et sic declinatur: *uespera, uespere*. Cauendum est ne aut *uespera* aut *uespere* aut *uesperum* pluralem numerum habere putentur'.

Virgilius Maro, *Epist.* I 4 'De Nomine' = Polara, 186–88; Huemer, 112 6 nominatiuus] nominatim **Br** 7 *uesperum*, etc.] uesperum riro **Br** 8 sic] si **Br** 10 aut (2°) *om.* **Br** [DRC §25, pp 132-33]

Virgilius is also cited in Brussels (fol. 87ᵛ) for definitions of *autumnus* and *hiems*, but only the latter appears in the published editions. Virgilius is cited twice in M (fols 12ʳ, 18ʳ), not under his own name but as Augustinus.[29]

It should be clear, then, from what we have seen that the Brussels manuscript reflects the computistical interests of certain seventh-century southern Irish schools, both in general and in detail. This manuscript contains the standard doctrine of those schools that had abandoned the Irish 84-year Paschal reckoning in favour of the Alexandrian cycle, which they derived from the combined writings of Victorius of Aquitaine and Dionysius Exiguus. This transitional period in the history of computistical studies in Ireland is perhaps best exemplified by the contents of the Munich computus, where a recension of DRT is accompanied by a detailed discussion of the older 84-year cycle. The Brussels manuscript, however, also contains references to the old Irish 84-year reckoning, many of which are identical with statements found in the Munich text.

In a discussion of the seven days of Easter week, for example, the Brussels computist has this to say:

Sciendum nobis quod quemadmodum hi uiri in .uii. paschae aetatibus discrepant. Laterci enim sectatores, qui .xiiii. luna usque ad .xx. septem aetates paschae numerant, a .ii. luna usque ad .uiii. lunam septem aetates

---

29 Clm 14456, fol. 12ʳ: 'Mensis a mensura dicitur, qui unusquisque eorum mensuratur. Augustinus ait: "Ueteres menses dicebant a mensa communi, quia terram suis fructibus quasi quibusdam dapibus replebit; chimales uero menses esse negabant; secundum spatia dicebant, quia nullum dapibus dant modum"; hucusque Augustinus'. Cf. Polara, 156 (*Epit.* XI 5, 4). I have noted the following passages quoted in Irish computi: Clm 14456: *Epit.* II 5, four times (twice as Augustinus); Sirmond MSS: *Epist.* I 4, 4-8; Brussels MS.: *Epist.* I 4, *Epit.* II 5 (twice).

initii conputant. Latini uero, .uii. aetates paschae a .xui. luna usque ad
.xxii. computantes, a .iiii. luna usque in .x. lunam septem initii aetates
numerant., Greci uero rationabilius, quos nos sequimur, a .xv. luna usque
in .xxi. lunam septem aetates paschae numerantes, a .iii. luna usque in
.uiiii. lunam septem aetates initii conputant.

Br fol. 104ᵛ [DRC §99, pp 204-5]
2 Laterci sectatores = *Followers of the 84-year cycle* 3 numerantes **Br**
4 initii] Initium Quadragesimae, *or* Lent (Ir. *Inid*) 6 rationabius **Br**
The same list, in slightly different wording, occurs in **M** fol. 33.

Now, this last citation brings us to the crucial problem facing the seventh-
century Irish computists: whether to calculate the date of Easter using the
paschal lunar terms .xiiii. to .xx. (as was the practice in the 84-year cycle) or
.xu. to .xxi. (in accordance with the Alexandrian reckoning). Cummian, in his
Letter, approached the problem in the following way:

Item in Exodo: *.vii. diebus comedetis azima usque ad diem .xxi.*; et hoc in
tractatibus diligenter inuestigaui, quid sentirent de .xxi. eruditissimi uiri,
quod Ieronimus pulcherrime explanat dicendo: 'Pascha immolat populus, et alias celebrat festiuitates; omnis eius sollenitas die finitur octauo'.
Prima dies in azimis .xv., dies octaua .xxi.

Ussher, *Sylloge*, 25 = MPL 87, 971 [*Cummian's Letter*, 58-60] Hieron *in
Aggaeum* II 11 -15, CCSL 76A, 734.

Because it was believed that this Jerome citation occurred nowhere in the
published corpus of that Father's writings, this was seen as the first of the
patristic sources that Cummian allegedly concocted in his own support. But
the citation is genuine and the very same passage (likewise ascribed to Jerome)
is found almost verbatim in the Brussels computus:

Sciendum nobis quo numero dierum sollempnitatem paschae Iudei
peragebant. Septem diebus uidelicet, ut Dominus illis conposuit ita
dicens: *.vii. diebus comedetis azyma et fermentum non inuenietur in domibus
uestris.* Sciendum nobis a qua lunae aetate hi .vii. dies incipiunt et in
quam aetatem dissiniunt. Secundum alios hi .vii. dies a .xiiii. luna usque
in .xx. conputantur, ut in Exodo dicitur: *Primo mense, .xiiii. die mensis
primi ad uesperam, comedetis azyma, usque ad .xx. unam diem eiusdem mensis
ad uesperam, .vii. diebus fermentum non inuenietur in domibus uestris.*
Secundum uero alios rectius principalis paschae dies, id est .xiiii. luna, in
.vii. azymorum diebus non conputatur, sed a .xv. luna usque in .xxi.
lunam .vii. dies azymorum conputantur, VT HIERONIMUS dicit: 'Pascha

immolat populus, et alios' azymorum .vii. dies 'celebrabat festiuitates'.
Quia 'ipse solus dies pasche immolatur in quo agnus immolabatur. Ceteri
uero azymorum dies dicuntur', qui a .xv. luna usque in .xxi. diem peru-
eniunt.

Br fol. 103ʳ⁻ᵛ [DRC § 96, pp 201-2] 5 Secundum alios] = *Followers of the
84-year cycle* 9 Secundum alios] *Followers of the Alexandrian cycle;* cf.
Orléans, Archives départmentales du Loire, MS. 75 (62), p. 241:
Hieronimus quoque ait: 'alia est enim sollemnitas paschae, alia sollemni-
tas azimorum. Omnis ergo sollemnitas apud Hebreos die octaua finitur'.
(Kindly supplied by Dr Jean Rittmueller). The text is an (eighth-century
?) Irish commentary on Matthew, for which see Bischoff, *Mitt. St.* 1,
244-45.

The Jerome text quoted above is clearly the same as that used by Cummian.
But the Brussels text is doubly important because the last two sentences also
occur in Cummian's Letter, as part of a citation from the mysterious work of
Pseudo-Origen:

Item perscrutans, inueni et Originem Calcenterum et uere Adamantinum
dicentem: 'Est quidem sollennis dies in mense primo: alia sollennitas
paschae, alia sollennitas azimorum, licet iuncta uideatur azimis, princip-
ium namque azimorum ad finem paschae coniungitur. Pascha autem ipse
solus dies appellatur in quo agnus occiditur. Reliqui uero azimorum .vii.
dies appellantur. Sic enim dicit: *Facies sollennitatem azimorum .vii.
diebus'*.

Ussher, *Sylloge,* 26 = MPL 87, 971 [*Cummian's Letter,* 62-64] 4 finem]
fidem **MS**

Therefore at least two of Cummian's 'patristic' sources hitherto regarded as
exclusive to his Letter were available also to the author of the Brussels computus. But a third text also appears in Brussels which is of interest at this point:
immediately following his citation from Pseudo-Jerome (above), Cummian
passed on to a text which we can identify as the *Liber Quaestionum* of
Ambrosiaster,³⁰ a late fourth-century work probably of Italian origin.
Cummian's Letter reads:

---

30 See Alexander Souter, *The earliest Latin commentaries on the Epistles of St. Paul* (Oxford 1927)
43; Jones, *Bedae opera,* 37. A. Souter (ed), *Liber Quaestionum Veteris et Novi Testamenti,* CSEL 50
(Vienna 1908) vi-vii, notes that there were three recensions of the work; Cummian used
Recension 1, of 150 questions.

Item xci. [questione]: 'Apostolus', inquit, 'falli non potuit, qui ait: *Pascha nostrum immolatus est Christus,* quod non suum utique, sed legis est uerbum, dicente Moyse: *Et erit cum dicent uobis filii uestri: "Quae est deseruitio haec?" Et dicetis: "Immolatio haec Pascha Domini est."* Quid amplius', inquit, 'necessarium est ad testimonium? Lex loquitur, apostolus probat; hoc superest, ut contradictor abiciatur ut peruicax. Manifestum est enim transitum post pascha fuisse. Sanguis igitur salutem prestitit, non transitus, quia, ut transitus non noceret, obsistit sanguis'.

Ussher, *Sylloge,* 26 = MPL 87, 971 [*Cummian's Letter,* 60]
4 Immolatio est hoc **MS** est *om.* **MS** 8 transitum est **MS**

Now in the Brussels computus, after a passage concerning the etymology of the word *Pascha* in which Augustine, Paschasinus and Isidore are cited successively, the text proceeds as follows:

Aliter [interpretatur] uero secundum Hieronimum *fasse* nomen Ebreicum est; *pascha* uero Grecum et immolatio interpretatur ita dicens: 'Requirendum est, si pascha transitus interpretatur, sicut Grecis uidetur. Apostolus falli non potuit, qui ait: *Pascha nostrum immolatus est Christus,* quod non suum utique, sed legis est uerbum, dicente Moyse: *Et erit cum dicent uobis filii uestri: "Quae est deseruitio haec ?" Et dicetis.. "Immolatio haec fasse Domini est".* Hoc tamen superest, ut contradictor ut peruicax abieciatur. Manifestum est enim transitum post immolationem fuisse. De sanguine enim agni immolati super postes hostii et super limen possuerunt, ut, transiens nocte angelus, noli percuteret domum in qua signum sanguis esse. Sanguis igitur salutem praestitit, non transitus'.

Br fols 99ʳ-100ʳ [DRC §84, p. 192] = *Liber quaestionium,* CSEL 50, 170-71
3 Quaerendum, *with* est *om.* Liber *Q.* (si pascha … uidetur *occurs verbatim in the letter of Paschasinus)* 5 est *om.* **Br**; *Et erit]* aderit **Br**; Immolatio pascha hoc. D. est *Lib. Q.* 7 ut] et **Br**

It will doubtless have been noted that in this citation, and in the previous one from the unidentified work of Pseudo-Origen, the Brussels computist gives a more complete text than that cited by Cummian. In fact, the Brussels computist reproduced *Quaestio* XCVI in its entirety (save for the words *Quid amplius … apostolus probat*), including the question itself. This at least proves that the Brussels text cannot have been copied directly from Cummian's Letter. The converse is also true: Cummian could not have copied directly from the Brussels computus, for there are minor, but significant, differences between the two texts, both here and in the previous citations. The only possible alternative interpretation of the evidence, therefore, is that both Cummian and the Brussels computist were drawing on common source-material. But such identity of what are sometimes unattested sources raises the obvious question: was Cummian, the author of the Letter to Ségéne of Iona, also the author of the Brussels computus?

There are several points in favour of the suggestion. Firstly, Cummian in his Letter shows that he was well versed in computistical studies and had access to a considerable body of computistical material, some of it hitherto regarded as unique. Such a man might be expected to compile a computistical manual for use in the school-room (as Bede, for example, was to do). The collection of primary texts in the Sirmond group of manuscripts would not have been suitable for classroom instruction, but the Brussels computus was clearly intended for just that purpose. Apart altogether from the *Sciendum nobis* formula which is used throughout, fol. 85^r of Brussels actually has an instance of the tell-tale ⊃–< sign denoting the Magister in a teacher-pupil dialogue. Such symbols (Δ, ⊃–<) are found in all manuscripts of DRT and we need not doubt that they were present in greater numbers in the exemplar of Brussels. Furthermore, the manner in which the work proceeds from the minutiae of time and time-reckoning up to a discussion of cycles and their manipulation is another strong indication that the Brussels computus is didactic, intended to lead the elementary student gradually through all the steps of the science. Indeed, if one were asked to picture the kind of computus-manual that Cummian might have been expected to compose, then the Brussels text would certainly fit the bill; for the sources used and the manner in which they were handled bear a marked resemblance to that scholar's work. We do not know if Cummian was in fact a monastic teacher (*fer légind*) but the level of scholarship that he showed in his Letter (and the fact that he, rather than someone else should have written it) clearly attests to his standing in the learned circles of southern Ireland in the first half of the seventh century. There are, besides, other indications that Cummian may have been a monastic scholar, possibly at Clonfert Brénainn (Co. Galway) but an examination of that evidence here would lead us too far away from our subject.[31] It will suffice for the present to point to his Letter (the authorship of which is undisputed) as the chief witness to his computistic skill. However, it is quite possible that Cummian did not regard himself primarily as a computist, but that the exigencies of the paschal controversy led him to acquire a more thorough familiarity with the material. Hence it may have been as a result of this interest that he set about (perhaps in his later years, *c*. AD 650?) compiling the kind of text we have in Brussels.

31 The ascription to Cummian of a Commentary on Mark and a descriptive list of Christ and the Apostles will be examined in our forthcoming edition of his Letter. [See now Walsh & Ó Cróinín, *Cummian's Letter*, 217-21, and Dáibhí Ó Cróinín, 'Cummianus Longus and the iconography of Christ and the apostles', in D. Ó Corráin, L. Breatnach & K. McCone (eds), *Sages, saints and scholars. Celtic studies in honour of James Carney* (Maynooth 1989) 268-79.]

Secondly, the Brussels manuscript mentions many of the texts that are found in the Sirmond group which preserves the southern Irish computistical collection of *c.* AD 658. These texts are, among others, the paschal letters of Paschasinus, Proterius, and Pope Leo, the works of Victorius and of Dionysius Exiguus, extracts from Boethius, Isidore and Augustine, and a collection of excerpts from Macrobius' *Saturnalia* which passed under the title *Disputatio Cori et Praetextati*.[32] Besides these texts there also occur the pseudonymous tracts of Anatolius, Cyril, Morinus, and Theophilus (otherwise known as the *Epistola Philippi* and the *Acta concilii Caesareae*). All these texts are cited by name in the Brussels computus, either in brief or at length; the latter four are cited also in Cummian's Letter. That he may have had some of the others to hand as well is possible, if not clearly demonstrable.

An example of this material in common is offered by the text of Brussels where the Dionysiac rule for finding the beginning of the First Month is discussed:

> UT DIONYSIUS dicit: 'Sed quod mensis hic, unde sumat exordium uel ubi terminetur, euidenter ibi non collegitur, praefati uenerabiles .ccc. x. et .viii. pontifices antiqui moris obseruantiam et exinde a sancto Moysi traditam, sicut in .vii. libro ecclesiasticis refertur historiae, solertius inuestigantes, ab .viii.a Idibus Martii usque in diem Nonarum Aprilis natam lunam facere dixerunt primi mensis initium; et a .xii. Kl. Apr. usque in .xiiii. Kl. Maii luna .xiiii. solertius inquirendum'. Et haec regula in diebus accensionis lunae primi mensis, et in .xiiii. luna euisdem, et in diebus dominicis pascha, per legalem conputationem et secundum angeli ordinationem et secundum lapidem Sileniten et secundum miraculum putei, qui in nocte pascha in Meltina manat, usque ad diem iudicii apud Christianos obseruabitur.

Br. fol 102ᵛ [DRC §94, pp 199-200]
1 DIONYSIUS] Dionysius Exig., *Ep. ad Petronium* (Krusch, *Studien* 2, 65)
3 minoris **Br** 5 uestigantes **Br** diebus **Br** Aprilis *om.* **Br**

The four authorities here cited in support of Dionysius' rule are easy enough to identify:

1. *The computatio legalis* is the Alexandrian reckoning referred to in the letter of Paschasinus, bishop of Lilybaeum in Sicily, addressed to Pope Leo on the

---

32 See Jones, 'Sirmond computus', EHR 52, 211. The collection exists now in the Sirmond group of MSS (to which add Tours, Bibl. mun., MS. 334 [*saec.* IXⁱ, Tours], which is in fact another copy of the same computus). It also occurs in Köln, Dombibliothek, MS. 83/2 and Vat. Reg. Lat. 586. 33 Edited by Krusch, *Studien* 1, 245-50. The passage here cited from the letter occurs verbatim in Brussels, fol. 103ʳ.

subject of the date of Easter in AD 444.[33] In remarking on the inaccuracy of the Roman cycle Paschasinus said: *In hoc ambiguo fluctuantes, ad Hebreorum, hoc est* LEGALEM, SUPPUTATIONEM *nos conuertimus, quae cum a Romanis ignoratur, facile errorem incurrunt.* Although not cited specifically by Cummian in his letter the work does occur in the manuscripts of the Sirmond group and may, therefore, also have been in his collection.

2. The second authority cited, the *ordinatio angeli,* refers to a legend which circulated in the West from at least the seventh century (and probably earlier) to the effect that Pachomius, founder of the cenobites of Egypt, had acquired the rules for computing the date of Easter from an angel.[34] The legend was attached to a mnemonic verse of nineteen lines, beginning *Nonae Aprilis norunt quinos,* which enabled the student to memorise the data for each year of the 19-year Alexandrian cycle, and the verses proved so useful that they circulated in almost every computistical manuscript of the Middle Ages. This is undoubtedly the Pachomian cycle to which Cummian refers in his list of ten cycles, and we may assume that he was familiar with the legend.

3. The third authority, the *lapis Silenitis,* derives from a curious anecdote in a letter ascribed (falsely) to Cyril of Alexandria[35] and which was much in vogue with Irish computists in the seventh century. Cummian cites at length from the Letter and the Brussels computus cites the identical passage:

> 'Scrutaminique', ut Cyrillus ait, 'quod ordinauit sinodus Nicena lunas quartasdecimas omnium annorum per decennouenalem cyclum' – quem Uictorius, per uicesimas et octauas uices, cum Kalendis .dxxxii. et bissextis .cxxxiii., in id ipsum, unde ortus est, redire fecit – 'ut non fallamur in luna primi mensis et celebremus pascha in sequenti Dominico, et non faciemus in luna .xiiii. cum Iudaeis et hereticis, qui dicuntur thesserescedecadite. Et constitutum est', inquit, 'in omnibus sinodis, preter sinodum Gangrensem et Cesariensem, ut non faceret ulla aecclesia uel ciuitas et omnis regio contraria his, quae statute sunt de pascha in Niceno concilio. Et si non scripsisset sinodus Nicena cyclum lunarem primi mensis, sufficeret cyclus lapidis Selenitis in Perside ad exemplum rationis paschalis, cuius candor interior cum luna primi mensis cresscit et decrescit'.

---

34 Charles W. Jones, 'A legend of St. Pachomius', *Speculum* 18 (1934) 198-210 [= *Bede, the schools and the computus,* chap. VII]. 35 Edited by Krusch, *Studien* 1, 344-9; cf. Jones, *Bedae opera,* 93-97. Note, however, the pertinent objections to the alleged Canterbury origin of the *Ep. Cyrilli* voiced by Kenneth Harrison, 'Lunisolar cycles: their accuracy and usage', in Margot H. King and Wesley M. Stevens (eds), *Saints, scholars and heroes. Studies in honour of Charles W. Jones* (2 vols, Minnesota 1979) 2, 65-78: 74. The lore about the Silenite stone is found also in Augustine, *De Civ. Dei* XXI 5, 1: 'In eadem Perside gigni etiam lapidem Silenitem, cuius interiorem candorem cum luna crescere atque deficere'. It arises from a misinterpretation of Pliny, *Hist. Nat.* XXXVII 101, 18: 'Selenitis ex candido tralucet melleo fulgore imaginem lunae continens redditque ea in dies singulos crescentis minuentisque sideris speciem, si uerum est'.

Ussher, *Sylloge*, 32-33 = MPL 87, 976 = **Br**, fol. 104ʳ [DRC § 98, pp 203-4]

1 UT CYRILLUS dicit *before* Scruteminique **Br**: Scrutemini quae diligentissimae **Br** 2 .xiiii. mas lunas **Br** 2-3 quem … fecit (5) *add. Cummian, om.* **Br** 4 fallantur **Br** 5 sequendi **Br** 6 Non faciamus **Br** heretricis **Br**; thesserescai.dechadite **Br** 8 atquae huic regulae poene omnes consentiunt, et qua nos utimur *add. after* thesserescai.dechadite **Br**, *which then cont.* : UT CIRILLUS dicit, *etc.*; inquit *om.* **Br** 8 praeter sinodum Gangressum et Cessariensum **Br** 8-9 ulla ciuitas uel regio uel ecclesia **Br** 9 hisq; **Br** 10 Et si … decrescit *om.* **Br**

Though it might at first appear that the Brussels computus here lacks the crucial reference to the Silenite stone that occurs in Cummian's Letter, in fact, however, if we recall the passage in Brussels that gave the names for the moon in the 'three principal languages' (fol. 92ᵛ, p. 106 above), we find that specific reference was there made to the name *Siline apud Aegyptios, unde lapis Silenitis dicitur,* which most probably derives from the Pseudo-Cyril letter.

4. The fourth authority cited in Brussels as support for the Dionysiac rule is another reference to the letter of Paschasinus, where that writer related to Pope Leo how, according to the testimony of his deacon Lollianus, there was a certain parish set in the most desolate parts of the country among rugged mountains and thick forests. In the baptistry of that little church the font regularly filled with water each Easter eve. But in AD 417, when the Church observed the Roman Easter on 25 March, the font had remained dry; but it filled miraculously at the usual hour on the eve of Sunday, 22 April, which was the date of Easter according to the Alexandrian reckoning.[36] The *miraculum Putei in Meltina* refers to this little village and its miraculous font. Whether Cummian was familiar with Paschasinus' letter *c.* AD 632 cannot be proved, since he does not cite it in his own. Nevertheless, the material we have examined so far strongly suggests that the doctrine propounded in the Brussels computus, based on Victorian-Dionysiac principles, was familiar to Cummian, and most of the texts on which that doctrine was based could have been available to him in a manuscript of the Sirmond group.

Is there any other support, then, for the suggestion that Cummian might also have been the author of our Brussels computus? In the manuscripts of the

36 Krusch, *Studien* 1, 249-50: 'Quaedam vilissima possessio Meltinas apellatur, in montibus arduis ac silvis densissimis constituta. Illic perparva atque vili opere constructa ecclesia est. In cuius baptisterio nocte sacrosancta paschali baptizandi hora, cum nullus canalis, nulla sit fistula nec aqua omnino vicina, fons ex sese repletur, paucisque qui fuerint consecratis, cum deductorium nullum habeat, ut aqua venerat, ex sese discendit. Tunc … cum apud occidentales error fuisset ortus … eum presbiter secundum morem baptizandi horam requireret, usque ad lucem aqua non veniente, non consecrati, qui baptizanti fuerant, recesserunt … illa nocte, qua lucscebat in diem dominicam, decima die kalendarum Maiarum fons sacer hora competenti repletus est. Evidenti ergo miraculo claruit, occidentalium partium errorem fuisse'.

Sirmond group there occurs a letter *De sollemnitatibus et neomeniis* which is usually ascribed to Jerome.[37] The letter has had mixed fortunes at the hands of modern computists.[38] It was first published in the Maurine edition of Jerome's works, although the editors did question its authenticity. It was subsequently re-edited by Hilberg in the Vienna *Corpus* (CSEL 56, 357-63, from the Vatican MS. Pal. Vat. 642, another MS. with Insular antecedents). Besides the manuscripts of the Sirmond group, however, the letter also occurs in Cologne, Dombibl., MS. 83² (*c.* AD 805, Cologne), another important representative of the seventh-century Irish computus, and was correctly catalogued by Krusch in his description of that manuscript.[39] Some years later, however, Krusch happened upon the letter again in Paris, Bibl. nat., MS. lat. 16361 (*saec.* XII) – a member of the Sirmond group – but failed to recognize it as the Pseudo-Jerome text which he had correctly identified at Cologne; Krusch republished the work as a 'lost' letter of Columbanus, basing his claim on the 'internal evidence'. The controversy that followed in the German journals concerning the authenticity of the letter nowhere made reference to the three previous editions, and so sure was Gundlach of Krusch's ascription that he published the work again as Letter VI in the MGH edition of Columbanus' works. Krusch subsequently withdrew his ascription to Columbanus, again on 'internal evidence'.[40]

Now, the letter *De sollemnitatibus* occurs, as I said, in the Sirmond group of manuscripts, but it is also cited by the Brussels computist. Immediately following the citation from Pseudo-Cyril (above, p. 103) the following passage occurs in the Brussels text:

> ET ISIDORUS dicit: 'Quicumque ante .xv. lunam pascha celebrari iubet, transgreditur mandatum Domini'. ITEM HIERONIMUS dicit: 'Cum Dominus, uerus agnus, uerum Pascha progreditur, in mundum aliquas

37 See Jones, *Bedae opera*,108-10. The text was also edited by Jean-Baptiste Pitra, *Spicilegium Solesmense* (2 vols, Paris 1852; repr. Graz 1962) 1, 6-13, from London, BL, MS. Cotton Caligula A XV (*saec.* VIII2) and Paris, BN, MS. lat. 16361 (*saec.* XII). Johannes W. Smit, *Studies on the language and style of Columba the Younger (Columbanus)* (Amsterdam 1971) 33 n. 1, remarks that 'nowadays the work is usually dated in the fifth century or even earlier', but he cites no authority for this statement. The work was considered but rejected as a possible letter of Pelagius by Georges de Plinval, *Pélage, ses écrits, sa vie et sa réforme. Étude d'histoire littéraire et religieuse* (Lausanne 1943) 43. The work may be Irish. An abbreviated version of the letter (beg. *De Pascha autem tamquam maximo sacramento*) also occurs in the MSS of the Sirmond group. [See also above, 'The computistical writings of Columbanus', 48-55.] 38 I follow the account by Jones, loc. cit. [See now below, 49-53.] 39 *Studien* 1, 195-205. 40 The work was re-edited among the *Dubia et spuria* by G.S.M. Walker, *Sancti Columbani opera*. Scriptores Latini Hiberniae 2 (Dublin 1957; repr. 1971) 198-206; cf. lx-lxi. Note, however, that Walker's statements concerning MS. affiliations are completely mistaken. For example, the BL, MS. Cotton Caligula A XV, fols 86ᵛ-90ʳ containing the *De sollemnitatibus* were dated by him '*saec.* XII/XIII', whereas Lowe, *Codices Latini Antiquiores* [CLA] 2 (Oxford 1935; 2nd rev. ed. 1972) No. 183, gives the date '*saec.* VIII²'.

permanere uolens custodiuit, aliquas non obseruare cupiens motauit'. Nam .xiiii. luna, umbralem relinquens et figuralem praeuidens, ueritatem per se expressam in dominicam diem cum luna pertransiuit.

Br fol. 104^(r-v) = **M** fols 31^v, 43v [DRC §99, p. 204]
2 Domini *om.* **M** HIERONIMUS] = Pseudo-Columbanus, *De sollemnitatibus* (Walker, 200, 14-15) 3 et uerum pascha progredituri **M** aliqua **Br M** alia non seruare **M** 6 per se et per suam **M**

The Pseudo-Jerome letter is not cited verbatim by Cummian but there are some grounds for believing that he knew it. An inferential reason for so believing is the fact (already stated) that he was familiar with much of the material in the Sirmond group of manuscripts in which both the Pseudo-Jerome letter and an epitome of it[41] occur close together. But there are also textual grounds for suggesting that Cummian knew the letter, which I cite here now:

> Quid plura ? Uenio ad apostolum item dicentem: *Fratres nemo uos seducat in parte diei festi aut neomenia aut sabbato, quae sunt umbra futurorum. Corpus autem Christi.* 'Dies festus', inquiens, 'pascha est, iuxta euangelistam Lucam dicentem: *Approprinquabat autem dies festus azimorum in quo necesse erat occidi Pascha.* Pascha occiditur et uiuificatur. Pars autem diei festi, .xiiii. luna, non totus dies, in qua seducimur; sed in parte et sabbato otioso, et neomenia bucinata, quae sunt umbra, non corpus, Christi; umbra occiditur, ueritas uiuificatur

Ussher, *Sylloge*, 28-29 = MPL 87, 973 [*Cummian's Letter*, 74]
4 festus iudaeorum *corr.* > azimorum MS. 5 ut uiuificatur MS., ueritas uiuificatur *conjectured by* Ussher (cf. 8 ueritas uiuificatur)

The citation, from Augustine, is another of Cummian's untraced sources, but that is not what concerns us here. What is interesting is that the wording of the Pauline citation (*Coloss.* 2, 16-17) NEMO UOS SEDUCAT occurs *only* in Cummian and in the Pseudo-Jerome letter.[42] It is of course possible (indeed, I think probable) that the Pseudo-Jerome letter is another Irish composition, and that both authors were drawing on the same Irish biblical text; but other passages in Cummian also suggest a dependence on the Pseudo-Jerome epistle; e.g.:

---

41 Cf. Walker, 200. The citation could thus have been taken from either the longer or the shorter version of the letter; but the short version has no ascription in the MSS. 42 This information I owe to the late Dr Hermann Frede of the Vetus Latina Institut, Beuron.

Deinde euangelio inueni Dominum meum Ihesum Christum dicentem: *Desiderio desideraui hoc pascha manducare uobiscum antequam patiar,* quod Ieronimus explanat: 'Finem', inquiens, 'carnali festiuitati uolens imponere umbraque transeunte paschae reddere ueritatem complens legem sicut dixit: *non ueni soluere legem sed adimplere,* hoc est addere'.

Ussher, *Sylloge*, 26 = MPL 87, 971 [*Cummian's Letter*, 120]

The Pseudo-Jerome citation here is another of Cummian's untraced sources, but the whole tenor of the passage seems to me very reminiscent of our Pseudo-Jerome letter, particularly the citation given above, p. 119.[43] There is another, more general, stylistic feature which the Brussels computist and Cummian have in common: in the Letter, Cummian endeavours to display an attitude of impartiality (as if that were possible !) in debating the Easter question. His opening remarks are a good example of his attitude:

> Ego enim primo anno quo cyclus quingentorum .xxx. duorum annorum a nostris celebrari orsus est non suscepi, sed silui; nec laudare nec uituperare ausus utpote Aebreos, Gregos, Latinos (quas linguas, ut Ieronimus ait, in crucis suae titulo Christum consecrauit) superare minime in scientia me credens.

Ussher, *Sylloge*, 24-25 = MPL 87, 969 [*Cummian's Letter*, 56-58]

The Brussels computist is likewise characterised by the judiciousness with which he compares the various conflicting computistical doctrines, setting them down side by side and debating their respective merits. An example is his treatment of the question *Sciendum nobis in qua aetate primitus creauit Deus lunam:*

> UICTORIUS OSTENDIT dicens: Luna 'die quarta existentis mundi, id est .v. Kl. Aprl. plena luna, hoc est .xiiii., iubente creatore inchoatione noctis exorta est'. Aliter AGUSTINUS dicit: 'Qualis etiam luna sit facta multi locacissime inquirunt. Dicunt enim ideo plenam factam, quia non decebat ut Deus inperfectum aliquid illo die faceret in sideribus, quo scripture est quod facta sint sidera. Qui autem resistunt, dicunt ipsa ergo debuit luna prima dici, non .xiiii. Quis enim incipit ita numerare ? Ego autem medius inter istos ita sum, ut neutrumque adseram, sed plane

---

43 The same tract may also have provided the inspiration for a curious phrase in Cummian's Letter, where he defends his elders and predecessors in the southern Irish churches against the strictures of Ségéne: *Seniores uero nostri, quos in uelamine repulsionis habetis*; cf. Pseudo-Jerome, who refers to his opponents as men *uelamine posito super faciem Moysi spiritus et ueritatis luce illuminari nequent* (Walker, 198).

dicam, siue primam siue plenam lunam Deus fecerit, fecisse perfectam. Ipsarum enim naturam Deus auctor et conditor.

Br fol. 94ʳ [DRC §67, p. 178]
VICTORIUS] *Prol. in cyclo paschal.* (Krusch, *Studien* 2, 23) 3 AGUSTINUS] *De Genesi ad litt.* (CSEL 28/2, 56) 7 debuit] debunt **Br** 8 neutrumque] que *om. De Gen.*

In summary, then, what is the case for the proposition that Cummian, author of the Letter to Ségéne *c.* AD 632/33 was the author also of the Brussels computus ? We may list the facts *seriatim* in order of importance:

1. The pseudo-patristic authorities cited by Cummian in the Letter occur also in Brussels and in *no other computus;*
2. The Brussels computist drew on a body of texts similar to that which Cummian used;
3. The Brussels computus shows, in its contents and doctrine and in the material which it has in common with the Munich and Milan computi, clear signs of a seventh-century Irish origin;
4. Even allowing for the inevitable similarity of terminology when discussing computistic material, stylistic features in both texts suggest a possibility of common authorship.

If it is accepted that the Brussels computus has its origins in southern Ireland in the mid-seventh century then the ramifications are many and important. In the first place, it would be possible to conclude with certainty that at least two of Isidore's works were in circulation in Ireland a generation or more before their appearance in England, for the Brussels computist draws extensively on the *Etymologiae* and on the *De natura rerum*.[44] Though there is evidence to show that 'unofficial' versions of the *Etymologiae* were circulating in Spain some years before Isidore's death in AD 636[45] there seems to be a general consensus that the official edition by Braulio of Saragossa did not leave the country for some time after that date. But the length of time between publication in Spain and reception in Ireland appears to have been remarkably short, for Bischoff, in his discussion of the dissemination of Isidore's works in the early medieval period,[46] has stated that the St Gall fragment containing a part

---

44 There are several passages, ascribed to Isidore, which I have not yet managed to identify.
45 Braulio of Saragossa, *Ep.* XII [IV] (cited by Lindsay, 8): 'Ergo et hoc notesco, libros etymologiarum, quos a te domino meo [sc. Isidore] posco, etsi detruncatos conrososque iam a multi haberi'. [For a suggestion that Isidore's works may have come to Ireland as a direct result of contact with Braulio, see above, 94 n. 44.]   46 'Die europäische Verbreitung der Werke Isidors von Sevilla', in Manuel C. Díaz y Díaz (ed), *Isidoriana. Estudios sobre San Isidoro de Sevilla en el XIV centenario de su nacimiento* (Léon 1961) 317-44; repr. in Bischoff's *Mittelalterliche Studien* I (Stuttgart 1966) 171-94.

of *Etym.* XI (which he thinks was written in Ireland) may, on palaeographical grounds, be dated close to the publication date of Braulio's edition, 'if not indeed to Isidore's own lifetime'.[47] The evidence hitherto available to scholars has been slight,[48] but the Brussels text would set the case for dating Isidore's reception into Ireland on an entirely new footing. More importantly, it would show that Fontaine's statement, that the *De natura rerum* was cited by no Irish writer before AD 685,[49] is quite mistaken; the text tradition of that work requires a complete re-examination. Not only does the Brussels computist draw on it, but so too does the contemporary *De ratione temporum* (before AD 658), indicating that Isidore's scientific works had already, by that time, been enthusiastically received into at least some of the southern Irish schools.

Besides, the evidence of Laidcend's *Ecloga de Moralibus in Iob* (before AD 661)[50] proves that Isidore's *De ortu et obitu patrum* was also available at Clonfert Mo-Lua, for Laidcend quotes a lengthy passage from the work. There are also strong grounds for believing that the Lorica ascribed to Laidcend in the oldest and best manuscripts drew on Isidore's *Etymologiae* and perhaps also his *De natura rerum*;[51] and Laidcend may well have been associated with Cummian.[52] Furthermore, if Bischoff is correct in proposing that the St Paul Kärnten Latin grammar known as the Anonymus ad Cuimnanum[53] was addressed to our Cummian then that too would provide clear proof that Isidore's writings were known in Ireland as early as the early seventh century, for that work clearly draws on his *Differentiae* and on DNR.[54] Cummian appears not to have used any of the

47 *Mittelalterliche Studien* I, 180: 'Zeitlich dürfte das St. Galler Stück in die Nähe der Veröffentlichung der Etymologiae durch Braulio, wenn nicht sogar noch in die Lebenszeit Isidors gehören'.   48 See Michael Herren, 'On the earliest Irish acquaintance with Isidore of Seville', in Edward James (ed), *Visigothic Spain: new approaches* (Oxford 1980) 243-50 [repr. in Michael Herren, *Latin letters in early christian Ireland*. Variorum Collected Studies CS 527 (Aldershot 1996) chap. III].   49 'On ne trouve aucune trace du *De natura rerum* dans les œuvres des écrivains irlandais antérieures à 685', in Jacques Fontaine (ed & transl), *Isidore de Seville, Traité de la nature, suivi de l'Épitre en vers du roi Sisebut à Isidore* (Bordeaux 1960) 76. Prof. Wesley Stevens has written to me that 'none of Fontaine's evidence for MS. A [of DNR] deriving from Northumbria is valid. Bede did not use Isidori DNR in that form (long version); his short form could have come from any part of England just as well. On the other hand the Anonymus ad Cuimnanum, which is addressed to a Cummian from an unknown place, did use Isidori DNR III in the FASB (long) version, and exists only in one Anglo-Saxon MS.' (letter of 23 Dec. 1981). See further n. 53 below.   50 See Marc Adriaen (ed), *Egloga quam scripsit Lathcen filius Baith de Moralibus Iob quas Gregorius fecit.* CCSL 145 (Turnhout 1969) 3.   51 Louis Gougaud, 'Le temoignage des manuscrits sur l'œuvre littéraire du moine Latchen', *Revue Celtique* 30 (1909) 37-46; Michael Herren, 'The authorship, date of composition and provenance of the so-called *Lorica Gildae*', *Ériu* 24 (1973) 35-51.   52 See esp. Mgr Michael Moloney, 'Beccan's hermitage in Aherlow: the riddle of the slabs', *North Munster Antiquarian Jnl* 9/3 (1964) 99-107. Further evidence for the possible association of the two will appear in our forthcoming edition of Cummian's Letter. [See now Walsh & Ó Cróinín, *Cummian's Letter*, 11-12.]   53 Benediktinerstift St Paul in Kärnten, MS. 25. 2. 16 (*saec.* VIII) fols 21-42; see Bischoff, 'Eine verschollene Einteilung der Wissenschaften', *Archives d'histoire doctrinale et littéraire du moyen-âge* 25 (1958) 5-20 = *Mittelalterliche Studien* I, 273-88, esp. 282-88. The precise origins of this text have yet to be determined.   Dr Vivien Law of Cambridge has suggested to me that the Epilogue (containing the

Spanish Father's corpus in his Letter of *c.* AD 632, and the obvious inference would seem to be that it had not yet reached Ireland by that date. The evidence for dating the Brussels computus, on the other hand, would seem to point more clearly to the mid-seventh century, by which time it may well have arrived.

A second important consequence of our mid-seventh-century dating of the Brussels computus and its localization in Ireland is that Michael Herren's[55] recently stated conclusion 'that the first literary use of Virgilius Maro Grammaticus that can be dated fairly securely occurred in England some time between 673 and 690' is contradicted. The fact that Virgilius is cited by name in our text on a number of occasions is itself sufficient evidence that he was known in Ireland at least twenty years before the earliest possible appearance of his works in England,[56] and the *De ratione temporum* (which existed in an archetype in AD 658) is confirmation of that general *terminus post quem non* in Ireland, for Virgil is cited in that collection as well.

That neither Isidore nor Virgilius Maro Grammaticus was cited by Cummian in the Letter need not, of course, tell decisively against the possibility of his having composed the Brussels computus, for it is more than likely that he had written the Letter before the appearance of Isidore's corpus or Virgilius' curiosities. But once they had made their appearance, it is to be expected that he (and those in his immediate circle) would have felt free to use both in the composition of the Brussels text There are, on the other hand, a number of details in the Letter and the computus which might give rise to doubt about the possibility of their common authorship. With reference to the lunar limits for the date of Easter, for example, the Letter reads:

> Unde ad passionem ueniens [Dominus] uetusque consummans testamentum et nouum inchoans, quinta feria, luna .xiiii. primi mensis, qui est aput Aebreos Nisan, apud Macedones Spantoriacos, aput Aegiptios Parmothi, *etc.*

> Ussher, *Sylloge*, 26 = MPL 87, 971 [*Cummian's Letter*, 64]

address to Cuimnanus) may have been grafted on to an eighth-century work. [See her more recent study, *Authority, wisdom and grammar*, cited p. 181 n. 1.] Professor Stevens has written: 'Correspondences of its text with Isidori DNR III are definite: variants of the text given by Hillgarth [see next note] are found in MSS A and S and perhaps in a corrector of B. According to Fontaine, MSS FASB form a group whose exemplar (perhaps A) derived from England and came to Fulda where it was copied. Yet, none of Fontaine's evidence for MS. A deriving from Northumbria is valid'. A final verdict on the work must await the appearance of the promised edition by Burchard Taeger and Bischoff. [See now Bengt Löfstedt & Bernhard Bischoff (eds), *Anonymus ad Cuimnanum, Expositio Latinitatis*. CCSL 133D (Turnhout 92) xxi-xxii.]   **54** See Jocelyn N. Hillgarth, 'Visigothic Spain and early Christian Ireland', PRIA 62 C 6 (1962) 167-94: 187-88.   **55** 'Some new light on the life of Virgilius Maro Grammaticus', PRIA 79 C 2 (1979) 27-71.   **56** For discussion of the date of Aldhelm's *Ep.* V *ad Heafridum*, which appears to cite a line from Virgilius, see Michael Lapidge and Michael Herren (transls), *Aldhelm. The prose works* (Ipswich 1979) 143-46. [See now also David Howlett, 'Seven studies in Hiberno-Latin texts', *Peritia* 10 (1996) 1-71: 57.]

The name of the first Macedonian month *Spantoriacos* does not accord with the name *Xanthicos* in the Calendar of Polemius Silvius and other early Latin lists of the months,[57] but the lists given in Brussels and H (p. 105 above) suggest how the form in Cummian's letter may come about. Insular uses of *n*, *p*, *r* and *s* were very often misread by continental scribes and the same might be expected of the Anglo-Norman scribe in England who transcribed the only surviving copy of the Letter. A form like *Psanticos* (Psanticus H) could easily have become *Spanticos*, and a marginal attempt to identify the *Macedones* with the *Sparticos* or some such may have multiplied the confusion if it later merged into some form like *Spantoriacos*. However it arose, the garbled name in the Letter need not preclude the use of a similar (or even identical) source by Cummian and by the author of the Brussels computus.

But there is another apparent disparity between the two texts on the subject of the *saltus lunae* ('moon's leap'), the calculation whereby the age of the moon was to increase artificially by one at a regular point in the 19-year lunar cycle. In his treatment in the Letter of the various cycles which he had to hand, Cummian remarked that they differed fron one another *alium in die, alium in luna, alium in mense, alium in bissexto, alium in epacta, alium in aucmento lunari (quod uos* [i.e. Ségéne] *saltum dicitis*)(= MPL 87, 975). We may compare the following passage from the Brussels computus (fol. 106ᵛ):

> Sciendum nobis est quot nomina saltus habet. Sex uidelicet. Id est natu-ralia .ii., augmentum lunare et incrementum lunare. Et haec duo nomina dum praeparatur sibi conueniunt. Quattuor uero in adnumeratione. Luna una cum apparet, adiectio lunae cum addit aetatem, ut .xxx. facit in .xi. Kl. Apr., motatio lunae, cum transilit [.x]xviiii. in .xxx.; et sic saltus dicitur, *quo nomine nos utimur.* (My italics)
>
> [DRC §110, pp 210-11]. Cf. **M** fol. 42ᵛ, which has the same material in slightly different wording. See also the Pseudo-Alcuin text *De saltu lunae*, MPL 101, 988D, where five names are listed. (The **Br** text should be emended accordingly.)

Here, however, it must be stressed that the difference is not significant and does not imply that Iona computists used the term *saltus*, while their southern-Irish counterparts used *augmentum lunare*. Rather, these words are further evidence

---

57 Cf. J.F. Mountford, 'De mensium nominibus', *Jnl Hellenic Studies* 43 (1923) 102-16; the Calendar of Polemius Silvius, in Theodor Mommsen (ed), *Corpus Inscriptionum Latinarum* 1, Inscriptiones Latinae Antiquissimae (Berlin 1863) 335-57, and Charles W. Jones, 'Polemius Silvius, Bede and the names of the months', *Speculum* 9 (1934) 50-56 [= *Bede, the schools and the computus*, chap. VI].

for the case made above, that at the time he wrote the Letter, Cummian did not regard himself primarily as a computist, but as an exegete; whence he invokes the technical term *saltus* (the meaning of which is not immediately clear to the uninitiated) in deference to the computists of Iona. That this was the case may be demonstrated by reference to an exactly parallel usage in the Irish Pseudo-Augustine's *De mirabilibus sacrae scripturae* (AD 655),[58] where that writer –though dealing with exegesis and not computus – gives a brief but succinct description of the use of (Victorian) cycles, in the following words:[59]

> Quorum [sc. cycles] unusquisque uniformi statu peractis quingentis triginta duobus annis in semetipsum, id est in sequentis initium reuoluitur, completis uidelicet in unoquoque solaribus octo uicenis nono decies et lunaribus decemnouenalibus uicies octies circulis. Post quos et in lunari supputatione per [annos] communes duodecim et embolismos septem per ogdoadem et endecadem et incrementum lunare, *quod computatores saltum nominabant.* (my italics)

The words *incrementum lunare, quod computatores saltum nominabant* are clearly those of a writer who felt himself to be primarily an exegete, one whose competence in matters computistical – though thorough – was only incidental. The same may be assumed for Cummian – at least for the time he composed his Letter to Ségéne. For that document is not, strictly speaking, a computistical one; it is the work of a biblical and exegetical scholar, a canon lawyer and an administrator, and only then a computist. The Cummian of the Letter had two terms for the 'moon's leap', the Brussels computist had six; that may be seen as a possible development of Cummian's computistical knowledge, but it cannot be taken as proof that he could not have composed the Brussels text.

There is, however, a passage in Brussels whose importance needs no emphasizing: an explicit citation from an otherwise unattested work of *Palumbus*. The only person of such a name in early Irish documents, to my knowledge, is Columbanus, who in his Epistola V, directed to Pope Boniface, signs himself by that name.[60] If this identification of Palumbus with the monk of Bangor can

---

58 MPL 35, 2149-200. See William Reeves, 'On Augustin, an Irish writer of the seventh century', PRIA 7 (1861) 514-22; Mario Esposito, 'On the pseudo-Augustinian treatise "De Mirabilibus Sacrae Scripturae"', PRIA 35 C 2 (1919) 189-207. [For further literature see now Michael Lapidge & Richard Sharpe, *A bibliography of Celtic-Latin literature 400-1200*. Royal Irish Academy, Dictionary of Medieval Latin from Celtic Sources, Ancillary Publications 1 (Dublin 1985) 79, No. 291.] 59 Book II 4 (MPL 35, 2176). The italics are mine. 60 'Rara avis scribere audet Bonifatio patri Palumbus', Walker, 36. See Smit, *Studies in the language and style of Columba*, 149-57. Since this paper went to press I have found citations of the *Palumbus* passage in 'St. Dunstan's classbook' Oxford, Bodleian Library, MS. Auct. F. 4/32, fol. 22ʳ (without identification of author), and in manuscripts of the Sirmond group (with a more complete text than the one in Brussels. The technical details of this passage will be discussed on another occasion. It should also be noted that extensive borrowings from the Brussels text are to to be found in the

stand (and there seems to be nothing to gainsay it) then the Brussels computus provides an important independent citation of Columbanus as an authority on the computus. The passage concerned occurs in a discussion of the First Month:

> Sciendum nobis, cum .ii. lunae in uno mense inueniuntur, quae est de illis luna ipsius mensis. Quae finitur in mense, ipsa est luna ipsius mensis. Luna uero sequens, si non pertingerit Kl. mensis sequentis, abortiua luna uocabitur, quam alii dicunt lunam esse embolismi, quod non est uerum, UT PALUMBUS: 'Illius mensis conputa lunam quae in eo finitur, non quae incipit. Unde quae primum prioris aut initium sequentis non tenet, abortiua dicitur'.

Br fol. 95^r. [DRC §70, p. 178]. This passage occurs also in Strasbourg, Bibl. Uni., MS. 326 (*saec.* XI) fol. 149^v, with the heading: DE DVABUS LVNATIONIBUS IN VNO MENSE ET DE LVNA ABORTIVA. I list the variants here as **S**

1 lunationes S 2 luna (1°)] lunationibus S lunatio S ipsa] ipse **Br**
3 sequentis S si *om.* S 4 embolisma S 5 illi mensi **Br** illius S

Now, such a reference to Columbanus (if indeed the reference is to him) could only come from an Irish monastery or from a Columban foundation on the continent. It has already been seen that some of the material in the Brussels computus occurs also in the Milan collection, which undoubtedly preserves a part at least of the computistical doctrine current in Columbanus' Frankish foundations, and the Munich Computus may have followed a similar route. The preservation in it of an otherwise unknown phrase from the letter of *Iohannes consiliarius* (AD 640) is one of a number of reasons for suggesting that M may have been compiled in the north (possibly Iona), and the compilation date of *c.* AD 718 is strikingly close to the time when Iona finally made the changeover to the 'Roman' Easter-reckoning – a transition which took place in AD 716. If M were indeed a northern (or Iona) compilation then the presence in it of the *Iohannes consiliarius* citation would be easily explained, for that text would have still had a relevance there that it had long since lost in the south. There are, in fact, very few tangible indications that the northern Irish in general adopted 'Roman' tables before Iona,[61] and the most likely source for

---

marginal commentary added to Angers, Bibl. munic., MS. 477 (*saec.* IX Breton ?), a collection of Bede's scientific works. [For St. Dunstan's 'Classbook', see R.W. Hunt (ed), *Saint Dunstan's 'Classbook' from Glastonbury (Oxford, Bodleian Library, MS. Auct. F. 4/32)*. Umbrae codicum occidentalium 4 (Leyden 1961), and 'Columbanus, the computistical writings', above, 48-55.]
61 Levison suggested that Adomnán, in his *Vita Columbae,* may have used one or two phrases from the introductory letter to Dionysius' Easter-table; see Gertrud Brüning, 'Adamnan's Vita Columbae und ihre Ableitungen', *Zeitschrift für celtische Philologie* 11 (1917) 213-303: 243-44. I

such texts would have been those monasteries in the south of Ireland which 'had long since learned to celebrate Easter in accordance with canonical custom'. Since it has been established that M drew verbatim on the passage in Pseudo-Augustine's *De mirabilibus* dealing with Victorian cycles, this too is evidence which suggests a northward flow of texts.[62] If this was indeed the background to the compilation of the Munich Computus it could be seen, perhaps, as marking the final stage in the paschal controversy among the Irish churches, while the Brussels text would belong to the previous generation and a different milieu.

In the final analysis, then, it seems fair to conclude that the Brussels computus does indeed derive from the same circle of thinking in which Cummian, the author of the Paschal Letter, was writing. Identity of particular material, stylistic similarities, and the basic structure of both texts would suggest as much. Whether Cummian was himself the author cannot, however, be proved conclusively from the evidence presently available. But the possibility should not be ruled out. If Cummian was indeed the author then we should have to presume a later date for his composition of the computus than for the Paschal Letter; a dating somewhere around the mid-seventh century would probably be a reasonable estimate. But whatever about its authorship, the computus is a not unworthy addition to the corpus of seventh-century Hiberno-Latin works.

ACKNOWLEDGEMENTS

I wish to thank Professor Gearóid Mac Niocaill, University College, Galway, and Jean Rittmueller and John Armstrong of Harvard, for reading a draft of this paper and suggesting corrections. I owe a particular debt to Professor Wesley Stevens, University of Winnipeg, who gave me the benefit of his deep erudition and made numerous corrections and suggestions for improvement. I also owe a special debt of gratitude to Professor Bernhard Bischoff, Munich, for invaluable help and advice regarding the manuscripts discussed in this paper. My wife Maura also provided stimulating criticism.

APPENDIX: THE DATE AND PROVENANCE OF BRUSSELS 5413-22

Date

The dating of the manuscript rests mainly on the material in fols 73^v-77^v. Fol. 73^v begins a set of synchronisins with the HEADING NUMERUS ANNORUM AB

---

have myself shown elsewhere that the evidence previously offered in support of the contention that the Dionysiac reckoning had been received at Bangor already before AD 610 is in fact spurious; see my paper 'Mo Sinu maccu Min and the computus at Bangor', *Peritia* 1 (1982) 281-95 [above, 35-47].   **62** I have discussed this northward flow of texts at greater length in a paper entitled 'The Irish background to Bede's computus', for which see n. 13 above [= 'The Irish provenance of Bede's computus', below, 173-80].

INITIO MUNDI SECUNDUM EUSEBIUM ET CETEROS USQUE IN PRAESENTEM ANNUM. The crucial passage of the text is here given in full:

> A natiuitate autem Christi usque ad praesens tempus secundum supputationes et cyclos et argumenta antiquorum patrum conputantur anni DCCCUIIII, qui simul collecti ab initio mundi usque ad praesentem. annum fiunt VI milia et VIII. [809 + Eusebian *anno mundi* 5199 = 6008]

This dating is confirmed by the passage that immediately follows, which ends this section of the synchronisms:

> Si uis scire annos ab initio mundi conputa quindecies/ [fol. 74ʳ] CCCCtos; fiunt VI milia. Adiece regulares, fiunt VI milia [et II]. Adde indictionem praesentis anni, utputa secundum [*leg.* sextum], fiunt simul anni VI milia et VIIII [*leg.* VIII]. Iste est numerus annorum ab initio mundi usque ad praesentem annum.

The first passage clearly gives AD 809 as the date of composition for the synchronism (though not necessarily for the manuscript). This date is supported by the second passage, despite its obvious corruptions. The first passage was noted by Henri Silvestre, 'Notices et extraits', *Sacris Erudiri* 5 (1953) 174-92: 181; but he assigned only a general dating 'saec. IX' to the manuscript as a whole. This is the dating also in J. Van den Gheyn, *Catalogue des manuscrits de la Bibliothèque royale de Belgique* 4 (Brussels 1904) 60-61. Neither of these works is referred to by François Masai and others, *Manuscrits datés conservés en Belgique 819-1400* (Brussels-Ghent 1968) 55, No. Al.

Masai refers only to H. Michel's *Les manuscrits astronomiques de la Bibliothèque royale de Belgique* (Brussels 1949) 199-200 (which I have not seen), where he says the date AD 807 was assigned to the section contained in fols 73ᵛ-77ᵛ. Michel's dating was based on the Carolingian additions made to the *Abbreviatio chronicae* that begins on fol. 74ʳ with the heading: IN DEI NOMINE SERIES ANNORUM AB INITIO MUNDI SECUNDUM HEBRAICAM UERITATEM, UT ALII DICUNT, which comprises a brief synchronism of the Six Ages of the World, ending (fol. 77ᵛ) with a notice of Charlemagne's reign:

> Et inde dominus carolus solus. regnum suscepit et deo protegente gubernat usque in praesentem. Feliciter qui est annus regni eius .xxxviiii. imperii. autem .vii. sunt autem totius summe ab origine mundi usque in praesentem annum. IIII (*sic*).

Masai rightly remarked that this date denoted only the year in which the synchronism was compiled, but that it need not necessarily provide a date for the transcription of the whole manuscript. He did not note, however, that the

Carolingian section of the synchronism had been published by Georg Pertz, 'Chronica de sex aetatibus mundi', in MGH *Scriptores* 2 (1829; repr. 1968) 256. According to Pertz, 'habetur in plurimis per Germaniam, Italiam, Galliamque codicibus … quos inter codex olim Salisburgensis iam Vindobonensis, sub Arnone archiepiscopo, saeculo nono exeunte exaratus, antiquitate et pulchritudine praestat'. (He probably meant Österreichische Nationalbibliothek, MS. 387 (AD 809-21).) Since the synchronism occurs in innumerable manuscripts, and since the Brussels copy is obviously defective in its figures, the text can offer no guide to the date of the manuscript. Pertz's text gives AD 810 as the final year of the synchronism: the Brussels manuscript (and Monte Cassino, MS. 3, p. 114, which also has it) gives AD 807. It is evident therefore that different scribes brought the work up to date, and Masai makes the point that since this was so, it would have been natural for a copyist to note such an event as Charlemagne's death, had it occurred. Since it is not noted in the Brussels manuscript he concluded that the transcription date for fols 73^v-77^v at least was 'après 807, probablement avant 814'.

In a letter of January 1982 Professor Bernhard Bischoff, with characteristic generosity, supplied the following detailed breakdown of the manuscript, with dates and (where possible to identify) provenances of the respective parts:

> fols 1-14; 15-41 (*saec.* IX², Rheims)
>
> fols 42-49　(*saec.* X¹)
>
> fols 50-62 (c. *saec.* IX-X, Rheims)
>
> fols 63-108; 117-24: 'die beiden Teile sind nicht von identischen, aber sehr ähnlichen Händen geschrieben, meines Erachtens s. IX² Nord-Frankreich';
>
> fols 109-116 'ist eine eingeschaltete Lage, s. X';
>
> fols 125-28 'bretonisch, *saec.* IX¹'.

Provenance

Silvestre, art. cit., 177, refers to an article by Nolte, 'Une lettre inédite de l'archevêque Hincmar de Reims', in *Revue des sciences ecclésiastiques*, 4th Ser., 6 (1877) 279-85, where it was apparently suggested that not only the section of the manuscript (front flyleaf) containing the letter of Hincmar to Hardvicus and Teutgaudus, but perhaps the whole codex was written by Hincmar himself; but Nolte apparently thought it more likely that the codex simply belonged to Hincmar's library. Silvestre regarded the suggestion as plausible. (I have not seen Frederick M. Carey, 'The scriptorium of Reims during the archbishopric of Hincmar (845-882 AD)', in Leslie Webber Jones (ed) *Classical and medieval studies in honour of Edward Kennard Rand* (New York 1938) 41-60.)

ADDITIONAL NOTE

In the course of a visit to Professor Wesley Stevens at Winnipeg (25-28 November 1982) I discovered the existence of a second manuscript of the computus discussed in this paper: Vatican MS. Reg. Lat. 1260 (*saec.* IX, Fleury ?) fols 87ᵛ-99ᵛ. The text in the two manuscripts is identical. [Not quite: the Vatican MS. has abbreviated some sections of the text; see Walsh & Ó Cróinín, *Cummian's Letter*, 107-9.]

10

An Old Irish gloss in the Munich computus[*]

The Munich, Bayerische Staatsbibliothek, manuscript Clm 14456 has been much discussed by computistical scholars[1] because it preserves the only substantial description of the early Irish 84-year Paschal cycle that we possess. The manuscript is a ninth-century copy, written at Regensburg in Bavaria, made from an Irish exemplar which itself was a compilation of *c*. AD 718. This original compilation comprised two tracts, one a discussion of the Alexandrian 19-year cycle, the other a section on the 84-year cycle just mentioned. Dating formulae within the text suggest the year AD 689 for the compilation of the 19-year tract, though the material incorporated into the text may be said to date roughly from the period after AD 655.[2]

The indefatigable Bartholomew Mac Carthy was the first to show[3] conclusively that the Munich computus was an Irish compilation, and in proof of his contention he published a long list of orthographical and other features from the manuscript.[4] Particularly significant in this list was a passage in a chapter *De mundo* which discussed the three great 'immovable years' in world history: the year of Creation, the year of Exodus from Egypt, and the year of the Passion. Concerning the precise date of Creation the author of the computus has this to say:

> Prima enim creatio in uere facta est, in .xii. K. Apr.; id est, ui hore resta-
> bant de .xii., die dominico. A .ui. hora dominici usque in .ui. horam dies
> lunes, .xi. K. Apr.; a .ui hora diei lunis usque in .ui. horam diei Martis,

---

[*] First published in *Éigse* 18 (1981) 289-90. 1 See Bruno Krusch, *Studien zur christlich-mittelal-terlichen Chronologie [1]: Der 84-jährige Ostercyclus und seine Quellen* (Leipzig 1880) 10 ff.; idem, *Studien zur christlich-mittelalterlichen Chronologie [2]: Die Entstehung unserer heutigen Zeitrechnung,* Abhandlungen der Preußischen Akademie der Wissenschaften, philol.-hist. Kl., 8, Jahrgang 1937 (Berlin 1938) 58; Eduard Schwarz, 'Christliche und jüdische Ostertafeln', *Abhandlungen der königl. Gesellschaft der Wissenschaften zu Göttingen,* phil.-hist. Kl., N. F., Nr. 8 vi (1905) 89-104; Bartholomew Mac Carthy (ed & transl), *Annals of Ulster* 4 (Dublin-London 1901) lxvii-lxxxiii. 2 See Charles W. Jones, *Bedae pseudepigrapha. Scientific writings falsely attributed to Bede* (Ithaca, N.Y. 1939) 48-51[= *Bede, the schools and the computus,* pt 2]. The author cites, among other texts, the Irish Ps. Augustine's *De mirabilibus sacrae scripturae,* which is dated to AD 655. 3 AU 4, lxviii-lxxi, correcting some of the errors of Krusch, 'Die Einführung des griechischen Paschalritus im Abendlande', *Neues Archiv* 9 (1884) 101-69, who, e.g., thought Pseudo-Augustine, *De mirabilibus,* was written *against* the Irish! 4 op. cit., clxxviii-ix, App. B 1.

.x. K. Aprl.; a .ui. hora Martis usque in .ui. horam *diei cetene,* .uiiii. K.
Apr.[5]

Here, for 'Wednesday', we have the form *dies cetene,* and Mac Carthy
(rightly, as I think) explained that the author – thinking in his native Irish –
seems to have been misled by the similarity of sound between the oblique cases
diei lunae = *dia luain,* and *diei martis* = *dia mairt,* into writing *diei cetene* as the
equivalent of the Latin *diei mercurii* in the third item of the jingle. He used the
form on two further occasions[6] in exactly the same circumstances, and similar
intrusions of Old Irish can be detected elsewhere in the Latin text.

Mac Carthy, however, overlooked another Irish gloss in the Latin text, a
form that bears out all his contentions about the origin of the computus. On
fol. 26[r], in a chapter entitled *De quattuor partibus mundi,* the author asks how
the smallest movements of the moon are calculated, and replies: *Cum sint
propria solis;* but he adds the caveat: *Siue* (MS. *sine*) *uerius Augustinus ait, 'a
parte solis numerantur', quia luna* tomel *diem solis,* i.e. the moon 'consumes' the
solar day! This occurrence of the Old Irish verb *do-meil* (with archaic pretonic
to-) is another clear indication of the seventh-century Irish origin of the
Munich computus.

---

5 Clm 14456, fol. 24[r]; Mac Carthy, op. cit., clxxx, App. B 2.   6 Fols. 24[r] 13-19 and 24[v] 6-15.

11

Early Echternach manuscript fragments with Old Irish glosses[*]

Among the manuscripts listed by E.A. Lowe in his great *Codices Latini Antiquiores* (CLA) as belonging to the monastery of Echternach in Luxembourg was a fragmentary volume, of which two folios survive in Paris, Bibliothèque Nationale, MS. lat. 10399, (Suppl. lat. 1894) fols 35 + 36.[1] This manuscript is a miscellany of various bits and pieces recovered from the bindings of other codices, brought together to form what a note on the flyleaf describes as *Fragmenta variorum codicum ad theologiam et ad jus spectantium.* The two leaves that concern us are badly worn in places and have lost parts of their texts as a result of the activities of the binder's knife. Enough survives, however, to enable a partial reconstruction of their former contents, together with a discussion of their possible provenance. Because the fragments contain a number of Old Irish glosses not previously noticed,[2] they have an importance belied by their present sorry state.

The principal reason for Lowe's ascription of our fragments to Echternach is the fact that they were recovered from the binding of a later codex from that monastery. He described the script (CLA V 585) as being a 'mixed Anglo-Saxon majuscule and minuscule, saec. VIII … written presumably in England, or possibly at Echternach, where the fragments were later used for binding purposes'. Here, however, the Bibliotheksheimat may have influenced Lowe's judgement of the Schriftheimat, for Professor Bernhard Bischoff has written more recently that 'Die Bestimmung von CLA V 585 als "angelsächsisch" war unvorsichtig wegen des eigenartigen Schriftcharakters … Es läßt sich nichts gegen irische Entstehung vorbringen, im Gegenteil (z. B. spelling)'.[3] Lowe in

---

[*] First published in Georges Kiesel & Jean Schroeder (eds), *Willibrord. Apostel der Niederlande, Gründer der Abtei Echternach. Gedenkgabe zum 1250. Todestag des angelsächsischen Missionars* (Luxemburg 1989) 135-43. [The Old Irish and Latin glosses were re-edited by me in 'The Old Irish and Old English glosses in Echternach manuscripts (with an appendix on Old Breton manuscripts)', in Michele Camillo-Ferrari, Jean Schroeder & Henri Trauffler (eds), *Die Abtei Echternach 698-1998* (Luxembourg 1999) 85-95: 92.] 1 CLA V 585. Lowe was, I think, mistaken in his belief that the single folio of Easter tables bound up with Paris, Bibl. Nat., MS. lat. 9527, as fol. 201, was part of the same manuscript. The dimensions of that single folio must have been quite different from those of the other two folios, and besides, the script is, in my view, by a different hand. See plates 5, 6, 7, 8. 2 They are not mentioned by Lowe, who in fact passed over one of them without comment, although he reproduced it in his CLA plate. 3 In a letter to the writer dated 22 January 1982.

his plate reproduced a part of the Paris fragments containing an Old Irish gloss – but without any comment. This single Old Irish gloss, however, was enough to awaken the suspicion that perhaps the manuscript was written by an Irishman rather than by an Englishman.[4] Further firsthand examination of the two Paris leaves has revealed the presence of five (possibly six) other Old Irish glosses (one of them a double-gloss). This being the case, it is time to look again at the manuscript and its contents in order to see how this new evidence can he brought to bear on the problem of establishing its provenance and authorship. Our findings will have obvious implications for the continuing debate about the earliest Echternach scriptorium and its personnel.

Lowe stated that the Paris fragments contain the text of Anatolius of Laodicea, *De Pascha*.[5] This was a work well-known to the Irish, and is cited as an authority by Columbanus in his letters to Rome AD 600 and to the Gallican bishops AD 603.[6] Anatolius is also cited by the southern Irish cleric Cummian in his letter on the Easter controversy addressed to abbot Ségéne of Iona, AD 632/3. In addition, the work is quoted (often at length) in every early Irish computistical collection known to me.[7] The great Bruno Krusch demonstrated over a century ago that the work is probably an Irish forgery of the sixth century, whose manuscript transmission is almost exclusively Irish or derived from Irish exemplars. Hence the nature of the text itself provides additional grounds for suspecting an Irish involvement in the production of the Paris manuscript.

In fact, however, the Paris leaves, fragmentary though they are, contain not just one text (as Lowe's description would suggest) but six, all of which I have been able to identify. Three of them are works usually regarded as Irish computistical forgeries (Pseudo-Athanasius, Pseudo-Anatolius, and Pseudo-Theophilus),[8] while the three others are excerpts from Augustine, *De Genesi ad litteram* II. 14, Gaudentius, *De paschae obseruatione*, and an excerpt from the Book of Numbers, also concerned with Easter. Hence the contents of the

---

4 The suggestion was first made in Dáibhí Ó Cróinín, 'Pride and Prejudice', *Peritia* 1 (1982) 352-62: 360-61; cf. idem, 'Rath Melsigi, Willibrord, and the earliest Echternach manuscripts', *Peritia* 3 (1984) 17-49: 26-28.   5 For the text, see Bruno Krusch (ed), *Studien zur christlich-mittelalterlichen Chronologie [1]. Der 84-jährige Ostercyclus und seine Quellen* (Leipzig 1880) 311-27. For commentary, see Charles W. Jones (ed), *Bedae opera de temporibus*. Medieval Academy of America Publications 41 (Cambridge, Mass. 1943) 82-87, and Maura Walsh & Dáibhí Ó Cróinín (eds & transl), *Cummian's Letter 'De controversia paschali' together with a related Irish computistical tract 'De ratione conputandi'*, Pontifical Institute of Mediaeval Studies, Studies and Texts 86 (Toronto 1988) 32-35.   6 Wilhelm Gundlach (ed), *Columbae sive Columbani abbatis Luxoviensis et Bobbiensis epistolae*. MGH Epistolae Merovingici et Karolini Aevi 1 (Berlin 1892) 154-190: 156-158, 162; G.S.M. Walker (ed & trans), *Sancti Columbani opera*. Scriptores Latini Hiberniae 2 (Dublin 1957) 2-59: 1 and 18.   7 See Walsh & Ó Cróinín, *Cummian's Letter*, 84-86.   8 Dáibhí Ó Cróinín, 'A seventh-century Irish computus from the circle of Cummianus', *Proceedings of the Royal Irish Academy* 82 C 11 (1982) 405-30. [See now above, 99-130.]

original manuscript, insofar as they can be reconstructed, seem to have dealt exclusively with the Paschal question.

The presence in the Paris fragments of a solitary Old Irish gloss – as was thought up to now – need have implied no more than that some Irishman at Echternach had glossed the text while reading through it. Now, however, with the realisation that there were many more glosses in Old Irish, at least six of which are still to be seen on the surviving folios, and that the contents of the manuscript were heavily biased in favour of Irish texts, there are surely much stronger grounds for believing that the manuscript itself was penned by an Irishman. All the glosses are apparently written by the prima manus and the orthography of the Old Irish ones suggests a very early date for the text. There is one small indication that the Old Irish glosses were copied from an earlier exemplar (one seems to be misplaced), and this would suggest on even older date for the archetype.

The present shorn and damaged state of the Paris fragments makes an accurate reconstruction of the original manuscript impossible, but the surviving evidence does suggest that the original measurements may have been *c*. 330 X *c*. 230 mm; the text was apparently written in two columns throughout. The quality of the texts is relatively good; what surprises is the unusual attributions of some: the Gaudentius excerpts are ascribed to Origen (*Originis*) while the tract known as Pseudo-Athanasius is here ascribed (uniquely) to Sulpicius Seuerus (*ut alii dicunt*).[9] The first few lines of Anatolius are lost, so we cannot say whether it was correctly identified or not, but the Augustine excerpts certainly were (*Augustinus hucusque*).

The known contents of the fragments allow some guesswork about the original extent of the manuscript. The two surviving folios have been inverted in the binding, so that fol. 35ᵛ should precede fol. 35ʳ, and fol. 36ᵛ should precede fol. 36ʳ. Following this revised order, the first text encountered is the end of Pseudo-Theophilus, *De Pascha*. The bulk of this text is now missing, however, but estimates based on the measurements (*c*. 330 X 230 mm) suggest that a full folio would have been required to accommodate the rest of the tract. Hence the present fol. 35 must have been preceded by at least one other folio. Following the end of Pseudo-Theophilus on the present fol. 35ᵛ are the excerpt from Numbers 9. 1-11 and Gaudentius ('Originis') *Tractatus I in Exodum (De Paschae obseruatione)*, which fill col. a of that page; col. b sees the opening of Anatolius, *De Pascha*, §l. Anatolius then continues on fol. 35ʳ a-b with §§1-3. The text then breaks off and is renewed on fol. 36v a with §§12-13, ending with the last section, §14, on fol. 36ᵛ b. This implies the loss of almost nine full

9 It is perhaps more than a coincidence that Aldhelm, in his letter to the British king Gerontius, has a confused reference to Sulpicius as author of the British/Irish 84-year tables; see Rudolf Ehwald (ed), *Aldhelmi opera*. MGH AA 15 (Berlin 1919) 480-86. For discussion of the work, see Jones, *Bedae opera*, 51-52, and Claude Barlow (ed), *Martini Ep. Bracarensis opera omnia* (New Haven 1950) 259-63.

sections of the printed edition, or approximately 200 lines of text. Reckoning on the basis of *c.*35 lines per column, this implies the loss of at least six columns or one full plus one half-folio. The present fol. 36^r begins with Augustine, DGAL, which is then followed by Pseudo-Athanasius/Pseudo-Martinus of Braga, *De ratione paschali*. If this text were transcribed in full into the original manuscript, we could reckon on the loss of four full columns, or one folio.

The upshot of these calculations is the probability that the surviving two folios were once accompanied by at least four others.

Although the bulk of Anatolius *De Pascha* has been lost in P, enough of the text survives to enable a comparison with other manuscripts. The readings in P at several points agree with those in the so-called 'Sirmond codex' of Bede's computus (S), which I have elsewhere demonstrated is derived from an Irish exemplar dated AD 658.[10] The relevant textual readings are as follows (reference is to Krusch's edition, cited by paragraph plus page- and line-number):

§1 (317.36):   et *(ter) om.* SP
§1 (318.1):   delucidii K stillicidii SP
§1 (318.1):   eloquiae K eloquentiae S aeloquentiae P
§1 (318.1-2):   sapientiae K scientiaeque S scientiae P
§2 (319.6):   luna soli K luna *om.* SP
§13 (326.11):   excedisset K excedens S excidens P
§13 (326.21):   Ab .viii. kl. ap. K Et ab .viii. kl. ap. SP
§13 (326.24):   sole discindente K d. s. S discendente s. P
§13 (326.26):   simili numero dierum K dierum *om.* SP

The texts in S and P are not identical, however. P sometimes has unique readings:

§1 (317.2):   contexerunt, *for* construxerunt K
§1 (317.4):   conprobandam, *for* probandam K
§1 (317.12):   ieurum, *for* Hieronymum K
§2 (318.21):   ex planiada, *for* ex Spaniada K
§2 (318.24):   praeponenti, *for* proponenti K
§13 (326.3):   Caeterum + est, *for* Caeterum K
§13 (326.4):   discensumque *om.*
§13 (326.4):   qui + in aequinoctio
§13 (326.9):   ex .xii. partibus, *for* ex .xii. partiunculis
§13 (326.13):   .*vii. diebus conmedes,* for *s. d. comedetis* K

---

10 See Dáibhí Ó Cróinín, 'The Irish provenance of Bede's computus', *Peritia* 2 (1983) 229-247 [= 173-90 below].

In drafting his statements about the earliest Echternach manuscripts, Lowe, as it seems to me, sometimes failed to appreciate the significance of some of the evidence. This case has already been made regarding the famous calendar known to have been in Willibrord's possession, and in particular the single-leaf Easter table which was bound in with the Calendar from an early date.[11] There seems now to be a general consensus emerging that this table must have been written *c*. AD 684, in which case it represents the earliest example of an Echternach hand, but one which must have received its training in the Irish monastery of Rath Melsigi.[12] The close relationship between the script of the Easter table and the hand that wrote the main entries in the Calendar, and also the Augsburg (*olim* Maihingen/Harburg) Gospels, has likewise led to the realisation that the first generation of Echternach scribes must have acquired their familiarity with this hand either in Ireland itself or from masters trained in Ireland.

That Rath Melsigi may have been the home of a thriving scriptorium, with Irish and Anglo-Saxon masters and pupils, is certainly not beyond the bounds of possibility. It is certainly significant that among the first generation of Echternach scribes are the names of at least two Irishmen, Laurentius and Virgilius, whose names are preserved in Echternach charters from the years AD 704 to AD 721/ 22.[13] To the weight of that evidence can now be added the newly-discovered Old Irish glosses in the Paris fragments. Bilingual glossing (Latin and Old Irish) is, of course, a distinctive feature of Irish manuscripts from the earliest period, and the glosses on Anatolius follow, therefore, in a long line of such practices developed in the Irish schools. We cannot say from the fragmentary evidence of the Paris leaves, however, whether text and glosses were written in Ireland or at Echternach. What we can say, on foot of the new evidence, is that the Irish input into Echternach manuscript production remained strong even after the transfer from Rath Melsigi. The orthography of the Old Irish glosses suggests an Irish presence at the very beginning, since spellings like *árem*, *córtdo* and *tólae* represent a stage of the language c. AD 700 (i.e. roughly contemporary with the oldest stratum of the Würzburg glosses on St Paul), while the technique of writing Old Irish words with horizontal dashes over most syllables likewise represents an early stage in the glossing practices of Irish scribes.[14]

All in all, therefore, the new Paris discoveries add more evidence for the argument that the earliest Echternach manuscripts and their scribes represent a thorough integration of Irish and Anglo-Saxon techniques and interests. In

---

11 See Ó Cróinín, 'Rath Melsigi, Willibrord, and the earliest Echternach manuscripts', 28-30 [= 145-72 below]. 12 See Bernhard Bischoff, *Paläographie des römischen Altertums und des lateinischen Mittelalters* (2nd ed. Berlin 1986) 126 n 75. 13 For a full description of the Echternach documents, see Camille Wampach, *Geschichte der Grundherrschaft Echternach im Frühmittelalter*. Publications de la section historique de l'Institut Grand-Ducal de Luxembourg 63, 2 vols (Luxembourg 1929-1930). 14 See Dáibhí Ó Cróinín, 'Mo-Sinu maccu Min and the computus at Bangor', *Peritia* 1 (1982) 281-95: 200 [See now below, 145-72: 153-56].

their choice of texts, in their bilingual glossing of those texts, and in their script, the Paris fragments provide important corroborative evidence that the genesis of Hiberno-Saxon cultural relations is to be sought not just in Northumbria but in Ireland as well.

TEXTS

The texts that follow are reproduced as they appear in the Paris fragments. I have printed between square brackets those letters and words that are no longer visible, but which can be safely restored since the texts have been identified. Manuscript abbreviations and contractions have been silently expanded, and minimal capitalisation has been introduced, to facilitate the reader. Punctuation is that of the manuscript, except where retention of it might confuse. The spelling of the fragments has been retained without change; where the text is lost I have assumed a certain consistency on the part of the scribe and used his spelling in preference to that of the editions.

Letters and words added between two diagonal slashes (//) indicate words or letters added by the scribe above the line. Words added between arrow brackets (<>) were omitted by the scribe, and I have restored them where necessary. The Latin and Old Irish glosses, with their lemmata, are printed following the six texts. Roman numerals are printed with a stop on either side, for clarity. A vertical line is used to mark line-ends.

PARIS, Bibliothèque Nationale, MS. lat. 10399, fols 35-36

I

35v a) ... [Has ergo .uii. lunas] similiter in P[ascha tenendo co[nsta]t [fuisse, con] | secrata sunt. Quando ergo /fit/ intra | [suum limitem ab .x]i. Kl. Ap[r]. <usque in .xi. Kl. Mai.> dies dominicus et luna | [ex illis sanctifica]ta sunt, Pascha nobís [iussum] est celeb | [rare]. Finit amen. [Deo gra | ti[as].

[Pseudo-Theophilus, *De ordinatione feriarum paschalium*, MPL 90, 607-10: 609-10]

II

5   [In nom]ine diuino | [Dei summi]
     [Loqutus est Dominu]s ad [Moysen] in [deserto] Sinai. anno | [secundo postqua]m egressi sunt de terra Aegipti mense | [primo dicens: Faciant] filii Israhel fasse in tempore suo | [.xiiii. die mensis huius ad uesper]am iuxta omnes queremo | [nias et iustificationes eius.] Et precipit Moyses filís Israhel ut | [facerent fasse.] Qui [fecerunt]
10 tempore suo .xiiii. die | [mensis ad uesperam in monte Sinai iuxta omnia quae mandauerat Dominus Moysi fecerunt filii Israhel. Ecce autem quidam] inmundi super [animam] | [hominis qui non poterant] facere phasse in [die] ill[o accedentes] | [ad Moysen et Aaron,] qui dixerunt eis: [inmundi sum]us | [super animam homin]is. [Quare] fraudimur ut non [u]alea | [mus oblationem] in tempore suo offer[re] inter
15 filios [Israhel. Quibus respondit] Moyses: State ut consulam quid [precipiat Dominus de] uobis. [Lo]qutus estque Dominus ad Moysen di | [cens: Loquere filís] Israhel: homo qui fuerit inmundus su | [per anima si]ue in uia procul in gente uestra, faciat [phasse Domino mense secundo, .xi]iii. die mensis ad uesperam:.

[Numbers 9.1-11]

III

Originis dicit: | [In exodo libro pariter nunc au]diuimus obersuatio paschae describitur
20 [et septem diebus eiusdem] sollempnita/ti/s azema comedenda mandatur. | [Precipit
tamen deus et h]oc ut si quis primo mense uel in anima /inmundus/ hominis | [id est
mortui attractu pol]lu[t]us. Uel extra electum sacrificís. hiru||[solimae locum in
lonqui]nquo itenere constitutus. pascha non [potuerit celebrare] .ii. mense celebraret
uidens quippe deus gen | [tium populos tunc ad]huc hominum mortuorum simulacris |
25 [inmundos et extra sanctum l]ocum sanctae aecclesiae. in lonquinquo pos||[itos – utique
nos] qui eramus longe. Et facti sumus prope | [in sanguine Christi da]t liquentiam ut si
primo mense non occur||[rit et dies domini]cus et congruus lunae numerus .ii. | [mense
celebremus.]:. Et ideo nec ante .xiiii. lunam. nec ultra | [uicesimam primam celebrare
po]ssumus. Quia .uii. sunt dies azemorum | [in qui]bus querimus dominicum diem:
30 Uult | [enim nos Christus promulga]tor legis et gratiae. Neque ligiti[mos] iuxt[a] |
[lunae cursum comp]ut[a]tos praeterire dies. Neque diem suae [resurrectionis otio
in]gr[ato] transcendere: Nam .ui. feria qua [hominem fecerat pro e]od[em] pasus. et die
dom[i]nica quae dicitur in scrip[turis prima sabbati in qua sumpserat mundus] exordium
resur[rexit ut qui prima die creauit caelum et terram unde postea hominem propter
35 quem fecerat mundum. Haec breuiter dixerim de ratione paschali.]

[Gaudentius, *Tractatus I in Exodum.* Ambrose Glück (ed), CSEL 68 (1936) 10-20]

IV

35v b) [De ratione ordinationis temporum ac uicissitudinum mundi dicturi diuersorum
computariorum scita ponemus qui lunae tantummodo] cursu c[onpu]tat[o] so[lis ascen-
sum discensumque | relinquentes diue[rsos circulos sibi contrarios] | e[t] in calculo uere
comp[uta]tionis [numquam in] | uentos a[die]ctís quibusdam pro[blesmatibus] |
5 contexe[r]unt c[um] certum sit [computationis] | rationem [ab]sque hís [am]bobus
[simul concur]|rentibus non esse conprob[an]d[am. Nam et in] | ue[t]er[ibus] exem-
plaribus [id est Hebraeís et] | [Grecís] uoluminibus non tantum l[unae cursum] | sed
et[iam] solis non solum gre[ssus sed per singula] ac min[utissi]ma horarum momenta
[que in suo] | tempore cum ratio poposcerit [proferimus in]uenimus conputata. E
10 q[uibu]s Hyppolitus] | .xui. annorum circulum qu[ibusdam ignotís] lunae cur[sib]us
conp[os]uit. Alii .xxu. alii .xxx.] | nonnulli .lxxxiiii. [anno]rum cir[culum computan]|tes
numquam ad uer[am] Pascha[e conponendi] | rationem per[uenerunt.] Uerum [maiores
nostri] | Hebreorum et Grecorum librorum [peritissimi Isi]|dorum et Heurum et
Clementum dico [licet dissimilia] | mensium principia pro d[iuersitate linguae
15 senserunt] | tamen ad unam eandemque Paschae [certissimam rati] | onem die et luna
et tem[p]ore [conuenientibus] | summa ueneratione dominicae res[urrectionis
con]senserunt. Sed et Originis omnium [eruditissimus] | et calculi conpon[en]di perspi-
cacis[simus] | qu[ippe qui et calcenterus uocatus] est l[ibellum de] | P[ascha
luculentissime edidit in quo adnuntians in die Paschae non solum lunae cursum et
20 equinoctii transitum intuendam sed et solis transcensum omnium tenebrarum tetras
insidias et offendicula auferentis et lucis aduentum ac totius mundi elimentorum
uirtutem et inspirationem adferentis esse seruandum ita dicens:]

(35r a) [I]n die inquid Paschae non d[ic]o obscr||[uandum ut] dies dominica inuenïatur et
lunae | [.uii. tantu]m dies non transeundi sed ut sol diuis||[ionem] ill[a]m lucis scilicet
ac tenebrarum in ex||[ordio] mundi domini dispensatione aequaliter con||[positam] tran-
scendat et á .i. in .ii. a [.ii.] in | [.iii. et a .i]ii. in .iiii. a .iiii. in .u. á .u. in .ui. horas | [luce
5 i]n solis ascensu crescente tenebrae | [decres]cant á [.c.] et .xl. numeri adiectione
con||[pleta] .xii. partes in uno eodemque die supplean||[tur.] Sed et ego si aliquid stilli-
cidii post quorum | [tam] exuberantia aeloquentiae ac scientiae | [flumi]na temptassem
inferre quid aliud esset | [creden]dum nisi iectantiae et ut uerius dicam | [dementiae] ab
omnibus esset credendum /uel scribendum / nisi nos | [paulisper] orationum tuarum
10 pullicitatum ani||[mauerit] auxilium, quia credimus orationibus | [et fidei tua]e nihil
esse inpossibile. Qua confi||[dentiae ro]burati profundissimum obscuratissimae |

[conputa]tionis et inprouissum pylagus consur|[gentibus] undique questionibus ac
problesma|[tibus in]tumescentibus ingredimur uerecondia | [contemp]ta:. Est ergo in
primo anno initium | [primi m]ensis quod est .x. et .uiiii. annorum | [circuli] princip-
15 ium secundum Aegiptios quidem | [mensis] Faminoth .xxui. die secundum uero |
[Macedon]es Distri m[en]sis .xx[ii. die secundum R]oman|[os uero Martii mensis .xxu.
die id est .uiii. Kl. Apr]l.

35ʳ b) [In qua die inuenitur sol non solum conscendisse primam partem uerum etiam
quadram iam in ea die habere, id est in prima ex .xii. partibus. Haec autem particula
prima ex .xii. uernale est aequinoctium et ipsa est] | [initium mensium et] capu[t]
circu[li et absolutio cur]|sus stellarum quae plane[tae id est uagae] | dicuntur ac finis
5 .xii. par[ticulae et totius] circuli terminus. Et ideo non p[arum delinque]re dicimus eos
qui ante initi[um hoc noui anni] | Pascha putant esse celebra[ndum. Sed nec] | á nobís
primís exordium sumit [haec ratio] | antiquís Iudeis fuisse conpr[obata monstra]|tur: et
ante aduentum Christi ob[seruata. sicut] | euidenter edocent Filo et Iose[phus sed et] |
eorum antiquiores Agathobol[us et ab eo cru]|ditus Aresthobulus ex Planiad[a qui] |
10 unus ex illís .lxx. senioribus [fuit qui missi] | fuerant á pontificibus ad T[holomeum
regem] | Ebreorum libros interpr<et>ari in Grecum ser]|monem. Quique multa ex
trad[itionibus Moysi] | praeponenti regi percunctan[tique responderunt.] | Ipsi ergo
cum questiones Exodi [exponerent dixer]|unt. Pascha non prius esse [immolandum.] |
quam equinoctium uernale [transiret.] | Aresthobulus uero etiam ho[c addit: in die]|
15 Paschae non solum obersuandu[m esse ut sol] | aequinoctium uernale tra[nscendat
uerum] | etiam et luna. Cum duo sunt a/e/q[uinoctia inquid] | ueris et autumpni
aequís spatís [derempta et] | .xiiii. die mensis primi sit statuta [sollempnitas] | post
uesperam. quando luna sol[i obposita e re]|gione depraehenditur sicut e[tiam oculis
probare] | licet. inuenitur utique uer[n]al[is aequinoctii] partem. sol obteniens luna
20 uer[o] é[contrario autum]|pnalis. Et ideo ... (text breaks off).

36ᵛ a) ... [nouissima pars uincitur .xiiii. die mensis primi qui non die sed lunae cursi]bus
[con]putatu[r Pasc]ha | [immoletur.] Quod qui[d]em ut domini [iussio]ne san|[citum
est et] catholicae fidei conueniens. om|[nibus annís an]|ticip[ar]i inlicitum | [ac
periculo]sum esse omni sa[p]ienti non est [dubium. Et i]deo hoc solum satis est omnibus
5 | [sanctis et cathol]icís uirís custodire ut pluri|[bus et diuer]sís opin<ion>ibus [ac
sen]ten[t]ís prae |[termissís intr]a terminos quos expossuimus | [sollempnita]tem
domin[ic]ae resurrectio|[nis conclud]ant:. Caeterum /est/ quod tuae | [epistolae
s]ubieceras ut solis ascensum | qui in aequinoctio in diminuti[one dierum] ac noctium
confi[cit]ur huic | [opusculo in]sinuare con[arer hoc] modo in | [choatur a]c consumi-
10 tur. P[er] .xu. dies et | [horae dime]dium sole ascend[en]te per singu | [la momenta] id
est per .iiii. in una die ab | [.uiii. Kl. Ian. in] .uiii. Kl. Apl. hora diminuitur. | IN qua
consummuntur .xii. | [horae et a]ssin id est prima pars. et ex ea | [inchoatur] particula
prima ex .xii. partibus | [In qua die] ad uesperum si luna .xiiii.ae | [aduenisset a]gnus
apud Iudeos immolabatur. | [Si autem e]xcidens numerum .xu. et .xui. lu|[na fuisse]
15 inuenta: in uespera eius diei | [in .xiiii. die se]cundae lunae eodem mensae | [natae ad]
uesperum Pasch[a c]eleb[ratur.] | [.uii. die]bus con<m>edent/e/ [az]ema usque|

36ᵛ b) [in diem .xxi. in uesperum. Nobis ergo similiter si eueniat ut .uiii. Kl. Apl. et dies
dominica et luna .xiiii. inueniatur Pascha celebrandum est. Sed si .xu. uel .xui. usque ad
.xx. lunam fuerat inuenta pro reuerentia dominicae resurrectionis | q[u]e [in die]
dom[inica] f[acta est nobís similiter celeb]|ra[ndu]m est. I[ta tam]en ut [pr]inc[ipium
5 Paschae finem] | so[llempnitatis eorum.] id est .xx. [lunam non excidat. et ideo] | non
paruum di[lin]quisse eos di/x/[imus qui anticipare] | uel excedere hunc numerum
[diuinae insertum scrip]|turae [au]si sunt. Et ab .uiii. Kl. Apl. in .uiii. Kl. Iulii per] |
.xu. dies [et] duas horas hora d[iminuitur per duo mom]|enta et dimedium. et .ui.
parte[m momenti per singulos] | dies sole ascendente. Et ab [.uiii. Kl. Iulii in .uiii. Kl.
10 Oct.] | similiter per .xu. dies et .iiii. hor[as hora diminuitur des]|cendente sole in
unaquaque di[e per eundem numerum] | momentorum. Et spatium quo[d super est
usque in .uiii. Kl.] | Ian. simili numero dierum at [horarum ac momentorum] | finitur.
Ita ut in .uiii. Kl. Iulii hora et horae dime]|dium hora habeat. Et .uiii. Kl. [Ian.

dimedi]|um hor[ae et] horam habea[t. Eo usque namque dies] | et nox diminuitur ut
15 .xii. ho[rae que in uerna]le | aequinoctio in pri[n]cipio [domini dispensatione
consti]itutae sunt. in .uiii. Kl. Iulii n[octe diminuta sole ascen] | dente per singulos quos
[supra diximus gradus] | .xuiii. in .xii. longiore spa[tio reperiantur adiunc] | tae. Et
iterum .xii. horae [que in autumpnale] | aequinoctio solis discens[u repleantur in .uiii.
Kl.] | Ian. .ui. horae in .xii. diuisa[e inueniantur disiunc]|tae. Nocte .xuiii. in .xii.
20 [diuisas tenente quae] | in .uiii. [K1.] Iulii similiter .ui. [in .xii. partitas tenebat.] | Hoc
autem non [ignores quod ista .iiii. quae supra] | prae[diximus temporum confinia] |
sci[licet mensium se]quentium kalendís ad[proximantur unumquodque | ta]men
medium temporis [id est ueris et estatis] | et autumpni et chemis [teneat et non exinde]
| temporum principia inch[oantur unde mensium] | kalendae initiantur. Sed ita
25 [unumquodque tempus inchoandum est ut a primo die ueris tempus aequinoctium diuidat et estatis .uiii. Kl. Iulii et autumpni .uiii. Kl. Oct. et chemis .uiii. Kl. Ian. similiter
diuidat.]

[Anatolius of Laodicea, *De Pascha*. Bruno Krusch (ed), *Studien zur christlich-mittelalterlichen Chronologie [1]. Der 84-jährige Ostercyclus und seine Quellen* (Leipzig 1880) 316-27:
316-19, 325-27.]

V

36ʳ a) [Itaque si hoc modo intellegamus] tem[pora] et dies et | [annos ut articul]os quos-
dam quos [per horologiam computamus] | [uel in caelo notissimos cum ab oriente usque
in] | [meridianam] sol altitudinem insurgit. Atque inde | [rursus usque in occi]dentem
uergit. Uti possit deinceps | [aduerti uel lunam] uel aliquod sidus ab oriente statim |
5 [post occasum solis] emergere:. Quod item cum ad medi|am caeli uenerit alti]tudinem.
medium noctis indicet. Tunc | [scilicet occasurum] cum sole radiente: fit mane: Dies |
[autem totos solis] ab o[riente usque ad occidentem] | [circuitus annos uero uel] istos
ussitatos solis [anfra]ctus non | [cum ad orientem quod] cotidie [facit sed cum ad eadem]
loca | [siderum redit – qu]od non facit nisi peractís [.ccc.tis] | [.lxu.] diebus. Et tribus
10 horís. [i]d est | [quadrante totius] diei quae [pars quater] ducta | [cogit interponi u]num
diem. quod Romani bissex | [tum uocant ut ad e]undem circuitum redeatur:. Uel |
[etiam maiores et] occultiores annos. Nam conple]|[tís aliorum siderum spatís ma]iores
anni fieri dicuntur: – | [...]logus phinicis: - Augustinus hucusque. |

[Augustinus, *De Genesi ad litteram* II. 14. Ioseph Zycha (ed.), CSEL 28 iii 2, 55]

VI

/De ratione <Paschae> uel Sulpici Se/ue/ri ut alii dicunt:./ | [Plerique mister]ium
15 Paschae narrare uoluerunt. | [simulque degerere] de ratione subputationis. In | [mense
et die et lu]na. siue scientiae:. siue sermonis | [inpossibilitate o]bscurius id relinquerunt.
Tan | [... ? quasi nihil inde] dixissent. Scio enim multos scru|[pulosius interro]gare
solitos. Quare secundum | [morem Iudeorum] ad lunae computationem diuersís |
[generibus Pas]cha celebremus. dicentes rectius. | [sibi uideri si do]minicae passionis
20 commemora | [tio agatur ut unum] anniuersarium [na]talem [di]em ob | [seruemus
sicut] et <a> [pler]ísque Gall[iaru]m aepisco|[pis est] usque ante non multum tempus |
[custoditum ut semper .u]iiii. Kl. Aprl. diem Paschae c/a/eleb|[rarent in quo facta
Christi resurrectio traditur. Placuit autem et mihi inquirenti curiose quid maiores nostri
secuti essent aperte exponere.]

25 36ʳ b) [Passio Christi redemptio est creaturae de qua apostolus ait quod s[u]b[i]ect[a] |
[fuerit seruituti non sua sponte] sed propter [eu]m | [qui subiecit eam in sp[em] quia et
[u]os creatura | [.] á curruptella interitus cum /omni/ libertat|[e filiorum Dei.] Haec
creat[ura est] spiritus uitae qui cr|[eauit omnia] terrena corporatura /[u]t corpora iam/
subiectus in | [eam spem ut de cur]ruptella interitus. Cum filiou|[m gloriae] liberetur:.
30 Quae utiquae [in] eo die [subiecta est ser]|uituti in quo mundus eff[ectu]s est | [quam
cum Christus] | per passionem suam liberare ueniss[et seruauit ut] | in eo tempore
[c]um patiretur. [in quo creatura] | subiecta fuerat seruitut[i ut] qui | [dies ille

    tris]|titiae fuerat. i[t]em laetitiae r[edderetur.] Quoniam uero huius sacraments m[agni
    tanta ut] | esset ueritas. ut ueritatis ipsius [etiam umbra] | proficeret. ad salutem.
35 liberandís. [Iudeís de] seruitute Pharaonis. Quasi iam [libe] | ratio creaturae. de
    seruitute cor[ruptellae] | figuraretur. Futurae passionis [Christi imago] | in aduentum
    salutis oper[ata] est. [et ideo dictum est] ad Iudeos. ut in primo mense an[ni .xiiii. luna]
    agnus inmaculatus anniculus im[molaretur] | de cuius sanguine domus suae sup[er
    limina] | consignarent. ne [á uas]tatore an[gelo tan]gerentur. at/que/ in [m]e[dio
40 [n]octe cones[to per domos] | agno. Quod esset Paschae /c/aelebra[tio.] | Tamen
    secundum figuram acciperunt ser[uitutem.] | Non obscura est figura. agnum i[nmac-
    ula]tum esse Ihesum Christum. huius ymmola[tione á] | serui[tu]te nos interitus
    li[ber]au[it. Nam sig] | no crucis eius [q]uassi aspersione /sanguinis/ [signati usque] |
    quo ad consum[mationem mundi á uastatoribus angelís uindicabimur. Hoc breuiter et
45 strictim dixisse sufficiat, ut id quod quaerere propositum est, rationem obseruationis et
    Paschae et mensis et lunae et diei, sine molestia multiloqui aperiamus.] (36^r b ends)

[Pseudo-Athanasius/Pseudo-Martinus Bracarensis, *De Pascha*. Claude Barlow (ed),
Martini Bracarensis episcopi opera (New Haven 1950) 270-71]

LATIN GLOSSES

35ᵛ	b	7	non tantum lunae cursum sed etiam solis, gl. id .xxx. diebus in ascensu solis
35ᵛ	b	8	minutissima horarum momenta, gl. id [si]ngul[a]
35ʳ	a	5	tenebrae decrescant, a .c. et .xl. numeri adiectione conpleta, .xii. partes in uno eodemque die suppleantur, gl. (1) id m[o]mentis; (2) ac .cxx. id bis [= bissexti];
35ʳ	a	6	(3) id horae
35ʳ	a	9	nisi nos paulisper orationum tuarum pullicitatum animauerit auxilium, gl. id est postule(?) nos(?)
35ʳ	a	14	quod est .x. et .uiiii. annorum circuli principium, gl. et eius circuli secundum Aegiptios, gl. id Marti. id .uii. Kl. Parmothi
35ʳ	a	15	secundum uero Macedones, gl. id Marti. id xi. Kl. Fa[rmothi(?)]
35ʳ	b	24	sicut euidenter edocent Filo et Iosephus, gl. […] numerato[r]
35ʳ	b	31	ut sol aequinoctium uernale transcendat uerum etiam et luna, gl. id .xiiii.
35ʳ	b	34	sicut etiam oculis probare licet, gl. id in di[e]
36ᵛ	a	12	id est prima pars. gl. id de bis [= bissexto]
36ᵛ	a	12	et ex ea inchoatur particula prima, gl. dies particula prima ex .xii. partibus, gl. id horís
36ᵛ	a	14	excidens numerum, gl. id .xiiii.
36ᵛ	a	15	in uespera, gl. id aequi [= aequinoctio]
36ᵛ	b	13	Et .uiii. Kl. Ian. dimedium horae et horam habeat, gl. id in noc[te]
36ᵛ	b	16	sole ascendente per singulos, quos supra diximus, gradus, .xuiii., gl. [aequi(?)]noc[tio(?)]
36ʳ	a	19	si dominicae passionis commemoratio agatur ut unum anniuersarium, gl. id […]st

OLD IRISH GLOSSES

35ᵛ	b	3	et in calculo, gl. ārem: 'counting, reckoning'; vn. of *ad-rími*. Royal Irish Academy, *Dictionary of the Irish Language* [DIL], A 197. Note the retention of -e- in the unstressed final syllable. The later spelling is *áram;* cf. Rudolf Thurneysen, *A grammar of Old Irish* (Dublin 1946) 105 §169.
35ᵛ	b	17	Origenis omnium eruditissimus et calculi conponendi perspicacissimus, gl. *cōrtdō:* archaic gen. of *cóirt*, (later *cúairt)* 'circle, circuit'. DIL., C 57-71. The

spelling -td- for -d- is unusual (cf. GOI 23 §31d), while the undiphthongised first syllable and the retention of the gen. sg. ending -o are evidence of archaism.

35r	a	13	problesmatibus (with ref. mark connecting this to *pylagus*), gl. *tolāe:* 'flood'; vn. of **to-uss-lin* or **to-fo-lin*. DIL, T 238. Note retention of *-ae* in the second, unstressed syllable (later *tóla*).
35r	b	20	utique uernalis aequinoctii partem sol obteniens, gl. *id for matin. id gīlē:* 'i.e., in the morning, i.e., (the) brightness'; *for* = prep. 'on' + acc./dat. *matin* (nom. *maten* <Latin *matutina.*); DIL, M 69. *gile*, DIL, G 82.
36r	a	21	usque ante non multum tempus, gl. *cō gaīr:* 'until recently'. Not the adverbial construction with prep. *co* but a slavish rendering of the Latin: *co* = usque, *gair* = non multum tempus.

The general impression given by the language of these glosses is that they represent a date in the early eighth century, perhaps even the seventh. The archaisms (undiphthongised long vowels, vowels between consonants in unstressed position not yet reduced to schwa, retention of full value in final vowels, absence of glide vowels) are such as are found in the oldest Irish texts: the Cambrai Homily, the *prima manus* of the Würzburg glosses, and the oldest stratum in the Book of Armagh Patrician texts. A date no later than AD 725 would seem appropriate. (I wish to thank Prof. Liam Breatnach, School of Irish, Trinity College, Dublin, for discussing these glosses with me.)

NOTES ON THE TEXTS

I	2	*Quando ergo fit intra:* the scribe first wrote *Quando ergo intra*, then added above the words *sit inter*, as a correction.
II	4	*Et precipit:* Not attested in Henri Quentin et al. (eds), *Biblia Sacra iuxta Latinam vulgatam versionem 3. Numeri-Deuteronomium* (Rome 1936). Most MSS have *praecip-itque*, though G* omits the *-que*.
II	7	*phasse: pascha* is the preferred reading in the Rome edition, though numerous MSS in fact have *phasse* or a variant.
II	9	*fraudimur: fraudamur* is the preferred reading in the Rome edition; MS. O has our reading.
II	9	*in tempore suo offerre:* the Vulgate text is *offerre oblationem Domino in t. s.;* our reading is not attested.
II	11	*Loqutus estque:* a peculiar reading; most MSS have either *locutusque est* or *loqutus est*.
III	1	*Originis:* an interesting ascription; the same spelling is found in MSS of Anatolius (Krusch, *Studien* 1, 317).
III	3	*in anima inmundus hominis:* the CSEL ed. reads: *immundus in anima hominis*.
IV	16	*.uii. diebus con<m>edete azema:* the scribe seems to have written *conedetis* (though the last two letters are no longer clearly visible, due to damage of the parchment. Above the second *-e-* was added the letter *-n-*, and above the final - *is(?)* was added *-e-* (both additions are clearly visible; the initial *con-* was written out in full, not abbreviated.
V	4	*uergit:* there is a *-p-* added above the first letter, though *uergit* is, in fact, correct.
V	13	[...]*logus phinicis:* I am unable to explain these words. [The first word is perhaps *Prologus*; the second might possibly be a 'Greek' spelling of *finit*.]
VI	14	<*Paschae*> the title is added between the lines, with the word *ratione* above the second *Paschae*, perhaps with the intention of incorporating the word in the title. The ascription of this work to Sulpicius Severus is, to my knowledge, unique.
VI	15	*de ratione:* above *-ne* is written *-ni*, perhaps as a correction.

VI   17   *relinquerunt. Tan* | [...]: the editions have nothing added between *relinquerunt* and *quasi.*

VI   26   *quia et uos:* the editions read: *quia et ipsa liberabitur a seruitute interitus cum libertate filiorum Dei* (= Rm 8: 20-21).

VI   27   *cum omni libertate: omni* not in the editions.

VI   28   *ut corpora iam:* not in the editions, perhaps a gloss.

PALEOGRAPHICAL DESCRIPTION

The two surviving folios measure 330 x 230 mm, but these have been trimmed by the binder. The writing area is *c.* 315 mm long, and the estimated breadth is *c.* 250 mm. Allowing for an average of *c.* 35 lines per page, with loss of 2-3 lines at the top of the page and 5-6 at the foot of the page, the original dimensions were probably in the region of *c.* 360 x *c.* 260 mm. The writing is in two columns, enclosed by single bounding lines.

Punctuation: The medial point is used for pauses; stops are indicated by the use of three dots (:.). Omissions are marked by *signes de renvoi.* Monosyllables and long *-is* in final syllables are accented. There is an extensive repertoire of construe-marks (though their use is not always clear).

Abbreviations: Besides the usual forms b:, q: = bus, que, dr̄, dn̄t = *dicitur, dicunt,* etc., some less regular forms occur: e.g. temp̄, = *tempus.* Insular abbreviations are frequent: ɔ = con/com (*comedenda*); 3 = *eius;* ÷ = *est;* id ÷ = *id est;* q:. = *quae;* ł = *uel.* Not noted by Lowe is the distinctively Irish f = *secundum.*

Spelling: Insular spellings are common: *pylagus (pelagus), problesma, lonquinquo, chemis (hiemis), sollempnitas,* but on the whole the orthography is good.

Script: Described by Lowe as a 'majuscule verging on minuscule', who noted also that the script changes into a crowded minuscule for the Gaudentius text on fol. 35ᵛ a. Uncial ∂ is the rule; half-uncial *n r* and *s* are regular, though the uncial forms do occur. Lowe described the bow of *q* as 'disproportionately large' and noted the stubbed, short descender of that letter. Ligatures are common: *ti, hi, mi, ni, fi, gn, nt,* with subscript *t* occurs once (36ʳ a). The ink is now brown, and according to Lowe the vellum was prepared 'in the Insular manner'.

12

Rath Melsigi, Willibrord,
and the earliest Echternach manuscripts[*]

It is over half a century now since the controversy first arose concerning the
date and provenance of certain early Insular manuscripts, particularly gospel
manuscripts like the Book of Durrow, the Lindisfarne Gospels, and the Book
of Kells.[1] It used to be the common belief in the last century and at the beginning of this one that all, or almost all, of these great codices were the products
of Irish scribes working in Irish scriptoria. In the course of the nineteen-twen-
ties and thirties, however, with the appearance of publications from such
scholars as A.W. Clapham,[2] E.T. Leeds,[3] and T.D. Kendrick,[4] there began to
emerge a rival theory: that these manuscripts – far from reflecting Irish crafts-
manship – were in fact Northumbrian-English in origin and the creations of
Anglo-Saxon scribes and artists whose main inspiration was drawn from their
heritage of Germanic artistic traditions and the direct Italian contacts of the
English church. This theory reached its apogée in 1947 with the appearance of
a book by the Belgian scholar, François Masai, entitled *Essai sur les origines de
la miniature dite irlandaise.*[5] In this book Masai maintained that the style of
manuscript illumination that had hitherto been termed 'Irish' ('la miniature
dite irlandaise') made its first appearance at the end of the seventh century not
in Ireland but in Northumbria, and more specifically at Lindisfarne.[6] The
earliest dateable witness to that style, Masai claimed, was the Lindisfarne
Gospels, which he dated to *c.* AD 700-720.[7] Masai argued further that this style

---

[*] First published in *Peritia* 3 (1984) 17-49. **1** For a convenient survey of the literature, see T. J.
Brown, 'Northumbria and the Book of Kells' [rev. ed., *Anglo-Saxon England* 1 (1972) 219-46].
[repr. in Janet Bately, Michelle Brown & Jane Roberts (eds*)*, *A palaeographer's view: Selected
writings of Julian Brown* (London 1993) 97-124.] **2** 'Notes on the origins of Hiberno-Saxon art',
Antiquity 8 (1934) 43-57. **3** *Celtic ornament in the British Isles down to AD 700* (Oxford 1933).
4 'British hanging-bowls', *Antiquity* 6 (1932) 161-84. **5** Les publications de Scriptorium 1
(Brussels 1947). See the replies by Françoise Henry, 'Irish culture in the seventh century', *Studies*
(Dublin) 37 (1948) 267-79, and Seán P. Ó Ríordáin, 'A note on the archaeological evidence', ibid.,
279-82. **6** 'Le Lindisfarnensis est sans doute le plus ancien manuscrit daté', *Essai* 52; 'Au départ
des missionnaires irlandais, en 664, la miniature anglo-irlandaise n'existait pas encore. Vers 720
elle produisait le Book of Lindisfarne. Ses débuts datent donc de la fin du VIIe siècle au plus tôt',
ibid., 103. **7** 'De la sorte la decoration de cet évangéliaire aurait été exécutée entre 698 et 740,
et plus précisément vers l'époque du changement d'évêque, soit vers 720-725', *Essai*, 50. For
Julian Brown's arguments in favour of a dating before AD 698, see 'Book of Kells', passim and the
literature there cited. For arguments against such an early date, see my review, 'Pride and
prejudice', *Peritia* 1 (1982) 352-62: 357-58.

of manuscript illumination owed nothing to Irish cultural ancestry but appeared, as it were, fully armed like Athena from the brow of Zeus.[8] There was in fact no Irish tradition of manuscript illumination, and the manuscripts that were usually cited as evidence for such a tradition must *ipso facto* be English or English-inspired, not Irish.[9] Thus at a stroke, one could almost say, the whole corpus of important early Insular illuminated manuscripts was claimed for Northumbria[10] and the two most illustrious of those that were of known Irish provenance, Durrow and Kells, were hailed by Masai as triumphs of the Lindisfarne scriptorium.[11] If I might be allowed to paraphrase Oscar Wilde, to lose one manuscript may be regarded as a misfortune; to lose both looks like carelessness.

The theory of a Northumbrian origin for Durrow, Lindisfarne and Kells received an added twist with the appearance of the two-volume facsimile edition of the Lindisfarne Gospels.[12] In his contribution to this work Professor Julian Brown advanced the theory (supported by his collaborator, Rupert Bruce-Mitford) that two others of this group of illuminated gospel codices,

---

8 'L'hypothèse d'une longue évolution, antérieure aux plus anciens monuments subsistants, ne trouve donc pas de confirmations dans l'étude attentive des procédés et des motifs employés. Elle se montre au contraire superflue et gratuite. L'examen du plus ancien codex fait même conclure à son invraisemblance. D'autres raisons vent nous en faire voir l'impossibilité complète. L'évolution séculaire est impossible – Malgré les lois exigeantes de l'évolution, la miniature "irlandaise" débute par des chefs-d'œuvre. Pas le moindre vestige d'une tradition, séculaire ou autre! Avant le Livre de Durrow, c'est-à-dire avant la fin du VIIe ou le début du VIIIe siècle, il n'y a rien', *Essai*, 60-61. 9 'Par consequent, les défenseurs de la thèse northumbrienne seront en droit de le prétendre, le laps de temps écoulé entre la sécession des Irlandais, en 664, et l'exécution de l'évangéliaire de Durrow, enclôt facilement le développement de la miniature "irlandaise", depuis ses premiers débuts jusqu'à son premier chef-d'œuvre', *Essai*, 64; 'C'est en Northumbrie en effet que plusieurs motifs "irlandais" s'élaborent par l'adaptation expressioniste de rinceaux de vigne et des oiseaux. Enfin les éléments les plus particuliers du vocabulaire, les plus aptes par conséquent à nous livrer le secret des origines, sont nettement anglais', ibid., 85; 'L'art dit irlandais était pour les irlandais tout aussi étranger que l'art mérovingien ou carolingien. Dès lors rien d'étonnant à ce qu'ils ne lui marquent aucune préférence. Les Irlandais suivent simplement la mode et subissent les influences du lieu et du temps où ils vivent. Les milieux anglo-saxons du continent, comme Echternach, voilà les centres de diffusion de la miniature "irlandaise"', ibid., 93-94. 10 Brown makes his views very clear in his Inaugural Lecture of the Chair of Palaeography in the University of London: 'Latin palaeography since Traube', *Litterae Textuales* [Codicologica] 1 (1976) 58-74: 66: 'After a good few years of minding their own business, Irish and English palaeographers will be better fitted to re-enter the archaeological conflict'. It seems now though that even the detritus of the tradition that was formerly left to Ireland is to be relocated in Northumbria; see T. J. Brown , 'The Irish element in the Insular system of scripts to circa A.D. 850', in Heinz Löwe (ed), *Die Iren und Europa im Frühmittelalter* (2 vols, Stuttgart 1979) 1, 101-19; esp. 109 [repr. *A palaeographer's view*, 201-20:211]. 11 'Le plus raisonnable est d'accorder à Lindisfarne le mérite des premières créations comme celui des premiers chefs-d'œuvre; sinon de tous', *Essai*, 127. On p. 126 of the same work Masai provides a diagrammatic representation of the development as he sees it: as products of the Lindisfarne scriptorium he lists Durrow, Echternach, Lindisfarne, Durham, and Kells, 'et d'autres manuscrits de Durham'. 12 T.D. Kendrick, T.J. Brown, R.L.S. Bruce-Mitford et al. (eds), *Evangeliorum quattuor Codex Lindisfarnensis* (2 vols, Olten and Lausanne 1956, 1960).

Durham, Cathedral Library, MS. A II 17, and the Echternach Gospels, Paris, Bibliothèque Nationale, MS. lat. 9389, were the work of one scribe-illuminator, whom he christened the 'Durham-Echternach Calligrapher'.[13] Brown further maintained that both manuscripts were produced in the Lindisfarne scriptorium at roughly the same date as the Lindisfarne Gospels. This theory has been reiterated in subsequent publications,[14] the most recent being the fine facsimile edition of the Durham Gospels.[15] But it is not really new; it is in fact a refinement and elaboration of Masai's original thesis and it is no surprise, therefore, to find Brown, in his Jarrow Lecture, openly avowing that it was 'as a follower of Masai' that he first came to this subject.[16]

In the discussion up to now the tendency has been to focus on the three principal manuscripts, Durrow, Lindisfarne and Kells, and attempt to set them in chronological order;[17] the others of the group would then fall into their 'natural' places in the series. The general consensus has been that Durrow is the earliest of the three and Kells the latest, with Lindisfarne occupying an apparently securely-dated position (AD 698) in the middle. But whereas Durrow used to be dated in the first half of the seventh century, the tendency now is to locate it in the second half;[18] and whereas Kells used to be dated to the late-eighth or early-ninth century, it now is dated *c*. AD 750.[19] But since the only grounds for such redating have been art-historical ones, we may take it that the chain of argument on which it is based is only as strong as its weakest link. Professor Brown has himself said that 'to be wrong about Kells – in itself a complete gallery of Hiberno-Saxon art – is to be wrong about Insular palaeography and Hiberno-Saxon archaeology in general'.[20] The axiom applies *mutatis mutandis* to all the other manuscripts in the discussion.

My own interest in this whole question arose out of work which I had been doing on another, unrelated topic, but one which led me by a roundabout route to look more closely at the arguments that had brought about the apparent triumph of the Northumbrian theory – for it seems to me that it is this view that currently holds the field. In particular, I was drawn to the corpus of

---

13 In his *Durham Gospels,* 45 (and not in the Jarrow Lecture, as I stated in *Peritia* 1, 352) Brown described him as 'one of the greatest masters of both formal and informal handwriting in the history of Europe'.   14 For example, in his *Codicologica* paper and in his contribution to *Die Iren* (p 18 n. 5) above.   15 C.D. Verey, T.J. Brown, E. Coatsworth et al. (eds), *The Durham Gospels. Early English Manuscripts in Facsimile* [EEMF] 20 (Copenhagen 1980).   16 'Book of Kells' 219. For my part I regard Masai's book as a disastrous intervention in the whole debate. His chapter 3 in particular ('Les vraisemblances historiques') is a travesty of historical method. 17 See the account in Brown, 'Book of Kells', passim, and Carl Nordenfalk, 'Before the Book of Durrow', *Acta Archaeologica* 18 (1947) 141-74.   18 See Brown, 'Book of Kells', 225; dated explicitly to the 670s by David H. Wright, 'The Irish element in the formation of Hiberno-Saxon art: calligraphy and metalwork', *Die Iren* 1, 99-100.   19 Brown now seems to be tending towards an even earlier date: 'before the middle of the eighth century', and he ascribes it to 'a centre under very strong Lindisfarne influence', which he has not yet managed to identify; see *Die Iren* 1, 108. 20 'Book of Kells', 220.

manuscripts which has survived from the monastery of Echternach[21] in Luxembourg, the foundation of Willibrord, because some of them happened to contain material which was relevant to my own computistical researches. Besides, these Echternach manuscripts, it seems to me, provide the linchpin for the general theory of Northumbrian origin, and one in particular – the Echternach Gospels – forms one of the twin foundations for Julian Brown's imposing creation, the Durham-Echternach Calligrapher. The Echternach manuscripts are important, too, because they are more susceptible of accurate dating than the others here mentioned, and the historical circumstances in which they were made can be more easily reconstructed. In what follows, therefore, I shall examine the history and background of this Echternach corpus, but I shall be drawing mainly on historical evidence, not the arguments of archaeology or art-history; because I believe that underlying the theory of Northumbrian provenance for these manuscripts especially there is a fundamental misconception about the historical origins of the Anglo-Saxon mission to the continent in general, and about the origins of the Echternach foundation in particular. The Echternach manuscripts are, in fact, crucial to our understanding of the development of Insular script and manuscript illumination.

The late-seventh-century Anglo-Saxon mission to the continent[22] which led to the foundation of Echternach *c.* AD 699 is one of two epoch-making ventures in the history of the churches in the British Isles. The other is, of course, the Northumbrian mission of the Irish monks from Iona. With the

---

21 See E.A. Lowe, *Codices Latini Antiquiores* [CLA] V 577, 578, 584, 585, 586, 588, 595, 596, 598, 605, 606a, 606b, and CLA IX 1364; Carl Nordenfalk, 'On the age of the earliest Echternach manuscripts', *Acta Archaeologica* 3 (1932) 57-62. There is a very valuable account of the history of the collection in Hermann Degering, 'Handschriften aus Echternach und Orval in Paris', in Georg Ley (ed), *Aufsaetze Fritz Milkau gewidmet* (Leipzig 1921) 48-85. [For the library and scriptorium of Echternach see now Michele Camillo-Ferrari, *Sancti Willibrordi venerantes memoriam. Echternacher Schreiber und Schriftsteller von den Angelsachsen bis Johann Bertels* (Luxembourg 1994), and idem (ed), *Analecta Epternacensia. Beiträge zur Bibliotheksgeschichte der Abtei Echternach* (Trier 2000).]   22 A good brief account is Wilhelm Levison's *England and the continent in the eighth century* (Oxford 1946) 45-69, and the same author's paper, 'St Willibrord and his place in history', *Durham University Jnl* 32 (1940) 23-41; repr. in Walther Holtzmann (ed), *Aus rheinischer und fränkischer Frühzeit* (Düsseldorf 1948) 314-29. Of no use for our purpose is Camille Wampach's *Sankt Willibrord, sein Leben und Lebenswerk* (Luxembourg 1953),which is a popularisation of his earlier, more detailed work (see below). There is a good detailed account of Willibrord's relationship with Wilfrid in A. van Berkum 'Willibrord en Wilfried: een onderzoek naar hun wederzijdse betrekkeningen', *Sacris Eruditi* 23(1978-79) 347-415; the author, however, has little or nothing to say about Willibrord's Irish years. On the other hand, he offers very effective criticism of the notion that Echternach and Northumbria were in exclusive contact throughout the period of Willibrord's missionary activity and that the monks of Rath Melsigi passed through northern England on their journeys to Frisia; see esp. 400-405. For the general background, see now Michael Richter, 'Der irische Hintergrund der angelsächsischen Mission', *Die Iren* 1, 120-137. [See now Michael Richter, *Ireland and her neighbours in the seventh century* (Dublin 2000).][See now also Doris Edel, 'The christianization of medieval Europe: Willibrord', in eadem, *The Celtic west and east. Studies in Celtic literature and the early Irish Church* (Dublin 2001) 121-36.]

establishment in AD 635 of an Irish community in Lindisfarne off the Northumbrian coast[23] the Irish churches entered on their third expansionary phase,[24] one which was to have momentous consequences not just for these islands. In a very real sense, however, this Iona connection has overshadowed the other, Anglo-Saxon, undertaking, so it may be useful at this point to retrace the historical events that led up to the Frisian mission.

The Frisian mission actually began as the result of an accident. It arose out of the troubled fortunes of bishop Wilfrid of York who, in AD 678, because of his opposition to the partition of his huge diocese, was driven out of Northumbria and determined to take his case to Rome.[25] He crossed the North Sea, landing in the Rhine delta, and spent the winter of AD 678-9 amongst the Frisians. With the onset of spring, however, Wilfrid renewed his journey to Rome, but not before he had spent a couple of the winter months preaching the gospel to the Frisians. Englishmen in later years came to look on this episode as the beginning of the Frisian mission.[26]

Wilfrid, however, did not himself take any further active part in the work of evangelization. This was to be the task of other Englishmen, but men who were resident not in England itself but in Ireland. This is a fundamental point: the Frisian mission of the Anglo-Saxons was an Irish-based undertaking from the start. The evidence is quite clearly stated in Bede's *Ecclesiastical History*, in that famous passage (III 27) where he related how 'large numbers of the English race' had taken themselves to Ireland in the first half of the seventh century in order to study at the feet of Irish masters.[27] Bede, in fact, gives the names of a dozen or so Anglo-Saxons who went to Ireland in the course of his History, and the names of others of what must have been a fairly sizeable group of exiles can be gleaned from other sources.[28] Moreover, Bede even mentions the principal

---

23 We are, strange though it may seem, still without a good, authoritative survey of this episode. [See D.A. Bullough, 'The missions to the English and the Picts and their heritage (to c. 800)', in Heinz Löwe (ed), *Die Iren und Europa im früheren Mittelalter*, 2 vols (Stuttgart 1979) 1, 80-98, and James Campbell, 'Elements in the background to the Life of St Cuthbert and his early cult', in Gerald Bonner, David Rollason & Clare Stancliffe (eds), *St Cuthbert, his cult and his community to AD 1200* (Woodbridge 1989) 3-19] 24 That is, taking the establishment of Iona as the beginning of the first phase, and Columbanus' departure in 590 as inaugurating the second. 25 See the account in Levison, *England and the continent*, passim. 26 See the comment of his biographer Eddius: 'Et primum ibi secundum apostolum fundamentum fidei posuit, quod adhuc superaedificat filius eius, in Hripis nutritus, gratia dei Willibrordus episcopus'; Wilhelm Levison (ed), *Vita Wilfridi I episcopi Eboracensis*, MGH SRM 6 (Hanover and Leipzig 1913) 163-263: 220. 27 Charles Plummer (ed), *Venerabilis Baedae opera historica* (2 vols, Oxford 1896; repr. 1969) 1, 192; Bertram Colgrave and R.A.B. Mynors (eds & transls), *Bede's Ecclesiastical History of the English people*. Oxford Medieval Texts (Oxford 1969) 312. It should be noted, however, that in a few passages crucial to our discussion the translation by Colgrave is seriously misleading; see, for example, 344-45 and 486-87. 28 Bede mentions the following: Ecgberct, Edilhun and Ediluin (III 27); Tuda (III 26); Willibrord (III 13); Higbald (IV 3); Uuictberct (V 9); Hewaldus Niger and Hewaldus Albus (V 10); Haemgils (V 12); Tilmon (V 10); Aldhelm records that the Heafrith to whom he was writing had studied in Ireland; cf. Rudolf Ewald (ed), *Aldhelmi et ad Aldhelmum*

site where these Englishmen were settled, Rath Melsigi, but this community is something of a lost colony, unmentioned almost in Irish or English documents,[29] and apparently lost without trace. And yet it can be shown that they provide a possible key to many of the problems facing the historians of Insular palaeography and learning. Not least, Rath Melsigi would provide an attractive alternative place of origin for some at least of the early manuscripts traditionally associated with Echternach.

The problem heretofore, of course, has been the inability of scholars to identify the Rath Melsigi site; that problem, however, may now have been solved. Mr Kenneth Nicholls of University College, Cork, has proposed that the site which occurs in some early charters as Cluain Melsige (now Clonmelsh, Co. Carlow) is identical with the Rath Melsigi of Bede's account.[30] There is no difficulty with the change in the first element of the name: *Cluain* in Irish means a meadow or pasture in a secluded area, often wooded, or a fertile 'island' in an area of bogland; *ráth*, on the other hand, means a ringfort.[31] But the onomastic difficulty here is only superficial, for a glance at the

---

epistulae, MGH AA 15 (Berlin 1919) 475–503: 488–94; Aethelwulf's *De abbatibus* (see p. 36 n. 3 below) mentions another Eadfrith who had been his teacher in Ireland; *Félire Óenguso* (hereafter Mart O), Whitley Stokes (ed), *Transactions of the Royal Irish Academy*, Irish MSS Series 1 (Dublin 1880) clxxxi, mentions a Benedict and a Cuthbert otherwise apparently unknown; Berchert of Tullylease is also commemorated on a stone slab still standing on the site; see John Ryan, 'Ecclesiastical relations between Ireland and England in the seventh and eighth centuries', *Cork Historical & Archaeological Society Jnl* 43 (1938) 109–12. [On the commemoration of the two Hewalds in Mart O, see now Pádraig Ó Riain, *Anglo-Saxon Ireland: the evidence of the Martyrology of Tallaght*. H.M. Chadwick Memorial Lecture 3 (Cambridge 1993).] 29 The name is written apparently as two words in the two earliest manuscripts of Bede's History: O. Arngart (ed), *The Leningrad Bede: an eighth-century manuscript of the Venerable Bede's Historia Ecclesiastica gentis Anglorum in the Public Library, Leningrad*. EEMF 2 (Copenhagen 1952) fol. 74ʳ; Peter Hunter Blair (ed), *The Moore Bede*, etc. EEMF 9 (Copenhagen 1959) fol. 67ᵛ; the name occurs as Ráith Maoilside in the Martyrology of Gorman (hereafter Mart G), Whitley Stokes (ed), *Félire hUí Gormáin: the martyrology of Gorman*, HBS 9 (London 1895) 238 (14 December); it is Ráth Maoilside in the Martyrology of Donegal, John O'Donovan, J. H. Todd and W. Reeves (eds), *The martyrology of Donegal* (Dublin 1864) 336 (14 December). A 'sanctus Congallus [= Comgall] abbas Rathurelfigi (*sic*) monasterij in Scotia' is commemorated at 12 May in the calendar of David Cameradus; see A.P. Forbes (ed), *Kalendars of Scottish saints* (Edinburgh 1872) 237 [ref. from Dr A.D.S. MacDonald, University College, Cork]. 30 The identification of Cluain Melsige with Rath Melsigi had been made independently by the late Éamon de hÓir, Irish Placenames Commission, as Breandán Ó Cíobháin kindly informs me. Fr Columcille Conway had suggested the same identification (see Aubrey Gwynn and R.N. Hadcock, *Medieval religious houses: Ireland* (London 1970) 402. Various other identifications have been suggested in the past, including some place in Connacht and Mellifont, Co. Louth (so Wampach, *Sankt Willibrord*, 193); these were rightly rejected by Plummer 2, 197. My late colleague, Thomas Fanning, suggested to me that Rath Melsigi may have been the important local secular settlement beside which the Anglo-Saxon foundation may have been located. He suggests further that the neighbouring Killogan may in fact have been the real ecclesiastical site. See his comments in the appendix to this paper. 31 Originally it denoted the rampart and ditch surrounding a site, then, by extension, the whole enclosure and the buildings within. The term is not restricted to ringforts alone, however, but can also denote an ecclesiastical site. The site of Clonmelsh, unfortunately, was levelled by quarrying

early nineteenth-century first edition of the Ordnance Survey map[32] shows Clonmelsh to be a clearing in a copse within which are clear traces of a ringfort or circular enclosure. In other words, the two sites could be identical: Rath Melsigi and Cluain Melsige could be one and the same,[33] and it may be from this site that the Frisian mission was despatched and coordinated, masterminded by the well-known figure of Ecgberct.

Bede related in detail how Ecgberct had spent many years already in Ireland when the great plague struck in AD 664.[34] Ecgberct vowed that, if he were spared, he would never again return to his homeland but would devote his remaining years to a spiritual and physical exile. Ecgberct was in fact spared and lived to the age of ninety, dying at last on 24 April 729, having allegedly converted the community of Iona to the orthodox reckoning of Easter in AD 715, and having spent the remaining fourteen years of his life on that island.[35] But the 'conversion' of the Iona community had not been Ecgberct's primary goal. Bede tells how, in fact, he had conceived the desire to preach the gospel to the continental Germans and how he had made elaborate plans to take up from where Wilfrid had left off on the Frisian mission.[36] But then two prophetic visions were related to him by a member of the Rath Melsigi community who had once been a monk of Melrose[37] in Scotland, in which Boisil, prior of Melrose, had told him in his sleep to warn Ecgberct against his new undertaking. On each occasion Ecgberct swore the monk to silence and tried to ignore the warnings, but when finally the ship which he had provisioned for the journey was wrecked in a storm Ecgberct decided reluctantly that his destiny was not to be with the Frisian mission. He chose instead for the task another of his companions at Rath Melsigi, a certain Uuictberct, who, likewise, had spent many years' exile in Ireland.[38] He took ship some time in the

and does not figure on the 2nd ed. of the OS map. **32** See the reproduction on p. 167 and the appendix to this paper. For the finished drawing of Fig. 1, I am grateful to Ms Angela Gallagher, Department of Archaeology, NUI, Galway. **33** Compare the reference, in the Genealogies of Irish saints, to 'Ernaine Dromma nó Cluana Railgech' (E. of Druim or Cluain R.); Anne O'Sullivan (ed), *The Book of Leinster* 6 (Dublin 1983) 1531. **34** HE III 27; Plummer 1, 192-93; Colgrave & Mynors, 312. **35** HE V 22; Plummer 1, 346-47; Colgrave & Mynors, 552-54. I do not believe that Ecgberct went to Iona in 712-13 and that he spent three years subsequently preaching to the Picts, before returning to Iona in 716, as claimed by Archibald A. Duncan. 'Bede, Iona, and the Picts', in R.H.C. Davis and J.-M. Wallace-Hadrill (eds), *The writing of history in the middle ages: Essays presented to Richard William Southern* (Oxford 1981) 1-42: 26-27. There is no justification for such a theory either in Bede's very clear account or in any other item of evidence. Plummer 2, 335, remarked of Ecgberct's 'mission' to Iona: 'Egbert seems to have taken his time in executing the commission which he received'! [50 years, in fact!] **36** HE V 9, Plummer 1, 296-98; Colgrave & Mynors, 474-8. It is interesting to note Bede's remark that Ecgberct had wished, in the event of his being unable to preach among the Germans, to undertake a pilgrimage to Rome. Ecgberct seems to have abandoned that notion also. [For an interesting additional item of information in Bede that originated in Melrose, see Colin Ireland, 'Boisil: an Irishman hidden in Bede's Historia Ecclesiastica', *Peritia* 5 (1986) 400-403.] **37** Note the provenance of the monk who had the visionary experiences. **38** 'Nam multos annos in Hibernia peregrinus anchoreticam in magna perfectione uitam egerat'; Plummer 1, 298; Colgrave &

680s and after reaching Frisia 'preached the word of life to that nation and to its king, Radbod'.[39] But Uuictberct met with no success, according to Bede, and after two years' fruitless labour he returned to 'his beloved place of exile' – to Ireland, that is, not England – and gave himself up to a life of devotion.[40]

This Uuictberct is never heard of again – or so we are told.[41] But he can in fact be rescued from the undeserved oblivion to which he has been assigned by the historians, by reference to *Cáin Adomnáin* 'The law of Adomnán' (of Iona).[42] This was a *lex innocentium* intended to protect non-combatants, and it was promulgated, according to the annals,[43] at an Irish midland synod of AD 697. The *Cáin* has attached to it a witness-list naming all those, both lay and ecclesiastical, who had subscribed to the terms of the decree. The authenticity of that list has recently been thoroughly vindicated.[44] One of the ecclesiastical witnesses is a man called *Ichtbricht epscop*: I believe this is our Uuictberct. Previous writers[45] have unanimously identified him with his more famous compatriot Ecgberct – overlooking Bede's explicit statement that Ecgberct died on 24 April 729, and the fact that he was not apparently a bishop.[46] Bede was particularly careful about that date because it had a very special significance for him.[47] But whereas Ecgberct is duly listed in the Irish martyrologies on 24 April,[48] Ichtbricht is commemorated on 8 December. We are clearly dealing with two separate individuals.[49] I believe, therefore, that it is Uuictberct and not Ecgberct who was present at the Birr synod of AD 697, so that in his case we have a definite instance of an Englishman who not only set out from Ireland on the Frisian mission, but who returned to Ireland (not England)

Mynors, 478. **39** 'Duobus annis continuis genti illi ac regi eius Rathbedo uerbum salutis praedicabat'; Plummer 1, 298; Colgrave & Mynors, 478. **40** 'Neque aliquem tanti laboris fructum apud barbaros inuenit auditores. Tum reuersus ad dilectae locum peregrinationis, solito in silentio uacare Domino coepit; et quoniam externis prodesse ad fidem non poterat, suis amplius ex uirtutum exemplis prodesse curabat'; Plummer 1, 298; Colgrave & Mynors, 478–80. **41** 'This priest is also mentioned by Alcuin in his *Life of Willibrord* but nothing further is known of him', Colgrave & Mynors, 478 n. 3; cf. Plummer 2, 287. **42** Kuno Meyer (ed), *Cáin Adamnáin, an Old-Irish treatise on the Law of Adamnan*. Anecdota Oxoniensia, Medieval & Modern Series 12 (Oxford 1905). **43** 'Adomnanus ad Hiberniam pergit et dedit legem innocentium populis', AU 696 (= 697), CS 693; 'Adhomnan tuc recht lecsa i n-Erind in bliadain-sea', AT [= 697]. **44** Máirín Ní Dhonnchadha, 'The guarantor list of Cáin Adomnáin, 697', *Peritia* 1 (1982) 178–215. The list had been rejected as spurious by D.A. Binchy, 'The date and provenance of Uraicecht Becc', *Ériu* 18 (1958) 44–54: 54 n. 2, and by Nora Chadwick, 'Bede, St Colmán and the Irish abbey of Mayo', in Nora Chadwick (ed), *Celt and Saxon: studies in the early British border* (Cambridge 1964) 186–205: 203 n. 2. **45** Meyer, *Cáin Adamnáin*, 40; Plummer 2, 285; Chadwick, *Celt and Saxon*, 203; Ní Dhonnchadha, 'Guarantor list', *Peritia* 1, 193–94. **46** HE V 22, Plummer 1, 347; Colgrave & Mynors, 554. Bede refers to him as *sacerdos*, which Plummer 2, 285, interpreted as meaning 'bishop'. **47** Ecgberct died on 24 April, a date three days beyond the traditional Irish Easter limit of 21 April. Hence the note of ill-concealed triumphalism in Bede's words: 'Mira autem diuinae dispensatio prouisionis erat, quod uenerabilis uir non solum in pascha transiuit de hoc mundo ad Patrem, uerum etiam cum eo die pascha celebraretur, quo numquam prius in eis locis celebrari solebat'; Plummer 1, 348; Colgrave & Mynors, 554. **48** 'Ecbrichti Saxonis', Mart T; 'Ecbricht', Mart G; not listed in Mart O.

when that mission failed. If, therefore, I were looking for a source of spiritual and material supply for the Frisian mission I would look, not to Lindisfarne, nor even to Northumbria, but to the English settlement at Rath Melsigi from which the earliest members of that mission set out. This was certainly the case with regard to Uuictberct and his successor, the great Willibrord (founder of Echternach); and I believe it can be argued also in the case of at least some early Echternach manuscripts.

A good example is provided by three fragments now bound up with two manuscripts in Paris, Bibliothèque Nationale, lat. 9527 (fol. 201) and lat. 10399 (fols 35-36).[50] These three folios were recovered from the bindings of known Echternach manuscripts and they contain Dionysiac paschal tables (for the years AD 706-778) and Anatolius *De Pascha*. In discussing these fragments, E. A. Lowe described the script as being 'a mixed Anglo-Saxon majuscule and minuscule, saec. VIII … written *presumably* [my italics] in England, or possibly at Echternach, where the fragments were later used for binding purposes'.[51] In this case Bibliotheksheimat (Echternach) has clearly suggested Schriftheimat (England). But it is as well to recall at this point a statement made by Lowe elsewhere: 'It is nothing strange if, when Insular manuscripts of the late seventh or early eighth century are in question, the palaeographer finds himself unable to say whether they were written by an English or by an Irish scribe, since at that period the English were still the imitators, following closely the methods of their Irish masters'.[52] In seeking to establish the origins of such

---

49 'Ichtbricht', Mart O; 'Ichtbritt', Mart G; Mart T is missing the December leaf. Note the remark of Hippolyte Delehaye: 'nulle part, la ténacité des habitudes populaires ne se manifeste avec plus d'évidence que dans la fidèle observance des jours fériés', *Les légendes hagiographiques*. Subsidia hagiographica 18 (Brussels 1973) 169. Despite many statements (e.g., by Chadwick, Duncan, and Ní Dhonnchadha) that Ecgberct was bishop and head of the English monastery at Mayo, there is, in fact, no evidence to support such a view; nor is it even likely, given that the members of that foundation left Lindisfarne rather than accept the orthodox Easter reckoning laid down by the synod of Whitby. Ecgberct's strict orthodoxy in this matter is a constant theme of Bede's account, who never mentions him in relation to Mayo. Thus Ní Dhonnchadha's citation of a late scholium in Mart O (p. 256) suggesting such a connection is misleading, since it omits a part of the Irish. The full scholium reads: *'Ichbricht áin* (this is not the diminutive but the adjective *án* 'famous') .i. ic Dun Geimin i Cianachta Glinde Geimin no i Connachta ata .i. a Maig Eo na Saxan i Cera (?) (Laud); .i. o Dun Gemin hi Ciannacht Glinne Geimin no hi Maig Eo na Sachsan i n-iarthur Chonnacht no hi Talaig Leis na Sachsan i nhuib Conaill Gabra (Rawl.); uel in alio loco diuersi duierse sentiunt, no o Thulaig Leis na Saxan a Mumain ⁊ Bercert a ainm, no Icht-bei ⁊l .i. Ichtbrit fil i Tig Saxain i nUib Eachach Mumán ⁊ brathair-sidhe do Dendict Tailcha Leis na Saxan ⁊ brathair doibh Cuitbrict ⁊ tair tarasarsen' (Franciscan MS.). The scholiast was clearly guessing and had no real knowledge of Ecgberct's alleged stay at Mayo. Besides, I have argued above that the 'Ichtbricht' of Mart O represents Uuictberct, not Ecgberct – though I do not believe that he had any connection with Mayo either. **50** CLA V 585. These fragments have not been discussed elsewhere, to my knowledge, except in my review of the Durham Gospels, *Peritia* 1 (1982), 360-61. Of necessity I repeat here some of the points made in that review. [See further: 'Early Echternach manuscript fragments and their Old Irish glosses', above, 133ff.] **51** See below, p. 33, for the logic behind Lowe's reasoning. **52** In the preface to CLA II (1972) XVI.

manuscripts, therefore, we need to be especially careful, and Bibliotheksheimat alone cannot offer a safe guide to place of origin. There are other criteria besides that of provenance which can help decide the ultimate origin of a codex, such as content.[53]

Anatolius, one of the surviving texts in the Paris fragments, is a computistical work well known to the Irish.[54] It is cited already as authoritative by Columbanus in his first two letters of AD 600 and 603.[55] It is cited also in the Letter of Cummian to Ségéne of Iona concerning the paschal question, *c.* AD 632/3.[56] and it is quoted at length in every early Irish computistical collection that I know.[57] Not only that, but Bruno Krusch in the last century demonstrated that the work is in fact probably an Irish forgery of the sixth century[58] the manuscript transmission of which is almost exclusively Irish.[59] Content, therefore, would at least suggest an Irish interest in the manuscript we are discussing, if not indeed an Irish origin. The case is strengthened by the presence in the text of an Old Irish gloss (*tólae*, not recognised or commented on by Lowe, although clearly visible in his plate).[60] This need, of course, imply no more than that an Irishman at Echternach penned and subsequently glossed the text – the subscriptions by Virgilius[61] in a couple of Echternach charters from the first years of the eighth century bear witness to the fact that there was at least one such Irish member of the community at the time; commonsense would suggest there may have been others.[62] But why not consider at least the

---

53 Lowe himself offered a list of seven such criteria in CLA IV (1947) xii-xiii. 54 For the text, see Bruno Krusch (ed), *Studien zur christlich-mittelalterlichen Chronologie* [1]: *Der 84-jährige Ostercyclus und seine Quellen* (Leipzig 1880) 311-27; for commentary, see Charles W. Jones (ed), *Bedae opera de temporibus*. Medieval Academy of America Publications 41 (Cambridge, Mass. 1943) 82-87. [A new ed., by D.P. McCarthy & Aidan Breen, will appear shortly.] 55 Wilhelm Gundlach (ed), *Columbae siue Columbani abbatis Luxoviensis et Bobbiensis epistolae*, MGH Epistolae Merovingici et Karolini Aevi 1 (Berlin 1892) 154-90: 156, 157,158, 162; G.S.M. Walker (ed & trans), *Sancti Columbani opera*, Scriptores Latini Hiberniae 2 (Dublin 1957) 2-59: 1 and 18. 56 First edited by James Ussher, *Veterum Hibernicarum epistolarum sylloge* (Dublin 1632) 24-35, No. XI: p. 21; = MPL 87, 964-78: 975. [See now Walsh & Ó Cróinín, *Cummian's Letter 'De controversia paschali'*, 32-35.] 57 See my paper, 'A seventh-century Irish computus from the circle of Cummianus', PRIA 82 C 11 (1982) 405-30 [=99-130 above.] 58 'An der britannischen Herkunft des Pseudo-Anatolius ist mithin nicht zu zweifeln', *Studien* 1, 312 (written at a time when Ireland was still regarded as part of Britain). 59 Bede knew the work through the Irish computus that he inherited at Jarrow; see my paper, 'The Irish provenance of Bede's computus', *Peritia* 2 (1983) 229-47 [= 175ff below]. 60 Note also the comments of the late Prof. Bernhard Bischoff, Munich, in response to a query of mine as to whether the Anatolius fragment might not just as likely have been written in Ireland as in England or Echternach: 'Die Bestimmung von CLA V 585 als "angelsächsisch" war unvorsichtig wegen des eigenartigen Schriftcharakters, auch ohne dass das irische Wort erkannt war. Es lässt sich nichts gegen irische Entstehung vorbringen, im Gegenteil (z. B. spelling)' (22 January 1982). 61 That he was Irish is suggested by the name, which is usually taken to be a latinisation of Fergal: cf. Genealogies of Irish saints in Anne O'Sullivan (ed), *Book of Leinster* 6, 1588: 'Tri filid in domain .i. Homer o Grecuib. ₇ Fergil o Latenaib (*sic leg.*). Et Ruman o Gaedelaib'. He also wrote a part of Paris, Bibliothèque Nationale, lat. 9382 (CLA V 577), containing the books of the minor prophets. 62 The Laurentius who penned the first part of Paris, Bibliothèque Nationale, lat. 10837 and a number of early eighth-

possibility that these Paris fragments were written in Ireland? Anatolius was, after all, a standard work in the Irish schools[63] and would doubtless have been familiar also to the English who studied there. And whatever about de luxe Gospel codices, a computus would have been a *sine qua non* of any missionary setting out on his journey.

This has particular importance with regard to another Echternach manuscript, Paris, Bibliothèque Nationale, lat. 10837,[64] which is in three parts: fols 2-33 contain a text of the Martyrologium Hieronymianum written by the scribe Laurentius; fols 34-41 + 44 contain the famous Calendar of Willibrord[65] and a paschal table; fols 42-43 contain later paschal tables for the years AD 760-797.[66] Lowe described the second section, Willibrord's Calendar (which contains, fol. 39ᵛ, a marginal entry in the saint's own hand)[67] as being penned in 'Anglo-Saxon majuscule, saec. VIII*in* (ante AD 728 … written in an Anglo-Saxon centre on the Continent, probably at Echternach, by the scribe of the Maihingen Gospels'.[68]

Lowe, however, did not quite appreciate the significance of the Easter table on fol. 44ʳ, which is a single leaf. Nor did he mention (what had been pointed out by Wilson, editor of the Calendar) that the script of this table was in a different – though stylistically related – hand.[69] The table covers the Easters of the nineteen-year cycle AD 684-702, but Lowe did not explain why an Echternach compiler of the early eighth century should have included such a list. What purpose could such a retrospective table have served? What relevance could the Easter date for those years have had for him at that time? It has not been explained why, if the table was already obsolete by the time the

---

century Echternach charters is also taken as Irish, though the reasons are nowhere stated clearly. Note also that Alcuin's life of Willibrord was based on an earlier work by an Irishman, presumably at Echternach; see the citation in Plummer 2, 287. **63** The work was being read even in those southern schools that had abandoned the Irish 84-year cycle, which Anatolius was believed to support. **64** CLA V 605, 606a, 606b. **65** H.A. Wilson (ed), *The Calendar of St Willibrord*. HBS 55 (London 1918). Wilson reproduced one page of the Martyrology as well. **66** It would be interesting to check whether the tables in Paris, Bibliothèque Nationale, lat. 10399, fols 35-36 (see 26 above) were copied from the tables in Willibrord's Calendar; as they now stand, however, they are acephalous. **67** Reproduced by Lowe, CLA V 606a. **68** Harburg, Fürstlich Öttingen-Wallersteinische Bibliothek, MS. I. 2. 4° 2, another of the so-called Echternach group. It is nowadays frequently referred to as the Harburg Gospels and contains (fol. 157ᵛ) the well-known acrostic verses whose resolution reads LAURENTIUS UIUAT SENIO, a reference apparently to the Laurentius mentioned in p. 154 n. 62 above. There are plates of the manuscript in E.H. Zimmermann, *Vorkarolingische Miniaturen* (Berlin 1916) pll 260-66, and J.J.G. Alexander, *Insular manuscripts, 6th to 9th century: a survey of manuscripts illuminated in the British Isles* I (London 1978) pll 115-16, 119, 124, 126; a useful discussion in Nordenfalk, 'The earliest Echternach manuscripts', passim. The occurrence in the manuscript of Old English and Old-High-German glosses does not necessarily determine its place of writing as being on the continent. [For a full colour facsimile, see now Dáibhí Ó Cróinín (ed), *Evangeliarium Epternacense (Universitätsbibliothek Augsburg, Cod. 1.2.4° 2)*. Codices Illuminati Medii Aevi 9 (Munich 1988). The MS. is now in the Augsburg university library.] **69** See the plate below, p. 221; the distinction of hands was duly noted by Kenney, *Sources*, 233, No. 69.

Calendar was being written, the scribe did not simply continue the original table for a further nineteen years on the verso page. But fol. 44ᵛ is blank, so that if its scribe were working 'saec. VIII*in*', as Lowe would have it, he must have drawn up his table in AD 701 or 702. But anyone familiar with the ways of computists will hardly believe that a scribe of *c.* AD 702 would pen a table for the nineteen-year cycle preceding that date, without continuing it for at least one further cycle of nineteen years.[70] That the cycle of AD 703-721 occurs in fact on a separate folio (40ᵛ) only confirms that the table on fol. 44ʳ was written before AD 702 – but how long before? It seems to me natural to assume that the table was written in or before the initial year of the cycle, AD 684;[71] the very purpose of an Easter table, after all, is to provide the dates of Easter in advance. But if this table was drawn up in or before AD 684 for Willibrord or one of his circle, then it must have been written in Ireland, for Willibrord was there until AD 690. Indeed, bearing in mind the initial year of the cycle, it is tempting to suggest that this table may originally have belonged to Uuictberct, who left on the Frisian mission, as we can infer from Bede,[72] some time in the 680s, perhaps even in that first year of the cycle. Having abandoned his missionary efforts then after two years, Uuictberct could have brought the table back with him to Rath Melsigi. It may well be that Willibrord then in turn brought the same table with him when he set out for Frisia in AD 690 and that it was subsequently bound in with the rest of his Calendar, as it is now.[73] It is hardly stretching the facts too much to assume that what property he had at Echternach in later years might have been his already in Rath Melsigi. It would likewise follow that the script of the Maihingen Gospels – written by the same hand as penned the Calendar, according to Lowe – might also reflect an Irish background, though it was doubtless written at Echternach, *c.* AD 702.

The suggestion of an Irish background for the Calendar can be buttressed by the internal evidence of the text itself. In terms of general content, of course, the Calendar contains nothing that is either peculiar or unusual, besides the fact that a number of the names have not been identified. Both English and

70 The tables of Dionysius Exiguus, on which the Echternach ones are based, extended from AD 532 to 626, i.e. a cycle of 5 x 19; the continuation of those tables by Felix 'Gyllitanus' covered the years AD 627-721 (i.e. another cycle of 95 years). I know of no other manuscript that contains a single cycle of 19 years.   71 For this statement I also have the endorsement of Professor Wesley Stevens of Winnipeg, *facile princeps* at present in the field of computistics. The table might conceivably have been written even earlier, since the practice was to prepare such tables a number of years in advance of the expiry date for the old cycle. Thus the 'Cyrillan' table of AD 437-531 that Dionysius adapted and extended was published by him in AD 525 – six years before the expiry of its last 19-year period.   72 HE V 9. It is not possible to deduce a precise year from Bede's words, though it must have been before 690, the year of Willibrord's departure.   73 Wilson, *Calendar*, x n. 2, refers to a paper (which I have not seen) of M.A. Reiners in *Publications de la section historique de l'Institut G.-D. de Luxembourg* 40 (1889) in which 'M. Reiners supposes the Calendar to have been written while St Willibrord was still in Ireland'. But he rejected this for the reasons given above.

Irish saints are well represented, as one would expect considering Willibrord's monastic formation in both countries. Oswald and Cuthbert appear among the English names, Patrick, Brigit and Colum Cille (in the form *Colum Cillae,* not Columbae) on the Irish side. One interesting absentee, perhaps, is bishop Wilfrid himself,[74] who not only began the Frisian mission but was also Willibrord's mentor at Ripon before his own departure from Northumbria in AD 678 and Willibrord's departure from Ireland.[75] But it is not safe to argue from silence, and since Wilfrid died in AD 709 the most that we could reasonably infer from his absence in the Calendar is that it was compiled or finished before that date.

But there is one name in the Calendar that does, I believe, have important implications for the theory of possible Irish origin: on 17 September there is entered the obit of a certain Cynifrid. According to H. A. Wilson, editor of the Calendar, 'this entry probably marks the obit of a contemporary otherwise unknown'.[76] I suggest that he is the Cynifrid who is mentioned by the author of the Wearmouth-Jarrow *Historia abbatum,*[77] writing in Bede's own monastery in Northumbria. The anonymous author, in his biography of abbot Ceolfrid, tells how Ceolfrid chose the monastic life in his late teens, and how he entered the monastery of Gilling in Yorkshire which had earlier been ruled by his elder brother, Cynifrid. But some years prior to Ceolfrid's entry into the monastery his brother Cynifrid had handed over the burden of administration to a kinsman and had taken himself off to Ireland 'in order to study the Scriptures'.[78] To judge from the general chronology of the *Vita,* this would have happened some time in the 650s. The Jarrow author further states that Cynifrid was one of the many Englishmen in Ireland who were carried off by the great plague of AD 664.[79] It seems possible, therefore, that the Cynifrid of the *Historia abbatum*

<hr />

74 The 'Wilfrid presbyter' who is commemorated at 17 February is clearly not the bishop of York, who died on 24 April.   75 Levison suggested that the two events were interconnected, *England and the continent,* 55, following Albert Hauck, *Kirchengeschichte Deutschlands vor der Reformation* 1 (Leipzig 1914; rev. ed. Leipzig-Berlin 1958) 435. Van Berkum, however, has disputed any such connection, 'Willibrord en Wilfried', 384-86.   76 *Calendar of Willibrord,* 40. 77 Edited by Plummer 1, 388-404. Cynifrid is not mentioned in Bede's *Historia abbatum* (Plummer 1, 364-87); one wonders why. A 'medicus Cynifrid' is mentioned by Bede, HE IV 19, but there is no obvious connection with the man named in the Calendar.   78 '[Ceolfridus], ubi octauum ferme et decimum agebat annum aetatis, deposito habitu saeculari monachus fieri maluit, intrauitque monasterium, quod positum in loco, qui dicitur Ingactlingum, religiosus ac Deo amabilis frater eius Cynefridus rexerat, sed non multum ante Tunberto cognato ipsorum regendum commiserat, qui postea Hagustaldensis aecclesiae antiste ordinatus est; ipse discendarum studio scripturarum Hiberniam secedens, simul et desiderio liberius Domino in lacrimis precibusque seruiendi', Plummer 1, 388. Henry Mayr-Harting seems to have been misled into thinking that Tunbert was the one who went to Ireland; see his *The coming of Christianity to Anglo-Saxon England* (London 1972) 106 and 290 n. 8.   79 'Nec multo post idem Cynefridus, pestilentia longe lateque grassante, cum aliis quoque Anglorum nobilibus, qui gratia legendi scripturas illo praecesserant, a morte transitoria perpetuam migrauit ad uitam', Plummer 1, 389.

is the Cynifrid of Willibrord's Calendar, the elder brother of no less a person-
age than Ceolfrid of Jarrow, Bede's own abbot.[80]

Now it is important to remember that Cynifrid left for Ireland some time in
the 650s. His name in the Calendar, therefore – if it does refer to him – can
hardly be the reflection of Willibrord's Northumbrian background, because
Cynifrid had left Northumbria even before Willibrord was born, in AD 658, and
hence they could not have met there. On the other hand, Cynifrid had died, it
seems, in Ireland in AD 664, if we can infer from the account in the *Historia
abbatum*,[81] so that they cannot have met in Ireland either, for Willibrord did not
leave Northumbria until his twentieth year, AD 677-8. The anonymous author's
account, however, seems to allow the reasonable inference that Cynifrid was
one of that group of Englishmen who made up the community at Rath
Melsigi. His commemoration in the Calendar (if he is the same man) must, I
think, reflect the memories of that Anglo-Saxon group in Ireland, not in
Northumbria, for it was in Ireland, after all, that he died.

But the survival of this memory is really no more than we would expect in
the circumstances. After all, Willibrord had been in Ireland for the twelve years
prior to his departure on the Frisian mission in AD 690. From AD 678 to AD 690,
therefore, he had lived and studied in that Anglo-Saxon community at Rath
Melsigi from which Uuictberct before him had been sent, and of which
Ecgberct was the acknowledged leader,[82] a site of which Bede said much and
yet so tantalisingly little. There was no comparable Northumbrian influence on
the missionary efforts of this group, but there was obviously a strong Irish
connection, if only by reason of the environment in which they were working.
Moreover, the continuity of this involvement is clear from Bede's statement
that two others of the group, Hewald the Black and Hewald the Fair, set out on
a similar mission to the Saxons, inspired by the example of their colleagues on
the Frisian mission.[83] Hence Rath Melsigi emerges clearly as the real source of

---

80 The anonymous Jarrow author believed that Ceolfrid had conceived the idea of a final
pilgrimage to Rome 'imitatus exemplum fratris sui Cynefridi, qui … studio uitae contemplatiuae
monasterii curam reliquit, et patriam propter Dominum spontaneo mutuauit exsilio', Plummer 1,
395.   81 So I would interpret the reference to the plague 'longe lateque grassante'; but the
transfer of Ceolfrid to Ripon, which the anonymous author (for reasons that are not clear)
mentions in the same breath as Cynifrid's death, is dated by Plummer to AD 661, though with a
query; chronological table, 2, xxi, and 196. Of course, the reference might also be to a later date,
such as the plague of AD 686, to which the anonymous author refers §14, Plummer 1, 393. Mr
William O'Sullivan has pointed out to me that Cynifrid's name occurs with that of Landberict,
bishop of Maestricht († before AD 706?). [William O'Sullivan died on 31 Dec. 2000.]   82 To the
objection that Bede (III 27) says the Rath Melsigi community was dispersed by the plague one can
compare the account of equal devastation of Jarrow in 686 related by the anonymous *Historia
abbatum*, Plummer 1, 393, where it is said that 'all who could read or preach or recite the
antiphons and responses were swept away, except the abbot himself and one little lad nourished
and taught by him'.   83 HE V 10, Plummer 1, 299-301; Colgrave & Mynors, 480-84. [See now
Pádraig Ó Riain, *Anglo-Saxon Ireland*, 7, 20.]

inspiration for this Anglo-Saxon missionary effort in the seventh and eighth centuries.

But not only did it provide the personnel for these undertakings, it must also have provided at least a few of the manuscripts for the initial missionaries, and the scribal expertise required to produce further ones. Thus the presumption of Northumbrian origin for most of these early Echternach codices rests, in fact, on little more than an ignorance of the true historical background to that monastery. Because Willibrord and his companions were Northumbrian by birth, Lowe (and others after him)[84] tacitly assumed that their closest contacts would have been with Northumbria. Thus Lowe, for example, in his discussion of the placing and dating of Insular manuscripts, said:[85] 'The Echternach Gospels, now in Paris ... a masterpiece of Insular calligraphy and decoration, belonged to St Willibrord,[86] himself a Northumbrian, who probably took it with him *from England*' (my italics). This is, of course, only a slip on Lowe's part, but the underlying assumptions which led to it have had an unfortunate effect on his estimations of all the Echternach manuscripts. In making these assumptions, however, Lowe was completely overlooking the explicit testimony of Bede and others that Willibrord and his companions had planned and supported the Frisian missionary effort from Rath Melsigi in Ireland, not from England.

There is one further piece of internal evidence from the Calendar which I think may possibly strengthen the case for this proposed Irish background. The May page[87] has two items of interest: on 26 May is the entry: *Dedicatio bassilicae sancti Martini*[88] *inuaedritlaeum*, the 29 May entry reads: *Dedicatio bassilicae sancti Pauli inrumleos*. Wilson, the editor, remarked at this point: 'The entries on these days record the dedication of two churches which were probably consecrated by St Willibrord, or had some special interest for him. It does not seem possible to identify the two places mentioned'.[89] This has certainly been the case up to now: neither of the placenames occurs, to my knowledge, in any of the 187 charters that have survived from Echternach,[90] nor in any other

---

84 For example, Brown, 'Book of Kells', 228, suggests that the Echternach Gospels was intended 'as a foundation gift [from Lindisfarne] for Willibrord's new monastery at Echternach', a theory he repeats in *Durham Gospels*, 43-44. Note also that Colgrave shares this mistaken preconception when he translates HE V 2: 'Postquam uero per annos aliquot in Fresia qui aduenerant docuerant', rendered as 'When those who had come *from Britain*' (my italics).   85 CLA II , xviii, Lowe further adds: 'If [the student] wants examples of authentic English performance he must go to the Lindisfarne Gospels and the Codex Epternachensis, to St. Willibrord's Calendar and Martyrology ... and to the Moore Bede. There he will find his criteria for Northumbrian calligraphy', ibid., xvi-xvii.   86 There is, in fact, no evidence to show that the codex 'belonged' to Willibrord personally in the sense that, for example, the Calendar clearly did.   87 See the reproduction on p. 222 below.   88 Wilson read this as 'sanctae Mariae', but the first word looks to me like the contraction *sci.*   89 *Calendar*, 30.   90 Edited with an excellent commentary by Camille Wampach, *Geschichte der Grundherrschaft Echternach im Frühmittelalter*, Publications de la section historique de l'Institut G.-D. de Luxembourg 63 (2 vols, Luxembourg 1929-30). There

source relating to Willibrord's continental foundations.[91] I should therefore suggest that the second at any rate may be an Irish placename: by supplying the radical *d* before the *r* we get *i nDrum Leos*, which looks very like the name *Druim Léas* (Drumlease, Co. Leitrim), an early foundation several times mentioned in the Patrician dossier in the Book of Armagh.[92]

If this proposed identification is correct then we have another strong argument in favour of an Irish background for the underlying text of the Calendar.[93] The Calendar was doubtless given its present form on the continent, possibly *c*. AD 702.[94] That it was the work of several hands writing at different times is obvious enough; but the accumulation of historical evidence would seem to indicate also that the initial compilation of its exemplar took place in Ireland.[95] I have argued as well that the Dionysiac Easter table on fol. 44[r] of the Calendar, covering the years AD 684-702, was most likely drawn up in the first of those years rather than the last – in which case it must certainly be of Irish origin. Since this single folio is clearly of Rath Melsigi provenance, and since a closely related hand was responsible for the other manuscripts mentioned, it is difficult to avoid the conclusion that the scriptorium in which these hands were developed was that of Rath Melsigi.[96] And the same arguments, to a greater or lesser extent, must apply to most of the other so-called

---

is a Rumlaos listed as a witness in one charter, 52, 12.Wampach did not consider the calendar entries.   **91** See the comment of Eugen Ewig, 'Die Kathedralpatrozinien im römischen und im fränkischen Gallien', *Historisches Jahrbuch* 79 (1960) 1-61; repr. Ewig, *Spätantikes und fränkisches Gallien* (2 vols, Munich 1976, 1979) 2, 260-317: 285: 'Ein Paulspatrozinium begegnet bei keiner Kathedrale Galliens. Es kommt auch bei den anderen Kirchen vor dem 7. Jh. selten oder gar nicht vor und gehört sicher einer jüngeren Schicht an'. In the accompanying note (238) he adds: 'Im 7. Jh. sind Paulskirchen häufiger zu belegen, meist aber in einem Zusammenhang mit Petruskirchen'. He does not mention the dedication in Willibrord's Calendar.   **92** Ludwig Bieler (ed & trans), *The Patrician texts in the Book of Armagh*, Scriptores Latini Hiberniae 10 (Dublin 1979) 158, 172: 'iuxta Druim Leas' (Tírechán), 'i ndruim Daro .i. Druim Lias'; 'du manchuib Drommo Lias'; 'altóir Drommo Lias'; 'for Druim Leas'; 'di muintir Drommo Léas' (Additamenta). *Druim Leas* is the oldest form attested in these documents; *Druim Lias* is the later development. The phonetics of the name, as it appears in the Calendar, present no difficulty to anyone familiar with Old Irish. Nasalisation of the initial after the preposition *i(n)* is the rule. **93** This applies to the entries by the principal hand. But it is quite clear that the entries by the *prima manus* generally reflect his Echternach milieu at time of writing, since they include names of people with whom Willibrord could only have come into contact on the continent.   **94** The entry relating to Pope Sergius I († 7 Sept. 701) is in the script of the *prima manus*. Mr William O'Sullivan has pointed out to me that the entry 'aodberto hecco' in cursive minuscule, *saec*. VIII, on fol. 44[v] may refer to the Adalbert (Aethelbert) who was a collaborator of Willibrord's; see Levison, *England and the continent*, 61.   **95** There is, unfortunately, no good, detailed palaeographical description of either manuscript.   **96** There may be significance in the fact that the Maihingen [Augsburg] codex has the oldest copy of Ailerán of Clonard's († AD 665) verses on the Eusebian canons, *Quam in primo speciosa quadriga*. Prof. Nancy Netzer, Boston Museum of Fine Arts, has pointed out to me that the poem contains the earliest reference to the 'beast canon tables' so prominent in Insular gospel codices. She discusses this point in chapter 6 of her forthcoming dissertation on the Trier Gospels. [See now Nancy Netzer, *Cultural interplay in the eighth century: The Trier Gospels and the making of a scriptorium at Echternach* (Cambridge 1994) 61, 82, 119.]

Echternach manuscripts. Once they have been removed from the spurious Northumbrian context they are free to find their most natural historical setting, which I believe was at Rath Melsigi in the south of Ireland.[97]

Rath Melsigi, however, provided material and spiritual support not just to the continent but to Willibrord's native Northumbria. Our evidence is in the poem *De abbatibus*[98] composed by the Northumbrian monk Aethelwulf between the years AD 803 and AD 821, and dedicated by him to bishop Ecgberht of Lindisfarne, successor to the Eadfrith to whom is ascribed the writing of the Lindisfarne Gospels. The poem relates the very interesting story of how Aethelwulf's monastery, unnamed but clearly located not far from Lindisfarne,[99] was founded as a daughter-house of that famous monastery *c.* AD 705-15.[100] The cell was established by one Eanmund, a Northumbrian nobleman who visited Eadfrith to seek advice about his undertaking. As a result of this conference he obtained a teacher from Lindisfarne to instruct his monks. A much more important and enduring role in the cell's establishment and development, however, was played by Ecgberct, the famous English exile in Ireland,[101] from whom Eanmund requested instruction on the education of his monks, an altar, and even advice on where to build the monastery.[102] The poem contains a lengthy account of Ecgberct's prophetic vision of the site and of his continued interest in its subsequent development.[103]

The passage that follows[104] in the *De abbatibus* has a particular relevance to the present discussion and to the general question of Insular illuminated manuscripts and their origins, for it describes some of the early inmates of Eanmund's monastery, amongst whom was one Ultán *preclaro nomine dictus.*

---

97 In his contribution to *Die Iren*, 1, 112, Brown has the following disarming statement: 'If the early Echternach scribes are not Northumbrians, like their founder Willibrord, they must have been Irish' [= *A palaeographer's view*, 212]. The comment is not elaborated upon and its possible implications for his theories are left unpursued. 98 Alistair Campbell (ed), *Aethelwulf De abbatibus* (Oxford 1967). See also David Howlett, 'The provenance, date, and structure of *De abbatibus,*' *Archaeologia Aeliana* 5/3 (1975) 121-30. Dr Howlett kindly sent me a copy of the revised text, to appear in 'The Anglo-Latin tradition', chapter 3 of *Alfredian books and their biblical models* (in the press). 99 See Campbell's introduction, pp xxv-xxvi. Dr Howlett suggests Bywell, about fifty miles from Lindisfarne. 100 The date is important, since Ecgberct was probably still in Ireland at the time, pace Duncan (see p. 24 n. 2 above). Aethelwulf describes Ecgberct as being 'Scottorum finibus'. Howlett stated that Eadfrith provided Ecgberct as instructor for Eanmund's cell, but he has acknowledged in a letter that such an interpretation is not warranted by the text, and he no longer holds that view. 101 'Haec inter famulus Christi dum noribus almum / pontifice discit Scottorum finibus esse / Ecgberctum, famulum cui fidum mittere curat, / poscens ut monachos firmaret rite libellis, / sanctificetque sibi uenerande altare tabellae, / atque memor uoti monstret, sint que loca digna, / quis possint sisti sacraria sancta tonanti'; *De abbatibus*, 11-13. 102 'Paret et obsequitur praesul uenerandus, euntem / confirmat dictis, quin sacro munere ditat: / mensa sacrata deo magni sub nomine Petri / aduolat et cellam nigro confirmat ab hoste'; *De abbatibus*, 13. 103 'Hacc dum gesta suo instituit mandare magistro, / nuntius ad patrem patris perferre loquelas / uenerat'; *De abbatibus*, 15. Note that the first messenger 'trusit per cerula puppim', again suggesting that Ecgberct was in Ireland. 104 *De abbatibus*, 19.

Ultán was an Irishman, as his name clearly indicates and as Aethelwulf himself remarks, 'and he could ornament books with fair markings and by this art he accordingly made the shape of the letters beautiful one by one, so that no modern scribe could equal him'.[105] It is as well to note that all this refers to the early years of the eighth century – immediately following that period (late seventh century) when, according to Julian Brown, not only the Lindisfarne Gospels but also the Durham and Echternach Gospels were in course of production at the Lindisfarne scriptorium. Yet this obscure and unnamed Northumbrian daughter-house of Lindisfarne has an Irish scribe-illuminator, not an English master from the scriptorium of the mother-house. Neither are we left in any doubt about Ultán's talents, for Aethelwulf expressly stated that there was not another scribe to match him.[106]

Where Ultán came from we do not know: he might have come from Lindisfarne, though Aethelwulf did not say so. He might plausibly have come from Iona or some such Irish foundation, but there is no evidence to suggest that he did. In the light of Ecgberct's known involvement in the establishment of Eanmund's monastery, however, and in view of the many palaeographical affinities that exist between the Durham Gospels and known Echternach manuscripts,[107] it is not unreasonable to ask whether he might have come from Rath Melsigi, Ecgberct's own foundation. I have suggested elsewhere[108] that Ultán might conceivably have been the scribe-illuminator of the Durham Gospels – a proposition which I believe matches the manuscript evidence far better than the theory of Lindisfarne origin which Julian Brown has proposed. If he did produce it then he may have done so either in his Northumbrian home or in his native Ireland.

But though the Calendar of Willibrord, the Maihingen [Augsburg] Gospels, and the Durham Gospels were probably not written at Rath Melsigi, but at Echternach or elsewhere, the scribal tradition that lies behind them must surely be Irish. We do well to recall Lowe s words: 'At that period the English were still the imitators, following closely the methods of their Irish masters'[109]

---

105 'Fama citat plures perfectam uisere uitam, / quam pater Eanmundus precultis moribus ornat. / a quibus est Vltan preclaro nomine dictus. / presbiter iste fuit Scottorum gente beatus, / comptis qui potuit notis ornare libellos / atque apicum speciem uiritim sic reddit amoenam / hac arte, ut nullus possit se aequare modemus / scriptor'; *De abbatibus*, 19. [For aguments against interpreting Aethelwulf's words as meaning an artist-scribe (not very convincing, in my view), see Lawrence Nees, 'Ultán the scribe', *Anglo-Saxon England* 22 (1993) 127-46.] **106** Indicative of Masai's methodology is his comment on this Ultán: 'On a depuis longtemps remarqué la nationalité de cet enlumineur, mais on a trop insisté sur ce fait et pas assez sur le circonstance important qu'il pratiquait l'enluminure à Lindisfarne', *Essai*, 127 n. 218. Ultán, of course, is not known to have worked at Lindisfarne, as Masai would have it; indeed, he seems oblivious of the fact that if he had, the consequences for his theory of English workmanship would have been disastrous. **107** See the detailed comparison in *Durham Gospels*, 42-49, and *Die Iren* 1, 111-12. **108** In a lengthy review of the facsimile Durham Gospels, *Peritia* 1 (1982) 352-62. **109** See p. 153 above; cf. T. J. Brown, 'An historical introduction to the use of Classical Latin authors in the

– men such as Ultán *preclaro nomine dictus.* That the influences which went to make up the scribal style of Rath Melsigi were Anglo-Saxon as well as Irish goes without saying. Indeed, it would not be going too far to suggest that there may have been Frankish elements in the mixture as well.[110] That might explain why, for example, in the opinion of art historians, the Book of Durrow has a number of decorative features that reflect Anglo-Saxon contacts rather than Celtic ancestry.[111] But if Rath Melsigi really were the location of a thriving seventh-century Hiberno-Saxon scriptorium, one would be surprised not to find such a 'foreign' presence reflected in the production of its close neighbour.[112] There were large numbers of Englishmen in Ireland during the formative period of Insular script and manuscript illumination,[113] not all of them based at Rath Melsigi. But even allowing for that fact, we should not forget the fundamental point demonstrated by Lowe[114] and accepted by all scholars since,[115] that the English learnt their script (and, I would argue, their techniques of manuscript illumination as well) from their Irish masters, and that they learnt these techniques in Ireland as well as in Northumbria.

If all the manuscripts traditionally associated with Echternach were the work of Rath Melsigi-trained scribes, one would have to assume a lengthy period of activity for the group in Ireland, before their transfer to Echternach in the early eighth century. That there was a reciprocal influence on the Irish in turn we need not doubt. In the dozen or so manuscripts[116] still surviving for which an Echternach provenance has been either demonstrated or posited, we find an impressive range of scripts and decorative techniques that bears clear

British Isles from the fifth to the eleventh century', *Settimane di Studio del Centro Italiano di studi sull'alto medioevo* 22 (1975) 237-99: 253-54: 'Until 669, then, Anglo-Saxon England was a cultural province of Ireland and evidently a province in which Latin learning flourished much less vigorously than in Ireland itself' [= *A palaeographer's view*, 141-77:150]. 110 Witness the presence of the Frank Acgilbert, later bishop of Paris, who had spent many years in Ireland in the 650s 'legendarum gratia scripturarum', as Bede puts it (HE III 7). 111 See Nordenfalk. 'Before the Book of Durrow' passim. [See now also, George Henderson, *From Durrow to Kells. The Insular gospel-book AD 650-800* (London 1987) 19 ff.] 112 I should make clear my belief that the Book of Durrow was made in and for Durrow, where it already was in the ninth century. Note the identical flourishes in Durrow and in Willibrord's Calendar (see plates 10, 11), and the more than superficial similarity of the scripts. Mr William O'Sullivan suggested to me a connection between the Book of Durrow and the Durham Gospels through the Irish and Iona connections of Ecgberct. For arguments in favour of a similar connection between Durrow and Iona, through the person of Adomnán, see Alfred P. Smyth, *Celtic Leinster: towards a historical geography of early Irish civilization A.D. 500-1600* (Dublin 1982) 94 and appendix, 118-22. In his 'Book of Kells', 242, Brown remarked that 'if Durrow were Irish, it would be another matter'. I hope to present further evidence for Durrow's Irish origin on another occasion. 113 See above, p. 151. 114 See above, p. 153. 115 Brown, 'Book of Kells', 221, reiterates 'the sound old view that the English had learned from the Irish' [= *A palaeographer's view*, 98]. 116 Cf. Lowe, CLA v 577, 578, 584, 585, 586, 588, 595, 596, 598, 605, 606a, 606b, ix 1364 [See also the additional Echternach manuscripts identified by Michele Camillo-Ferrari, *Sancti Willibrordi venerantes*, 20-23]; Brown, 'The Insular system of scripts', passim, suggests other candidates. There is an annotated catalogue in Degering's 'Handschriften aus Echternach', 71-82.

witness to the work of a practised scriptorium. A style is already set *c.* AD 684, in the Dionysiac Easter table from Paris, Bibliothèque Nationale, MS. 10837, fol. 44ʳ, and another closely related one in the *prima manus* of Willibrord's Calendar, fols 34-41 of the same manuscript. It might be suggested that those Echternach manuscripts in particular that show Insular traits in the preparation of the vellum could have been written at Rath Melsigi.[117] When exactly (and how many of) the Rath Melsigi scribes transferred to Echternach we cannot say for sure, but it may be significant that the names of Laurentius and Virgilius do not appear in charters there before 704 and 709 respectively.[118]

There is, unfortunately, nothing either in the Maihingen [Augsburg] or Echternach Gospels to provide a clue as to their precise date or origin, unless the presence in the Maihingen [Augsburg] manuscript of Ailerán's poem is taken as evidence for an Irish environment. It is certainly curious that the Echternach Gospels seem to have exercised no obvious textual influence on the later Echternach scriptorium,[119] for the scribe of the Trier Gospels[120] – another closely related manuscript – drew on two separate exemplars for his text: one similar to the Maihingen and Maeseyk Gospels[121] (whose texts are virtually identical), but the other of no discernible relationship to any of the Echternach group, including the Echternach Gospels themselves.[122] It may be, therefore, that the Echternach Gospels are to be dated considerably later than the Calendar and the other early Echternach manuscripts. But until such time as a thorough study of all these manuscripts is undertaken we will not be in a position to offer definite views as to their relative chronology. However, there

---

117 BN lat. 9382 (Prophets), written by Virgilius [CLA V 577]; BN lat. 9527, fol. 201 + BN lat. 10399, fols 35-36 (Dionysius Exiguus, Anatolius, etc.) [CLA V 585]; BN lat. 9538 (Aug., *De Trinitate*) [CLA V 588]; BN lat. 10399, fol. 50 (Greg. Mag., *Moralia*) [CLA V 596]; BN lat. 10400, fols 107-8 (Bede, *In Apocalypsin*) [CLA V 598]; BN lat. 10837, fols 2-33 (*Martyr. Hieron.*), written by Laurentius [CLA V 605]; BN lat. 10837, fols 34-41 + fol. 44ʳ (Calendar) [CLA V 606a], written by the scribe of the Maihingen [now Augsburg] Gospels. 118 Wampach, *Geschichte* 2, Nrs 8 (p. 30), 1 May 704 (Laurentius); 16 (p. 46), 21 May 709 (Virgilius); 17 (p. 48), 29 July 710 (Laurentius); 28 (p. 70), 24 Oct. 718 (Laurentius); 31 (p. 75), 721-2 (Virgilius); 32 (p. 76), 721-2 (Laurentius Virgilius [*sic*]). 119 Though the illumination in several Echternach books certainly was influenced by it. Alexander, *Insular manuscripts*, 53b, sees influence on the Trier Gospels. See now Martin Smith, 'A note on the Echternach Gospels', *Chiba Review* 3 (1981) 25-58. Smith's findings have important implications for the theory of a 'Durham-Echternach Calligrapher'. [Subsequent scrutiny of the Echternach Gospels revealed that Smith's theory of a singleton as first leaf of the MS. was mistaken. I believe that Brown's 'Durham-Echternach Calligrapher' was his finest achievement in a wide range of valuable palaeographical contributions.] 120 Trier, Domschatz, MS. 134 (6l): CLA IX 1364; Alexander, *Insular manuscripts*, pls 108-14, 125, 127. 121 Church of St Catherine, Trésor, s.n., fols 6-132, another one of this group of illuminated gospels; see Alexander, *Insular manuscripts*, pll 87-107. Like the others, it is usually assumed to be of Northumbrian provenance. 122 This important information I owe to the kindness of Nancy Netzer, Museum of Fine Arts, Boston, who has discussed the question in chapter 3 of her forthcoming dissertation on the Trier Gospels. [See n. 96 above. Dr Netzer is now Professor at Boston College.]

are sufficient historical data to hand for us to be able to say with a fair degree of certainty that the scriptorium in which the first-generation Echternach scribes received their formation was at Rath Melsigi in Ireland.[123][*]

123 I leave the last word to Nordenfalk, *Celtic and Anglo-Saxon painting*, 11: 'By localizing in Northumbria all those key manuscripts that show the Hiberno-Saxon style of book decoration in full maturity, some scholars have gone so far as to deprive Ireland of the honor of having played an essential part in the creation of what has been considered its greatest national exploit'.
[*] This is the annotated text of a paper delivered to a joint meeting of the Pontifical Institute of Medieval Studies and the Centre for Medieval Studies in the University of Toronto on 26 October 1982, and to a meeting of the Medieval and Renaissance Guild of the Universities of Winnipeg and Manitoba on 24 November 1982. I wish to thank in particular Profs. Leonard Boyle, Virginia Brown, and Jocelyn Hillgarth in Toronto, and Prof. Wesley Stevens in Winnipeg for their help and encouragement while preparing the paper. I have deliberately retained, as much as possible, the style of the talk as it was delivered. It was read in draft by Mr William O'Sullivan, former Keeper of Manuscripts, Trinity College, Dublin, who made many very helpful suggestions for its improvement and who saved me from numerous errors. I am very grateful for his help and encouragement. I am grateful also to the Trustees of Trinity College, Dublin, and the Bibliothèque Nationale, Paris, for permission to publish the plates in this paper. P. Dr Édouard Jeauneau, Paris, kindly procured for me the photograph of BN lat. 10837, fol. 44[r], and my colleague Dr Anders Ahlqvist kindly sent me photographs of BN lat. 9527, fol. 201.

Some field monuments in the townlands of Clonmelsh and Garryhundon, Co. Carlow

Thomas Fanning (†)

Department of Archaeology,
University College, Galway

On the first edition of the Ordnance Survey (OS) 6-inch map, sheet 12, for Co. Carlow there are a number of monuments marked which are relevant to the foregoing article by my colleague Dáibhí Ó Cróinín. A third monument, marked as a church, deserves a brief mention but does not share the antiquity of the other sites. The latter monument is in the townland of Clonmelsh and is located within the north-east corner of a small graveyard directly south of Clonmelsh house, roughly four miles due south of Carlow town. In 1833 this church is stated by the local historian Ryan to be the parish church.[124] His brief reference implies that the plain simple building was in use at the time, and this is borne out by the fact that the word 'church' is not marked in Gothic lettering on the OS map. Today all that survives within the square-shaped walled graveyard are the ivy-covered lower walls of the church and the headstones noted by Ryan. These eighteenth- and nineteenth-century tombstones and their inscriptions, by and large, commemorate the Protestant gentry from the nearby 'big houses' of Clonmelsh and Garryhundon – the former was the local rectory. There is no evidence either within or without the graveyard of medieval or earlier features.

Roughly half a mile to the south-east of the above monument, in the same parish of Clonmelsh but in the next townland of Garryhundon, there was a fairly substantial, roughly oval-shaped enclosure which was marked in the usual hachured manner on the first edition of the OS map (fig. 1, p. 167). This earthwork, about sixty metres in greatest diameter, was, apparently, a single-banked earthen enclosure and was situated within a small copse or plantation of trees. On the later editions of the OS maps nothing is shown of either the plantation or the enclosure. Whether this earthwork, which would be classified as a ringfort or rath, could have had any connection with the Rath Melsigi referred to by Bede we shall never know, for not only has the monument itself been removed but the area in which it was located is badly scarred by quarry-

---

124 J. Ryan, *The history and antiquities of the county of Carlow* (Dublin 1833) 337.

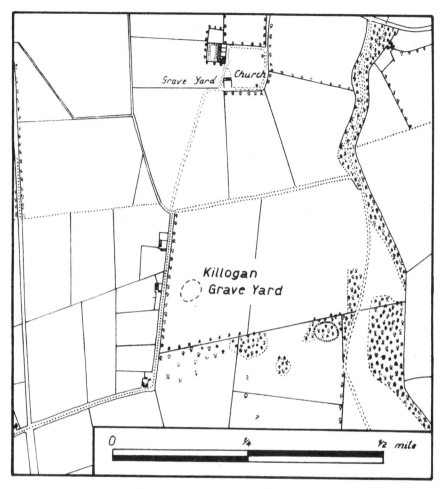

Fig. 1 Location map of the field monuments in the townlands of Clonmelsh and Garryhundon, Co. Carlow (based on the OS 6-inch map by permission of the Government, Permit No. 4318).

ing and dumping, as can be seen from the aerial photograph taken in 1967 (pl. 1a).

About a quarter of a mile to the west of where the rath was located, and in the same townland, another enclosure is marked on all editions of the OS 6-inch map. The site is located on a low ridge close to the 200 foot contour and is marked in Gothic lettering as 'Killogan Grave Yard' in the first edition (fig. 1) and as 'Killogan Burial Ground (disused)' in subsequent editions.[125] The

125 There is a brief mention of the site in John O'Donovan and others, *Ordnance Survey letters for Co. Carlow* (1837) 59-60. The exact location is Co. Carlow OS 6-inch sheet 12:6:3, 39 cm from western margin and 38.5 cm from southern margin, NGR S 723690.

Plate 1(a) Aerial view showing Killogan burial ground in the centre (north).
Copyright Cambridge University Collection.

placename is the one referred to as Kelogan in the Baltinglass charter along
with Cluain Maelsige. The monument is not hachured on the OS maps but is
shown with a broken line to indicate a much-levelled or almost destroyed
earthwork (fig. 1).

The site, today, consists of a low defaced earthen bank enclosing an irregu-
lar oval-shaped area measuring approximately 56 by 34 metres from crest to
crest of the bank (pl. 1a). The bank can be best traced on the east and south and
is only barely perceptible on the west and north. There is no visible trace of a
surrounding fosse or an entrance feature. A modern fence of large concrete
posts and wiring is located on the remains of the enclosing bank. Scattered
within the earthwork but mainly in the western and northern sectors beneath
the small trees and scrub are a number of eighteenth- and nineteenth-century
headstones commemorating some local, Catholic, interments.

Plate 1(b) Killogan from west, with remains of earthern bank and cross.

Standing approximately in the centre of the enclosure is a small ringed or wheeled cross of granite (pl. 1b). This monument is not marked on any edition of the OS 6-inch maps and only came to light in the summer of 1892 when it was found, buried in the ground.[126] The shaft, detached from the cross-head, lay beside the socket-stone or base until last year, when the cross was repaired and re-erected on its base.[127] The cross, which appears complete, except for one section of the ring, is 125 cm in height and 85 cm wide across the arms and has an average thickness of 20 cm (pl. 2a). The small socketstone in which it is set measures 65 by 40 cm and is 25 cm in height. Both main faces of the cross are similar, with the solid ring ornamented with a small central boss and outlined by a low moulding (pl. 2b). A similar moulding is carved along the edges of the cross-head, arms and shaft, and apart from this there is no other trace of decoration or of figurative or abstract art.

Similar small, granite crosses, mainly with solid rings, are to be found on other early sites in the immediate locality,[128] and the cross at Nurney, a mile or so to the south, provides the closest parallel. This latter cross displays the low moulding and small central boss as found on the Killogan example and also exhibits the unusual feature of a straight appearance to the upper section of the ring, as if the ring was skeuomorphic of timber braces.[129] Amongst the other

---

126 Cf. *Jnl Roy. Soc. Antiq. Ire.* 23 (1893) 87.   127 This work was tastefully executed by members of the Old Carlow Society under the direction of Mr Alec Burns.   128 Cf. H.S. Crawford, 'A descriptive list of the early Irish crosses', JRSAI 37 (1907) 218-19.   129 See Seán P. Ó Ríordáin, 'The genesis of the Celtic cross', in Seán Pender (ed), *Féilscríbhinn Tórna* (Cork 1947) 113-14.

Plate 2(a) Cross at Killogan burial ground.

Plate 2(b) Close-up of cross head.

sites in Co. Carlow close to the river Barrow, where such crosses, or fragments thereof, have been found are Old Leighlin, Kildreenagh (Newtown), Agha, and Templeowen.[130] These crosses are usually regarded as a sub-type of the so-called Granite or Barrow Group of high crosses which are known from St Mullins in the south of Co. Carlow (where the cross, though larger, is of somewhat similar proportions to that from Killogan) northwards to the other important early christian monastic sites of Castledermot, Moone and Old Kilcullen in Co. Kildare.[131] They can be dated, in general terms, to the period extending from the late eighth to the early tenth century AD.

The nature of the enclosure at Killogan, and particularly the presence of the cross, point to the existence of an early monastic site or cell, clearly one of a number in the immediate area. The Rath Melsigi of Bede inhabited *c.* AD 664 by the Saxon monks could have been the principal house of the group of cells. It is somewhat unusual to find the prefix *rath* associated with a monastery, but famous sites, like Armagh, are referred to in the literature as 'the Rath'.[132] Since the term in old Irish signified the rampart or enclosing bank of a fort it could also have been utilized on occasion to denote the earthen *vallum* of a monastery. Was the site referred to by Bede one of the monastic sites in the area which is now known under another placename, or was it a large enclosure dominating the area later referred to as Cluain Melsigi? We shall probably never know the answers to these questions, though the destroyed *rath* referred to above may have contained some helpful information.

The cross at Killogan and its companions in the surrounding countryside are indicative of monastic activity in the area, and the probable relationship between this minor group and the more important figured crosses at nearby Moone and Castledermot has already been referred to. These latter monuments, located on documented Columban sites, are notable for the parallels they provide with similar monuments in Scotland and northern England. The slender shape and certain figured panels on the Moone cross can be compared with the two famous crosses of the Cumbrian school, viz. the Ruthwell cross in Dumfrieshire and its neighbour across the border at Bewcastle, erected in the middle of the eighth century.[133] The finding at Castledermot, some years ago, of the only known example from Ireland of a hogbacked, recumbent monument of a type well known from the Scandinavian settlements in northern England[134] also points, in a tenuous manner, to some continuing link with that

130 See B. Fitzmaurice. 'A survey of the pre-Norman stone crosses of Co. Carlow', *Carloviana* I/ 19 (1970) 31-32, and another notice in the same journal No. 30 (1983) 32-33.   **131** Françoise Henry, *Irish high crosses* (Dublin 1964) 27.   **132** See Françoise Henry, *Irish art during the Viking invasions (800-1020 AD)* (London 1967) 40. Monastic sites whose placenames incorporate this prefix include Rathmichael, Co. Dublin; Rahan, Co. Offaly; and Ratass, Co. Kerry.   **133** Rosemary Cramp, 'The Anglian tradition in the ninth century', in J. F. Lang (ed), *Anglo-Saxon and Viking age culture*, British Archaeological Reports, British Series 49 (1978) 7.   **134** J.F. Lang, 'The Castledermot hogback', JRSAI 102 (1972) 154-58.

region in the subsequent centuries. Certain comparisons have also been drawn between the crosses of the Barrow group, such as those at Moone and Castledermot, and the surviving crosses at Iona,[135] and hence the comment by Bede that Ecgberct, one of the Saxon monks resident at Rath Melsigi, ended his days at Iona in 729, may have an added significance.

The cells of Cluain Melsigi and Kelogan mentioned in the charter can be traced from the placename and cartographic evidence, and Killogan, at least, has been located on the ground. The archaeological evidence provided by the presence of the cross indicates that the latter site was in existence sometime during the eighth to tenth centuries. Any further or more tangible evidence of a possible Hiberno-Saxon connection can only be furnished by means of archaeological excavation. Such evidence, if it survives, could well be of particular importance for a clearer understanding of the nature of monastic and other cultural links between the Irish and Anglo-Saxons in the centuries preceding the Viking incursions.

135 Françoise Henry, *Irish high crosses*, 27-8.

13

The Irish provenance of Bede's computus[*]

In his great studies of Bede's works 'On Times' Charles W. Jones assembled a large and hitherto unknown body of manuscript material on which to base a history of Insular computistical writings in the seventh century.[1] *Computus*, the study of time-reckoning and ecclesiastical calendar calculations at all levels, from initial learning of numerals themselves up to the mastery of methods and tables for constructing and manipulating such calendars, was one of the three principal subjects of the medieval monastic curriculum.[2] In the narrower sense, however, computus can also denote an individual tract or collection of tracts or rules *(argumenta)* concerning Easter calculations, so that a computus can range in length from the nine brief formulae ascribed to Cassiodorus,[3] up to the massive compilation in Milan, Biblioteca Ambrosiana, MS. H. 150 Inf., which contains a huge variety of *argumenta*, computistical verses, letters, tracts, tables and a calendar.[4] It has of course been long known that the Paschal controversy developed computistical knowledge and skills in Ireland and England to a degree which was far in advance of anything on the continent during the previous few centuries.[5] Professor Jones showed that this knowledge was based principally on a collection of Spanish (and in some cases ultimately African) origin which had reached Ireland by *c.* AD 630, and which travelled subsequently from there to England, where (by the end of the seventh century) it formed the basis of Bede's own computistical library at Jarrow.

The bulk of this collection comprised paschal letters of Pope Leo, Proterius of Alexandria and Paschasinus of Lilybaeum, the paschal cycles of Theophilus and Cyril of Alexandria and their continuator Dionysius Exiguus, together

---

[*] First published in *Peritia* 2 (1983) 229-47. 1 Charles W. Jones, 'The "lost" Sirmond manuscript'. [Unfortunately, the crucial last six pages of the original article have been accidentally omitted from the reprint].; idem, *Bedae pseudepigrapha· scientific writings falsely attributed to Bede* (Ithaca, N.Y. 1939) [= *Bede, the schools and the computus*, pt 2]; idem (ed), *Bedae opera*. I am at all times heavily indebted to the work of this great Bedan scholar, a gentleman and a good friend. [Charles W. Jones died 25 June 1989.] 2 This fact has been obscured by the tendency of many writers to see the 'liberal arts' as the backbone of Irish monastic curricula in particular. 3 See Paul Lehmann, 'Cassidorstudien II: Die Datierung der Institutiones und der Computus paschalis', *Philologus* 71 (1912) 278-99 (297-99 = text). 4 Ludovico Muratori (ed), *Anecdota quae ex Ambrosianae Bibliothecae codicibus primum eruit Ludovicus Antonius Muratorius* (6 vols, Padua 1713) 3, 109-209 = MPL, 129, 1273-1372. This collection contains material from Columbanus' Burgundian foundations, some of it dating from the seventh century. 5 Jones, 'Sirmond manuscript', 207 [= *Bede, the computus and the schools*, chap. X].

with various other computistical tracts and tables. To these items in the computus the Irish added a number of texts of native origin, among them the Anatolian *Canon Paschalis*,[6] the *Epistola Cyrilli*,[7] and the tract of pseudo-Morinus,[8] which the Irish then in turn compared with older tracts on the subject of the 84-year cycle. It is quite clear that the reception into Ireland in the 630s of the 'Roman' methods of dating Easter caused a ferment of argument and discussion in the Irish schools concerning the respective merits of the various tracts. This transition period between the old and new cycles can be observed in the evidence of Cummian's famous Paschal letter[9] and also in such computistical collections as are contained, for example, in Munich, Bayerische Staatsbibliothek, Clm 14456 (*saec.* IX$^{1/4}$, Regensburg),[10] in the Milan collection previously referred to,[11] and in the computus which I recently discovered in Brussels, Bibliothèque Royale, MS. 5413-22 (*saec.* Xin, partly Reims), and Vatican, Biblioteca Apostolica Vaticana, MS. Reg. Lat. 1260 (*saec.* IX, Fleury?).[12] These collections, however, clearly show that the debate was a long-drawn-out one and that the adoption of the 'Roman' Easter was a gradual process in which Irish computistical scholars tried and tested the respective cycles by practical observation.[13] The situation with regard to seventh-century England, however, is not so clear.[14]

Our main source of information is, of course, Bede who, in his account of the synod of Whitby (AD 664) and the events that led up to it[15] gives some idea

6 See Bruno Krusch (ed), *Studien zur christlich-mittelalterlichen Chronologie* [1]: *Der 84-jährige Ostercyclus und seine Quellen* (Leipzig 1880) 311-27. Commentary in Jones, *Bedae opera*, 82-87. [A new ed., by D.P. Mc Carthy and Aidan Breen, will appear shortly.]   7 Ed. Krusch, *Studien* 1, 344-49. Commentary in Jones, *Bedae opera*, 93-97.   8 Ed. Jean-Baptiste Pitra, *Spicilegium Solesmense* (2 vols, Paris 1852; repr. Graz 1962) 1, 14-15; Alfred Cordoliani, 'Les computistes insulaires et les écrits pseudo-alexandrins', *Bibliothèque de l'École des Chartes* 106 (1945-6) 5-34: 30-34.   9 First edited by James Ussher, *Veterum epistolarum Hibernicarum sylloge* (Dublin 1632) 24-35, No. XI; slightly emended in MPL 87, 969-78. A new critical edition with commentary, by Maura Walsh and myself, is ready for the press. [See now Walsh & Ó Cróinín, *Cummian's Letter 'De controversia paschali'*.]   10 See Krusch, *Studien* 1, 10-23; *Studien* [2]: *Die Entstehung unserer heutigen Zeitrechnung*. Abhandlungen der Preußischen Akadademie der Wissenschaften, Jahrg. 1937, phil.-hist. Kl., Nr. 8 (Berlin 1938) 58; Bartholomew Mac Carthy, in Hennessy & Mac Carthy (eds & transls), *Annála Uladh, Annals of Ulster* (4 vols, Dublin 1887-1901) 4, lxvii-lxviii; Eduard Schwarz, 'Christliche und jüdische Ostertafeln', *Abhandlungen der königlichen Gesellschaft der Wissenschaften zu Göttingen*, phil.-hist. Kl., N.F., 8, Nr. 6 (Berlin 1905) 89-103.   11 For a discussion of the relationship between these various collections, see my paper, 'A seventh-century Irish computus from the circle of Cummianus', PRIA 82 C 11 (1982) 405-30 [= 99-130 above].   12 An edition of this work will accompany our new edition of Cummian's Letter (see 230 n. 5 above). [This is the text *De ratione conputandi* which forms the second part of Walsh & Ó Cróinín, *Cummian's Letter and the 'De ratione conputandi'*.]   13 I have shown elsewhere that the evidence cited by previous scholars in support of the claim that the Dionysiac cycle was known in Ireland before AD 610 is entirely spurious. See my paper 'Mo Sinu maccu Min and the computus at Bangor', *Peritia* 1 (1982) 352-62. [= 35-47 above.]   14 See Jones, *Bedae opera*, 78-113; Kenneth Harrison, *The framework of Anglo-Saxon history to AD 900* (Cambridge 1976) 52-75.   15 *Historia Ecclesiastica* III 25 (hereafter HE); Charles Plummer (ed), *Venerabilis Baedae opera historica* (2 vols, Oxford 1896; repr. London 1969) 1, 181-94; Colgrave and Mynors (eds), *Bede's Ecclesiastical*

of how he, at least, saw the development of current practice; but even Bede is so vague on the crucial points of technical importance that modern scholars have been unable to agree about his intentions.[16] We are on sure enough ground for Northumbria after AD 635, for with the foundation of Lindisfarne and the establishment of the Irish mission there the Irish 84-year cycle clearly became the basis for subsequent Easter reckonings.[17] But the discord that had arisen in the 630s among the churches in Ireland manifested itself shortly thereafter in Northumbria, for Bede tells us that during the episcopacy of Fínán, Aidan's successor at Lindisfarne (AD 651-661), an Irishman named Rónán, 'who had learned the true rules of the church in Gaul or Italy', disputed the Easter question vehemently with Fínán, but to no lasting effect. Though Rónán succeeded (according to Bede) in winning over many to his point of view, the Lindisfarne abbot remained unmoved and 'on the contrary', to use Bede's extraordinary words, because 'he was a man of fierce temper, Rónán made him the more bitter by his reproofs and turned him into an open adversary of the truth'.[18] What the *regula ecclesiasticae ueritatis* was that Rónán so assiduously championed Bede, unfortunately, does not say.[19] Neither is he more specific about the practice of James the Deacon, 'who kept the true and Catholic Easter with all those whom he could instruct in the better way'.[20] Nor does Bede say exactly how the Northumbrian queen Eanfled was instructed by the priest Romanus, whom she had brought with her from her native Kent, a man 'who followed the catholic observance'.[21] That Bede himself understood the 'catholic observance' to be the one that involved use of the Dionysiac paschal tables can hardly be doubted, but he was too good a scholar to believe that what was 'catholic' in his day was 'catholic' also in the seventh century, and his reluctance to specify those tables by name in his discussion has led modern scholars to doubt whether, in fact, they were known in England (north or south) before the mid-seventh century.[22]

History, 294-309. **16** Jones, *Bedae opera*, 102-4; Harrison, *Framework*, 59-63. **17** Harrison, *Framework*, 62. That the Iona community decided finally in AD 715 to abandon the 84-year tables was doubtless due to their having discovered from comparison with the Victorian/Dionysiac over the full 84-year cycle that theirs was the less accurate table: 715-84 = 631, roughly the date when, according to Cummian's Letter, the Alexandrian reckoning was first introduced into southern Ireland. I do not accept any of the speculations on this point in A.A.M. Duncan, 'Bede, Iona, and the Picts', in R.H.C. Davis and J.M. Wallace-Hadrill (eds), *The writing of history in the Middle Ages* (Oxford 1981) 1-42. **18** HE III 25: 'quin potius, quod esset homo ferocis animi, aceruiorem castigando et apertum ueritatis aduersarium reddidit'; Plummer 1, 181; Colgrave & Mynors, 296. Colgrave and Mynors (296 n. 1) suggest that Rónán was the one with the 'fierce temper', wrongly in my view. **19** Jones thought that the Victorian tables might have been meant, *Bedae opera*, 104. If this were the case then Bede's silence would be understandable, since the principal purpose of his *De temporum ratione* was to counter the influence of Victorius. **20** HE III 25: 'uerum et catholicum pascha cum omnibus, quos ad correctiorem uiam erudire poterat'; Plummer 1, 181; Colgrave & Mynors, 296. **21** Bede, loc. cit. **22** Harrison, *Framework*, 62: 'It would seem that Dionysiac tables were not known, even in Kent, before 654, or known only in a superficial way'. The possible exception considered by him is Birinus, bishop of Wessex from AD

The circumstances of this dispute over the correct method of calculating the date of Easter have been seen by Harrison as one of the motives for the departure of Wilfrid (later bishop of York) to Rome in AD 654.[23] According to Bede, Wilfrid received instruction at Rome from Archdeacon Boniface and learned, amongst other things, 'the correct method of calculating Easter, as well as gaining, under his teacher's guidance, a knowledge of many other matters of ecclesiastical discipline which were unknown in his own country'.[24] The role played by Wilfrid subsequently at the Whitby synod, and the pane-gyric verses inscribed on his tomb, are viewed by Harrison as confirmation of the general impression that 'Wilfrid is being credited with the promotion in England of the Dionysiac cycle':[25]

> Paschalis qui etiam sollemnia tempora cursus
> Catholici ad iustum correxit dogma canonis,
> Quem statuere patres, dubioque errore remoto,
> Certa suae genti ostendit moderamina ritus.

But this theory lays rather too much stress on the alleged continental prove-nance of the 'catholic observance', at the expense of other, more immediate and (in my view) more likely sources for such instruction. More importantly, it ignores the fact – long since established by Jones – that the bulk of Northumbrian computistical material came from the Irish. 'Bede's works show that Northumbrian education [in the computistical field, at any rate] owed comparatively little to Rome and the Augustinian mission',[26] and apart from those works which Bede assembled expressly for the composition of his History, there is 'no indication of a stream of literature from the south which in any way equals the obvious stream from Ireland'.[27] The basis for these state-ments was Jones' important discovery that the computus which Bede himself used at Jarrow could be recovered almost in its entirety by an examination of four computistical manuscripts:[28] Vatican, Biblioteca Rossiana, MS. Lat 247 (*saec.* XI) [R], Paris, Bibliothèque Nationale, MS. lat. 16361 (*saec.* XII) [P], Geneva, Bibliothèque de l'Université, MS. 50 (AD 804, Massai [G], and Oxford, Bodleian Library, MS. Bodley 309 (*saec.* XI, Vendôme) [S]. To these may now be added Tours, Bibliothèque Municipale, MS. 334 (AD 819, Tours) [T], which in fact is the exemplar of P. All of these manuscripts (except P)

634; but there is in fact no evidence to show what tables, if any, Birinus followed. **23** Harrison, *Framework*, 62-63. **24** HE V 19: 'computum paschae rationabilem [didicit] et alia multa, quae in patria nequiuerat, ecclesiasticis disciplinis accommoda eodem magistro tradente percepit'; Plummer 1, 324; Colgrave & Mynors, 590. **25** Harrison, *Framework*, 75. **26** Jones, *Bedae opera*, 112-13. **27** Ibid., 113. **28** See esp. 'The "lost" Sirmond manuscript', *passim*, and *Bedae opera*, 105-13. Note that the Tours MS. 334 (formerly 42) is now made up of four parts, one at Tours and the others comprising Paris, Bibliothèque Nationale, Nouv. acq. 1612, 1613, 1614. For simplicity, however, I use the siglum T to cover all parts. (Note that in *Peritia* 1, 296, I accidentally gave the folio reference in T; the text concerned occurs in S on fol. 106ᵛ).

were copied independently from a now lost exemplar whose text is best preserved by S, a codex which once belonged to the French scholar Jacques Sirmond; whence Jones coined the term 'Sirmond group of manuscripts'.[29] The purpose of this paper will be to demonstrate that the exemplar of this whole group (which Bede undoubtedly used at Jarrow) was compiled in southern Ireland in AD 658, and passed from there shortly after to Northumbria and Jarrow.

It is an extraordinary quirk of fortune in the circumstances that Professor Jones – having established his case for the Irish provenance of Bede's computus on irrefutable textual grounds – should have overlooked an explicit statement in four of the manuscripts that he examined which would have clinched his argument beyond cavil. The passage concerned occurs in a collection of short synchronistic notes, culled mainly from the Prologue of Victorius of Aquitaine. I give the text here from S and in the apparatus the variants from G, P and T.

'Omnibus annis temporibus diebus ac luna maxime, que iuxta Hebraeos menses facit, rite discussis, a mundi principio usque in diem, quo filii Israhel paschale mysterium initiauere anni sunt III DCLXXXVIIII, praecedente primo mense VIII Kl. Aprilis, luna XIIII, VI feria. Passum autem dominum nostrum Ihesum Christum peractis VCCXX & VIII annis ab exortu mundi, eadem cronicorum relatione monstratur, VIII Kl. Aprilis primo mense, luna XIIII', VI feria.

Inter primum pascha in Aegypto et passionem domini anni sunt I DXXXVIIII. R,. Ex domini uero passione usque in pascha quod secutum est suibini filii commanni anni sunt DCXXXI. A pascha autem supradicto usque ad tempus praefinitum consummationis mundi, id est sex milibus consummatis, anni sunt CXLI.

1-8 Victorius, *Prologus in cyclo paschali* (Krusch, *Studien* 2, 24)
2 facis (underlined) S fac T usque *eras.* P a principibus *corr.* K > a principio P 3 annui G 4 luna XVII TG anni et G 6 reuelatione TP 9 R *in marg.* S, *in text* TGP domino G 9-10 sequu/um ÷ sui n̄ri filii communi T, sui n̄ri r̄ filii commamni G, sui.N̄ri.r̄., *with* filii – dcxxxi. *om (gap left)* P 12 XCLI GP

From the information contained in the final passage we can calculate not only the date of composition for the text, but also deduce a precise location for

---

29 A full list of contents is given by Jones, 'Sirmond manuscript', 213-19, and *Bedae opera*, 106-7. These include unpublished texts of 'Palumbus' and Patrick which I hope to discuss in the next volume of *Peritia*. [See 'New light on Palladius', above, 28-34, and 'Columbanus, the computistical writings', above 48-55.] [For the contents of the Sirmond manuscript, see further below, 202-3.]

its compilation. The mathematics of the formulae are simple enough: (1) From the year of Our Lord's Passion to the year of writing is 631 (DCXXXI) years. Since Victorius says that the number of years to the Passion is Anni Mundi 5228 (Passum autem ... peractis VCCXX & VIII annis), the total number of years (AM) elapsed = 5228 + 631 = 5859; subtracting the number of years to the Nativity (5201) we get 658. In other words, to convert Victorius' *annus passionis* dating to its AD equivalent, add 27: 631 + 27 = AD 658. (2) The second clause in the dating formula provides corroboration of this: from the time of writing to the end of the world (traditionally calculated at AM 6000) is 141 years. Subtracting 141 from 6000 leaves 5859 AM. To reduce a Victorian AM dating to AD we subtract 5201 (as above): AM 5859-5201 = AD 658.

Both these formulae, therefore, give the date of composition as AD 658. More important, however, is the precise wording of the text at this point: according to the dating clause, 631 years had elapsed from the year of Christ's Passion *usque in pascha quod secutum est suibini filii commanni* 'the Easter of Suibine mac Commáin' which had followed. In other words, the computist was working with a Victorian Easter-table in the margin of which, beside the data for the current year, was noted the death of one Suibine mac Commáin. The text thus comprises one of our earliest dateable Irish annals and is alone sufficient refutation – if such were needed – of the argument that our earliest Irish annals do not derive from such Easter-tables. All the evidence of the text: dating formulae, the form of the Irish name,[30] and the orthography of the manuscript[31] show clearly that we have here a genuine, mid-seventh-century document, and the annal is in fact preserved independently in the Annals of Inisfallen, s.a. 658, where that text reads:

> Kl. Dub Tíre ua Maíl Ochtraig ⁊ Conaing mac Muricáin ⁊ Suibne mac Commáin.[32]

---

30 Trisyllabic *Suibine* is a pre-syncope form very rare in documents after the mid-seventh century; see James Carney, 'Aspects of Archaic Irish', *Éigse* 17 (1978-9) 417-35, esp. 421-30. Note that in the Life of St Aldegunde *(Bibliotheca Hagiographica Latina*, No. 244, ed. Chesquière, 321) the same trisyllabic form occurs as the name of an Irish abbot at Nivelles *(cuidam uiro religiose Subino)*; see Paul Grosjean, 'Notes d'hagiographie celtique 39', *Analecta Bollandiana* 75 (1957) 397 n. 2, who emends unnecessarily to *Subino*.   31 The use of short horizontal dashes over every syllable of an Irish word is a feature, e.g., of the Schaffhausen MS. of Adomnán's *Vita Columbae*, where they serve the same purpose as italicisation in modern type. Such horizontal dashes occur also in the Reichenau MS. of the seventh-century Irish commentary on the Catholic Epistles (see below, 150 n. 46) and in the Würzburg MS. M. p. th. f. 61 (glosses) which I discussed in the paper cited on p 174 n. 13 above. In later Irish MSS (e.g. the Book of Armagh) acute accents have replaced these horizontal dashes.   32 Seán Mac Airt (ed), *The Annals of Inisfallen*, 94. The annal is added in the lower margin, with a reference-mark indicating its place in the main text; see Richard I. Best and Eoin Mac Néill (eds), *The Annals of Inisfallen reproduced in facsimile*, etc. (Dublin 1933) fol. 11ᵛ (lower margin).

Of the first two persons named here nothing further is known to me,[33] but Suibine mac Commáin (the man mentioned in the computus) would seem to have been quite an important figure in mid-seventh-century Ireland, and the information which we have concerning him allows us to make a good guess as to where the computistical text was written,

Suibine mac Commáin belonged to the Uí Fothaid branch of the Déisi,[34] a south-Munster tribal group settled mainly in the area of modern-day Co. Waterford. From the accounts in the annals and genealogies it can be shown that one of his daughters, Uasal, was married to Faélán mac Colmáin († AD 666),[35] king of the north Leinster dynasty of Uí Dúnlainge and the man chiefly responsible for the rise to power of that dynasty in the seventh century.[36] One earnest of Faélán's dominance is the fact that a brother of his, Áed Dub, was abbot and bishop of Kildare and was styled by the genealogists *ríg-epscop Cilli Dara ⁊ Lagen uli* 'royal bishop of Kildare and of all Leinster'.[37] According to Cogitosus, the biographer of St Brigit who was writing probably in the mid-seventh century,[38] the foundation of Kildare was 'a great metropolitan city' where the treasures of kings were kept, doubtless implying that (in his view at least) Kildare was claiming to be the chief church in Leinster. That the Uí Dúnlainge king under whose patronage Kildare flourished should marry a daughter of Suibine mac Commáin clearly implies that Suibine was a figure of power among the neighbouring Uí Fothaid of the Déisi to the south. There may also be some significance in the fact that Cummie,[39] who was married to Faélán mac Colmáin's father, was also a Déisi woman.

A second daughter of Suibine, Faílend, was (again according to the genealogies)[40] married to Crundmaél mac Rónáin († AD 656), king of the other great Leinster dynasty of Uí Cennselaig. This Faílend – 'a queen who reigned but kept her powder dry' – seems to have been a woman of some repute, to judge by a remark in the genealogies to the effect that the stories about her and

33 Conaing mac Muricáin is perhaps the Conaing mac Marcáin mentioned in the Déisi genealogies; see O'Brien (ed), *Corpus genealogiarum Hiberniae* 1, 397. A son of his, Fland Suanach Érand (or Coraind) is mentioned there as 'rí inna nDésse' ('king of the Déisi'). 34 O'Brien, *Corpus*, 340, 400. 35 See Whitley Stokes (ed), 'The Annals of Tigernach', *Revue Celtique* 17 (1896) 186: 'Bass Uasle ingine Suibne Maic Colmain i. rigan Faelain ríg Laigen'; though AU has only 'Mors hUaisle filiae Suibni', there is no good reason to doubt the identification. However, these annals seem to have been misconstrued by F. J. Byrne, *Irish kings and high-kings* (London 1973) 154. [For additional confirmation of the Uasal-Faélán connection, see now my paper, 'Lebar Buide Meic Murchada', in T.C. Barnard, Dáibhí Ó Cróinín & K. Simms (eds), *A Miracle of Learning'. Essays for William O'Sullivan* (Aldershot 1999).] 36 For an outline of his career see Byrne, *Irish kings*, 154. 37 O'Brien, *Corpus*, 339; Byrne, *Irish kings*, 152. 38 MPL 72, 775-90. See Kenney, *Sources for the early history of Ireland* 1: Ecclesiastical (Columbia, N.Y. 1929; repr. Dublin 1993) 359-60, No. 147; Mario Esposito, 'On the earliest Latin Life of St Brigid of Kildare', PRIA 30 C 2 (1912) 307-26; Kathleen Hughes, *The church in early Irish society* (London 1966) 83-85; Richard Sharpe, '*Vitae S Brigitae*: the oldest texts', *Peritia* 1 (1982) 81-106; Kim McCone, 'Brigit in the seventh century: a saint with three lives?', *Peritia* 1, 107-45. 39 O'Brien, *Corpus*, 340. 40 Ibid.

Crundmaél were famous; but the genealogist (doubtless for good reasons) thought better of reciting the details of her adventures.⁴¹ Besides providing daughters as wives to these two leading dynasts, Suibine also had a son, Congal († AD 701) who put his name to *Cáin Adomnáin* 'The Law of Adomnán' (promulgated in AD 697) as *rí inna nDéissiu* 'king of the Déisi'.⁴²

There can be no doubting, then, that Suibine mac Commáin was a powerful and influential figure in mid-seventh century Irish politics – certainly noteworthy enough for his death to warrant mention in an annal. The dating formulae in the Sirmond group of manuscripts thus set the date and location as *c.* AD 658, in the south-east region of Ireland. This immediately brings to mind the group of scholars, mainly exegetical, who have been traditionally associated with the monastery of Lismore, Co. Waterford, and other foundations in the south-central area of the country.⁴³ These are Manchianus (Manchéne) of Min Droichit († AD 652);⁴⁴ Laidcenn mac Baíth Bannaig of Cluain Ferta Mo Lua († AD 661); a Breccanus of unknown location; two other Déisi-men: Bercannus mac Áedo and Banbanus (mac Donngaile? † AD 685/6, of unknown location) or Baithanus (Baíthéne); and the unknown author of the *De mirabilibus sacrae scripturae* (flor. *c.* AD 655).⁴⁵ The names of the first five of these have been recovered from an important Irish commentary on the Catholic Epistles (Karlsruhe, Badische Landesbibliothek, MS. Aug. CCXXXIII [*saec.* IX¹, Reichenau]),⁴⁶ composed probably in the mid-seventh century.⁴⁷ Manchianus is cited there as *doctor noster* and the others are cited also as being exegetical authorities. Their connection with the author of the *De mirabilibus*

41 'Is airrdirc trá seanchas na Faílinde seo ⁊ Crundmaíl meic Rónáin a fir ⁊ a raind do-rochtad ⁊ ideo nech scribo', *Corpus*, 340.   42 Kuno Meyer (ed), *Cáin Adamnáin: an Old-Irish treatise on the Law of Adamnan*. Anecdota Oxoniensia, Medieval and Modern Series 12 (Oxford 1905) 18. See Máirín Ní Dhonnchadha, 'The guarantor list of *Cáin Adomnáin*, 697', *Peritia* 1 (1982) 178-215: 200. Another son of Suibine's, Conamail, figures in Irish legend, for which see Seán Ó Coileáin, 'The structure of a literary cycle', *Ériu* 25 (1974) 88-125.   43 See Paul Grosjean, 'Sur quelques exégètes irlandaises du VIIe siècle', *Sacris Erudiri* 7 (1955) 67-98. There are, however, strong grounds for believing that this scholarly circle centred on Cluain Ferta Mo Lua rather than Lismore, as Grosjean argued; the arguments are laid out in the work by McGinty, cited below. [For a vindication of the existence of this group of scholars (against some recent writers who would wish them out of existence) see my paper 'Bischoff's "Wendepunkte" fifty years on', *Revue Bénédictine* 110/3-4 (2000) 204-37, and Charles D. Wright, 'Bischoff's theory of Irish exegesis and the Genesis commentary in Munich Clm 6302: a critique of a critique', *Jnl Med. Latin* 10 (2000) 115-75.]   44 There are no good grounds for Grosjean's claim that the Manchianus here discussed was the saint of Liath Mancháin (Co. Offaly).   45 MPL 35, 2149-200. See William Reeves, 'On Augustin, an Irish writer of the seventh century', PRIA 7 (1861) 514-22; Mario Esposito, 'On the pseudo-Augustinian treatise "De Mirabilibus Sacrae Scripturae"', PRIA *(C)* 35 (1919) 189-207; Kenney, *Sources*, 275-77, No. 104. I have derived much profit from the new edition by Dom Gerard McGinty, OSB, 'The treatise *De Mirabilibus Sacrae Scripturae*', unpubl. PhD dissertation, 2 vols, University College, Dublin, 1971.   46 Robert E. McNally (ed), *Scriptores Hiberniae Minores* 1, CCSL 108 B (Turnhout 1972); for the names, see Alfred Holder, 'Altirische Namen im Reichenauer Codex CCXXXIII', *Archiv für celtische Lexicographie* 3 (1907) 266-67.

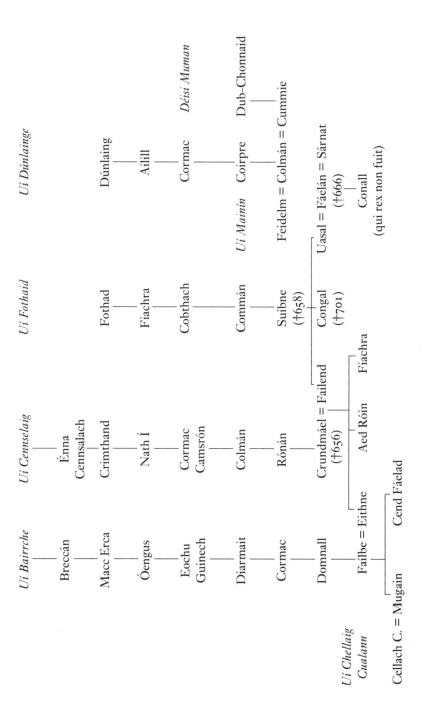

lies in the fact that he too mentions Manchianus by name in a passage which is significant in this context for a number of reasons, and which should therefore be cited here in full.

The subject under discussion is the miracle recounted in Joshua 12-14, when the sun and moon halted in their courses at the command of Joshua son of Nun; the author of the *De mirabilibus,* however, is at pains to explain that this did not disrupt the cyclical revolution of sun and moon, and he does so by referring to the computus:

> Ut enim hoc manifestis approbationibus pateat, cyclorum etiam ab initio conditi orbis recursus in se breuiter digeremus, quos semper post quingentos triginta duos annos sole ut in principio et luna per omnia conuenientibus nullis subuenientibus impedimentis in id unde coeperant redire ostendemus. Quinto namque cyclo a mundi principio anno centesimo quarto decimo generale totius mundi diluuium sub Noe uenit, qui post diluuium quadringentesimo decimo octauo defecit; et inde alius incipiens, id est sextus, in octauo aetatis Abrahae anno finitur. Et nono eius anno septimus incipiens, tricesimo quinto anno egressionis filiorum Israhel de Aegypto quinquennio ante mortem Moysi concluditur. Post quem octauus, in quo etiam istud signum, in sole et lune factum, tricesimo sexto anno egressionis Israhel de Aegypto incipiens in tricesimum primum annum Asa regis Iuda incedit: cuius tricesimo secundo anno nonus exordium capiens in quo etiam aliud signum in sole Ezechiae regis tempore, de quo paulisper dicemus, factum legitur, centesimo octauo anno post templi restaurationem quae sub Dario facta est, sui cursus spatium consumauit: donec decimus inde oriens nonagesimo secundo anno post passionem Saluatoris, Alia et Sparsa [= Auiola et Pansa] consulibus cursibus consumatur. Post quem undecimus a consulatu Paterni et Torquati ad nostra usque tempora decurrens, extremo anno Hiberniensium moriente Manchiano inter ceteros sapientes peragitur. Et duodecimus nunc tertium annum agens ad futurorum scientiam se praestans, a nobis qualem finem sit habiturus ignoratur.[48]

His reference to cycles of 532 years shows clearly that the author was working with Victorian tables, from which he also took the names of the consuls. Indeed, Krusch[49] long ago pointed out that the curious distortion in the consular names Alia et Sparsa has its closest congener in the Victorian tables of the Sirmond codex (S): Aulia et Parsa – another indication, perhaps, that this manuscript represents a direct witness to the Irish computistical tradition.

---

47 Cf. McNally, ed. cit., x-xvii.   48 Book II 4 = MPL 35, 2175-6. I have changed the text slightly in accordance with McGinty's readings.   49 Krusch, 'Die Einführung des griechischen Paschalritus im Abendlande', *Neues Archiv* 9 (1884) 101-69: 159.

More importantly, however, the mention of Manchianus in such a context proves that his obit must likewise have been marked as an annal in the margin of a Victorian table, beside the Easter data for AD 652.[50]

Manchianus of Min Droichit is indeed recorded in the annals as having died in that year.[51] Moreover, this very passage in the *De mirabilibus* was cited verbatim by the compiler of the Munich Computus, writing probably not long after[52] –showing once again that exegesis and computistics were the common preoccupation of seventh-century Irish scholars. Indeed, a study of Irish manuscripts shows that computists, exegetes, hagiographers and even grammarians all drew on a common body of materials;[53] the separation of these disciplines is a modern departure from medieval practice.

That there was a circle of scholars active in southern Ireland, in all these fields, throughout the course of the seventh century is evident from the contents of the Reichenau commentary on the Catholic Epistles and the *De mirabilibus*, as well as from other Hiberno-Latin texts. The letter of Cummian (*c.* AD 632), who was probably bishop or *fer légind* of Cluain Ferta Brénainn, shows that he had to hand an extraordinarily rich collection of computistical tracts, besides an uncommonly broad selection of patristic, canonical and exegetical materials. My discovery in two Brussels and Vatican manuscripts of a computus, which, if not Cummian's own composition, almost certainly emanates from his immediate circle, indicates that he also had access subsequently to Isidore's works, the writings of Virgilius Maro Grammaticus, and a number of other Latin grammatical texts. Computistical manuscripts bear clear witness to the fact that such esoteric authors as Virgilius Maro were just as familiar to the computists as they were to the grammarians,[54] just as computistical tracts frequently appear in the writing of Insular hagiographers and exegetes. Thus Cogitosus, the author of probably the oldest *Vita Brigitae*, draws on Victorius for the wording of his Prologue, as also does the anonymous author of the Lindisfarne *Vita Cuthberti* (*c.* AD 700).[55] The convergence of

---

50 The Manichaeo (= *Manchiano*) of the printed editions gave rise to an extraordinary theory of Krusch's (158-60) that the author was anti-Irish(!) and that he was here referring to 'der irische Manichäer d.i. kein anderer als Bischof Aedan von Holy Island' (= Lindisfarne) and that 'also 654 ist die Berechnung geschrieben, offenbar im Reiche Oswius'. The gaffe was pilloried by Mac Carthy, AU 4, lxx, and by Esposito, 202 n. 1. Unfortunately, the ghost of this 'Irish Manichaean' was insufficiently exorcised, for it re-appears in the otherwise exemplary paper by Anna-Dorothee von den Brinken, 'Marianus Scottus, unter besonderer Berücksichtigung der nicht veröffentlichten Teile seiner Chronik' *Deutsches Archiv* 17 (1961) 191-238. 238, where the reference to a *Manicheus Hibernensium* in a twelfth-century text is taken by her to be a criticism of Marianus by one of his opponents! The passage is in fact copied directly from the *De Mirabilibus*. **51** Mac Carthy, AU 4, lxx; Stokes, 'Annals of Tigernach', 192.   **52** The passages are cited in parallel by Mac Carthy, lxx, and Esposito, 200; the Munich MS. is the basis for the restoration *Manchiano* for the *Manichaeo* of the printed editions (McGinty 1, 133).   **53** I hope to discuss this point at greater length on another occasion. [See now below, 191-200.]   **54** His *Epit.* XI 5 is cited, e.g. in Bede's DTR, cap. XXXV; cf. *Bedae opera*, 369. In fact Bede cites Virgilius Maro also in his *De orthographia*.   **55** See the Prologue, in Bertram Colgrave (ed & trans), *Two 'Lives' of Saint*

sources is perhaps best illustrated by a comment of the anonymous Hiberno-Latin (?) author writing at the end of the seventh century, whose tract *De ordine creaturarum*[56] draws on the *De mirabilibus*, and which was drawn on then in turn by Bede.[57] In a chapter of the work entitled *De sole et luna* (V 10) the anonymous has this to say:

> De cursibus autem solis et lunae nec temporis nec [loci] istius est breui-tatis deserere, quos idcirco in hoc opusculo neglegentius adsequor, quia et ipsius conpendiosa breuitas non patitur et in usum paene omnibus lectoribus dierum festorum conpotandorum gratia conuersi sunt.[58]

As far as he was concerned, those who would read exegesis would be equally at home in matters computistical, and doubtless also in the writings of hagiographers. We need not be surprised, therefore, that Cummian has had ascribed to him also a commentary on the Gospel of Mark,[59] and that he appears to have been closely associated with Laidcend mac Baíth Bannaig of Cluain Ferta Mo Lua, about twenty miles south-east of Cluain Ferta Brénainn.[60] We know that Laidcend composed an epitome of Gregory the Great's *Moralia in Iob*[61] (in which he cites Isidore's *De ortu et obitu patrum* at length) and we have already seen him cited as an authority in the Reichenau commentary. Manchianus, who is cited as *doctor noster* in the same commentary, was apparently the man at whose instigation the author of the *De mirabilibus* composed his work,[62] and it

---

Cuthbert (New York 1969) 60-62. **56** Manuel C. Díaz y Díaz (ed & trans), *Liber de ordine creaturarum: un anónimo irlandés del siglo VII*. Monografías de la Universidad de Santiago de Compostella 10 (Santiago de Compostella 1972). Professor Jones has remarked to me privately, however, that he believes the work could be Northumbrian (either from Lindisfarne or Whitby), a judgement which he bases on the contextual evidence of some MSS with which Díaz y Díaz was not familiar. **57** See esp. Charles W. Jones, 'Some introductory remarks on Bede's commentary on Genesis', *Sacris Erudiri* 19 (1969-70) 115-98. **58** Díaz y Díaz, ed. cit., 118. **59** See Bernhard Bischoff, 'Wendepunkte in der Geschichte der lateinischen Exegese im Frühmittelalter', *Sacris Erudiri* 6 (1954) 189-279 = *Mittelalterliche Studien* 1 (Stuttgart 1966) 205-73: 257-58, No. 27 (and 213-15). I am not convinced by the counter-arguments of Clare Stancliffe, 'Early "Irish" biblical exegesis', *Studia Patristica* 12 [Texte und Untersuchungen 115] (1975) 361-70: 365-66 [though they are certainly superior to the nonsense in Michael Gorman, 'A critique of Bischoff's theory of Irish exegesis: the commentary on Genesis in Munich Clm 6302 (Wendepunkte 2)', *Jnl of Medieval Latin* 7 (1997) 178-233, to which my article cited in n. 43 above is a reply.] The question of Cummian's alleged authorship will be discussed in our forthcoming edition of his Letter. [See now Walsh & Ó Cróinín, *Cummian's Letter*, 217-21.] **60** It may be worth noting that the monastery of Min Droichit, with which Manchianus is associated, was about 3 miles east of Cluain Ferta Mo Lua. The names *CVMMENE* and *Ladcen* (the one in capitals, the other in majuscule) are found together on a slab at Peakaun, Aherlow (Co. Tipperary), which is not far distant; see Mgr Michael Moloney, 'Beccan's hermitage in Aherlow: the riddle of the slabs', *North Munster Archaeological Jnl* 9 (1964) 99-107. **61** Marc Adriaen (ed), *Egloga quam scripsit Lathcen filius Baith de Moralibus Iob quas Gregorius fecit*, CCSL 145 (Turnhout 1969). **62** If such is the correct interpretation of the obscure Prologue: 'Ab uno enim uestrum, id est Baithano (Banbano?), post patrem Manchianum, si quid intelligentiae addidi, et ab altero, ut credo, saliua oris eius uicem laborum causam suscepi'; MPL 35, 2152.

may be that we should see in him the leading light of the circle.[63] Be that as it may, there can be no reasonable doubt that the compilation of the 'Sirmond' computistical collection is to be seen against this background of intense scholarly activity in southern Ireland in the mid and late seventh century.

The question now arises as to how this corpus of computistical texts made its way to Jarrow. I stated at the outset that the path of dissemination seemed to lead from southern Ireland to southern (or south-western) England, and thence northwards to Bede. Indeed, I would now suggest that all (or almost all) of the Hiberno-Latin texts which we know Bede used: the *De ordine creaturarum*, Pseudo-Hilary on the Catholic Epistles, Virgilius Maro, and the Irish computus, travelled this same route. That the computus at least did not come to him via Iona seems to me demonstrable from the fact that – despite his frequent references to it – Bede never seems to have laid eyes on an Irish 84-year cycle.[64] Knowing what we do of Bede's methodology, it is scarcely conceivable that he would not have quoted from such a table (if he had one), if only to refute it. That he did not do so can surely be laid down to the fact that the manuscripts of the 'Sirmond' group show no trace of ever having contained such 84-year material. The Irish computus which Bede inherited was concerned almost exclusively with the Alexandrian cycle and represented the combination of the doctrines of Victorius and Dionysius Exiguus. Such a synthesis could not have come to Bede from Iona, where we know the 84-year cycle survived in use until AD 716; it seems clear, on the other hand, that this Irish material had reached Jarrow long before that time and had comprised the standard teaching of that school probably before Bede himself began to teach there.[65]

It may be possible, however, to trace the steps by which the Irish computus reached Jarrow, beginning with the text tradition in England itself. Our first clue is a passage in Aldhelm's *Epistola ad Geruntium* (AD 672?)[66] which has puzzled modern computists. In the letter, Aldhelm states that he had recently been present at a national synod of the British bishops[67] and that, at the request of these bishops, he was now writing to Geraint (a king *occidentalis regni*) to inform him of the errors of the British. A part of the letter deals with the Easter-question:

---

63 Grosjean's theories need to be throughly revised in the light of McGinty's more recent and detailed work. 64 Bede refers only to *dubii circuli*, a curiously vague description from a professed chronologist. 65 Jones, *Bedae opera*, 130-31. 66 Rudolf Ehwald (ed), *Aldhelmi opera*. MGH AA 15 (Berlin 1919; repr. 1961) 475-503: 480-86, *Ep.* 4. Ehwald seemed to argue for a date *c.* AD 705 for the letter, though he quotes with some approval (480-81 n.) a suggestion by Hahn that it should be dated closer to AD 680. The dating here given is that of Michael Herren, in M. Lapidge and M. Herren (trans), *Aldhelm: the prose works* (Ipswich 1979) 103-4. 67 'In concilio episcoporum, ubi ex tota paena Brittania innumerabilis sacerdotum caterua confluxit', Ehwald, 480.

> Est autem altera crudelior animarum pernicies, quod in sacrosancta paschali solemnitate CCCXVIII patrum regulam non sectantur, qui in Niceno concilio decemnovenalem laterculi circulum per ogdoadem et endicadam usque ad finem mundi recto tramite decursurum sagaci solertis sanxerunt et a quinta decima luna usque ad vigesimam primam supputationis seriem et paschalis calculi terminum tradiderunt, quem anticipare et transgredi contra ius et fas illicitum fore censuerunt. Porro isti secundum decennem nouennemque Anatolii computatum aut potius iuxta Sulpicii Seueri regulam, qui LXXXIIII annorum cursum descripsit, quarta decima luna cum Iudaeis paschale sacramentum celebrant, cum neutrum ecclesiae Romanae pontifices ad perfectam calculi rationem sequantur; sed nec Uictorii paschalis laterculi curriculum, qui DCCCII annorum circuli continetur, posteris sectandum decreuerunt.[68]

The references to the 'cycle of the 318 bishops' (= Dionysius) and to Victorius are both clear enough; what puzzles modern computists is Aldhelm's statement that Sulpicius Seuerus was the author of the 84-year cycle.[69] I believe that here, as in so many other instances, Professor Jones was on the right track. He rightly dismissed Aldhelm's attribution as unbelievable, pointing out that Cummian, for example, had said that the place, date and author of the 84 were unknown, and that Bede – who was apparently familiar with the letter[70] – had referred only to *dubii circuli*.[71] Jones then noted a passage which occurs in all but one of the Sirmond group of manuscripts and which he thought might explain Aldhelm's confusion; the passage occurs immediately after the dating formulae which we discussed above:

> SVLPICIVS. 'Christus natus est Sabino et Rufino consulibus .VIII. Kl. Ianuarii'. Christus passus duobus geminis consulibus. A natiuitate domini Sabino et Rufino consulibus usque ad passionem eius Rufo uidelicet et Rubellio consulibus geminis, sub quibus Christus crucifixus est in die .VIII. Kl. Aprilis, sunt anni .XXXI. et menses tres.
>
> S fol. 95 bis[r] T fol. 17[v] G fol. 133v P p 242
> Sulpicius Severus, *Chron.* II 27 (Karl Halm (ed), *CSEL* I (Vienna 1866) 82)

68 Ehwald, ed. cit., 483.   69 Note that both Mac Carthy, AU 4, cxlvi, and Jones, *Bedae opera*, 101, misconstrue the words of Aldhelm to mean that Rome had rejected the Victorian tables, when in fact the rejection was by the British (and Irish). Lapidge and Herren, 158, have translated the passage correctly.   70 Herren, 142, argues that 'Bede had no copy of Aldhelm's letter before him and was ignorant of the date of the work' and further, that 'he seemed to possess scant knowledge of it'.   71 Jones, *Bedae opera*, 93.

The passage, as Jones remarked, looks at first sight like a short prologue to an Easter-table. But it is in fact made up of a statement from Sulpicius' Chronicle[72] about the Nativity and an item from a Victorian computus. We may suggest that perhaps Aldhelm had seen a manuscript of the Irish computus, which contains the text of Anatolius' *Canon paschalis* – frequently cited by the Irish in support of their usage – as well as the above passage from Sulpicius, and that a rather vague memory associated the two in his mind.[73]

If we could be sure, then, that the archetype of the Sirmond group of manuscripts was in Wessex by the third quarter of the seventh century we would be that much closer to tracing the point at which it entered England. The most obvious suggestion would be that the manuscript was brought to Malmesbury by Maéldub, founder of that monastery and (apparently) Aldhelm's predecessor there as abbot.[74] Unfortunately, we know nothing about Maéldub's Irish background, and his influence on Aldhelm has lately been placed in question.[75] Nevertheless, we know from Aldhelm's own writings that he was thoroughly familiar with the teachings of the Irish schools in his time[76] – he cites a line from Virgilius Maro Grammaticus[77] – and he seems to have been god-father to Aldfrith, the Northumbrian king whose Irish connections are well-known.[78]

English connections with southern Ireland are well attested for the seventh century, as all readers of Bede's History will know. Indeed, there is some

---

72 Bischoff, *Mittelalterliche Studien* 1, 232. The *Chronicle* was rare in the seventh century, but was used extensively by Adomnán; see Denis Meehan (ed), *Adamnan's 'De locis sanctis'*. Scriptores Latini Hiberniae 3 (Dublin 1958) 58, 70. 73 *Bedae opera*, 101. [For arguments in support of Aldhelm and in favour of the theory that Sulpicius was, in fact, the author of the 84-year table mentioned by him, see now D.P. McCarthy, 'Easter principles and a fifth-century lunar cycle used in the British churches', *Jnl of the History of Astronomy* 24 (1993) 204-24, and idem, 'Origins of the *Latercus* paschal cycle of the Insular Celtic church, *Cambrian Medieval Celtic Studies* 28 (Winter 1994) 25-49.] 74 See Plummer 2, 310-11. 75 Lapidge, in Lapidge and Herren, *Aldhelm, the prose works*, 7, 9. This work labours under an excessive reluctance to admit any Irish debt in Aldhelm's life and work. [For recent arguments in favour of strong Irish influence on Aldhelm, see now Michael Herren, 'Scholarly contacts between the Irish and the southern English in the seventh century', *Peritia* 12 (1998) 24-53.] 76 Witness his letters to the Anglo-Saxons Wihtfrith and Heahfrith, Ehwald, *Epp* III and V. 77 In the letter to Heahfrith, Ehwald, 494.1. [On which see now David Howlett, 'Seven studies in seventh-century texts', *Peritia* 10 (1996) 1-70: 57]. Herren and Lapidge suggest (7) that Aldhelm may have known the (Irish?) *Hisperica Famina*, though the statement (182 n. 13) that Aldhelm thereby provides a *terminus ante quem* for that work must be revised in the light of the present article. There are traces of 'Hisperic' vocabulary in the Irish computus, which would establish familiarity with the genre in Ireland a generation earlier than Aldhelm. Note too that Díaz y Díaz argues for Aldhelm's familiarity also with the *De ordine creaturarum* (37). 78 Lapidge and Herren, 12; Byrne, *Irish kings*, 104, 111. [See now Colin Ireland, 'Aldfrith of Northumbria and the learning of a *sapiens*', in Eve E. Sweetser, Claire Thomas & Kathryn Klar (eds), *A Celtic florilegium in memory of Brendan O Hehir* (Lawrence, MA 1996) 63-77, and the same author's more recent *Old Irish wisdom attributed to Aldfrith of Northumbria: an edition of Bríathra Flainn Fhína maic Ossu* (Tempo, AR 1999.]

ground for saying that the English presence in Ireland has been unduly over-shadowed by the more obvious role which the Iona paruchia played in the development of Northumbrian schools. Travellers such as these could have been the means by which the Irish computus passed first to England and then to the continent. Besides the Irish themselves, the Anglo-Saxons at Rath Melsigi undoubtedly remained in close contact with Northumbria, and they also had important contacts in Francia.[79] The Frank Acgilbert, for instance, who spent the years AD 635-40 as a missionary in Wessex and some further years there as bishop of Dorchester before moving to Northumbria, was for many years before his English sojourn *legendarum gratia scripturarum in Hibernia*.[80] His role at the synod of Whitby (AD 664) as leader of the 'Roman' party against the Irish of Lindisfarne shows clearly where his sympathies lay in the matter of the Easter-question, and his knowledge of the 'orthodox' cycle may have been obtained during his Irish years. Acgilbert's close association with Wilfrid, both at the Whitby synod and in subsequent years,[81] strongly suggests that the Frankish group in southern Ireland in the seventh century were located close to, if not indeed in the same place as, the Anglo-Saxons, namely Rath Melsigi. Only such ties can explain the extraordinary fact that when, in AD 656, the Austrasian mayor of the palace, Grimoald, attempted his coup against the Merovingians, the young royal son Dagobert II was despatched in the company of bishop Desiderius of Poitiers to Ireland, and that after the passage of some years one of the warring parties in Austrasia asked Wilfrid to arrange for the boy's return to Francia.[82] For Wilfrid to have had such power he must have had close, personal contacts in southern Ireland,[83] and the obvious place to look for such men is among the group of

79 See esp. Annethe Lohaus, *Die Merowinger und England*. Münchener Beiträge zur Mediävistik und Renaissance-Forschung 19 (Munich 1974), and Eric Fletcher, 'The influence of Merovingian Gaul on Northumbria in the seventh century', *Medieval Archaeology* 24 (1980) 69-86. [See also my paper, 'Rath Melsigi, Willibrord and the earliest Echternach manuscripts', below, 145-65.] 80 Bede, HE III 7; Plummer I, 140-41; Colgrave & Mynors, 234; Lohaus, 46-47. 81 Acgilbert was bishop of Paris from c. AD 667/8 to c. AD 680; after Wilfrid's expulsion from his see at York in AD 678, he travelled to Rome and was entertained on the way both by Acgilbert and by the Merovingian king Dagobert II. According to tradition at Jouarre, Acgilbert was a brother of the first abbess there, and hence a nephew of Ado's, the founder. Since Ado was a brother of Audoin, Acgilbert must have had connections also with Rouen. He eventually retired to the family monastery at Jouarre and was buried there. Such powerful connections doubtless helped Irish monks in Francia, as well as Anglo-Saxons, See Eugen Ewig, 'Die fränkischen Teilreiche im 7. Jahrhundert', *Trierer Zeitschrift* 22 (1953) 85-144: 130 and n. 176 = *Spätantikes Gallien* (2 vols, Munich 1976-77) I, 173-230: 216 and n. 176. 82 See Eugen Ewig, 'Noch einmal zum Staatsstreich Grimoalds', *Spätantikes Gallien* I (Munich 1976), 573-77; Paul Grosjean, 'Chronologie de S. Feuillen', *Notes d'hagiographie celtique* 38, *Analecta Bollandiana* 75 (1957) 379-93. [For a different interpretation of the evidence, see also Jean-Michel Picard, 'Church and politics in the seventh century: the Irish exile of King Dagobert II', in idem (ed), *Ireland and northern France, AD 600-850* (Dublin 1991) 27-52.] 83 I cannot agree with Grosjean's claim, 391-92 n. 3, that Iona was the place of Dagobert's exile, and not Ireland. It seems to me unlikely that Wilfrid would have been on such good terms with the monks of Iona after the events of

Anglo-Saxon and Frankish scholars there. It was possibly by these channels, and not by the better-known route from Iona to Northumbria, that the Irish computus made its way to Jarrow.

We do not know for certain, then, at what date the Irish collection travelled to England. One theoretical means of transmission has been suggested above in relation to Aldhelm, but there are other routes possible and the date of first reception in England could likewise be different. Bede himself is the source for our knowledge that many prominent Anglo-Saxon clerics in the late-seventh or early-eighth century had been Irish trained, some even (like Tuda, a bishop of the Northumbrians) educated and consecrated in Ireland. Any one of these, or of the group located at Rath Melsigi, could have brought a transcript of the collection directly or indirectly to Northumbria. It may have been in circulation in Northumbria before the foundation of Wearmouth in AD 674 and of Jarrow in AD 681/2. We have seen that it may also have been available to Aldhelm at roughly the same time. Both these suggestions would seem to support the manuscript evidence that the collection received its definitive form in southern Ireland *c.* AD 658 and that it may have been taken to England shortly thereafter. When and how it travelled to the continent is a question that cannot, I think, be answered with the available evidence.

Scholars have laboured to show that Bede admired and revered the Irish – except in the matter of the Easter-question. Even so careful a scholar as Charles Jones has been led to remark that 'to fervent pro-Irish historians who belabor Bede for his unfriendly remarks, it must be pointed out that practically all our evidence of early Irish intellectual activity comes to us from or through Bede'.[84] It is a curious defence, surely. Bede learned a great deal from the Irish, particularly in the computistical field,[85] and yet his comments on the Irish Easter only once make the point that the southern Irish, at least, 'had long since learned to celebrate Easter in accordance with canonical custom'.[86] But even this grudging statement was intended more as condemnation of the northern Irish than as praise of their southern compatriots. Jones suggests that Bede did not know the provenance of the Jarrow computus, which may have been accumulated before his interest in it; even so 'it is notable that no Irish teacher or school or even the word *Scotti* is mentioned throughout his computistical

Whitby. **84** *Bedae opera*, 99 n 2. **85** This is the whole thrust of Jones' pioneering work. Subsequent research has shown that, if anything, he underestimated the extent of Bede's debt to the Irish. **86** HE III 3 (Plummer 1, 131; Colgrave & Mynors, 218). Note, for example, that Bede, in his *Vita Cuthberti*, cap. XXXIX (Colgrave, *Two 'Lives' of Saint Cuthbert*, 282-84) has Cuthbert utter the following words on his deathbed: 'Cum illis autem qui ab unitate catholicae pacis uel pascha non suo tempore celebrando, uel peruerse uiuendo aberrant, uobis sit nulla communio'; in fact, however, Cuthbert left Ripon some years before Whitby rather than accept the Roman Easter! (Plummer 2, 323). For a critical appraisal of Bede's views on the Irish, see Margaret Pepperdene, 'Bede's *Historia Ecclesiastica*: a new perspective', *Celtica* 4 (1958) 253-62. [See now also Alan Thacker, 'Bede and the Irish', in L.A.J.R. Houwen & A.A. MacDonald (eds), *Beda Venerabilis, historian, monk and Northumbrian* (Groningen 1996) 31-59.]

works'.[87] Bede nowhere makes acknowledgement of what he had come to know about the 'orthodox' Easter-reckoning from the Irish, and very little of what the monks of Iona and Lindisfarne had contributed to the development of Northumbrian schools. In this, as in so many things, he was a man before his time.[88]

87 Jones, *Bedae opera*, 131.   88 I wish to thank Prof. Wesley Stevens, University of Winnipeg, for reading a draft of this paper and for making some helpful suggestions for its improvement. [Alan Thacker's paper (see previous n.) was written partially in pained response to my 'bitterly epigrammatic conclusion' voiced above. Faith Wallis, *Bede: The Reckoning of Time*, Translated Texts for Historians 29 (Liverpool 1999) lxxviii remarks: 'Ó Cróinín even accuses Bede of deliberately suppressing information about the Irish origin of his material, *presumably out of dislike for the Irish*' [my italics]. This is to read rather more malice into my words than they really contain! Still, I wonder what Bede made of that dating-clause when he read it.]

14

The date, provenance and earliest use of the works of Virgilius Maro Grammaticus[*]

'Of all the grammarians with Insular connections, none is as puzzling as Virgilius Maro Grammaticus. His two grammars, the *Epitomae* and *Epistolae*, have provided material for endless scholarly speculation. His date, his nationality, even the purpose of his writings, are all disputed. Hypotheses as to his origin range from fifth-century Gaul to seventh-century Spain or Ireland, and even into ninth-century France'.[1] These comments of the most recent writer on the subject serve to set the scene for any study of Virgil, and Dr Law's chapter on the subject offers the best brief summary to date of the *status quaestionis*. At the same time, however, it must be said that the criteria used to date and locate Virgil have not always been sound, and the criticism applies no less to recent authors than to their predecessors.[2] Dr Law, for instance, has this to say on the subject:

'The most serious problem is the transmission of Virgilius' works. With one possible exception,[3] all the grammarians who use Virgilius before the ninth century – Aldhelm (?), Boniface and Bede – are English; and the early ninth-century works which borrow from him, whether directly or via a collection of excerpts, are of Continental origin ... A related difficulty is the fact that Boniface and Bede (and also Alcuin in his *De orthographia*) use only the *Epitomae;* apart from the single contestable reference in Aldhelm, the *Epistolae* appear first on the Continent in the ninth century'.[4]

---

[*] First published in Günter Bernt, Fidel Rädle and Gabriel Silagi (eds), *Tradition und Wertung: Festschrift Franz Brunhölzl* (Sigmaringen 1989) 13-22. 1 Vivien Law, *The Insular Latin grammarians*. Studies in Celtic History 3 (Woodbridge 1982) 42. [See now Vivien Law, *Wisdom, authority and grammar in the seventh century: Decoding Virgilius Maro Grammaticus* (Cambridge 1998).] 2 See, for example, the exemplary demolition of Virgil's alleged connection with Toulouse by Louis Holz, 'Irish grammarians and the continent in the seventh century', in H.B. Clarke & Mary Brennan (eds), *Columbanus and Merovingian monasticism*. British Archaeological Reports, International Series 113 (Oxford 1981) 135-152: 137-138. It may be suggested here that the reading 'cum in hiborum/cum hi bonorum', etc of *Epitoma* V 1, which has been variously emended as 'cum in Hebraicorum' or 'cum in Hibernorum' or 'cum in Hibonorum', should perhaps be read as 'hiberbatonicorum' [= grammaticorum], as in the seventh-century Irish *Anonymus ad Cuimnanum*. 3 'The anonymous source used by "Malsachanus" and Clemens Scottus, which antedates 700 and may have been of Irish origin – though whether from Ireland itself or from from Irish circles on the Continent is at present impossible to decide', Law, *Insular Latin grammarians*, 49 n. 45. 4 Law, *Insular Latin grammarians*, 49.

In taking Virgil's use of Isidore, *Etymologiae,* as the terminus post quem Dr Law follows previous authorities, such as Michael Herren,[5] though Louis Holtz prefers the later date offered by the citation of Virgil in a letter of Aldhelm (c. AD 690).[6] But her consideration of all the evidence, primary and secondary, leads her to the following conclusion:

'Two things stand out: first, that Virgilius' early eighth-century connection with England is much more clearly documented than any connection at any time with Ireland, and his use of Priscian's *Institutiones grammaticae* links him with the Anglo-Saxon writer Aldhelm, the only other Insular author to use the *Institutiones* before the ninth century; and secondly, that the *Epitomae* were at all times very much better known than the *Epistolae,* which survive in a single early ninth-century manuscript. The *Epitomae* only were used in eighth-century England (always exepting the one questionable borrowing in Aldhelm), and they were the only work of Virgilius known to most ninth-century excerptors ... At the risk of adding yet another unprovable theory to an already inflated list, one might surmise that the *Epitomae* and the *Epistolae* were the work of an author based in Britain, whatever his ultimate origin, and that their transmission to the ninth century rested in English hands.'[7]

None of the above statements is correct, and the evidence to refute several of them has already appeared in print.[8] This author has previously stated that the use of Virgil's compositions in Ireland can be demonstrated for the mid-seventh century (before AD 658);[9] since, however, the evidence offered in support of this contention has recently been questioned[10] – without good reason, in my view – it may be as well to review the evidence here and to present in full the citations from Virgil that are found in the various seventh-century Irish computistical texts that I was using.

Citations from Virgilius Maro Grammaticus are normally encountered in grammatical texts, and the evidence from Hiberno-Latin grammatical sources

---

5 Michael Herren, 'Some new light on the life of Virgilius Maro Grammaticus', PRIA 79 C 2 (1979) 27-71. 6 Besides the article referred to above, see also his *Donat et la tradition de l'enseignement grammatical* (Paris 1981) 271-74, 315-18. 7 Law, *Insular Latin grammarians,* 51. 8 For detailed refutation, see the reviews of Law by: Dáibhí Ó Cróinín, *Studia Hibernica* 22/23 (1982/83) 149-56; Anders Ahlqvist, *Cambridge Medieval Celtic Studies* [CMCS] 6 (Winter 1983) 100-1; Michael Herren, *Peritia* 2 (1983) 312-16; Pádraig A. Breatnach, *Celtica* 16 (1984) 182-86. 9 Dáibhí Ó Cróinín, 'A seventh-century Irish computus from the circle of Cummianus', PRIA 82 C 11 (1982) 405-30: 424-25. [=99-130 above.] 10 See Marina Smyth, 'Isidore of Seville and early Irish cosmography', CMCS 14 (Winter 1987) 69-102: 94-100. I should say here that I find Dr Smyth's thesis, that Isidore's works were not known or generally used in Ireland before the mid-seventh century, on the whole thoroughly unobjectionable; our differences concern only the texts to be discussed below. [It should be remarked, however, that Dr Smyth, in her article, 'Isidore and early Irish cosmography', and in her full-length monograph, *Understanding the universe in seventh-century Ireland.* Studies in Celtic History 15 (Woodbridge 1996), has taken her earlier views about knowledge of Isidore in 7th-century Ireland to greater extremes, and now denies that Irish authors had any access to Isidore before *c.* AD 700; see my review of her book in *English Historical Review* 113, No. 451 (Apr. 1998) 397-99.]

is ably discussed by Law. It was long known, however, that Virgil was also cited in the Irish *Collectio canonum Hibernensis* LIIIIa ('bestia de bessu dicta, hoc est more feritatis'),[11] and twice in another Hiberno-Latin commentary entitled *Interrogationes uel responsiones tam de ueteri quam de nouo testamenti*, first brought to light by Bernhard Bischoff.[12] There are possible instances of dependence on Virgil in one or two other Hiberno-Latin biblical commentaries also.[13] However, neither the grammatical material nor the biblical commentaries can be accurately dated, and so the problem remains very much as it was before.

The distinctive feature of computistical texts, as compared to grammars and biblical commentaries, is that they more often than not offer precisely what is lacking in examples of the other two genres: a precise date of composition. Medieval computists, in every country and in every period, invariably illustrate the rules of their trade by reference to the *annus praesens*, and these data are very often preserved even in later copies. It is frequently the case, of course, that recopying of a text induces the copyist to bring his examples up to date, by reference to the year in which he himself is writing, and the original date of composition is thereby often – though by no means always – lost. On the other hand, no copyist ever projects the *annus praesens* backwards, from his own year to an earlier one.

In arguing for an Irish acquaintance with Virgilius Maro Grammaticus in the mid seventh century this writer referred to a dating clause which is found in several of the manuscripts which Charles W. Jones had demonstrated were copies of Bede's own computus.[14] Unaware of the dating clause, Jones demonstrated from the internal evidence of the manuscripts, and from Bede's own computistical manuals, *De temporibus* and *De temporum ratione*, that this 'Sirmond Group' of manuscripts was a precious record of the very materials which Bede himself had used at Wearmouth-Jarrow. My discovery of the dating clause – common to all but one of the group and therefore clearly present in the exemplar – allowed the dating of the archetype of the 'Sirmond' collection to AD 658, and its location in south-east Ireland.[15] Since this dating-clause is clearly crucial to the argument (and since Dr Marina Smyth has attempted to undermine its importance) it will be useful to give the text again here:

---

11 See Hermann Wasserschleben (ed), *Die irische Kanonensammlung* (Leipzig 1885) 213; the Book is entitled 'De bestiis mitibus'　12 Bernhard Bischoff, 'Wendepunkte in der Geschichte der lateinischen Exegese im Frühmittelalter', *Sacris Erudiri* 6 (1954) 189-281 = *Mittelalterliche Studien* 1 (Stuttgart 1966) 206-270, No. 1c.　13 See Aidan Breen, 'Some seventh-century Hiberno-Latin texts and their relationships', *Peritia* 3 (1984) 204-14: 210-14.　14 Charles W. Jones, 'The "lost" Sirmond manuscript of Bede's "computus"', EHR 52 (1937) 204-19; idem (ed), *Bedae opera* 105-10.　15 Dáibhí Ó Cróinín, 'The Irish provenance of Bede's computus', *Peritia* 2 (1983) 229-47 [= 173-80 above]; see also idem, 'Early Irish annals from Easter tables: a case restated', *Peritia* 2 (1983) 74-86 [= 76-86 above].

Omnibus annis temporibus diebus ac luna maxime, que iuxta Hebraeos menses facit, rite discussis, a mundi principio usque in diem, quo filii Israhel paschale mysterium initiauere anni sunt $\overline{\text{III}}$ DCLXXXVIIII, praecedente primo mense VIII Kl. Aprilis, luna XIIII, VI feria. Passum autem dominum nostrum Ihesum Christum peractis $\overline{\text{V}}$ CCXX & VIII annis ab exortu mundi, eadem cronicorum relatione monstratur, VIII Kl. Aprilis primo mense, luna XIIII, VI feria.

Inter primum pascha in Aegypto et passionem domini anni sunt $\overline{\text{I}}$ DXXXVIII. Ex domini uero passione usque in pascha quod secutum est Suibini filii Commanni anni sunt DCXXXI. A pascha autem supradicto usque ad tempus praefinitum consummationis mundi, id est sex milibus consummatis, anni sunt CXLI.[16]

The data clearly refer to AD 658, and the double-dating (from the Passion and from the *tempus consummationis mundi*) establishes the year beyond any reasonable doubt. The question raised by Smyth is whether this date applies to everything in the exemplar of the Sirmond group, or just to one part of it. Since her argumentation is at times confused it will be as well to quote her *ipsissima verba:* '... It does not follow that the observation cited above was first written down in the year 658. Why would the writer talk about the Easter of the death of Suibne, when he could simply talk about "this Easter" or "last Easter"? In fact what he does say is *"that* Easter", which seems to indicate that it was not the most recent one, though perhaps it is a mistake to lay too much emphasis on *supradicto.* This could equally well be interpreted as the comment of someone writing later but referring to an Easter table in which the last *obit* happened to be that of Suibne.'[17]

It is not my wish to draw the reader into a tangled web of technicalities, so I shall try to explain why this reasoning cannot be sound. That a writer working some time after the year AD 658 would insert a dating clause referring to an earlier year (which in this instance 'happened to be that of Suibne'), but without reference to his own year of writing, is to ignore the evidence of computists and their ways. It is true that writers will sometimes refer to events that predate the time of writing by a couple of years, but the actual *annus praesens* is always the basis of the calculation.

For example, the Irish author of the synchronistic poem *Deus a quo facta fuit,*[18] writing in AD 645, dates his composition internally by reference to the Anno Mundi reckoning of AM 5845 for that year *(octingenti ... / quadraginta quinque anni / atque quinque milia).* Like the author of the dating-clause in the Sirmond collection, he also adds a second calculation based on the millennar-

---

16 Ó Cróinín, 'Irish provenance of Bede's computus', 234. 17 Smyth, 'Isidore and early Irish cosmography', 98. 18 For what follows, see Ó Cróinín, 'Early Irish annals from Easter tables', passim [= 76-86 above].

ian date AM 6000, saying that 155 years remain (*a quo centum in futurum / est annorum spatium / Finem usque quinquaginta / quino ad sex millium*). He also has a reference to an event which took place three years previously (the death of Domnall mac Áedo, *rex Scottorum*), but there is no doubt about which is the actual *annus praesens*. In other words, it is inconceivable that our author would have composed his poem several years after AD 642, without indicating the fact with a reference to his current year.

A very similar instance is found in the Irish Pseudo-Augustine's *De mirabilibus sacrae scripturae*, though in this case the dating is by reference to Great Paschal Cycles. Our author states that the tenth cycle ended in the ninety-second year after the Passion, in the consulship of Aviola and Pansa (erroneously given as = AD 19, based on the tables of Victorius of Aquitaine); the eleventh began in the following year, in the consulship of Paternus and Torquatus. The final year of the eleventh cycle (= AD 652) is identified by the death of Mainchéne (of Min Droichid), amongst others (*extremo anno Hibernensium moriente Manchiano inter ceteros sapientes*). In the third year of the twelfth cycle the treatise was written (*Et duodecimus nunc tertium annum agens*). Here again there is mention of an event predating the year of writing, but again the *annus praesens* is the basis of the calculation. The only valid reason, therefore, for referring to Suibne mac Commáin in the Sirmond dating-clause, without the indication of any other *annus praesens*, is that he died in the year of writing.

Dr Smyth, it must be said, clearly had doubts about her own argument, and therefore offers an alternative solution: '... Seventh-century Irish scholars believed that the world had been created on 25 March and would end on that same date, *sex milibus consummatis* as our computist phrases it. Since Our Lord's Passion also traditionally took place on 25 March, as mentioned a little later in this group of computistical notes, an event occurring on that day in any year could be located with great precision within the desired framework – there would be no need to worry about fractions of years. Now, Easter fell on 25 March in AD 658 ... Since this had not happened for quite some time (the last occurrence was in AD 585), could it be that this Easter was felt to be especially significant? If this suggestion corresponds to reality – and, given the Irish propensity for noticing such patterns in history, this seems likely – it may well be that this computistical "bit" was composed within the decade following AD 658: ... the next Easter falling on that date occurred already in AD 669.'[19]

---

19 Smyth, 'Isidore and early Irish cosmography', 98. It is perhaps possible that the word *Pascha* was either dropped from the dating-clause by haplology or was implied by the genitive of the name: 'Usque in pascha quod secutum est [Pascha] Suibini filii Commanni', which would give an *annus praesens* of AD 659 (i.e. 'the Pasch that followed that of Suibne mac Commáin'). The examples given above from other Hiberno-Latin texts suggest that, even if Suibne's obit did precede the time of writing, it cannot have been by more than two or three years.

Allowing for the fact that 'such patterns in history' were a commonplace of computistical studies everywhere in the church, and the Irish were not the only ones who alluded to them, the above argument still lacks all conviction. The dating-clause nowhere alludes to the special significance of Easter on 25 March, and in fact Smyth's observation that Easter would fall on that date again in AD 669 only points up the incongruity. If the scribe's interest were solely in the millennarian doctrine, then there would have been no cause to mention Suibne mac Commáin at all. The wording in the clause clearly demonstrates that the millennarian element was only secondary; the mention of Suibne mac Commáin by name can only be explained as a reference to the death of a contemporary, a death which occurred in the year of writing.

Smyth's final sally against the dating-clause in the Sirmond manuscripts is to argue that the archetype was made up of groups of texts, so that '[i]t is at least possible that at some earlier time one of these groups formed a smaller collection which was then incorporated into the exemplar'.[20] However, this is to go against the considered judgement of Charles Jones, whose minute analysis of the Sirmond group led him to conclude that not only the items in fols 80ʳ-140ʳ of Bodley 309 [i.e., including the dating-clause] were derived from Bede's computus, 'but additional study shows that all items in the first folios were also known to Bede and are therefore probably a part of that codex into which he copied DTR'.[21] It is therefore not possible to isolate that section of the archetype which contained the dating-clause, and consign it to an earlier period than that of the rest of the collection. There is not the space here to discuss Smyth's attempts at separating out groups of texts in the Sirmond collection, but it is clear that her arguments are based on an inadequate firsthand familiarity with the manuscripts. One further instance will suffice to demonstrate that her late-seventh-century dating of the Sirmond collection cannot stand.

At the close of her discussion Smyth states that 'Judging from the selections available in print and from perusal of the relevant texts in a microfilm of MS. Bodley 309, I would assign this collection, as we have it, to a later period, probably the end of the seventh century'.[22] Now, fols 98-99ʳ of the Bodleian manuscript contain the Prologue of Theophilus, bishop of Alexandria, with the rubric *Incipit prologus Theophili Alexandrini episcopi ad Theodosium.* The end of the text, however, reads as follows: *Finit de exemplaris cosmographiae. Incipit prologus Theophili.* Clearly, the archetype originally contained either the original or a copy of the famous *Liber Cosmographiorum* which abbot Ceolfrid gave to king Aldfrid of Northumbria in return for eight hides of land.[23] Hence Smyth's conclusion that 'just how long [the Sirmond collection was] available in Northumbria, we cannot say'[24] is also open to refinement. Since we know

---

20 Smyth, 'Isidore and early Irish cosmography', 99.   **21** Jones, *Bedae opera*, 106.   **22** Smyth, art. cit., 99-100.   **23** See Charles Pummer (ed), *Baedae venerabilis opera historica* (2 vols, Oxford 1896; repr. 1969) 1, 380 (*Historia abbatum auctore Baeda*, cap. XV).   **24** Smyth, art. cit., 99.

that Aldfrid succeeded his brother Ecgfrith after the latter's death in the battle of Nechtansmere in May 685, we can deduce that the *Liber Cosmographiorum* must have been at Wearmouth-Jarrow before that date, and was probably brought back from Rome *(quem Romae Benedictus emerat)* at the latest in (?) AD 684, when Benedict returned from his last trip there. The archetype of the Sirmond collection must, therefore, have been at Wearmouth-Jarrow already by the mid-680s, at the latest (and it may even have been present in Northumbria before the foundation of either monastery). Contrary to what Smyth says, there is no internal evidence to suggest that any one or more parts of the collection circulated separately before their inclusion in the archetype of AD 658. All the surviving manuscript witnesses preserve the texts in the same sequence, and though there is evidence of some dislocation, her theory that 'we cannot discount the possibility that [Items 21 to 26, which include the dating-clause] were copied from some earlier independent collection' – while not unreasonable as a hypothesis – is not supported by the evidence. The reference to 'a few brief computistical non-sequiturs' is especially misleading, since it is precisely the miscellaneous items in the collection that preserve the oldest computistical texts, such as those of Palumbus/Columbanus and Palladius.[25] The only text in the collection, as Bede had it, which can definitely be said to be an addition to the Irish archetype is the *Liber Cosmographiorum;* everything else would be thoroughly at home in a mid-seventh-century Irish computus.

On the basis of the foregoing discussion we can, I believe, accept the date AD 658 given in the dating-clause of the Sirmond collection. Its location in south-east Ireland needs no further demonstration. That much said, it is clear that the citations of Virgilius Maro Grammaticus in the text *De ratione temporum uel de compoto annali* (items 3-6 of the Sirmond collection) and separately in the same collection, constitute the earliest known references to that author by any English or Irish writer. The other text cited below, *De ratione conputandi,* while it lacks a dating-clause such as occurs in the Sirmond group, is nevertheless so similar to DRT in content and style that it seems reasonable to date it to roughly the same period (though a date in the last third of the seventh century would not be unacceptable). The famous Munich Computus (Bayerische Staatsbibliothek, Clm 14456) is twice dated by reference to computistical rules, once to AD 689 and again to AD 718, and almost certainly derives from Iona around the period (AD 716) when that community is known to have abandoned the old Irish 84-year Easter reckoning in favour of the Victorian/Dionysiac tables.[26]

---

25 For Palumbus/Columbanus see Ó Cróinín, 'A seventh-century Irish computus', 426-27 [above 125-6], and Walsh & Ó Cróinín, *Cummian's Letter*, 176-77 (cap. 70 n. 5); for the Palladian text see Dáibhí Ó Cróinín, 'New light on Palladius', *Peritia* 5 (1986) 276-83 [above 28-34].

26 I demonstrated elsewhere that the compilation preserves a citation – not found in Bede – from the letter of AD 640 addressed by the papal curia to the northern Irish churches; see Ó Cróinín, 'A seventh-century Irish computus', 409 [above, 103-4].

1. *De ratione temporum uel de compoto annali,* cap. XXVI

>—< Haec ergo quattuor tempora ita nominantur: uer aestas autumnus hiemps. Δ Uer, unde nomen accepit? >—< Hoc, uer dicitur eo quod in eo cuncta uernent, id est uirescunt, de uiriditate, quia in illo tempore tellus uirescit et florere uidetur. Δ Aestas, unde nomen accepit? >—< Ab aestu, hoc est a calore solis maturandis frugibus. Δ Autumnus, quid est? Autumnus ab autumnatione, id est collectione fructuum; augmentum dicitur ab augmentatione frugum quae in eo colliguntur, siue autumnus abundantia dicitur uel maturitas [cf. *Epitoma* XI 5-6; Polara, 156].²⁷

2. Oxford, Bodleian Library, MS. 309, fols 105ᵛ-106ʳ + Tours, Bibliothèque Municipale, MS. 334 (*saec.* IX) fol. 44ᵛ:²⁸

Uirgilius dicit: Est etiam uesper uespere uesperum uespera; hic cassus nominatiuus quadruplex est. Uesper quidem dicitur quotiescunque sol nubibus uel luna ferruginibus quacunque diei aut noctis hora obtegatur, et neutrum nomen est: hoc uesper huius uesperis, et reliqua; at nominatiuo uespere uocatur ab hora nona sole discensum inchoante; sed hoc nomen declinationem nullam habet. Uesperum autem cum sole occidente dies deficit, et sic declinatur: uesperum uesperi uespero, et reliqua. Uespera est cum lucis oriente aurora nox finiatur, etenim sicut dies noctis successu uesperum habet, sic et nox diei ex hoc ortu uesperam habet, et est nomen primae declinationis. Cauendum est tamen ne haec nomina pluralem numerum habeant [cf. *Epistola* XIV, 4-8; Polara, 186-88].

3. *De ratione conputandi,* caps. 2, 22, 25, 42, 43 (cf. M. Walsh & D. Ó Cróinín (eds), *Cummian's Letter 'De controversia paschali', together with a related Irish computistical tract 'De ratione conputandi'.* Pontifical Institute of Mediaeval Studies, Studies and Texts 86 (Toronto 1988) 114, 128, 129, 131, 148-49, 150, 151):

---

27 Text from my unpublished edition, for which Bodley 309 is the principal manuscript. Reference throughout is to the edition by Giovanni Polara, *Virgilio Marone Grammatico, Epitomi ed Epistole.* Nuovo Medioevo 9 (Napoli 1979). 28 A miscellany of pieces on the Roman calendar added to the account in Macrobius, *Saturnalia,* excerpted in the Sirmond group and known to Bede as *Disputatio Cori et Praetextati*; the description in Jones, *Bedae opera,* 107 (items 35 and 36 of the Sirmond collection) as 'Notes based on Etym.' and 'Computistical notes partially unpublished' gives no adequate idea of the contents. [For further discussion, see below, 201-12.] [Marina Smyth's dismissal of them as 'a few brief computistical non-sequiturs' (see above) is equally misleading.] The Tours MS. preserves an older orthography.

ISIDORUS dicit: 'Sol dictus est eo quod solus' luceat, uel soliditate luminis aut de solemnitate lucis. Unde AGUSTINUS: 'Quia solus per diem sui fulgoris ui obtonsis cum luna stellis totum mundum inlustrat' [cf. *Epitoma* XI 1, 8; Polara, 148].

Ita dies diuidendo lucem a tenebris dicta, uel eo quod 'iucundus sit diis' [cf. *Epitoma* XI 5, 2; Polara, 156].

Sciendum nobis unde nox nomen accepit. ISIDORUS dicit: 'Nox est absentia' lucis. Hinc 'dicta quod humanis negotiis uel oculorum obtutibus noceat, uel quod fures et bestias humanis rebus nocere facit liberius operantes' [cf. *Epitoma* XI 5, 2; Polara, 156].

UIRGILIUS demonstrat dicens: 'Est etiam uesper, uespere, uesperum, uespera. Hic cassus nominatiuus quadruplex est, cuius differentia est, quod uesper quidem dicitur quociescumque sol nubibus aut luna ferruginibus quacumque diei ac noctis hora obcecatur. Et hoc neutrum "uesper, uesperis" facit. Aut nominatiuo uespere uocatur, ab hora nona sole discensum inchoante. Hoc nomen declinationem non habet. Uesperum est cum lucis oriente aurora nox finitur, et sic declinatur: uespera, uespere. Cauendum est, ne aut "uespera, uespere" aut "uesperum" pluralem numerum habere putentur' [cf. *Epistola* XIV, 4-8; Polara, 186-88].

Sciendum nobis unde [tempus] nominatum est. A temperamento, ut ISIDORUS dicit: 'Tempus a temperamento' quodam siderum 'nomen accepit, quia diebus' ac noctibus, 'mensibus' et 'annis, frigore aestateque conponitur' [cf. *Epitoma* XI 5, 3; Polara, 156].

Sciendum nobis quod dicunt alii Greca esse haec nomina temporum, et ita interpretantur, id est uer fructificatio, estas calor, autumpnus copiositas, 'hiems frigus uel sterilitas' [cf. *Epitoma* XI 5, 5; Polara, 156]. Item UIRGILIUS dicit: 'Autumnus uocatur' ab 'autumatione fructuum qui in eo colliguntur' [cf. *Epitoma* XI 5, 5; Polara, 156].

4. München, Bayerische Staatsbibliothek, Clm 14456 (*saec*. IX, Regensburg) 10r, 12ʳ, 17ʳ, 18ʳ:

Dies gemine appellari solet, proprie a solis ortu donec rursum oriatur, abusiue a solis ortu usque dum ueniat occasum solis; siue dictus est dies a diis, eo quod diis iocundus [cf. *Epitoma* XI 5, 5; Polara, 156].

Mensis a mensura dicitur, qui unusquisque eorum mensuratur. Augustinus ait: 'Ueteres menses dicebant a mensa communi, quia terram suis fructibus quasi quibusdam dapibus replebit; chimales uero menses esse negabant, secundum spatia dicebant, quia nullum dapibus dant modum'; hucusque Augustinus [cf. *Epitoma* XI 5, 4; Polara, 156]. Tempus temperamentum dicitur, eo quod designationem .iiii. tempora anni temperat [cf. *Epitoma* XI 5,3; Polara, 156].

Sol dicitur quia solus per diem sui fulgoris uim obtonsis luna cum
stellis totum mundum inlustrat [cf. *Epitoma* XI 1, 8; Polara, 148].

For the sake of completeness I include the following (undated) citation, which has not hitherto been recognized.

Oxford, Bodleian Library, MS. Digby 63 (*saec.* IX, provenance
Winchester), which contains much pre-Bedan Irish material (cf. Jones,
Bedae opera, 369)²⁹ fol. 30ᵛ:

Quare dicatur ver, aestas, autumnus, et iemps? Sanctus Atanasius ita
dicit: Vocatur autem ver eo quod in eo cuncta uernant, id est uires-
cant. Estas ab estu, quia in eo maturandis frugibus dantur. Autumnus
de autumnatione, qia [*sic*] in eo colliguntur. Iemps uero ab octoribus
[*sic*] frugus intemperatus dicitur [cf. *Epitoma* XI 5-6; Polara, 156].

As a final contribution, I give here the verbatim citation of Priscian,
Institutiones grammaticae, which occurs in DRT cap. VII, as additional
proof that the *Institutiones* were, in fact, known in Ireland before the
ninth century:³⁰
In multis enim nominibus, quae in Greco aspirationem habent, nos pro
aspiratione s ponimus, ut pro hex sex et pro hepta septem, sicut pro
herpillo herba illum [= *Etym.* III 3]. Item Priscianus hoc confirmat
dicens: In aliis dictionibus quibusdam solent Eolos sequentes uel in
digamma uel in s conuertere aspirationem, ut hemis semis, hex sex, hepta
septem [cf. *Institutiones grammaticae,* ed. Martin Hertz, *Grammatici
Latini* 3 (Leipzig 1859; repr. Hildesheim 1967) 16, 18-20].

---

29 The text given by Jones is not quite accurate. [On Digby 63 see Dáibhí Ó Cróinín, 'Sticks and
stones', *Peritia* 2 (1983) 257-60.]   **30** There are, of course, other passages in DRT which may
likewise derive from the *Institutiones*, but this one is the most clear-cut example.

15

Bede's Irish computus[*]

In the first of his many valuable contributions to the study of Insular computistics in the seventh century and after, Charles W. Jones announced in 1937 his rediscovery of the supposedly lost Sirmond manuscript of Bede's computus.[1] The 'Sirmond manuscript' was the eleventh-century Vendôme codex owned by the great French Jesuit scholar Jacques Sirmond (1559-1651) and loaned by him in turn to the Flemish chronologist Gilles Bouchier (Aegidius Bucherius) for his edition of Victorius of Aquitaine's Paschal table,[2] and to the more erudite and influential French contemporary Denis Petau (Dionysius Petavius) for use in his great compendium on technical chronology, *Opus de doctrina temporum* (2 vols, Paris 1627).[3] After Sirmond's death, his books were transferred to the Jesuit library in Paris, but because the Vendôme manuscript disappeared shortly thereafter it was described by all subsequent commentators as lost. In fact, however, it had been acquired by the English scholar Edward Bernard (author of the first great catalogue of English manuscript libraries, *Catalogi librorum manuscriptorum Angliae et Hiberniae*, Oxford 1697) and on his death in 1698 it came with his collection of books into the Bodleian Library at Oxford, where Jones subsequently happened upon it. The manuscript had never been called from the shelves by any previous visiting scholar, it seems, not even the great Mommsen, who had read at the Bodleian without realising that the codex contained Bede's chronicles and some unique Vendôme annals. Jones' discovery of the manuscript, therefore, allowed him 'to purge away many of the surmises of the intervening centuries'.[4] Furthermore, he was able to show that 'the Sirmond manuscript combines with three others, hitherto virtually unused, to provide definite knowledge of the Insular *computus*'.[5]

In the original article announcing his important discovery, and in his subsequent edition of Bede's *De temporum ratione* and *De temporibus*, Jones gave an itemised list of contents for the Sirmond codex, having established in the intervening years that the entire collection (and not just the second part of the

---

[*] Published here for the first time. 1 C.W. Jones, 'The "lost" Sirmond manuscript'. Unfortunately, the crucial last six pages of the original article have been accidentally omitted in the reprint. 2 Aegidius Bucherius, *De doctrina temporum commentarius in Victorium Aquitanum* (Antwerp 1634). 3 For a valuable discussion of these seventeenth-century chronological researches, see Anthony T. Grafton, 'Joseph Scaliger and historical chronology: the rise and fall of a discipline', *History and Theory* 14 (1975), 156-85. 4 Jones, *Bedae opera*, ix. 5 Ibid., 105.

manuscript, as he had first thought) represented a faithful copy of Bede's own computus at Jarrow. That inventory has been reprinted more recently by the Canadian scholar Faith Wallis in her excellent English translation of Bede's works,[6] but because neither Jones' original list nor Dr Wallis' more recent discussion of it has identified all of the material in the collection – in particular the brief excerpts and short tracts that are crucial to the task of locating and dating the exemplar from which the Sirmond codex was copied – I propose here to repeat Jones' inventory of the manuscript, but to identify and print those texts that have hitherto escaped notice.[7] I give a short-title description of each text, with relevant bibliographical details, where necessary.

1.	fols 3v–61v	Bede's *De temporum ratione*
2.	fol. 61v	A list of Greek numbers
3.	fol. 62r–v	Prologue and capitula to the Irish computus *De ratione temporum uel de compoto annali*
4.	fols 62v–64v	*Sententiae Sti Augustini et Isidori in laude compoti*
5.	fols 64v–73v	*De .xiiii. diuisionibus temporum*
6a.	fols 74r–76r	*De bissexto*
6b.	fols 76r–78r	*De saltu lunae pauca dicamus*
7.	fol. 78r–v	Argumentum *De saltu lunae monstrando*
8.	fol. 78v	Argumentum *De materia bissexti*
9.	fols 78v–79r	Argumentum *Si nosse desideras augmentum lunare*
10.	fols 79r–80r	Computistical poem *Annus solis continetur*
11.	fol. 80r	Bede, DTR XXIII
12.	fol. 80r–v	Bede, DTR XIX
13.	fols 80v–81r	Three uncanonical Dionysiac argumenta
14.	fols 81r–82r	Dionysiac argumenta I–X
15.	fol. 82r–v	Dionys. arg. XIV *Incipit calculatio quomodo reperiri*
16.	fol. 82r–v	*Exemplum suggestionis Boni sancti primicerii, De sollemnitatibus et sabbatis.* The rubric is that of the *Exemplum Boni*, but the text is the pseudo-Columbanus letter *De sollemnitatibus*
17.	fols 84r–85r	Letter of Paschasinus to Pope Leo
18.	fols 85r–86r	Dionysius Exiguus to Boniface and Bonus
19.	fols 86r–87v	Dionysius to Petronius
20.	fols 88r–89v	Proterius of Alexandria to Pope Leo
21.	fols 89v–90v	Epistola Cyrilli *De Pascha*
22.	fols 90v–93v	Anatolius of Laodicea, *De ratione paschali*
23.	fols 93v–94r	Excerpts from Eusebius, Gennadius, Jerome, etc., about Anatolius
24.	fol. 94r–v	Pseudo-Morinus, *De Pascha*

---

6 Faith Wallis, *Bede: The Reckoning of Time*. Translated Texts for Historians 29 (Liverpool 1999) lxxii–lxxix.

25. fols 94v-95v   *Epistola Philippi de Pascha* [= Pseudo-Theophilus, *Acta Synodi*]
26. fols 95v-95²r   'Computistical bits' (Jones)
27. fol. 96r-v   Victorian argumenta
28. fols 96v-97r   Letter of Pope Leo to the Emperor Marcian
29. fol. 97r-v   Excerpt from *De sollemnitatibus* (No. 16 above)
30. fols 97v-98r   Tract on finger-reckoning
31. fols 98r-99r   Prologue to Easter table of Theophilus of Alexandria
32. fol. 99r-v   Argumenta
33. fols 99v-101r   Prologue of (Pseudo-)Cyril of Alexandria
34. fols 101r-5v   Excerpts from Macrobius, *Saturnalia* I 15, 5-6, known to Bede as *Disputatio Cori et Praetextati*
35. fols 105v-6v   Excerpts from Isidore, *Etymologiae*
36. fols 106r-7v   'Computistical notes partially unpublished' (Jones)
37. fol. 107v   Heading for a Cyrillan Alexandrian Easter table
38. fol. 108r   Rota of lunar and solar months
39. fol. 108r   Gennadius, *De uiris illustribus*, on Victorius
40. fols 108r-10v   Letter of Archdeacon Hilarus to Victorius of Aquitaine, plus Victorius's Prologue
41. fol. 110v   (originally blank; additions by later hand)
42. fols 111r-13r   Excerpts from Chronicle of Eusebius-Jerome
43. fols 113r-20r   Victorius' 532-year Easter table
44. fols 120r-31v   Dionysiac Easter tables, AD 532-1042 (lacunose)
45. fols 132r-40v   Victorius' *Calculus*
46. fols 141r-65v   Computistical items of later date

Jones proved conclusively that 'Bede's works indicate that Northumbrian schools largely depended upon Irish knowledge and methods' and that 'Northumbrian education owed comparatively little to Rome and the Augustinian mission'.[8] 'Except for those works which Bede expressly assembled for the composition of his *History* [he added], like the selections from the *Liber Pontificalis* and Gregory's letters, I can find no indication of a stream of literature from the south which in any way equals the obvious stream from Ireland'.[9] That verdict has been accepted also by Faith Wallis, the most recent writer on the subject. And yet neither scholar adverted to the text in the Sirmond collection that is expressly attributed to Patrick *(Patricius in prologo suo)*, or the extract from the tract *De luna abortiua* explicitly ascribed to Columbanus (here called *Palumbus*, a form of the name which he himself used in his letters), nor – strangest of all – to the dating-clause in the manuscript,

---

7 I drew attention myself to some of these texts in the various articles printed above; but there are some other, previously unidentified excerpts that are worth publishing here for the light they cast on the question of what books were known to the Irish in the seventh century. **8** *Bedae opera*, 11, 112. **9** Ibid., 113.

which is preserved also, but in more garbled form, in the other related manuscripts referred to by Jones in his 1937 article and again in his great edition of Bede's works 'On Time', and that was therefore clearly contained in the Irish exemplar from which all these later copies ultimately derive. I have printed the dating-clause and these previously unnoticed texts in articles published elsewhere in this volume,[10] and there is no need here to rehearse the arguments concerning their authenticity. But it is perhaps opportune at this point to print those items, described as 'computistical notes' by Jones and a 'miscellany of computistica' by Faith Wallis (and as 'a few brief computistical non-sequiturs' by Marina Smyth),[11] in their entirety, to illustrate the context in which they are found, and also the range of sources – some of them extremely rare – drawn upon by the compiler of the original Irish computus. The items on fols 105v-107r of the Bodleian manuscript are here given first (with a minimum of editorial interference, in order to illustrate the characteristically Irish aspects of the spelling; direct citations are indicated by use of italic font).

[I] ISSIODORUS dicit: *Tempora autem momentis, horis, diebus, mensibus, annis, lustris, saeculis, aetatibus diuiduntur.* Atomos in diuisione temporis non est; similiter et minutum. Quadras quarta pars assis, id est .iii. unciae. Inde, propter similem numerum, annua praeparatio bissexti, in qua fiunt .iii. horae, quadras translato nomine uocatur.

[II] *Uesperus stella est occidentalis, quam cognominatam perhibent ab Hespero Hispaniae rege. Est autem et ipsa ex quinque stellis planetis, noctem ducens et solem sequens. Fertur autem quod haec stella oriens luciferum, occidens uesperum facit.* Uirgilius dicit: *Est* autem *uesper, uespere, uesperum, uespera. Hic cassus nominatiuus quadruplex est,* cuius deferentia haec erit, quod *uesper autem dicitur quotienscumque sol nubibus* aut *luna ferruginibus quacumque diei uel noctis hora obtegitur. Et neutrum* nomen est: hoc *uesper,* huius *uesperis,* et reliqua. *At* nominatiuo *uesper uocatur ab hora nona sole descensum inchoante; sed hoc nomen nullam declinationem habet. Uesperum* autem est *cum sole occidente dies deficit, et sic declinatur: uesperum, uesperi, uespero,* et reliqua. *Uespera est cum lucis oriente aurora nox finiatur. Etenim sicut dies noctis successu uesperum, sic et nox diei exortu uesperam habet, et* sic declinatur nomen *primae declinationis. Cauendum est tamen, ne* haec nomina *pluralem numerum habeant.*

[III] Quaeritur cur Kalendae, hoc est principia mensis, ab accensione lunae conposita esse dicuntur, cum aliquando in principio memsis luna, quae ei deputatur, extinguitur, et alterius luna poene in suo initio accensa fere tota contra eum decurrit. Hoc ita est, quod in primo anno tantum-

---

10 'The computistical writings of Columbanus', above 48ff; 'New light on Palladius', above 28ff. The long-promised edition of the *Disputatio Chori et Praetextati* will appear elsewhere before very much longer. 11 Marina Smyth, 'Isidore of Seville and early Irish cosmology', CMCS 14 (Winter 1987) 69-102: 99.

modo conponendorum mensium haec ratio effecta fuerit, quae quintanas septemque Nonas mensibus praebuit, et tricenos, undetricenos secundum ordinem statum esse efficit, quam ratio (id est, a lunae incensione menses incipere) Macrobius, stultam esse coarguens, hoc modo inquit: *Romulus, cum ingenio acri* quidem, *sed agresti statum proprii ordinaret imperii, initium cuiusque mensis ex illo summebat die quo nouam lunam contigisset uideri, quia non continuo euenit ut eodem die semper appareat, sed modo tardius, modo celerius ex certis causis uideri solet, contigit ut, cum tardius apparuit, praecedenti mensi plures dies, aut cum celerius, pauciores darentur; et ex singulis quibusque mensibus perpetuam numeri legem primus cassus addixit. Sic factum est ut alii triginta et unum, alii undetriginta sortirentur dies. Omnibus tamen mensibus ex die Nonarum Idus nono die representari placuit; et inter Idus ac sequentes Kalendas constitutum est .xvi. dies esse numerandos. Ideo mensis uberior .ii. illos quibus augebatur dies inter Kalendas suas et Nonas habebat. Hinc aliis .v. a Kalendis dies, aliis .vii. Nonas facit* de uarietate diuidendorum dierum mensibus inter stipites suos, quod, ut placuit sacerdotibus, factum est.

Kalendas autem Nonas et Idus propter dies festos Romani instituerunt, uel propter *officia magistratuum. In his enim diebus conueniebatur in urbibus. Quidam* autem *Kalendas a colendo appellari existimant. Apud ueteres enim omnium mensium principia colebantur, sicut et apud Hebraeos. Idus autem plerique Latinorum ab edendo dictum putant, quod hi dies apud ueteres epularum essent. Nonae a nundinis uocatae; nundinae enim sunt publicae conuentiones siue commercimonia.*

[IV] Quaeritur utrum secundum solem an lunam Aegyptii numerant. Augustinus ostendit dicens: *Annus quoque, si in circuitu lunari triceni* dies *numerantur, senario numero pollet. Restant tamen quinque dies ut sol impleat cursum suum.* Item Issiodorus: *Itaque luna per tricenos dies duodenis uicibus suum cursum perficiens consummat annum, secundum Hebraeos aliquibus diebus adiectis.*

[V] Item sciendum, si secundum lunam enumerant, cur non cum duobus annis lunae, communi scilicet uel embolismo, concordant. Et notandum quod bissextus in luna numeratur, quem Aegyptii in principio sui anni ponunt. Hoc ita est, quod Issiodorus ostendit dicens: *Aegyptii autem primi propter lunae uelociorem cursum, et ne error conputationis eius uelocitate accideret, ex solis cursu diem mensis adinuenerunt, quoniam tardior solis motus facilius poterat conprehendi.* Item, secundum solem alia ratione adnumerantes, totum solarem cursum terminant, dicente Macrobio: *Post hoc emitatus Aegyptios, solos diuinarum rerum omnium conscios, ad numerum solis, qui diebus .ccclxv. et quadrante conficit cursum, annum dirigere contendit.*

[VI] Quaeritur utrum ignorantia an scientia Aegyptii .xii. tricenorum mensium ratione, secuti sunt. Alii dicunt quod ignorantia erroreque

decepti hanc rationem tenuerunt, Dionisio dicente: *Nec hoc praetereun-*
dum esse putauimus, quod nimis errent, qui lunam peragere cursum sui circuli
.xxx. dierum spatiis estimantes, .xii. lunares menses in .ccclx. diebus annu-
merant, quibus etiam .v. dies adieciunt, quos interkalares appellauit
antiquitas, ut solarem annum adimplere uideantur.

[VII] Sciendum cur hanc rationem propriae tenuerunt. Hoc ita est, de
quo iure alius calcenterus hoc modo dicens inquit: *Menses* tantummodo
per tricenarium numerum computantes in .ccclx. diebus cursum .xii. explica-
bant mensium, secuti tempus illud dilui Geneseos scriptura tricenos dies currere
monstratur. Quinque scilicet dies qui supersunt, ad annum finiendum in memo-
riam fabricae Dei uacui nominabantur. Quinque enim diebus fabricatus est
mundus. Homo uero sexto die post omnia factus est; ex qua etiam die ad .xii.
percurrendos menses compotus dierum fuit tricentorum sexaginta in pridie diei
illius, quem primo constituit Dominus. Quinque deinde uacui fuerant dies
usque in pridie natiuitatis, qui primo finxtus est.

[VIII] *Sed cum tres menses uernum habeat tempus, horum* trium *medius est,*
qui initium mundo dedit. Neque solum mensis medius, sed etiam dies mensium
medius est. Ex .v. Idus enim Febroarii (ueris inchoatio) in .v. Idus Martii
unus mensis est; ex .v. Idus autem *Martii in .viii. Kl. Aprilis .xv. dies sunt,*
id est medietas mensis. Ita unus et dimedius mensis subsequitur, hoc est in .v.
Idus Maias. *Ex .v. Idus Maias in .v. Idus Augusti,* secundum hanc
rationem, *tempus aestatis* est. *Ex .v. Idus Augusti in .v. Idus Nouimbris,*
autumni tempus est; item *ex .v. Idus Nouimbris* licet dissimiliter *in .v. Idus*
Februarii, hiemale tempus est. Patricius, in prologo suo, secundum
rationem Anatolii, hoc ius ostendit.

[IX] *Notandum est quod in .xviiii. ciclo quattuor anni contrariae regulae*
inueniuntur, quorum ratio diligenter arguteque animaduertenda est. Hoc est
annus .viii. lunae, secundum rationem Grecorum, et annus .xxvii; item, secun-
dum rationem Latinorum, .iiii. lunae annus et .xxx. Item tribus annis in
.xviiii. ciclo eadem aetas super Kl Aprilis et Maii inuenitur, hoc est in anno
.xxvi. lunae super Kl. Ianuarii et in anno .xxviiii. et in anno .xxvii.

[X] Palumbus dicit: *Nunc de luna pauca tractanda sunt. Luna maior*
lunaque minor in anno sunt, sed uicissim (ut quidam putant) sibi semper
alterno succedunt cursu; licet unius temporis alios intellexisse breues.
Sciendum est similiter absque una abortiua quae, si tunc illo euenerit tempore,
nulla conputanda (ut aiunt). Mensis nimirum neutri mensis Kalendis uindi-
cata. Primum scilicet diem prioris non tenens ac usque ad secundi initium non
pertingens, e medio quodammodo proiecto deprehenditur ceteraque lunas
similiter breues esse, id est Iunii et Septimbris et Nouimbris; et conputata
ratione ab eis. Sed illam mensis computa lunam quae in eo finitur, non quae
incipit. Inde, quae primum prioris aut initium sequentis non tenet, abortiua
luna dicitur. Hoc licet alio lapsu saltus.

Omnis enim .xiiii. luna semper facit anno. Idcirco, dum per menses .vi., ut
supradictum est, id est aut per tres ueris et alios tres supra iam nominatos, aut
(ut plus firmant) per alternos uices .vi. lunae .xxviiii. sunt et per .vi. alios
.xxx. inueniuntur.

The sources of these extracts are as follows: (I) Isidore, *Etymologiae* V 29.1, 3-6
(cf. *Etym.* VI. 17. 25; XVI. 25.17); (II) Virgilius Maro Grammaticus, *Epistola* I.
4, 4-8; (III) *Disputatio Cori et Praextextati* (= Macrobius, *Saturnalia* I. 15, 5-6);
(IV) Augustinus, *De Trinitate* IV. 4; (V) Isidore, *De natura rerum* XIX. 2; (VI)
Isidore, *Etymologiae* V. 33.2; I.14.3 (VII) Dionysius Exiguus, *Praefatio in cyclo*
paschali (Krusch, *Studien* 2, 65); (VIII) Q. Iulius Hilarianus, *Expositum de die*
paschae et mensis (MPL 13, 1105-14: 1107); (IX) Pseudo-Athanasius/Pseudo-
Martinus Bracarensis, *De Pascha* (Barlow, *Martini ep. Bracarensis opera*, 273);
Pseudo-Augustinus, *De temporibus anni* (MPL 129, 1292); Patricius, *Prologus in*
cyclo paschali (deperditus); (X) Palumbus (= Columbanus) *De ratione lunae*.

It cannot seriously be doubted that a collection that contains material on the
luna abortiua (a term used exclusively by Irish computists)[12] composed by
Columbanus (alias Palumbus), which is otherwise found only in the Irish
computus *De ratione conputandi*[13] and in the famous 'Classbook' of St Dunstan
(otherwise known – significantly, no doubt – as the *Liber Commonei*,
'Cummian's Book'), and excerpted in only two other (derivative) computistical
collections,[14] must itself be Irish in origin. The fact that Patrick *(Patricius)* is
cited by name in the same set of excerpts can only copper-fasten that suggestion. If, in addition, we point to the dating-clause in the collection, which was
clearly also in the underlying exemplar of all the surviving copies, and which
locates the original in southern Ireland in AD 658, then it seems hard to avoid
the conclusion that Jones' original assessment of Bede's indebtedness to the
Irish was, if anything, understated. The only puzzling feature of all this is the
fact that Bede and his two modern commentators passed by these Irish texts in
silence.

The dating-clause in the Sirmond computus is found in a miscellany of
brief biographical excerpts from Eusebius and Jerome on Anatolius of
Laodicea, Gaudentius of Brescia *De Pascha*, Victorius' prologue, biographical
scraps on Victorius from Gennadius' *De uiris illustribus*, and a citation from
Sulpicius Severus' Chronicle.[15] I have published the text of the dating-clause
more than once already in this collection and need not repeat it again here, but it
might be useful to give at this point that section of the miscellany immediately

---

12 See Walsh & Ó Cróinín, *Cummian's Letter*, 89.237, 177-79.   13 Walsh & Ó Cróinín, loc.cit.
14 Oxford, Bodleian Library, MS. Digby 63 (saec. IX, Winchester provenance) and in the
annotations to Angers, Bibl. mun., MS. 477 (saec. IX/X), which contains Bede's *De temporum*
ratione.   15 Of these only Morinus is mentioned by Wallis, *Bede: The Reckoning of Time*, lxxv-
lxxvi.

following the end of Anatolius *De Pascha* (fol. 93v 16, No. 22 in Jones' inventory), which is as follows:

[I]... FINIT LIBER ANATOLII. EVSEBIVS CAESARIENSIS dicit: *Dignum mihi uidetur dicere quod Anatholius de Pascha senserit.* '*Est ergo*', dicens, '*in primo anno, initium primi mensis*', et reliqua.

[II]... HIERONIMVS DICIT: *Anatholius Alexandrinus, Laodiciae Syriae episcopus, sub Probo et Caro imperatoribus floruit, mirae doctrinae uir in arithmetica, geometria, astronomia, rethorica, dialectica, grammatica. Cuius ingenii magnitudinem de uolumine quod 'Super Pascha' composuit, et 'De .x. libris arithmeticae instructionis', uix intelligere possumus.*

[III]... EVSEBIVS dicit: *Anatholius Laodiciae episcopus in doctrina philosophorum plurimo sermone celebratur. ccxlviiii. a passione Domini sub primo anni Probi scripsit .lxxii. in ordine scriptorum a Petro. Octauo recursu nunc agitur circulus eius.*

[IV]... *Oportuno tempore Dominus Ihesus beatissimam festiuitatem Paschae uoluit celebrari, post autumni nebulam, post horrorem hiemis, ante aestatis ardorem. Oportebat enim solem iustitiae Christum et Iudaeorum caliginem et frigus /uel rigorem/ gentium ante ardorem futuri iudicii placido resurrectionis lumine* remouere, *cunctaque in stat*utum *tranquillis primordiis reuocare, quae fuerant uelamine tetro confusa ab illo principe tenebrarum. Nam ueris temperiae Deus condidit mundum. Martio enim mense dixit* ad *M*oysen *Deus: 'Mensis hic uobis initium mensium primus est in mensibus anni'* [Exod. 12], *quem mensem uerax utique Deus primum non diceret, nisi primus esset. Filius ergo Dei, 'per quem facta sunt omnia'* [Io 1], *eodem die, eodemque tempore, prostratum mundum propria resurrectione resuscitat, quo eum ipse prius creat ex nichilo, ut enim reformarentur 'in Christo, quae in caelis et quae in terra sunt'* [Eph. 1, 10]; '*quoniam ex ipso*', *ut ait apostolus,* et reliqua. *Nec turbari quisquam nostrum debet, si interdum secundo mense, id est Aprili, Pascha nos celebrare lunaris ratio et dies cogit dominicus. Secundum enim lunae cursum in scripturis diuinis numerantur dies. Caeterum Kalendas et Idus et Nonas et mensium nomina ac dierum gentiles posuerunt, ut puta quem uetustas humanae memoriae primum mensem tenebat, paganus hunc a Marte Martium nuncuparet; et diem* secundum *quem septimum rationabilium corda seruabant ille Saturni diem statueret appellandum. Scripturae autem sanctae cum de temporibus aliquid uel referunt uel iubent ita loquuntur: 'Decima die mensis secundi, id est luna decima, aut quinta decima die mensis septimi, aut uicesima die mensis noni, aut .xiiii. die mensis primi', ut in Exodi libro /* 94ra) *pariter audiuimus* [Exod. 12; cf. Lev. 23] , *ubi obseruatio Paschae describitur, et .vii. diebus sollemnitatis azima comedenda mandantur. Praecepit tamen Deus et hoc, ut si quis primo mense, uel immundus in anima hominis, id est mortui, a*ut *tactu pollutus, uel extra electum sacri*s *Hierusolimae locum, in longinquo itinere constitutus Pascha non potuit celebrare, secundo mense cele-*

*braret. Praeuidens quippe Deus gentium populos tunc adhuc hominum mortuo-
rum simulacris immundos extra locum sanctum ecclesiae in longinquo positos,
utique nobis 'qui eramus longe, et facti sumus prope in sanguine Christi'*
[Ephes. 2, 13]; *dat licentiam, ut si primo mense nobis non occurrerit et dies
dominicus, et congruus lunae numerus secundo mense celebremus. Et ideo nec
citra .xiiii. lunam nec ultra uicesimam primam celebrare possumus, quia
septem sunt dies azimorum paschalium in quibus quaerimus dominicum diem.
Vult enim nos Christus, promulgator legis et gratiae, nec legitimos iuxta lunae
cursum praeterire dies. neque diem suae resurrectionis otio ingrato transcendere. Nam .vi. feria, qua hominem fecerat, pro eodem passus est, et die
dominica quae dicitur in scripturis prima sabbati, in qua mundus sumpserat
exordium, resurrexit, ut qui prima die creauit caelum et terram (unde postea
hominem faciens figurauit) primo etiam die omnem hominem reparet, propter
quem fecerat mundum.*

[V] Disputatio Morini Alexandrini Episcopi de ratione Paschali
[No. 24 in Jones' inventory]. This is the text of Pseudo-Morinus, another
'Irish Paschal Forgery'; it extends over fol. 94r-v and is followed, fols
94v-95v by another supposed 'Irish Forgery', the work known as Pseudo-
Theophilus, *Acta Synodi Caesariae* (No. 25 in Jones' inventory, here given
the rubric *Epistola Philippi de Pascha*). This in turn is followed immediately by Jones' 'computistical bits' [No. 26 in his inventory], beginning
(fol. 95vb 8) with an account of Victorius:

[VI]... Uictorius, in quo ordine scriptorum? Id est .ccxxii. post Petrum.
De genere Romanorum est, ab Aquitania prouincia, ut Gennadius dicit.[16]
Cursum paschalem ratione certissima composuit. Sub Leone minore et
maiore conscripsit, anno .iiii. regni eorum. Quanto tempore ab initio et
cruce Christi conscripsit? Hic est circulus annorum .xviiii. octauies
centies, secundum saltum lunae. Et hic est circulus annorum .xxviii.
nondecies, secundum bissextos solis. In hoc circulo ogdoades sunt .xxviii.
In hoc circulo endecades similiter .xxviii. In hoc circulo saltus sunt
.xxviii. In hoc circulo bissexti sunt .cxxxiii.

[VII]... *Omnibus annis temporibus diebus ac luna maxime, que iuxta
Hebraeos menses faci*s *rite discussis, a mundi principio usque in diem, quo filii
Israhel paschale mysterium initiauere, anni sunt .iii.dclxxxviiii, precedente
primo mense, .viii. Kl. Aprilis, luna .xiiii., .vi. feria. Passum autem
Dominum nostrum Ihesum Christum, peractis .vccvx. et .viii. annis ab exort
mundi eadem cronicorum relatione monstratur, .viii. Kl. Aprilis, primo mense,
luna .xiiii., .vi. feria.*

[VIII]... Inter primum Pascha in Aegypto et passionem Domini, anni
sunt īdxxxviiii. Ex Domini uero passione usque in Pascha quod secutum

---

16 A paraphrase only of Gennadius; see Ernest C. Richardson (ed), *Hieronymus 'Liber de viris
illustribus', Gennadius 'Liber de viris illustribus'* (Leipzig 1896) 92.

est Suibini filii Commanni, anni sunt .dcxxxi. A Pascha autem /95*bis* r)
supradicto usque ad tempus praefinitum consummationis mundi, id est
sex milibus consummatis, anni sunt .cxli. Ab .viii. luna usque in .xxvi.
lunam ogdoas. Ab .viiii. luna crescit usque in .xxviii. luna endecas currit.,
[IX]... SULPICIUS. *Christus natus est Sabino et Rufino consulibus .viii. Kl.*
Ianuarii. Christus passus duobus geminis consulibus. A natiuitate domini
Sabino et Rufino consulibus usque ad passionem eius R*ufo* uidelicet *et*
Rubellio consulibus geminis, sub quibus Christus crucifixus est in die .viii.
Kl. Aprilis, sunt anni .xxxi. et menses tres.[17]
[X]... Hilarus, in quo ordine episcoporum in Roma? Id est .xliiii.to. Et
quanto tempore rexit ecclesiam? Id est .iii. annis et tribus mensibus et .x.
diebus.
[XI]... Apud Hebraeos 'niman', et apud Syros et Caldaeos. Apud
Graecos autem 'arithmus', et altera ratione cyclis. Apud Aegyptios 'later-
cus'. Apud Macedones 'calculus'. Apud Latinos 'compotus' uocatur.
[XII]... .īi.dccclxxx. momentorum Ionas in medio coeti.
[The verso side of the added leaf 95*bis* is blank].[18]

The sources for items I and III above are Eusebius' *Historia Ecclesiastica*
VII.32, in Rufinus' Latin translation (Schwarz-Mommsen, 718-21, 722-3). The
Jerome citation [II] is from his *De uiris illustribus* §73 (MPL 23, 683;
Richardson, 40). The long citation in IV is from Gaudentius, *De Pascha* (MPL
20, 843-8). Section V need not be discussed here; the reference to Gennadius
[VI] is to his *De uiris illustribus* §89,[19] and this in turn is followed by a truncated
citation [VII] from the prefatory letter of Victorius of Aquitaine to Archeacon
(later Pope) Hilarus, introducing his Paschal tables (Mommsen, *MGH*
Auct.Antiq. IX, 682 (§9). After this comes the dating-clause [VIII] discussed
above, the brief citation from Sulpicius' Chronicle [IX], a brief passage [X] *not*
from the *Liber Pontificalis* on (Pope) Hilarus, then an excerpt from the *De*
ratione conputandi (or some other Irish computus) on the etymology of the
word *numerus* in the various ancient languages (DRC §3; Ó Cróinín 117-18; cf.
MPL 129, 1306),[20] and finally a playful computistical calculation of the
number of days spent by Jonah inside the belly of the whale.
    None of these sources is exceptional, save the Chronicle, which is very rare
in this period and which has survived in only one manuscript copy (*saec.* XI). It
was known, however, to Insular writers, including Adomnán of Iona.[21] That

17 Karl Halm (ed), *Sulpicii Severi libri qui supersunt*, *Chronica* II. 27, *Corpus Scriptorum*
Ecclesiasticorum Latinorum I (Vienna 1866) 82.   18 There is no significance whatever in the fact
that the leaf containing the dating-clause is an inserted one; there are several other such vellum
fragments inserted at other points in the manuscript, where lacunae in the text had to be filled by
the corrector.   19 In fact, only the detail concerning Victorius' Aquitanian origin is in
Gennadius.   20 Some such question as *Sciendum est nobis quomodo uocatur numerus in*
principalibus linguis is understood, though not expressed.   21 See Bernhard Bischoff,

Sulpicius' name was also associated with a computus is attested by a letter of Aldhelm to the British king Geraint (AD 672?),[22] in which Aldhelm states that Sulpicius was the author of an 84-year Easter table *(iuxta Sulpicii Seueri regulam, qui lxxxiiii annorum cursum descripsit)*. What had previously been a puzzle to modern commentators has recently been solved by Dan McCarthy,[23] who demonstrated that the 'Irish' 84-year Easter table was, in fact, the work of Sulpicius, thus vindicating Aldhelm and at the same time lending further weight to the possibility that his Chronicle may have come to Ireland in the company of that Easter table. It is worth remembering that in the Paris Irish fragments from Echternach which contain just this kind of miscellany of texts on the Pasch,[24] the excerpt from Pseudo-Athanasius/Pseudo-Martinus Bracarensis is headed: *De ratione Paschae uel Sulpici Seueri, ut alii dicunt.* The Echternach miscellany has excerpts from Pseudo-Theophilus, *De ordinatione feriarum paschalium* (the so-called *Acta Synodi* contained in the Sirmond MS. under the rubric *Epistola Philippi de Pascha*; see above), an extract from the Book of Numbers concerning the Jewish observation of Passover, the same passage of Gaudentius, *De Pascha* that we find in Bodley 309, followed by Anatolius, *De Pascha* and an extract from Augustine, *De Genesi ad litteram* on the Roman calendar, and finally the 'Sulpicius Severus' passage from Pseudo-Athanasius/Pseudo-Martinus Bracarensis. The computistical interests of the two compilers are almost identical, and the Sirmond codex clearly reflects, in every detail – down to its preservation of Victorius' long outdated tables – the self-same methods and materials of the seventh-century Irish computists. That being clearly the case, the 'computistical bits' in the Sirmond codex referred to by Jones provide valuable evidence for knowledge of all these texts in Ireland at an early date (i.e., before the end of the seventh century at latest, and quite possibly as early as AD 658).[25]

Elsewhere in this essay collection[26] I have reprinted evidence, passed over by previous commentators, which might enable us to determine more precisely the date when this Irish computus arrived in Northumbria. On fols 98r-99r of

'Wendepunkte in der Geschichte der lateinischen Exegese im Frühmittelalter', in idem, *Mittelalterliche Studien. Ausgewählte Aufsätze zur Schriftkunde und Literaturgeschichte*, 3 vols (Stuttgart 1966-7, 1981) I, 205-73: 232; Denis Meehan (ed & trans), *Adomnan's 'De locis sanctis'*, Scriptores Latini Hiberniae 3 (Dublin 1958) 58, 70. **22** For discussion of the date, see my 'Irish provenance of Bede's computus', 242 n. 4 (above, 185). **23** Daniel McCarthy, 'The origin of the *Latercus* Paschal cycle of the Insular Celtic churches', CMCS 28 (Winter 1944) 25-49, esp. 37 ff. **24** See 'Early Echternach manuscript fragments with Old Irish glosses', above, 133-44. **25** Whether it can be argued that the Sirmond collection approximates to that compiled by Cummian aleady by the early 630s is a moot point; the case has been made by Wallis, *Bede: The Reckoning of Time*, lxxviii n. 201. If Cummian really was the author of the *De ratione conputandi*, then he must have composed it after the arrival of Isidore's work in Ireland; Isidore is nowhere cited in Cummian's Letter, but he does feature prominently both in the DRC and in the Sirmond collection. **26** 'The date, provenance, and earliest use of the works of Virgilius Maro Grammaticus', above, 191-200.

the Sirmond codex there is found the Prologue of Theophilus, patriarch of Alexandria, to an Easter table (No. 31 in Jones' inventory) with the rubric *Incipit prologus Theophili Alexandrini episcopi ad Theodosium*. The end of the text, however, reads as follows: *Finit de exemplaris cosmographi. Incipit prologus Theophili*. In my 1989 paper I suggested that the reference here must be to the famous *Liber Cosmographiorum* which Ceolfrid, Bede's abbot at Wearmouth-Jarrow, is reported as having given to king Aldfrith of Northumbria in return for eight hides of land.[27] Since we know that Aldfrith succeeded his brother Ecgfrith after the latter's death at the hands of the Picts in the battle of Nechtansmere in 20 May 685 (less than one month after Ecgfrith had attended the foundation ceremony at Jarrow, 23 April) we can assume that the *Liber Cosmographiorum*, which had been brought back from Rome by Benedict Biscop (*quem Romae Benedictus emerat*, in Bede's words) at the latest in AD 684, when Benedict returned from his last journey to the Eternal City, was in the library of Wearmouth-Jarrow by that date. If the reference in the Sirmond codex to the *exemplar cosmographi* is to this Roman book, or a copy of it, then it must have been united with the Irish computus *before* AD 684, the date when Aldfrith purchased it from Ceolfrid. That would seem to provide us with a precious *terminus post quem non* for the arrival of that computus in Northumbria. Whether and how much earlier than that it may have arrived there are questions that still await satisfactory answers, but of one thing we may be certain: research carried out since Jones' path-breaking discovery of 1937 indicates that his verdict in BOT, that Bede owed almost all he knew in the field of computistics to the Irish, has been thoroughly vindicated.

27 Bede, *Historia abbatum*, cap. 15; Charles Plummer (ed), *Baedae opera* (Oxford 1896) 1, 380.

Plate 1 St John's College, Oxford, MS. 17, fol. 71v. The Old Irish names for the days of the week are in the lowest roundel.

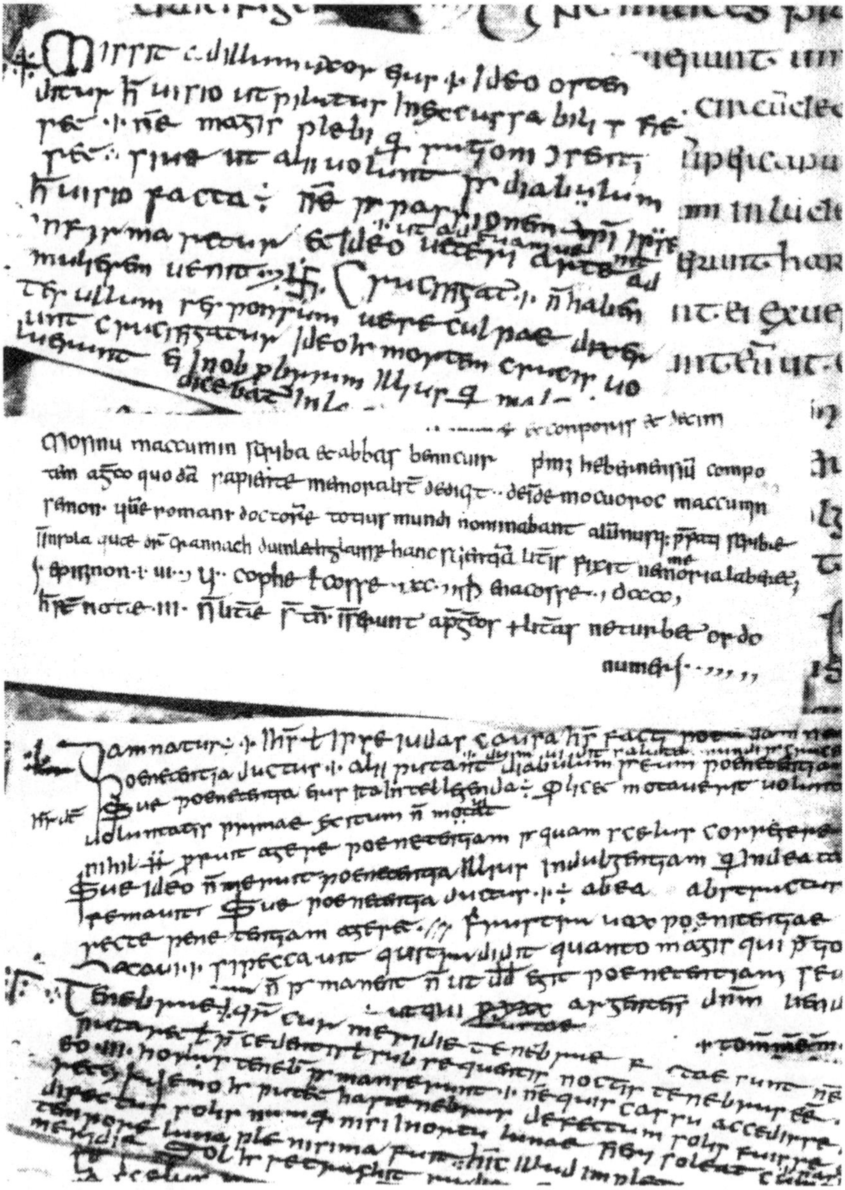

Plate 2 Würzburg, Universitätsbibliothek, M.p.th.f. 61, inserted fol. 29r. The item about Mo Sinu moccu Min is in the second of the inserted leaves.

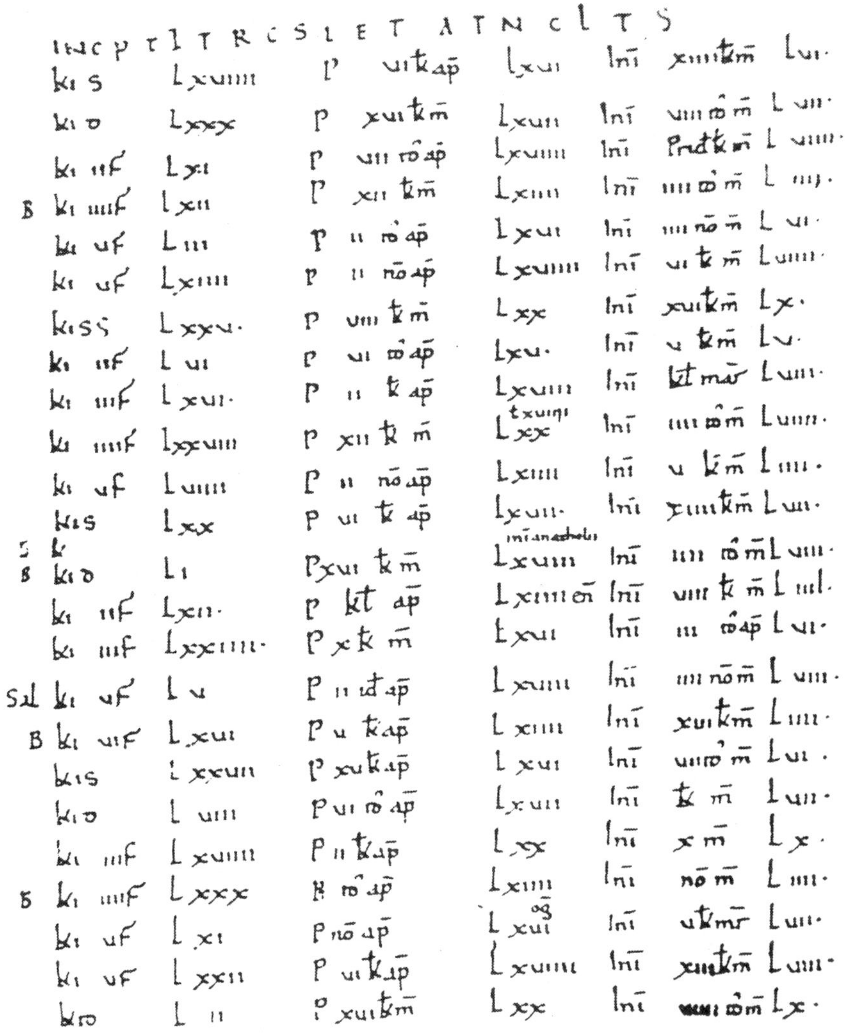

INCP IT I T RCSLET ATNCLTS

	kl s	L xuiiii	P uitkap	L xui	lni	xiiii kl m	L ui·
	kl d	L xxx	P xuii kl m	L xuii	lni	uiii id m	L uii·
	kl iif	L xi	P uii id ap	L xuiiii	lni	Prid kl m	L uiiii·
B	kl iiif	L xii	P xii kl m	L xiiii	lni	iiii id m	L iiii·
	kl uf	L iii	P ii id ap	L xui	lni	iiii no m	L ui·
	kl uf	L xiiii	P ii no ap	L xuiiii	lni	ui kl m	L uiiii·
	kl s s	L xxu·	P uiii kl m	L xx	lni	xuii kl m	L x·
	kl iif	L ui	P ui id ap	L xu·	lni	u kl m	L u·
	kl iiif	L xuii·	P ii kl ap	L xuiii	lni	kl mar	L uiii·
	kl iiif	L xxuiii	P xii kl m	L xx (txuiiii)	lni	iiii id m	L uiiii·
	kl uf	L uiiii	P ii no ap	L xiiii	lni	u kl m	L iiii·
	kl s	L xx	P ui kl ap	L xuii·	lni	xiiii kl m	L uii·
S / B	k / kl d	L i	P xuii kl m	L xuiii (intanacholu)	lni	iii id m	L uiii·
	kl iif	L xii·	P kl ap	L xiiii en	lni	uiii kl m	L iii·
	kl iiif	L xxiiii·	P x kl m	L xui	lni	iii id ap	L ui·
Sal	kl uf	L u	P ii id ap	L xuiiii	lni	iiii no m	L uiii·
B	kl uif	L xui	P u kl ap	L xiiii	lni	xui kl m	L iiii·
	kl s	L xxuii	P xu kl ap	L xui	lni	uiii id m	L ui·
	kl d	L uiii	P ui id ap	L xuii	lni	kl m	L uii·
	kl iiif	L xuiiii	P ii kl ap	L xx	lni	x kl m	L x·
B	kl iiif	L xxx	P ii id ap	L xiiii	lni	no m	L iiii·
	kl uf	L xi	P no ap	L xui (og)	lni	u kl m	L uii·
	kl uf	L xxii	P ui kl ap	L xuiiii	lni	xuiii kl m	L uiii·
	kl d	L ii	P xui kl m	L xx	lni	uiii id m	L x·

Plate 3 Padua, Biblioteca Antoniana, MS. I 27, fol. 76r.
The opening page of the Irish 84-year Easter table.

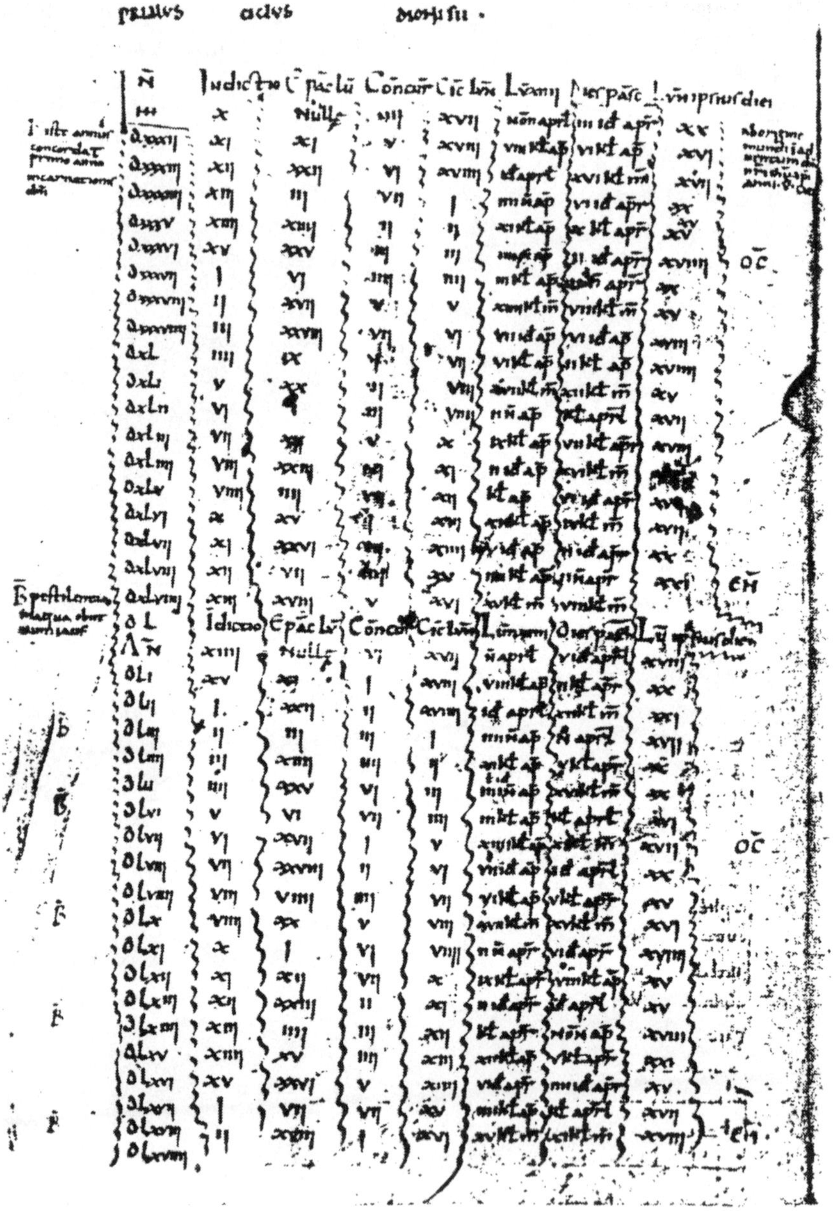

Plate 4 Angers, Bibliothèque Municipale, MS. 477, fol. 36v. The obit of Finnian
of Clonard (Uinniaus) is added in the left margin, beside the year 549 (Dxlviiii).

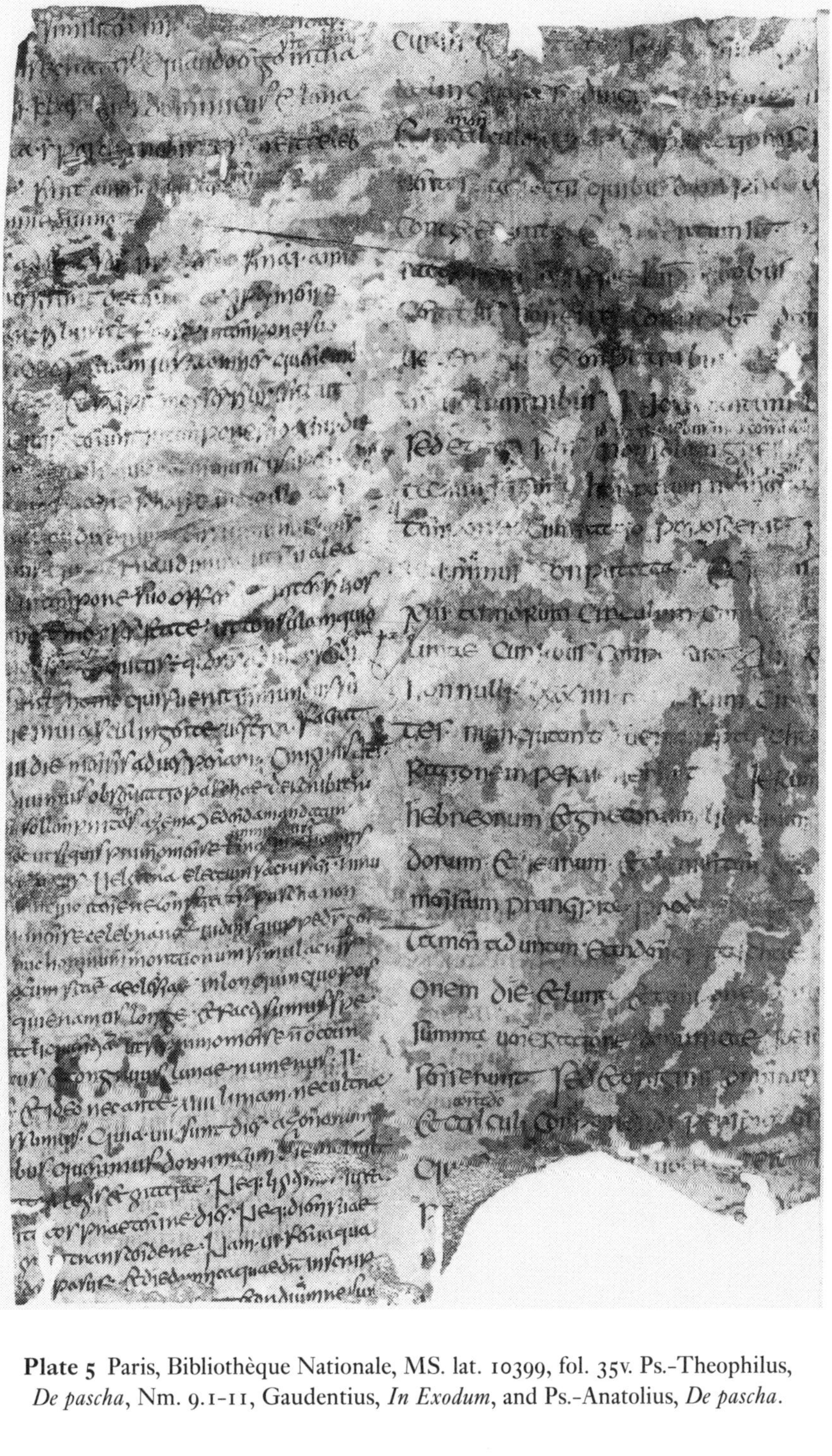

Plate 5 Paris, Bibliothèque Nationale, MS. lat. 10399, fol. 35v. Ps.-Theophilus, *De pascha*, Nm. 9.1-11, Gaudentius, *In Exodum*, and Ps.-Anatolius, *De pascha*.

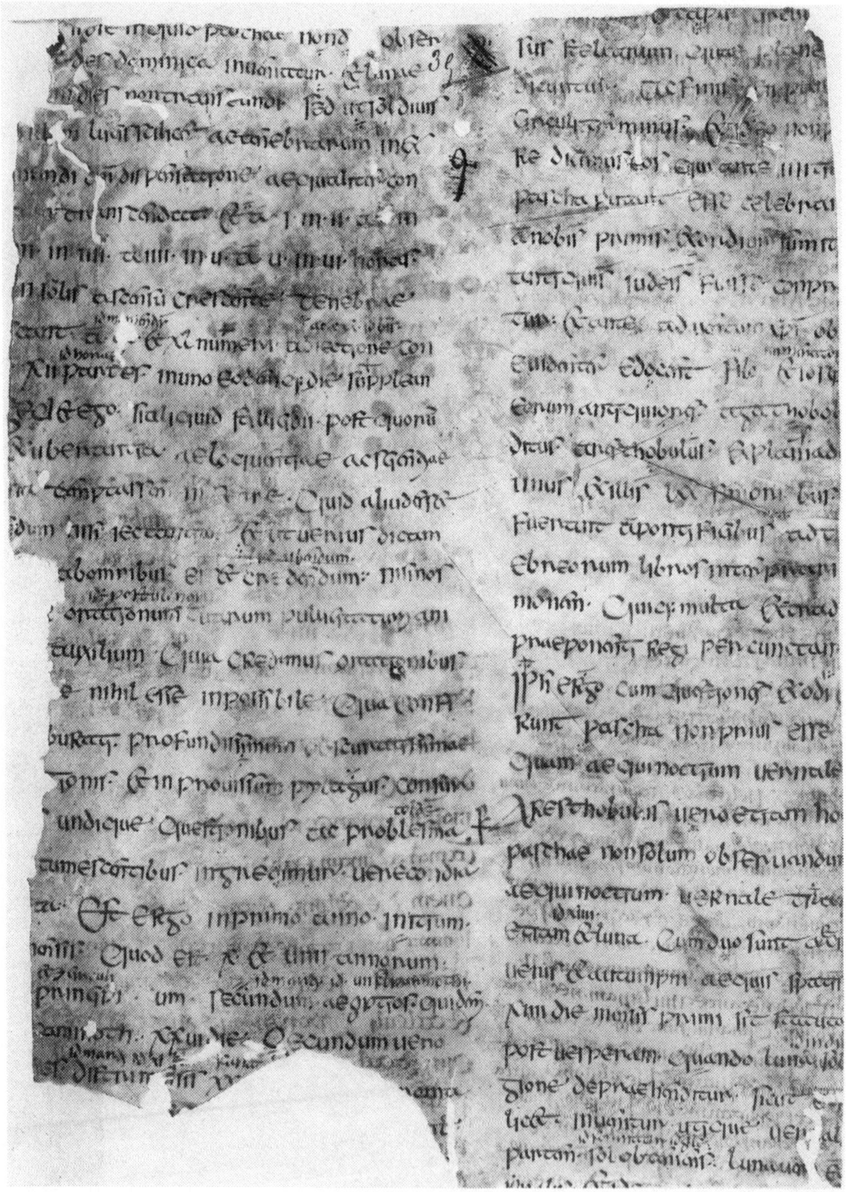

Plate 6 Paris, Bibliothèque Nationale, MS. lat. 10399, fol. 35r.
Ps.-Anatolius, *De pascha* (ctd)

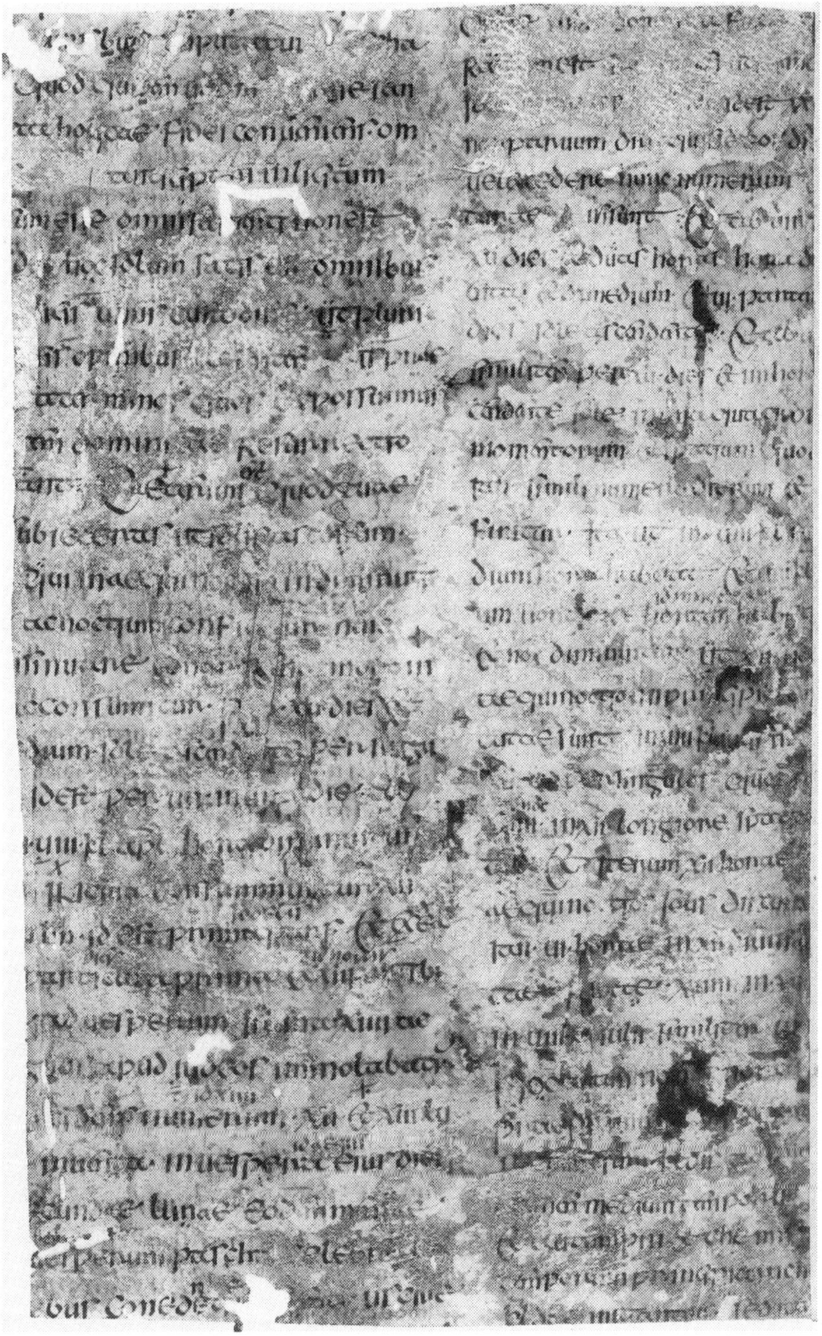

Plate 7 Paris, Bibliothèque Nationale, MS. lat. 10399, fol. 36v.
Ps.-Anatolius, *De pascha* (ctd)

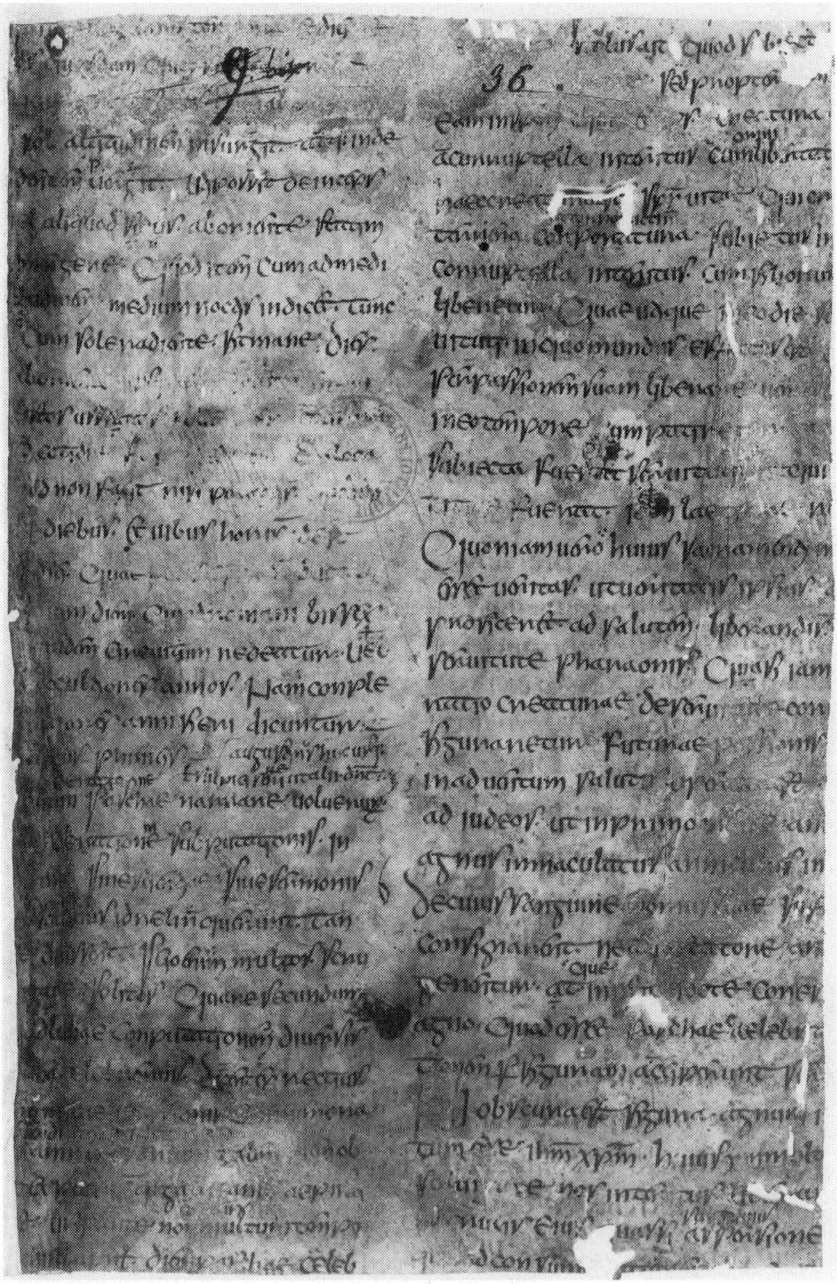

Plate 8 Paris, Bibliothèque Nationale, MS. lat. 10399, fol. 36r.
Augustine, *De Genesi ad litteram*, and Ps.-Athanasius, *De pascha*.

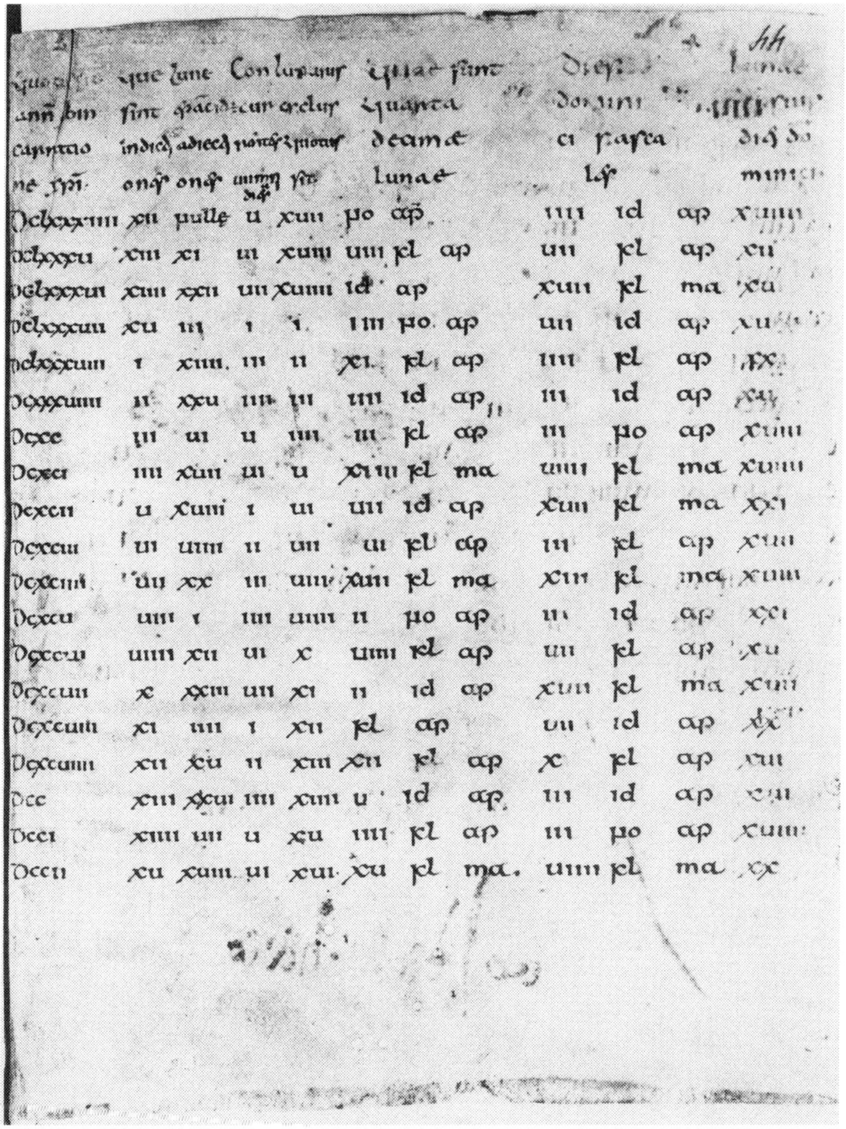

Plate 9 Paris, Bibliothèque Nationale, MS. lat. 10399, fol. 44r. Dionysiac Easter table for the years AD 684-702, bound up with Willibrord's Calendar.

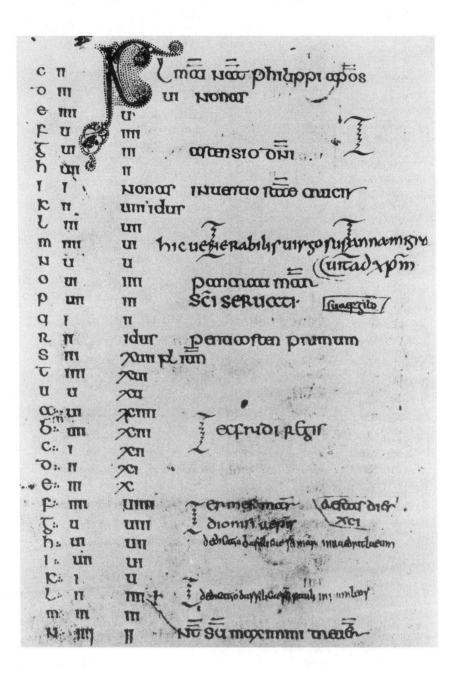

Plate 10 Paris, Bibliothèque Nationale, MS. lat. 10399, fol. 30v.
Willibrord's Calendar, May page, with church dedications.

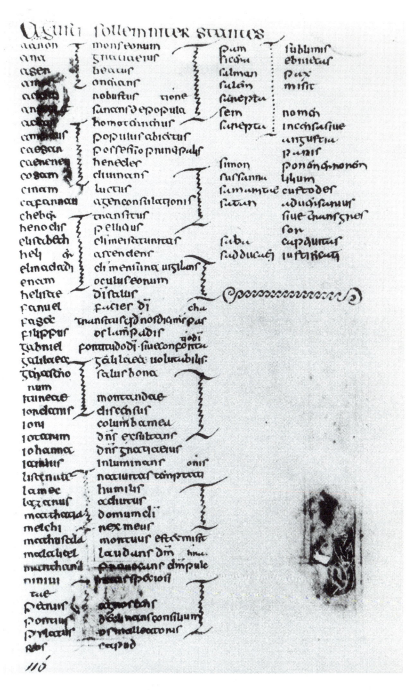

Plate 11 Trinity College Dublin, MS. 57 (A.4.5), fol. 124r.
Hebrew Names with space fillers between columns.

CAVAN COUNTY LIBRARY

Index

Index of Manuscripts Cited